中国双向投资报告 2024

中国国际投资贸易洽谈会组委会
国务院发展研究中心信息中心　　编著
国务院发展研究中心对外经济研究部

中国商务出版社
·北京·

图书在版编目（CIP）数据

中国双向投资报告 . 2024=China Two-way
Investment Report 2024：汉英对照 / 中国国际投资贸
易洽谈会组委会，国务院发展研究中心信息中心，国务院
发展研究中心对外经济研究部编著 . -- 北京：中国商务
出版社，2024.12. -- ISBN 978-7-5103-5498-4

　Ⅰ . F832.48

中国国家版本馆 CIP 数据核字第 2024QV2738 号

中国双向投资报告 2024

中国国际投资贸易洽谈会组委会
国务院发展研究中心信息中心　　　　　编著
国务院发展研究中心对外经济研究部

英文翻译： 张高平　陈旭　等
出版发行： 中国商务出版社有限公司
地　　址： 北京市东城区安定门外大街东后巷 28 号　　邮　编：100710
网　　址： http://www.cctpress.com
联系电话： 010-64515150（发行部）　　　　010-64212247（总编室）
　　　　　　010-64269744（事业部）　　　　010-64248236（印制部）
责任编辑： 郭舒怡
编辑助理： 孙柳明
排　　版： 北京天逸合文化有限公司
印　　刷： 北京建宏印刷有限公司
开　　本： 889 毫米 × 1194 毫米　1/16
印　　张： 31.5　　　　　　　　　　**字　数：** 509 千字
版　　次： 2024 年 12 月第 1 版　　　　**印　次：** 2024 年 12 月第 1 次印刷
书　　号： ISBN 978-7-5103-5498-4
定　　价： 198.00 元

课题组成员

课题顾问

隆国强　国务院发展研究中心副主任

庄荣良　厦门市委常委、厦门市人民政府副市长

课题负责人

李慧莲　国务院发展研究中心信息中心主任

张　琦　国务院发展研究中心对外经济研究部部长

张建斌　中国（厦门）国际投资促进中心主任

课题协调人

奚剑明　国务院发展研究中心信息中心副研究员

宗芳宇　国务院发展研究中心对外经济研究部研究室主任

总报告课题组成员

罗雨泽　国务院发展研究中心对外经济研究部副部长

吕　刚　国务院发展研究中心对外经济研究部副部长

杜奇睿　商务部贸研院副研究员

詹晓宁　全球经济特区联盟主席、世界投资大会执委会主席

高庆鹏　国务院发展研究中心对外经济研究部研究室主任

贾卢魁　国务院发展研究中心信息中心副研究员

杨彩霞　国务院发展研究中心信息中心副研究员

钟运琴　国务院发展研究中心信息中心副研究员

胡豫陇　国务院发展研究中心信息中心副研究员

葛顺奇　南开大学中国式现代化发展研究院教授

李　锋　南京大学自贸区综合研究院研究员

陈文水　投洽（厦门）会展有限公司总经理

专题报告合作单位与专家

北京市商务局

上海市商务委

浙江省商务厅

海南省商务厅

中国外商投资企业协会投资性公司工作委员会

中资企业（新加坡）协会

德勤中国／德勤东南亚

国务院发展研究中心金融研究所：张丽平　孙飞

国务院发展研究中心市场经济研究所：黄千员

中国电子信息产业发展研究院：关兵　陈禄平　杨济菡　高雅

上海市外商投资协会：黄峰　丁隧亮

上海市外商投资咨询有限公司：邹妍琪　万天南

Members of the Research Group

Project consultant

Long Guoqiang	Deputy director of the Development Research Center of the State Council
Zhuang Rongliang	Member of CPC Xiamen Municipal Committee, Vice Mayor of Xiamen Municipal People's government

Project Leader

Li Huilian	Director of the Information Center of the Development Research Center of the State Council
Zhang Qi	Minister of the Department of Foreign Economic Research at theDevelopment Research Center of the State Council
Zhang Jianbin	Director of China (Xiamen) International Investment Promotion Center

Project Coordinator

Xi Jianming	Associate Researcher at the Information Center of the Development Research Center of the State Council
Zong Fangyu	Director of the Research Office of the Department of Foreign Economic Research at the Development Research Center of the State Council

Member of the general report group

Luo Yuze	Deputy Director of the Department of Foreign Economic Research at the Development Research Center of the State Council
Lü Gang	Deputy Director of the Department of Foreign Economic Research at the State Council Development Research Center

Du Qirui	Associate Researcher at the Chinese Academy of International Trade and Economic Cooperation
Zhan Xiaoning	Chairman of the Global Economic Special Zone Alliance
	Chairman of the World Investment Conference Executive Committee
Gao Qingpeng	Director of the Research Office of the Department of Foreign Economic Research at the Development Research Center of the State Council
Jia Lu Kui	Associate Researcher at the Information Center of the Development Research Center of the State Council
Yang Caixia	Associate Researcher at the Information Center of the Development Research Center of the State Council
Zhong Yunqin	Associate Researcher at the Information Center of the Development Research Center of the State Council
Hu Yulong	Associate Researcher at the Information Center of the Development Research Center of the State Council
Ge Shunqi	Professor at the Institute for the Study of Chinese-style Modernization Development, Nankai University
Li Feng	Researcher at the Comprehensive Research Institute of the Free Trade Zone at Nanjing University
Chen Wenshui	General Manager of the Investment and Trade Promotion (Xiamen) Exhibition Co., Ltd.

Collaborating Units and Experts for the Thematic Report

Beijing Municipal Bureau of Commerce

Shanghai Municipal Commission of Commerce

Department of Commerce of Zhejiang Province

Department of Commerce of Hainan Province

Investment Company Working Committee of the China Foreign Investment Enterprises Association

China Enterprises Association (Singapore)

Deloitte China/Deloitte Southeast Asia

Institute of Finance, Development Research Center of the State Council: Zhang Liping, Sun Fei

Institute of Market Economy, Development Research Center of the State Council: Huang Qianyuan

China Electronic Information Industry Development Research Institute: Guan Bing Chen Luping　　Yang Jihan　　Gao Ya

Shanghai Foreign Investment Association: Huang Feng　　Ding Suiliang

Shanghai Foreign Investment Consulting Co. , Ltd. : Zou Yanqi, Wan Tiannan

序　言

　　跨境直接投资不但是跨国公司国际化经营与全球供应链布局的主要方式，也是东道国和投资来源国之间非常重要的经济联系纽带。近年来，受疫情冲击、地缘政治博弈、通货膨胀、汇率波动等因素交织影响，全球跨境直接投资规模连续下行，给经济全球化与世界经济复苏蒙上阴影。面对严峻复杂的国际形势，中国坚持扩大市场开放的决心毫不动摇，坚定以合作共赢推动经济全球化与可持续增长。

　　中国高度重视引资工作，2023年将"更大力度吸引和利用外资"作为年度重点任务之一，密集推出一系列高水平开放和投资促进政策举措，力度之大，前所未有。中国持续扩大市场准入，落实外资企业国民待遇，先后出台两个吸引外资的"24条"，加快构建与国际高标准经贸规则相衔接的制度体系，并推出深化金融业开放、鼓励外资在华开展科技创新合作、举办外资企业圆桌会议、打造"投资中国"品牌等务实举措，要素跨境流动便利度不断提高，营商环境进一步优化。此外，有针对性地解决跨国公司在华投资经营关切的问题，进一步提升外籍人员办理签证证件便利化水平，打通外国友人来华商旅的痛点堵点。2023年，在全球跨境投资持续下滑的背景下，中国吸收外资取得"量稳质升"的难得成就，实际利用外资额达1633亿美元，为历史第三高，继续保持全球第二大外资流入国地位。

　　中国继续鼓励对外投资，不断优化管理体制机制，完善以监管政策、支持政策和服务促进为核心的对外投资政策和服务体系，建立了"管理分级分类、信息统一归口、违规联合惩戒"的对外投资管理模式，提升对外投资便利化水平。中国积极引导企业海外合规经营，完善金融服务"走出去"政策，加强境外机构和人员安全管理制度，深化"一带一路"合作机制，推动对外投资合作数字化和绿色化发展，助力东道国经济社会发展，对外投资取得新进展。2023年，中国对外直接投资金额达1772.9亿美元，居世界第三位，对外投资大国地位进一步稳固。

　　无论"引进来"还是"走出去"，中国都与相关方实现了互利共赢。在华外资企业有力地促进了中国经济发展，也享受到中国市场机遇和发展红利，实现了自身的盈利增长。中国美国商会2024年发布的调查报告显示，约68%的受调查企业预计在华利润率达到或超过全球平均水平。中国企业的海外投资运营既为东道国带来积极的经济效益，也显著促进了当地经济社会发展与民生福祉改善。党的十八大以来至 2023 年底，中国企业累计向东道国缴纳各种税金 5185 亿美元，年均提供超过 200 万个就业岗位。

"中国的发展惠及世界，中国的发展离不开世界。"展望未来，尽管跨境投资合作面临诸多困难和挑战，但经济全球化发展大势不会逆转。因为从根本上说，全球化有利于发挥各国比较优势，通过优化资源配置实现更有效率的增长，通过互补合作做大共赢蛋糕，这既符合经济规律和国家利益，也系各国人民所盼。无论国际环境如何复杂、风云如何变幻，中国都会保持战略定力，坚定不移扩大对外开放、以互利共赢引领双向投资发展。

党的二十届三中全会明确提出，"开放是中国式现代化的鲜明标识"，并对进一步扩大制度型开放、深化外商投资和对外投资管理体制改革作出部署。中国具有超大规模的市场、完善的产业配套、丰富的人才资源和不断完善的营商环境等诸多优势，随着经济高质量发展和开放水平的进一步提升，必将创造出更多的投资机遇，拓展出更广阔的投资蓝海。

多家跨国企业负责人指出，与中国同行就是与机遇同行。中国张开双臂欢迎跨国公司来华投资兴业，也支持跨国企业参与共建"一带一路"、与中国企业一道拓展第三方市场，投资合作的空间巨大，共赢发展的机遇众多，"投资中国"未来可期。

Preface

Cross-border direct investment is not only a primary means for multinational corporations to operate internationally and arrange global supply chains, but also serves as a vital economic link between host countries and source countries of investment. In recent years, affected by factors such as the pandemic, geopolitical tensions, inflation, and exchange rate fluctuations, global cross-border direct investment has experienced a continuous downturn, resulting in a negative impact on economic globalization and world economic recovery. In the face of this challenging and complex international environment, China remains unwavering in its commitment to expanding market openness and steadfastly promotes economic globalization and sustainable growth through mutually beneficial cooperation.

China places great emphasis on attracting investment. In 2023, "making greater efforts to attract and utilize foreign investment" was designated as a key task for the year, with a series of high-level policies and measures for opening up and investment promotion being intensively introduced, showing an unprecedented level of commitment. China has consistently expanded market access, implemented national treatment for foreign enterprises, and successively introduced two "24 Measures" for attracting foreign investment, aimed at accelerating the alignment of domestic systems with international high-standard economic and trade rules. Practical steps have been taken, including deepening the opening up of the financial sector, encouraging foreign capital to pursue technological innovation in China, hosting Roundtable Meetings for foreign enterprises, and building the "Invest China" brand. These initiatives have continuously improved the ease of cross-border factor flows and further optimized the business environment. Additionally, targeted efforts have been made to address issues faced by multinational companies investing and operating in China, enhancing the facilitation of visa processing for foreign personnel, and alleviating pain points for international visitors. Despite a global decline in cross-border investment, in 2023, China achieved remarkable progress with "improved quality and stable volume" in foreign investment, with actual utilized foreign capital reaching USD 163.3 billion, marking the third-highest in history and securing China's position as the second largest foreign capital inflow destination in the world.

China continues to encourage outbound investment, which is able to consistently optimize management systems and mechanisms and enhance an outbound investment policy and service system centered around regulatory policies, supportive policies, and service promotion. A management model for outbound investment has been established, characterized by "graded and classified management, unified information management, and establishment of punitive measures for violations", which improved the facilitation of outbound investments. China actively guides companies to conduct compliant operations overseas, improves financial services for "going global" policies, strengthens security management for overseas institutions and personnel, deepens cooperation mechanisms under the Belt and Road Initiative, and promotes digitalization and green development in outbound investment cooperation, thereby supporting the economic and social development of host countries, and achieving new progress in outbound investment. In 2023, China's outbound direct investment reached USD 177.29 billion, ranking third globally and further solidifying China's position as a major outbound investor.

Regardless of whether it is "introducing FDI" or "going global," China has achieved mutual benefits with relevant partners. Foreign-invested enterprises in China have significantly contributed to China's economic development while also benefiting from China's market opportunities and development dividends, thereby achieving their own profit growth. A survey report released in 2024 by the American Chamber of Commerce in China indicates that approximately 68% of surveyed enterprises expect their profit margins in China to reach or exceed the global average. Chinese companies' overseas investments not only bring positive economic benefits to host countries but also substantially promote local economic and social development and improve the well-being of local populations. From the 18th National Congress of the Communist Party of China until the end of 2023, Chinese enterprises have cumulatively paid USD 518.5 billion in taxes to host countries and have provided over two million jobs annually.

"China's development benefits the world and China cannot develop in isolation from the rest of the world." Looking forward, despite the numerous difficulties and challenges faced by cross-border investment cooperation, the trend of economic globalization will not be reversed. Fundamentally, globalization helps countries leverage their comparative advantages, achieving more efficient growth through optimized resource allocation and expanding the pie of common interests through complementary cooperation. This aligns with economic principles and national interests and reflects the aspirations of people worldwide. Regardless of the complexity of the international environment and changing global dynamics, China will maintain its strategic focus, unwaveringly expand its opening up to the world, and lead two-way investment development through mutual benefits.

The Third Plenary Session of the 20th CPC Central Committee explicitly stated that "Opening up is a distinct hallmark of Chinese modernization" and outlined plans to further expand institutional opening up and deepen reforms in the management systems for foreign investment and outbound investment. China has numerous advantages, including an ultra-large market, well-established industrial support, abundant human resources, and an improving business environment. As China's economy continues its high-quality development and as its level of opening up increases, more investment opportunities will emerge, and a broader investment landscape will be cultivated.

Executives from multiple multinational companies have noted that partnering with China means partnering with opportunities. China warmly welcomes multinational corporations to invest and operate in China and also supports them in participating in the Belt and Road Initiative and in exploring third-party markets alongside Chinese enterprises. There is vast potential for investment cooperation, numerous opportunities for mutual development, and a promising future for "Investing in China".

前　言

　　2023 年，受全球经济复苏乏力、地缘政治冲突加剧、产业链供应链继续深度调整等多重因素影响，全球跨境投资表现疲软，全球直接投资流量比 2022 年下降 2%。若排除少数"管道经济体"因素，实际降幅达到 10%，处于十年来第二低的水平，仅略好于 2020 年疫情时期。展望未来，全球跨境投资的前景仍面临多重挑战，融资条件收紧、跨国公司海外业务拓展更加谨慎、金融市场波动及部分国家对外国投资监管趋严，可能导致跨境投资持续低水平徘徊。但与此同时，推动全球投资恢复增长的积极因素依然存在。跨国公司作为投资主体，2023 年整体利润情况较好，一些行业和区域投资也呈现出亮点。例如，可再生能源等绿色投资缺口较大、需求迫切，2023 年绿地投资项目总数增加 2%；对人工智能和数字基础设施的投资保持增长；制造业和关键矿产投资较快增加，服务业直接投资持续引领全球 FDI 增长，占比为 72%；发展中经济体引资下降，但亚洲、拉美和非洲等新兴市场引资潜力逐步显现。与此同时，全球跨境投资出现新趋势新特点，主要受技术创新和产业革命、可持续发展和地缘政治经济格局变革等影响，全球产业链供应链正在经历重大调整，韧性与安全驱动全球价值链出现区域化、多元化，产业链数字化和轻资产化，服务业与制造业一体化，基础设施、蓝色经济与绿色发展成为投资重点。

　　面对复杂严峻的国际环境和全球跨境投资下滑的不利影响，中国坚持更大力度吸引和利用外资，坚持发挥两个市场、两种资源联动效应，2023 年继续保持全球第二大外资流入国地位，对外直接投资居全球第三位，双向投资量稳质升、亮点突出。

　　一方面，中国双向投资的开放支持政策不断完善。2023 年以来，中国相继推出一系列政策举措，力度之大，前所未有。为进一步优化外商投资环境、加大引资力度，国务院先后发布两个吸引外资的"24 条"意见和方案，在扩大市场准入、提高引资质量、保障外资企业国民待遇、持续加强外商投资保护、提高投资运营便利化水平、加大财税支持力度等方面提出一揽子举措；提出了在自贸试验区 / 港对接高标准经贸规则、推进高水平制度型开放的措施；提出了在特定地区试点对互联网数据中心等六项增值电信业务取消外资股比限制的措施；提出了在安全有序前提下放宽数据跨境流动限制的措施，授权自贸试验区制定跨境数据流动负面清单。此外，中国进一步提升外籍人员办理签证证件便利化水平，来华单方面免签国扩大到 15 个。这些政策都受到了跨国企业和外籍人士的广泛好评。与此同时，中国持续健全对外投资政策和服务体系，不断深化合作机制建设。2023 年，中国与有关国家共同发布《数字经济和绿色发展国际经贸合作框架倡议》，对促进跨境投资数字化、绿色化发展起到重要的促进作用。

另一方面，中国双向投资质量持续提升。商务部数据显示，从利用外资看，尽管受全球跨境投资形势影响，2023 年中国实际利用外资金额同比有所下降，但仍达到 1633 亿美元，是历史第三高的成绩；根据联合国贸发会议发布的数据，占全球比重为 12.3%，仅次于美国、居全球第二。商务部数据显示，2024 年 1—7 月，全国新设立外商投资企业 31654 家，同比增长 11.4%，延续了 2023 年以来新设外资企业较快增长的趋势。在引资结构方面，利用外资质量进一步提升，2023 年高技术产业和制造业占实际使用外资金额比重分别达到 37.4%、27.9%；2024 年 1—7 月，医疗仪器设备及仪器仪表制造业、专业技术服务业、计算机及办公设备制造业实际使用外资以人民币计分别增长 87%、41.3% 和 32.4%。在投资来源地方面，欧盟、美国、日本在华新设外资企业数量实现增长。中国贸促会、在华美国商会和欧盟商会的问卷调查结果均显示，大多数受访外资企业对中国经济前景和营商环境充满信心；华南美国商会调查报告显示，受访企业普遍认为在中国能获得较高的投资回报率，九成美资企业在华盈利，"外资企业不仅进得来，也能在中国发展好"，这是跨国公司持续加码投资中国的重要动力。

从对外投资看，商务部和联合国贸发会议数据显示，2023 年中国对外直接投资金额为 1772.9 亿美元，较上年增长 8.7%，连续 11 年稳居世界前三。对外投资存量 2.96 万亿美元，遍布 190 多个国家和地区，连续 6 年保持世界前三，对外投资大国地位日益巩固。其中，"一带一路"投资合作稳步推进，中国企业在"一带一路"共建国家非金融类直接投资 318 亿美元，同比增长 22.6%。一批标志性项目和"小而美"民生项目稳步实施，推动高质量共建"一带一路"走深走实。境外中资企业经营成效良好，制造业对外投资和对"一带一路"共建国家投资持续增长，金融机构"走出去"成效显著，中国企业国际竞争力、国际化经营水平和信心不断提升。

中国吸引外资的优势不断累积提升。当前，中国加快推动经济高质量发展，引资优势正在从低成本要素优势向基于超大规模市场、全产业链配套和创新应用等综合优势转变，这些是支撑中国引资长期稳定发展的有利因素。第一，中国超大规模市场带来广阔发展机遇。作为世界第二大经济体，随着经济高质量发展的深入推进，中国在先进制造业、消费升级、新型城镇化等方面将持续释放出巨大需求，成为与跨国企业分享发展机遇的新优势。第二，产业配套完备高效、供应链快速响应和投资环境全球领先。中国是全世界产业体系最完整、产业配套能力领先的国家，制造业规模连续13年居世界首位，培育了45个国家级先进制造业集群，能为外商投资提供高效率、高可靠性的供应链支撑。同时，中国持续扩大市场开放、坚持维护外商投资合法权益，为各国企业来华投资营造极具吸引力的营商环境。第三，基于科技创新和人力资本的新兴优势日益增强。中国高度重视科技创新在产业升级中的重要作用，2023年研发经费支出居全球第二位，创新场景开发和规模化应用优势凸显，创新能力综合排名提升至全球第12位，并且拥有全球规模最大的科技人才队伍，为跨国企业在华研发、提升供应链效率与服务全球市场提供了坚实基础。第四，高水平开放平台的引领作用进一步凸显。中国以自贸试验区和自由贸易港、国家级经开区等开放平台为重要载体，积极对标国际高标准经贸规则，推进高水平开放先行先试，将为外资在华投资提供重要支撑。总体上看，中国正在依托超大规模的市场、完备的产业链、科技创新等多重优势，形成对全球要素资源的强大吸引，为各国企业在中国拓展业务与市场提供更大空间和便利化服务。

中国双向投资促进与世界互利共赢。中国稳步扩大制度型开放，持续深化外商投资和对外投资管理体制改革，实现了双向投资互利共赢，也为全球经济注入了更多确定性和正能量。第一，外资企业看好中国市场巨大机遇，在华业务为全球业务发展提供重要支撑。外资企业充分利用中国的政策红利和市场红利，交出了亮眼的成绩单。根据国家统计局数据，2023年，外商及港澳台商投资企业营业收入27.2万亿元，利润总额1.8万亿元，营业收入利润率为6.6%。中国美国商会的年度报告表明，尽管仍然面临突出挑战，约40%的受访企业对未来两年在华盈利潜力持乐观态度，高于2023年的33%，44%的受访企业表示对中国市场增长感觉良好；日本贸易振兴机构表示，近90%的受访日本企业将在中国维持或加大投资；中国德国商会的企业调查显示，一半以上德国企业计划在未来两年内增加在华投资。第二，中国企业对外投资有力促进了东道国经济社会发展。近年来，中国企业"走出去"步伐不断加速，为助力东道国基础设施完善，增加当地就业和税收，集聚技术、人才等要素作出了重要贡献，促进了东道国长期发展能力和自主发展能力提升，形成了互利共赢的良好局面。第三，中国双向投资为全球经济注入了信心和活力。中国超大规模市场优势与高水平营商环境叠加，为各国企业提供了广阔的市场空间。在全球供应链脆弱性上升的背景下，中国依托强大高效的产业体系，为稳定全球供应链发挥了关键作用。中国加快建设科技强国，积极布局新赛道新领域，为全球经济发展注入了新活力。

投资链接世界，机遇惠及全球。中国共产党二十届三中全会对中国坚定不移扩大高水平开放作出了重要部署，指出"必须坚持对外开放基本国策，坚持以开放促改革，依托我国超大规模市场优势，在扩大国际合作中提升开放能力，建设更高水平开放型经济新体制"，释放了进一步扩大制度型开放的信号。《中共中央关于进一步全面深化改革　推进中国式现代化的决定》提出，要深化外商投资和对外投资管理体制改革，营造市场化、法治化、国际化营商环境，依法保护外商投资权益；完善促进和保障对外投资体制机制，推动产业链供应链国际合作。

展望未来，加强国际投资合作，以互利共赢引领全球贸易投资发展、保持产业链供应链稳定有序，可以为全球数字化、绿色化转型发展提供资金支持，为世界经济复苏注入新动能，为推动落实全球发展倡议、实现可持续发展议程提供重要支撑。

有跨国企业讲，与中国同行就是与机遇同行。我们相信，一个经济稳健前行、不断扩大开放的中国，必将为世界经济注入强大动力，为国内外投资者提供巨大的市场机遇和广阔的发展前景。携手中国，就是赢得未来！

国务院发展研究中心党组成员、副主任

2024 年 9 月

Foreword

In 2023, global cross-border investment was influenced by factors such as a sluggish global economic recovery, escalating geopolitical conflicts, and continued deep adjustments in industrial and supply chains, so it showed a weak performance, with global direct investment flows down by 2% compared to 2022. Except for a few "pipeline economies," the actual decline reached 10%, marking the second-lowest level in a decade, slightly better than the pandemic period in 2020. Looking forward, Global cross-border investment still faces multiple challenges. Tightened financing conditions, a cautious approach by multinational companies to expanding their overseas operations, market volatility, and stricter foreign investment regulations in certain countries may result in cross-border investment remaining at a low level. Nonetheless, there are still positive factors that can drive a recovery in global investment. Multinational companies, as the main investment entities, had relatively strong profits overall in 2023, and certain industries and regions displayed some highlights. For instance, there is an urgent demand in renewable energy, with a substantial investment gap; the total number of greenfield investment projects increased by 2% in 2023. Investment in artificial intelligence and digital infrastructure continued to grow; investment in manufacturing and critical minerals increased rapidly, and the service sector continued to lead global FDI (foreign direct investment) growth, accounting for 72%. Though developing economies experienced a decline in investment inflows, investment potential of markets such as Asia, Latin America, and Africa is gradually emerging. At the same time, new trends and characteristics in global cross-border investment are emerging. Driven by technological innovation, industrial revolutions, sustainable development, and changes in geopolitical and economic landscapes, the global supply and value chains are undergoing significant adjustments. The emphasis on resilience and security is leading to regionalization and diversification in global value chains, digitalization and asset-light operations in supply chains, integration of services and manufacturing, and a focus on infrastructure construction, blue economy, and green development.

To respond to a complex and challenging international environment and the adverse impacts of declining global cross-border investment, China remains committed to attracting and utilizing foreign investment on a larger scale, leveraging the synergies of both domestic and international markets and resources. In 2023, China maintained its position as the world's second-largest foreign investment inflow destination and the third-largest source of outbound direct investment globally, achieving steady growth in both volume and quality, with notable highlights.

On the one hand, China's policies in favor of opening up in two-way investment have continued to improve. Since 2023, China has introduced a raft of unprecedented policies and measures. To further optimize the foreign investment environment and enhance investment attraction, the State Council released two sets of "24 Measures" for attracting foreign investment, which involved the following aspects: outlining comprehensive measures for expanding market access, improving the quality of investment inflows, ensuring national treatment for foreign-invested enterprises, continuously strengthening the protection of foreign investments, enhancing the ease of investment operations, and increasing fiscal and tax support. Additionally, China issued measures to align free trade pilot zones/ports with high-standard economic and trade regulations and promoted institutional opening up at high levels. Measures were also introduced to remove foreign ownership restrictions in six value-added telecom services, including internet data centers, in specific regions. Furthermore, steps were taken to relax restrictions on cross-border data flows under safe and orderly conditions, authorizing free trade pilot zones to establish a negative list for cross-border data flows. China also enhanced the facilitation of visa processing for foreign nationals, expanding unilateral visa-free access to 15 countries. These policies have been widely welcomed by multinational companies and foreign nationals. Meanwhile, China has continued to improve its outbound investment policy and service system, deepening cooperation mechanisms. In 2023, China and relevant countries jointly issued the *Initiative on International Trade and Economic Cooperation Framework for Digital Economy and Green Development*, playing a significant role in promoting the digitalization and green development of cross-border investments.

On the other hand, the quality of China's two-way investment has continued to improve. Data from the Ministry of Commerce shows, in terms of foreign investment utilization, despite the global cross-border investment situation, the actual utilization of foreign capital in China in 2023 reached USD 163.3 billion, a slight decline year-over-year, but it remained the third-highest amount in history; According to data from the United Nations Conference on Trade and Development, accounting for 12.3% of the global total, second only to the United States. According to data from the Ministry of Commerce, from January to July 2024, 31,654 new foreign-invested enterprises were established in China, an 11.4% increase year-over-year, continuing the trend of rapid growth in new foreign enterprises since 2023. In terms of investment structure, the quality of foreign investment utilization improved further, with high-tech industries and manufacturing accounting for 37.4% and 27.9% of actual foreign capital utilization, respectively, in 2023. In the first seven months of 2024, the actual foreign capital utilization in the manufacturing sectors of medical instruments and devices, professional technical services, and computer and office equipment grew by 87%, 41.3%, and 32.4% year-over-year, respectively. In terms of investment sources, the number of new foreign-invested enterprises from the EU, the United States, and Japan increased. Survey results from the China Council for the Promotion of International Trade, the American Chamber of Commerce in China, and the EU Chamber of Commerce showed that most surveyed foreign-invested enterprises are confident in the Chinese economy and business environment. A report by the American Chamber of Commerce in South China indicated that surveyed companies generally perceived high returns on investments in China, with 90% of American enterprises in China being profitable, "foreign-invested enterprises are able to not only come in but also flourish in China," making the attractive business environment a key driver for multinational companies to increase their investments in China.

From the perspective of outbound investment, data from the Ministry of Commerce and the UN Trade and Development (UNCTAD) shows, China's outbound direct investment in 2023 was USD 177.29 billion, an 8.7% increase year-over-year, marking its position in the global top three for eleven consecutive years. China's outbound investment stock stands at USD 2.96 trillion, spanning over 190 countries and regions, and maintaining its position in the global top three for six consecutive years, further solidifying its status as a major outbound investor. Among these, investment cooperation under the Belt and Road Initiative has steadily advanced, with Chinese enterprises' non-financial direct investment in Belt and Road partner countries reaching USD 31.8 billion, a 22.6% year-over-year increase. A series of flagship projects and "small and beautiful" livelihood projects have been implemented, promoting the high-quality development of the Belt and Road Initiative. Overseas Chinese enterprises have performed well, with continued growth in outbound investment of the manufacturing sector and the investment in Belt and Road partner countries, significant achievements by financial institutions in "going global", and continuous enhancement of the international competitiveness, operational levels, and confidence of Chinese enterprises.

China's advantages in attracting foreign investment are continuously accumulating and improving. Currently, as China accelerates high-quality economic development, its advantages in attracting investment are shifting from low-cost factors to a comprehensive edge based on a super-large market, complete industrial support, and innovation in application. These are favorable factors supporting China's long-term, stable investment inflows. First, China's super-large market offers vast development opportunities. As the world's second-largest economy, with the deepening of high-quality economic development, China will continue to unleash significant demand in areas such as advanced manufacturing, consumption upgrading, and new urbanization, becoming a new advantage for sharing development opportunities with multinational enterprises. Second, China boasts complete and efficient industrial support, a highly responsive supply chain, and a globally leading investment environment. China has the world's most complete industrial system and top-tier industrial support capabilities. Its manufacturing scale has ranked first globally for thirteen consecutive years, with 45 national advanced manufacturing clusters that can provide foreign investment with high-efficiency and reliable supply chain support. Meanwhile, China is continually expanding market opening up, steadfastly protecting the legitimate rights and interests of foreign investments, and fostering an extremely attractive business environment for companies from around the world. Third, China's emerging advantages based on technological innovation and human capital are increasingly prominent. China places great importance on technological innovation in industrial upgrading. In 2023, China ranked second globally in R&D expenditure, with notable advantages in innovation scenario development and large-scale application, elevating its comprehensive innovation capacity ranking to 12th in the world. China also possesses the largest pool of scientific and technological talent globally, providing a solid foundation for multinational companies to conduct R&D, enhance supply chain efficiency, and serve global markets. Fourth, the role of high-level open platforms as leaders is becoming increasingly evident. Through platforms like free trade pilot zones, free trade ports, and national-level economic development zones, China actively aligns with international high-standard economic and trade rules, promoting high-level opening-up in pioneering ways, which will provide critical support for foreign investment in China. Overall, China is forming a powerful attraction for global resources by leveraging its super-large market, complete industrial chain, and technological innovation, offering greater space for global enterprises to expand their business and markets in China.

China's two-way investment promotes mutual benefit and win-win cooperation with the world. China has steadily expanded institutional opening up, continued to deepen reforms in the management of foreign and outbound investment, achieving mutual benefits in two-way investment and injecting more certainty and positive energy into the global economy. First, foreign-invested enterprises are optimistic about China's massive market opportunities, where their operations provide critical support for their global business development. Foreign-invested enterprises have fully utilized China's policy and market dividends, achieving impressive results. According to data from the National Bureau of Statistics, in 2023, foreign-invested and Hong Kong, Macao, and Taiwan enterprises achieved a total operating income of CNY 27.2 trillion, with total profits of CNY 1.8 trillion and an operating income profit margin of 6.6%. The American Chamber of Commerce in China's annual report indicates that despite facing prominent challenges, approximately 40% of surveyed enterprises remain optimistic about their profit potential in China over the next two years, an increase from 33% in 2023, and 44% expressed positive feelings about market growth in China. The Japan External Trade Organization reported that nearly 90% of surveyed Japanese companies planned to maintain or increase their investment in China. The German Chamber of Commerce in China's survey showed that over half of the surveyed German companies planned to increase their investment in China over the next two years. Second, Chinese enterprises' outbound investments have effectively promoted economic and social development in host countries. In recent years, Chinese enterprises have accelerated their "going global" efforts, making significant contributions to host countries by helping improve infrastructure, creating local jobs, increasing tax revenues, and gathering technical expertise and talent. This has strengthened host countries' long-term development capabilities and self-sufficiency, fostering a mutually beneficial and win-win situation. Third, China's two-way investment has injected confidence and vitality into the global economy. China's super-large market advantages, combined with a high-level business environment, provide broad market space for companies worldwide. Amid rising vulnerabilities in the global supply chain, China's robust and efficient industrial system plays a critical role in stabilizing the global supply chain. China is accelerating the construction of a scientific and technological powerhouse, actively engaging in new industries and sectors, and injecting new vitality into the global economy.

Investment links the world, and opportunities benefit the globe. At the Third Plenary Session of the 20th CPC Central Committee, China released significant plans to unwaveringly expand high-level opening-up, stating that"adhering to the basic policy of opening-up, promoting reform through opening up, leveraging China's super-large market advantages, and enhancing openness through international cooperation is essential to building a new high-level open economic system". This released a strong signal to further expand institutional opening-up. The *Resolution of the Communist Party of China (CPC) Central Committee on Further Deepening Reform Comprehensively to Advance Chinese Modernization* calls for further reforming the management systems for foreign investment and outbound investment, we will foster a first-rate business environment that is market-oriented, law-based, and internationalized and protect the rights and interests of foreign investors in accordance with the law. We will refine the institutions and mechanisms for promoting and protecting Chinese investment abroad, and facilitate international cooperation in industrial and supply chains.

Looking ahead, strengthening international investment cooperation and leading global trade and investment development through mutual benefit and win-win cooperation can maintain stability and order in industrial and supply chains. It can also provide financial support for the global shift towards digitalization and green development, inject new momentum into global economic recovery, and support the implementation of the global development initiative and sustainable development agenda.

As some multinational companies have stated, partnering with China means partnering with opportunities. It is believed that an economically stable and forward-moving China that continues to expand its opening-up will inject strong momentum into the world economy, offering immense market opportunities and a broad development prospect for both domestic and international investors. Partnering with China is a step towards a prosperous future!

Member of the Party Leadership Group and Deputy Director,
Development Research Center of the State Council
September 2024

目　录

Contents

Association Section 361

总报告

第一章 全球 FDI 趋势和前景

受疫情危机、世界经济不景气、地缘政治紧张，持续的地区冲突和贸易争端等因素影响，近年来，全球国际投资持续低迷，并呈现七大特征。短期内，全球跨国投资将在低位徘徊。从中长期来看，全球产业链正在经历重大调整，未来国际投资与国际生产将向着十大方向转型。同时，可持续投资、数字化转型、新兴市场崛起、区域合作加强、产业的韧性与创新，将为各国带来新的机遇。

一、全球 FDI 趋势

2023—2024 年全球外国直接投资呈现七大特征。

（一）投资总量持续在低位徘徊

2023 年全球 FDI 流动实际下降了 10%，降至 1.3 万亿美元。即使将三大过境外资国（荷兰、卢森堡和爱尔兰）的大幅逆转计入全球投资流动总额，全球 FDI 仍比 2022 年下降 2%，接近十年来的触底水平。目前来看，2024 年全球 FDI 增长乏力，持续在低水平徘徊（见图 1-1）。

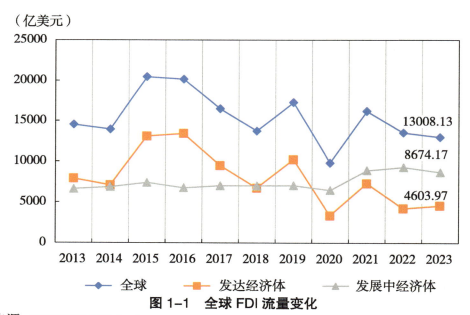

图 1-1 全球 FDI 流量变化

资料来源：UNCTAD FDI database.

（二）发达经济体 FDI 处于历史低点

2023 年流入发达经济体的 FDI 增加了 9%，仅为大幅下降之后的较小回升，且为非实质性增长。主要由三大过境外资国的大幅逆转所致，三国由负流入 1060 亿美元转为正流入 160 亿美元。最值得关注的是，欧盟的 FDI 流入从 2019 年的 6270 亿美元降至 2022 年的负 850 亿美元。2023 年，欧盟的 FDI 流入 580 亿美元，与非洲持平，仅为亚洲 FDI 的近 10%、中国 FDI 的 1/3（见图 1-2）。美国的 FDI 流入减少了 6%，降至 3110 亿美元，跨境并购大幅减少了 40%，降至 810 亿美元，仅为过去十年平均水平的一半。

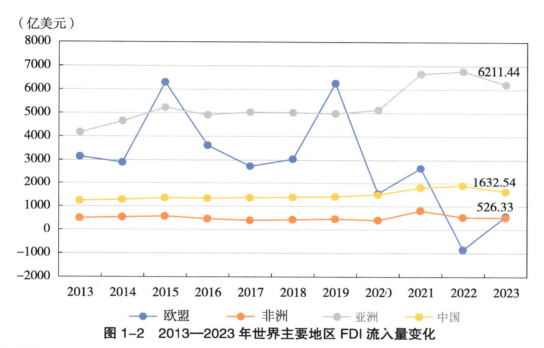

图 1-2　2013—2023 年世界主要地区 FDI 流入量变化

资料来源：UNCTAD FDI database.

（三）发展中经济体 FDI 增长势头减弱

根据联合国贸易和发展会议 FDI 数据库，发展中经济体的 FDI 下降了 7%，降至 8670 亿美元，扭转了过去几年的增长态势。亚洲作为发展中经济体 FDI 增长的主要推动力，FDI 下滑了 8%。非洲和拉丁美洲的 FDI 也分别下降了 3% 和 1%。

（四）制造业 FDI 正在复苏

制造业的 FDI 增加，扭转了过去十年增长停滞的局面。这一增长主要由地缘政治驱动，特别是"近岸外包"和"友岸外包"。由技术应用驱动的 FDI 也促进了这一趋势，包括人工智能相关技术的溢出效应。

（五）行业间 FDI 发生重大转变

根据《金融时报》FDI Intelligence 的报告，2023 年和 2024 年上半年，全球 FDI 由大型资本密集型项目推动，尤其是可再生能源、电池和金属行业。FDI 在软件与 IT 服务行业势头减弱，从 2022 年的第 6 位跌至 2023 年第 11 位。这是自 2013 年以来，该行业首次未能进入 FDI 前十大领域（见图 1–3）。

图 1–3　行业投资矩阵

资料来源：金融时报 FDI Intelligence。

（六）服务业 FDI 持续引领全球 FDI 增长

服务业跨境投资增长是一个长期趋势。自 1990 年以来，服务业 FDI 每十年都显著增长，2000 年增长了五倍，2010 年增长了四倍，2020 年再次增长 50% 以上。第三产业 FDI 的增长速度远远超过了第二产业和第一产业 FDI 的增长速度。目前，服务业投资占 FDI 总量的 72%，服务业 GDP 占全球的 67%（见图 1–4）。

（十亿美元）

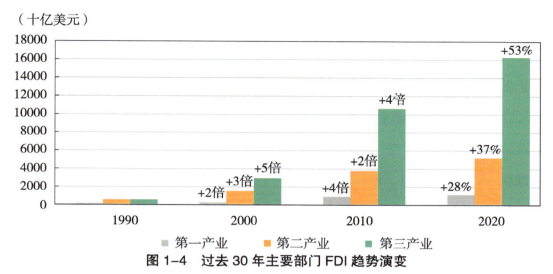

图 1-4 过去 30 年主要部门 FDI 趋势演变

资料来源：James X.Zhan（詹晓宁），基于 UNCTAD 数据。

（七）主权基金成为 FDI 的新来源

公共养老金基金（PPFs）的资产激增，2018 年为 18 万亿美元，2023 年达到 23 万亿美元。与此同时，主权财富基金（SWFs）的资产从 7 万亿美元增加到 11 万亿美元，两类资金管理总额达到 34 万亿美元。包括 PPFs 和 SWFs 在内的主权投资者越来越多地将资金投资于基础设施、能源、房地产和制造业等领域。

二、全球 FDI 面临的挑战与机遇

（一）挑战

1.地缘政治紧张局势

持续的地区冲突和贸易争端，特别是主要经济体之间的争端，带来了不确定性和风险，使投资者更加谨慎。

2.经济不确定性

宏观经济条件（三高：高利率、高债务、高通胀水平；三低：GDP 低增长、贸易流动低、生产率低）以及大幅波动的金融市场，导致经济环境面临挑战，这些因素大幅拉高了投资成本，降低了跨境投资的吸引力。

3. 监管变化

主要国家对外资的监管更加严格，特别是在技术和基础设施等敏感行业，使投资过程变得复杂、投资的政策风险增大。此外，政策不确定性（全球 70 多个经济体选举及选后政策调整）给长期投资带来了更大的挑战。

4. 供应链受阻

全球供应链持续受阻，增加了企业对外投资的成本和物流障碍。五大全球供应链中转点易受到气候变化和地缘政治冲突的影响，关键全球航运路线的受阻——苏伊士运河、巴拿马运河和黑海海峡——给全球贸易带来了前所未有的挑战，影响着每个地区的数百万人的生活。红海航运遭遇的攻击严重影响了通过苏伊士运河的航运，正在重塑全球贸易路线。

5. 技术适应

为适应日新月异的技术变化，需要在新技术和技能上进行大量投资，这可能对某些地区尤其是发展中国家构成障碍。

（二）机遇

1. 可持续投资

对可持续和绿色投资的关注日益增加，各国政府为可再生能源、可持续基础设施和环保技术项目提供激励措施。联合国在全球范围内协调可持续发展目标的实施也为国际投资拓展了更大的空间。

2. 数字化转型

对数字基础设施、人工智能以及其他先进技术的投资预计将增长，企业持续的数字化转型趋势日益显著。

3. 新兴市场

像亚洲、拉美和非洲地区因其增长潜力和不断扩大的消费市场而继续吸引 FDI，这些地区为希望进入新市场的投资者提供了重大机会。

4. 区域合作

不断增加的区域合作和贸易协议可以创建更为一体化的市场，减少跨境投资的障碍，使投资者在多个国家运营变得更加便利。

5. 韧性与创新

企业越来越多地寻求能够提升其韧性和创新能力的投资，包括对自动化、先进制造业以及提高运营效率的技术投资。

总体而言，得益于技术进步、政府政策以及日益增长的全球需求，可再生能源和数字基础设施领域有望实现显著增长。应对挑战并利用机遇，对希望未来几年吸引和受益于 FDI 的国家和公司至关重要。投资者应密切关注全球发展动态，并据此调整策略。

三、全球 FDI 的前景

（一）短期内全球 FDI 持续低迷

2024 年全球经济增长率预计为 2.6%，连续 3 年低于 2015—2019 年疫情前的 3.2% 平均水平（见图 1–5），全球贸易和投资也在低水平上停滞不前。根据世界贸易组织的数据，全球商品贸易量预计 2024 年增长 2.6%（见图 1–6）。过去 4 年，全球跨境投资一直在低位徘徊。在此背景下，2024 年，全球国际直接投资将持续低迷。2025—2026 年，全球国际投资有望回升，但多为恢复性反弹、结构性调整，而非大幅扩张性投资，难以恢复到疫情前的最高水平。

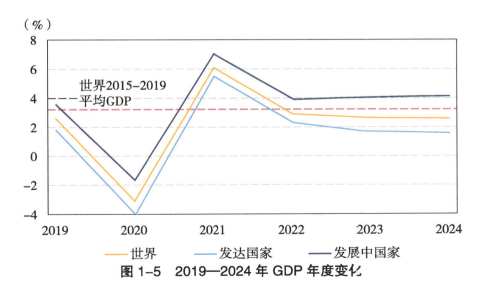

图 1–5　2019—2024 年 GDP 年度变化

资料来源：UNCTAD。

图 1-6　2018—2025 年全球商品贸易量与 GDP 增长

资料来源：WTO。

注：2024 年和 2025 年的数字是预测。2010 年至 2023 年间，商品贸易平均每年增长 2.5%，而 GDP 平均增长 2.7%。

（二）FDI 前景看好的产业

尽管全球 FDI 总体上在低水平徘徊，但以下行业将成为投资亮点，为寻求利用新兴趋势和技术的投资者提供了广阔前景。

1. 可再生能源

随着全球对可持续发展的推动，包括太阳能、风能和水力发电在内的可再生能源项目预计将获得大量 FDI，该行业对于实现气候目标和减少碳排放至关重要。

2. 技术与数字经济

对技术的投资，特别是在人工智能、网络安全和数字基础设施等领域，预计将持续增长。企业的数字化转型和对技术的日益依赖推动了这一趋势。

3. 医疗保健与生物技术

医疗保健行业，包括生物技术和制药领域，因医疗研究、药物开发的持续进展以及对医疗服务需求的增加，继续吸引 FDI。

4. 基础设施

对基础设施项目的投资，如交通、通信和城市发展，仍然是优先事项，这些项目对于经济增长和改善连接性至关重要。

5. 碳捕集、利用与存储（CCUS）

随着减少碳排放的努力加剧，CCUS 行业正成为 FDI 的重要目的地，该行业为环境影响和经济发展提供了机遇。

四、全球产业链大转型：贸易与投资的重新配置

从中长期来看，受技术创新和产业革命、可持续发展浪潮以及地缘政治经济三大要素的影响，全球产业链正在经历重大的结构调整和重组，国际投资与国际生产将向着以下十大方向转型（见表 1-1）。

（一）全球产业链的十大转型方向

表 1-1　全球产业链演变的十大方向

主要方面	十大方向
产业链重塑	产业链区域化
	产业集群化
	产业链数字化和轻资产化
	服务业和制造业一体化
	韧性与安全驱动的产业链多元化
投资贸易模式变化	全球效率型 FDI 下降，区域市场型 FDI 增加
	中间品贸易下行压力增大
	从规模化生产向定制化生产转变
	基础设施和公共服务领域 FDI 增长
	绿色、蓝色和循环经济投资成为投资重点

资料来源：①詹晓宁、齐凡、吴琦琦：百年变局背景下国际直接投资趋势与政策展望，《国际经济评论》，2024 年第 2 期，第 1-24 页。

②Zhan J.X."GVC Transformation and a New Investment Landscape in the 2020s: Driving Forces, Directions, and a Forward-looking Research and Policy Agenda", Journal of International Business Studies, 2021, 69（4）：206-220.

1. 产业链区域化

跨国公司正在将其全球生产网络重组为多个区域和次区域生产中心，从而使全球产业链区域化。区域价值链在全球生产体系中的作用将不断增强，依赖于区域内资源禀赋优势的本地化生产将不断增长，但区域价值链不是封闭的或排他的，国际投资包括区域外的投资，仍是区域价值链的主要驱动因素，各区域价值链之间仍将通过投资贸易进行合作。

2. 产业集群化

现代制造业中的全球产业链更倾向于简化环节并尽可能地本地化，从而使产业内的价值链更短，碎片化程度更低，价值链附加值将更加集中，最终形成产业集群化。价值链区域化以及发达经济体竭力推动的产业回流也是导致价值链变短的影响因素。与此同时，分布式制造作为价值链创新的重要手段，在保证价值链活动更加集中的基础上，实现生产在全球范围内的高效运作。特别是 3D 打印技术的广泛应用以及产业链的数字化可以使企业生产分布范围更广，价值链长度更短、单个地点的附加值更加集中。

3. 产业链数字化和轻资产化

大型数字化跨国公司将通过数字化全球产业链提供数字化基础设施，从而使产业链表现出轻资产化。此外，凭借大型数字跨国公司提供的数字平台，全球产业链治理的数字平台形式将取代传统跨国公司治理模式，最终实现多平台驱动下的价值链治理模式。

4. 服务业国际化及与制造业一体化

增强型数字科技的广泛应用，深度影响服务业，特别是高附加值服务业。其中，高附加值服务业，包括专业和商业服务，以及金融、工程和相关营销活动，在价值链中的比重将不断上升。在劳动力成本套利的驱动下，数字技术的增强使服务业成为离岸外包的新前沿，助力服务业的全球化。传统的中高附加值服务将越来越多地通过远程办公由海外提供。此外，制造业的服务化同样值得关注。在服务与数字化的相互影响下，制造业将越来越多地与数字服务相结合。

5. 韧性与安全驱动的产业链多元化

地缘政治和经济改变了许多国家对全球经济一体化和相互依存的看法，成本和效率不再是国际投资和国际生产布局的最重要因素。与此同时，数字技术也为价值链多元化提供了便利，但多元化本身也放弃了一定程度的规模经济。制造业回流的本地化生产尝试、友岸化生产的生产布局模式以及全产业链体系构建日渐兴起，成为当前全球产业链多元化的重要特征之一。

6. 全球效率型 FDI 下降，区域市场型 FDI 增加

价值链的垂直专业化是吸引效率寻求型 FDI 的基础。随着技术的发展，劳动力红利逐渐消失，数字化跨国企业资产配置的重心由固定资产、有形资产转向流动资产和无形资产。跨国公司更加强调通过市场寻求型投资在各地区复制生产过程，获得市场优势，提高产业链韧性，推动 FDI 从效率寻求型向区域市场寻求型转变。

7. 中间品贸易下行压力大增

全球产业链近岸化、本地化，生产流程及附加值在地理上更加集中，将减少中间投入和零部件的跨境贸易，特别是跨区域贸易，中间产品贸易已经开始减少，其缩减幅度将持续增加。与此同时，跨国公司由效率导向型向市场导向型投资的转变，将直接服务于消费市场。

8. 从规模化生产到定制化生产的转变

基于 3D 打印等新兴生产技术的支持，先进制造业具备规模小、本地化生产以及靠近市场的特点，这一技术改变了传统的国际生产模式。在新兴技术的扶持下，制造业实现了分布式生产，从大规模生产和规模经济向定制化生产和范围经济的转变。除此之外，制造业的服务化也推进了定制化进程，制造商提供的高级定制服务同样可以创造价值，并形成了更加高效且以客户为中心的全球产业链的重要一环。在大数据和物联网的支持下，制造业的服务化将对跨国公司未来的贸易和投资产生深远的影响。

9. 基础设施和公共服务领域 FDI 增长

可持续发展、全球产业链重构以及数字经济的发展均对基础设施提出了新的要求，各国都在努力促进基础设施投资。在政策上，长期以来，仅面向国内投资的公共服务（如医疗保健、教育）、公用事业和数字基础设施等领域，出现了对外资扩大准入的趋势，从而为这些领域的外国投资创造了新的机会。

10. 绿色、蓝色和循环经济投资成为投资的重点

全球可持续发展势在必行，绿色经济、蓝色经济和循环经济具有巨大的国际投资潜力。跨国公司越来越多地使其投资决策、生产过程、产品和服务与可持续发展目标保持一致。统一 ESG 标准，加强企业问责制将对跨国公司及其全球供应网络进一步施压，督

促它们的投资决策兼顾可持续目标。当前可持续发展目标正逐渐被纳入投资政策制定的主流，投资促进和便利化战略也重新定位于可持续发展目标。可见，绿色经济、蓝色经济和循环经济在政治议程上正逐步获得优先地位，未来将受益于更大的政策支持。

（二）未来国际生产新格局

虽然当前全球产业链正朝着区域化趋势发展，但并不意味着全球产业链的解体，而是全球产业链在区域层面上进行新的布局，从而对未来国际投资格局产生重要影响。从近年来全球主要经济体及主要区域 FDI 流动趋势看，未来国际生产格局将呈现以下特点：

1. 中美欧将在未来全球生产格局中保持三足鼎立地位

美国跨国企业在计算机、电子和光学产品、高端设备的制造等诸多领域继续处于全球产业链的上游位置。美国企业将继续把产品生产环节分解至各国或地区进行，但大部分环节在美国政策支持下可能回流国内或近岸市场，对优势产业价值链的掌控能力得到加强。欧洲跨国企业也广泛深度参与全球产业链分工体系，其与美国相似，专注于高端制造业与服务业。虽然近年来吸收外资和对外投资均有所下降，但其全球产业链参与度仍居全球前列。中国是全球最大的制造业大国，拥有全球最全的产业链和战略产业集群，在全球价值链和国际分工中不断向高附加值环节攀升。近期内，由地缘政治所引发的产业回流、生产近岸化与友岸化所引致的投资转移，对中国产生了重大压力和影响，但中国仍将是国际投资，特别是高科技国际投资的重要吸收国。在未来的国际生产体系中，中国、美国和欧盟三大经济体将继续在全球产业链分工体系中处于核心地位，并主导着国际投资的资金走向。

2. 东亚、北美和西欧三大区域产业链分工体系的新拓展

未来几年，全球外资流向将持续重大调整。一是东亚，尤其是东北亚（中、日、韩）资本和传统产能南下，向东南亚和南亚扩张，东盟十国外资流入的增长尤为明显。二是北美资金及产能由北美或其他地区转移或回流至中美洲和加勒比地区，以墨西哥为代表的中美及加勒比地区逐步出现新的出口导向型产业集群。三是欧洲地区的迁移态势，目前欧洲资本已由多年来的由西向东扩张，开始回转为由东向西回流，并向南延伸至环地中海沿岸。

总之，2023 年全球国际直接投资持续低迷，2024 年将在低水平徘徊。2025—2026

年全球国际投资有望回升，但多为恢复性反弹、结构性调整，而非大幅扩张性投资，难以恢复到疫情前的最高水平。中长远来看，全球产业链绊构将持续重大调整，从十大趋势朝着区域化和多极化的方向发展，最终形成中美欧"三足鼎立"的全球三大生产体系。

第二章 中国双向投资实现新发展

近年来，面对复杂严峻的国际环境和全球跨境直接投资下滑的不利局面，中国坚持"引进来"和"走出去"并重，将"更大力度吸引和利用外资"作为中央经济工作会议确定的 2023 年年度重点任务之一，不断提升双向投资便利化水平。2023 年，中国继续保持全球第二大外资流入国地位，对外直接投资居全球第三位，双向投资量稳质升、亮点突出。

一、双向投资政策不断完善

（一）连续推出更大力度吸引外资政策

利用外资是中国对外开放基本国策的重要内容。在构建新发展格局过程中，外资企业在联通国内国际双循环、优化配置资源要素方面发挥着独特的纽带桥梁作用。2022 年底，中央经济工作会议提出，将"更大力度吸引和利用外资"作为年度重点任务之一。2023 年以来，中国相继推出一系列高水平开放和投资促进举措，力度之大，前所未有。外资准入门槛进一步降低，要素跨境流动便利度不断提高，加上深化金融业开放、举办外资企业圆桌会议、打造"投资中国"品牌等务实举措，市场化、法治化、国际化一流营商环境加快形成。

1. 扎实推进高水平开放

2023 年以来，中国以《外商投资法》为基础，不断扩大高水平制度型开放，完善外资管理体制，在扩大外资市场准入、制造业稳外资、保障外资公平待遇、扩大服务业开放、鼓励设立研发中心、对接国际高标准经贸规则方面出台了一系列政策（见表 2-1），对优化营商环境起到了重要作用。

两个吸引外资"24 条"受到跨国公司高度关注和欢迎。2023 年 8 月，国务院发布《关于进一步优化外商投资环境加大吸引外商投资力度的意见》（外资 24 条），提出提高引资质量、保障外资企业国民待遇、加强外商投资保护、提高投资运营便利化水平、加大财税支持力度、完善外商投资促进方式等六个方面举措，以更好地营造市场化、法治化、国际化一流营商环境，更大力度吸引和利用外商投资，推进高水平对外开放。同时，鼓励各地区因地制宜出台配套举措，增强政策协同效应。2024 年 3 月，国务院办公厅发布了《扎实推进高水平对外开放更大力度吸引和利用外资行动方案》（新外资 24 条），在扩大市场准入的同时，提出要优化公平竞争环境，做好外资企业服务，推动相关政策落实落地生效；印发招标投标领域公平竞争审查规则，着力破除地方保护、所有制歧视等问题；出台政府采购本国产品标准，要求在政府采购活动中对内外资企业生产的符合标准的产品一视同仁、平等对待等。

加快构建与国际高标准经贸规则相衔接的制度体系。2023 年 6 月，国务院发布《关于在有条件的自由贸易试验区和自由贸易港试点对接国际高标准推进制度型开放若干措施》，从推动货物贸易创新发展、推进服务贸易自由便利、便利商务人员临时入境、促进数字贸易健康发展、加大优化营商环境力度、健全完善风险防控制度六个方面提出了一系列制度创新举措，目前各项试点措施已全面落地，形成了一批引领性成果。2023 年 12 月，国务院发布《全面对接国际高标准经贸规则推进中国（上海）自由贸易试验区高水平制度型开放总体方案》，支持上海自贸试验区在服务贸易、金融开放、数字贸易等多个领域，率先对接高标准经贸规则，加大先行先试力度。目前相关举措正在加快落地实施中，部分领域已取得积极进展。

鼓励外资在华开展科技创新合作是中国新时代吸引外资政策的重要内容。2023 年 1 月，国务院办公厅转发商务部科技部《关于进一步鼓励外商投资设立研发中心的若干措施》，提出完善科技创新金融支持、畅通政府项目渠道、支持研发数据依法跨境流动、提高知识产权执法水平等 16 个方面举措。其中有许多值得关注的亮点，如支持外资研发中心使用大型科研仪器、提升外籍人员工作许可便利度等，有利于为外资研发中心营造良好发展环境，更好发挥其在全球创新资源配置中的独特优势。

表 2-1　2023 年以来中国出台的鼓励外商投资的综合性政策

发布时间	文件名称	印发机关	主要内容
2024 年 7 月	《关于加强商务和金融协同，更大力度支持跨境贸易和投资高质量发展的意见》	商务部等部门	稳外贸、稳外资、深化"一带一路"经贸合作和对外投资合作等
2024 年 4 月	《数字商务三年行动计划（2024—2026 年）》	商务部	推动商务各领域数字化发展

续表

发布时间	文件名称	印发机关	主要内容
2024 年 3 月	《扎实推进高水平对外开放更大力度吸引和利用外资行动方案》	国务院办公厅	新一轮更大力度吸引外资的 24 条举措
2023 年 8 月	《关于进一步优化外商投资环境加大吸引外商投资力度的意见》	国务院	优化外商投资环境、加大引资力度 24 条举措
2023 年 6 月	《国务院关于在有条件的自由贸易试验区和自由贸易港试点对接国际高标准推进制度型开放若干措施的通知》	国务院	对接高标准国际高标准、推进制度开放
2023 年 3 月	《商务部等 17 部门关于服务构建新发展格局推动边（跨）境经济合作区高质量发展若干措施的通知》	商务部等 17 部门	深化区域开放
2023 年 1 月	国务院办公厅转发商务部科技部《关于进一步鼓励外商投资设立研发中心若干措施的通知》	商务部科技部	支持科技创新

资料来源：根据公开资料整理。

2. 进一步放宽外资准入

党的十八大以来，在自贸试验区先行先试基础上，中国《外商投资法》确立了外资准入前国民待遇加负面清单管理制度。2021 年修订出台的自贸试验区版和全国版外资准入负面清单分别压缩至 27 条和 31 条，制造业限制性措施在自贸试验区实现"清零"，金融、交通运输、商贸物流、专业服务等领域有序放开，为外资企业提供更广阔的市场空间。2023 年，习近平主席在第三届"一带一路"国际合作高峰论坛开幕式上提出，全面取消制造业领域外资准入限制措施，彰显了中国不断扩大开放的决心。

逐步放宽外商投资准入限制。2024 年 3 月，国务院办公厅印发《扎实推进高水平对外开放更大力度吸引和利用外资行动方案》，在扩大市场准入方面提出合理缩减外商投资准入负面清单、开展放宽科技创新领域外商投资准入试点、扩大银行保险领域外资金融机构准入等措施，开放力度大，含金量高。例如，全面取消制造业领域外资准入限制措施，持续推进电信、医疗等领域扩大开放；允许北京、上海、广东等自由贸易试验区选择若干符合条件的外商投资企业，在基因诊断与治疗技术开发和应用等领域进行扩大开放试点；在保障安全、高效和稳定的前提下，支持符合条件的外资机构依法开展银行卡清算业务。

扩大增值电信领域对外开放试点。中国增值电信领域市场规模巨大，外资企业高度关注。工业和信息化部 2024 年 4 月发布《增值电信业务扩大对外开放试点方案》，提出在北京市服务业扩大开放综合示范区、上海自贸试验区临港新片区及社会主义现代化建设引领区、海南自由贸易港、深圳中国特色社会主义先行示范区率先开展试点，取消互联网数据中心（IDC）、内容分发网络（CDN）、互联网接入服务（ISP）、在线数据处理与交易处理，以及信息服务中信息发布平台和递送服务（互联网新闻信息、网络出版、网络视听、互联网文化经营除外）、信息保护和处理服务业务的外资股比限制，标志着中国电信市场扩大开放取得重要突破，将吸引更多外资企业在华开展增值电信业务。

推进统一市场建设与公平竞争。市场监管总局、国家发改委、财政部、商务部 2023年 6 月发布《关于开展妨碍统一市场和公平竞争的政策措施清理工作的通知》，全面清理妨碍市场准入和退出、妨碍商品和要素自由流动等妨碍统一市场和公平竞争的有关政策措施，有助于进一步营造公开透明、竞争有序的市场环境，为外资企业拓展中国市场提供良好的制度保障。

3. 金融业对外开放不断深化

金融开放是高水平开放的关键环节，事关跨国公司在华长远战略布局。2018 年以来，中国全面持续推进金融高水平对外开放，中国人民银行等金融管理部门先后推出 50多项金融对外开放政策举措，为营造市场化、法治化、国际化一流营商环境，为吸引更多外资和长期资本来中国开展业务、落地生根创造了积极有利的条件。

2023 年中央金融工作会议进一步强调，要着力推进金融高水平开放，确保国家金融和经济安全，坚持"引进来"和"走出去"并重，稳步扩大金融领域制度型开放，提升跨境投融资便利化，吸引更多外资金融机构和长期资本来华展业兴业。

当前，中国金融开放在多个领域有序推进。一方面，金融服务业对外开放力度不断加大。已完全取消银行、证券、基金管理、期货、人身险领域的外资持股比例限制，在企业征信、评级、支付等领域给予外资机构国民待遇，放宽对外资机构在资产规模、经营年限等股东资质方面的要求，大幅扩大外资机构业务范围，在开展碳减排支持工具等新业务试点时对中外资机构一视同仁。另一方面，资本市场开放有序实施。逐步推动债券、股票、金融衍生品市场对外开放，沪深港通、基金互认、债券通、沪伦通、互换通等互联互通机制相继建立并持续完善，QFII 和 RQFII 全面取消额度限制，粤港澳大湾区跨境理财通业务试点不断优化，外资参与中国金融市场的便利度进一步提升。人民银行资料显示，截至 2023 年 9 月末，境外机构持有境内股票、债券等人民币金融资产规模合计 9.3 万亿元。2024 年 3 月，《扎实推进高水平对外开放更大力度吸引和利用外资行动方案》明确提出扩大银行保险领域外资金融机构准入，拓展外资金融机构参与国内债券市场业务范围，深入实施合格境外有限合伙人境内投资试点。

4. 促进数据跨境安全有序流动

随着数字经济开放创新浪潮的不断推进，数据跨境安全有序流动已成为跨国公司关注的焦点问题之一。在 2023 年 9 月发布《规范和促进数据跨境流动规定（征求意见稿）》的基础上，国家互联网信息办公室于 2024 年 3 月公布《促进和规范数据跨境流动规定》，提出在保障数据安全的前提下促进数据依法有序自由流动的有关举措，主要包括：一是明确重要数据出境安全评估申报标准；二是明确免予申报数据出境安全评估、订立个人信息出境标准合同、通过个人信息保护认证的数据出境活动条件；三是设立自由贸易试验区负面清单制度；四是调整应当申报数据出境安全评估、订立个人信息出境标准合同、通过个人信息保护认证的数据出境活动条件；五是延长数据出境安全评估结果有效期，增加数据处理者可以申请延长评估结果有效期的规定。总体上看，数据跨境流动的便利度明显提升，有助于降低企业合规成本、扩大高水平对外开放，受到跨国公司积极肯定。

5. 持续打造"投资中国"品牌

当前，全球经济增速放缓，地缘政治风险显著上升，各国引资竞争日趋激烈，外部环境的复杂性、严峻性、不确定性上升对中国吸引外资带来一定挑战。2023 年 3 月起，商务部举办"投资中国年"系列活动，统筹各方资源，推动招商引资的常态化、系列化和多元化。一方面，积极"请进来"，通过举办主旨论坛等综合性活动以及有关省份举办的专场推介和"进博会走进地方""跨国公司地方行"等活动，搭建平台、畅通渠道，展示全国各省市的投资机遇，亮出"投资中国"的金字招牌。另一方面，主动"走出去"，充分发挥展会平台、驻外经商机构和投资促进机构作用，支持各省市和企业到海外市场开展重点推介，多层次、多形式开展招商引资活动，为国内外投资对接创造平台和桥梁。全国各省市在"投资中国"品牌下，结合各自区位优势、资源禀赋、产业特点，举办系列配套活动，形成全国引资"一盘棋"。"投资中国"系列活动展示了中国持续扩大市场准入、打造高水平营商环境的决心，也展示了中国作为全球第二大消费市场的潜力与活力，坚定了外资企业关注中国、投资中国的信心。

专栏2-1　商务部建立外资企业圆桌会议制度

自2023年7月起，商务部建立外资企业圆桌会议制度，定期召开会议听取外资企业反映困难问题和意见建议。圆桌会议鼓励企业畅所欲言，部分问题在会上当场得到解决，对于尚未解决的难点和共性问题建立工作台账，与有关部门深入会商研究，针对性出台务实举措。

一是紧抓快办一批重点问题。在外资企业圆桌会议制度的推动下，商务部会同财政部、税务总局继续对外资研发中心采购国产设备全额退还增值税；财政部、税务总局将外籍个人有关津补贴个人所得税政策延续至2027年底；国家发展改革委明确绿色电力交易规则；市场监管总局发布《外商投资企业参与我国标准化工作"十问十答"》，支持外资企业平等参与中国标准制定工作。

二是改进完善一批政策规定。在外资企业圆桌会议制度的推动下，外交部发布新版外国人来华签证申请表，便利外籍人员来华；国家移民局签发启用新版外国人永久居留身份证，便利外籍人员工作、学习、生活；市场监管总局修订《特殊医学用途配方食品注册管理办法》，完善特殊医学用途配方食品管理。

三是解释说明一批热点关切。圆桌会议由商务部搭台、各部门参与，主动对接中国美国商会、中国欧盟商会、中国日本商会等主要外国商协会及重点外资企业，就数据跨境流动、出口管制、反间谍法、最新外资政策等热点关切针对性开展政策解读。"面对面"答疑释惑，增强政企互信，有力提升政策透明度和可预期性。

截至2024年1月底，商务部已召开16场外资企业圆桌会，共400余家外资企业、外国商协会参会，解决会上反映的问题诉求300余件。同时，各省也建立"圆桌会议"制度，共召开140余场圆桌会，2200余家外资企业、外国商协会参会，已解决问题诉求900余件。

6. 为外国人来华工作生活提供便利

2023年以来，中国先后出台20余项政策措施，便利外籍商务人员往来，稳定来华发展预期，助力营造一流营商环境和外商投资环境[①]。一是持续优化外籍人员来华政策措施。2023 年 8 月，公布延续实施外籍个人津补贴等有关个人所得税优惠政策，对持普通护照急需来华从事商贸合作、访问交流、投资创业、旅游观光等外籍人员提供口岸签证入境便利。二是积极为国际商务人员提供签证便利。扩大免签国家范围，对法国、德国、意大利、荷兰、西班牙、马来西亚等国家持普通护照人员试行单方面免签政策，后又扩大至瑞士等国。截至 2024 年 7 月，中国位于 19 个省（自治区、直辖市）的 41 个对外开放口岸，对 54 个国家人员实施 72 小时或 144 小时过境免签政策。对在华从事商贸合作、投资创业等商务活动的外籍人员，有正当合理事由需多次往返的，可签发 5 年内多次入境有效签证，并可就近就便办理签证延期换发或者补发。三是持续优化移民出入境政务服务。建设启用多语种政府网站和政务新媒体平台，及时公布外籍人员来华政策及签证证件申办规定。

（二）对外投资政策逐步健全完善

对外投资是整合全球创新资源、优化资源配置、促进国内产业升级、畅通国内国际双循环的重要途径。中国坚持"政府引导、企业主导、市场化运作"的原则，鼓励和支持企业稳妥有序开展对外投资，深度参与全球产业分工和合作。持续健全对外投资管理服务体系，不断推进对外投资便利化、完善事前事中事后监管，引导对外投资企业提升合规经营水平，支持数字经济与绿色发展领域的对外投资合作，提升对外投资的质量和水平。

1. 健全对外投资管理服务政策体系

中国持续优化对外投资管理体制机制，逐步建立起以监管政策、支持政策和服务促进为核心的对外投资政策和服务体系。一是健全投资管理。建立对外投资事前事中事后全周期、全流程管理体系。依托《境外投资管理办法》，实行"备案为主、核准为辅"的对外投资备案（核准）管理模式，做好对外投资真实性合规性审核。开展对外投资"双随机、一公开"检查工作，督促企业落实合规工作要求。做好企业境外并购事项前期报告和对外投资备案核准环节风险提示工作，指导企业防范对外投资风险。二是完善投资促进。推进对外投资便利化，实施对外投资备案（核准）无纸化管理，推动对外

---

① http://www.scio.gov.cn/live/2024/33491/tw/，国家移民局外国人管理司负责人贾同斌答记者问。

投资电子证照制发应用，累计制发电子证照超 3 万份，对外投资政务服务效能显著提升。依托进博会、广交会、服贸会、投洽会、消博会等重大展会，为企业开展对外投资合作搭建平台，助力企业"走出去"。三是做好权益保障。积极推动多双边投资合作工作组建设，与 130 多个国家和地区签署双边投资保护协定，与 29 个国家和地区签署 22 个自由贸易协定，与 60 多个国家建立 70 多个双边投资合作工作组，为企业开展对外投资合作营造良好外部环境。四是加强海外综合服务。商务部建立完善"走出去"公共服务平台，为企业提供政策咨询、业务办理、信息共享等一站式普惠性公共服务。定期发布《对外投资合作别国（地区）指南》等公共服务产品，涵盖 170 多个国家和地区，从投资环境、法律法规、产业发展等方面为"走出去"企业提供信息支持和服务。五是完善对外承包工程管理工作。我国对外承包工程对带动产品技术服务"走出去"、服务构建新发展格局、实现我与相关国家互利合作发挥了重要作用。2024 年 5 月，商务部发布《对外承包工程项目备案和立项管理办法》[1]，进一步优化监管。

2. 推动对外投资合作数字化和绿色化发展

数字化和绿色化转型发展是推动世界经济增长的新动能。中国一直是数字和绿色领域国际合作的积极倡导者和参与者，习近平主席在 2021 年第四届中国国际进口博览会开幕式上表示，"中国将深度参与绿色低碳、数字经济等国际合作"。2023 年 10 月，第三届"一带一路"国际合作高峰论坛贸易畅通专题论坛期间，中方与有关国家共同发布《数字经济和绿色发展国际经贸合作框架倡议》，包括数字领域经贸合作、绿色发展合作、能力建设、落实与展望等四个部分，并设置营造开放安全的环境、提升贸易便利化水平、弥合数字鸿沟、增强消费者信任、营造促进绿色发展的政策环境、加强贸易合作促进绿色和可持续发展、鼓励绿色技术和服务的交流与投资合作等七个支柱。目前，第一批确认加入该倡议的国家有 35 个[2]，联合国贸发会议、联合国工发组织和国际贸易中心等国际组织表示支持，上述框架落地生根，为各参加方带来实实在在的好处。引导企业

---

[1] http://www.mofcom.gov.cn/article/xwfb/xwsjfzr/202405/20240503510979.shtml.

[2] 分别为阿富汗、阿根廷、白俄罗斯、文莱、柬埔寨、喀麦隆、中非、智利、中国、库克群岛、科特迪瓦、埃塞俄比亚、匈牙利、伊朗、肯尼亚、吉尔吉斯斯坦、老挝、蒙古、莫桑比克、缅甸、尼加拉瓜、尼日利亚、纽埃、巴基斯坦、巴布亚新几内亚、菲律宾、塞尔维亚、塞拉利昂、斯里兰卡、塔吉克斯坦、坦桑尼亚、泰国、土库曼斯坦、乌兹别克斯坦、赞比亚。

积极落实《对外投资合作绿色发展工作指引》《数字经济对外投资合作工作指引》，培育对外投资合作数字、绿色发展新动能，与 44 个国家签署 76 份数字、绿色、蓝色经济等领域投资合作文件，深化相关领域双边投资合作。

3. 完善金融服务"走出去"政策

一是持续完善对企业海外投融资的支持政策。2023 年 10 月，财政部发布《"一带一路"债务可持续性分析框架（市场融资国家适用）》。该分析框架与 2019 年发布的《"一带一路"债务可持续性分析框架（低收入国家适用）》互为补充，全面覆盖共建"一带一路"低收入和中等收入国家，为国内企业参与"一带一路"投融资提供指引。2023 年 7 月，国家外汇管理局发布《汇率风险情景与外汇衍生产品运用案例集》，运用大量真实案例，使企业充分了解汇率避险的积极意义和关键操作，积极支持对外投资企业管理"走出去"过程中的汇率风险。二是金融业自身"走出去"稳步推进，为服务企业"走出去"提供保障。根据中国银行研究院数据，截至 2023 年 6 月末，五大行已在境外 67 个国家和地区设立了经营性机构，基本覆盖了主要国际性、区域性金融中心。三是金融机构根据企业"走出去"的实际需求，不断创新产品与服务。如国家开发银行、国家进出口银行等充分发挥政策性金融作用，支持企业发挥优势，支持中欧班列高质量发展。四是人民币跨境支付等金融基础设施持续优化，为企业"走出去"提供便捷的资金结算服务。根据人民银行《2023 年支付体系运行总体情况》，2023 年人民币跨境支付系统（CIPS）处理业务 661.33 万笔，金额 123.06 万亿元，同比分别增长 50.29% 和 27.27%。

4. 完善境外机构和人员安全管理制度

2023 年 11 月 7 日，在第六届中国国际进口博览会"跨境投资高质量发展圆桌会"期间，商务部与中国对外承包工程商会共同发布第三版《境外中资企业机构和人员安全管理指南》。作为中国首个针对"走出去"企业境外安全风险管理工作的指导性文件，该指南首版发布于 2012 年，此后不断修订完善，全面梳理了境外中资企业和人员面临的各类风险，系统总结了风险管理的相关原则，从风险识别、评估预警、安全管控、应急处置等七个维度，为开展跨境投资业务的中国企业提供了务实有效的参考借鉴。

5. 继续深化"一带一路"合作机制

2023 年 10 月，在第三届"一带一路"国际合作高峰论坛绿色发展高级别论坛上，启动绿色发展投融资合作伙伴关系并纳入高峰论坛主席声明和多边合作成果文件清单。

绿色发展投融资合作伙伴关系由"一带一路"绿色发展国际联盟与中外合作伙伴共同发起，遵循开放包容、互利共赢、市场运作的原则，旨在发挥合作伙伴各自专业优势，积极推动绿色发展投融资合作，探索开展绿色投融资与绿色项目评价工作，完善项目的ESG 评价和管理，为解决绿色"一带一路"建设中面临的投融资瓶颈，打造沟通合作平台并提供务实解决方案。

二、双向投资质量效益持续提升

（一）利用外资处于历史高位、保持全球第二位

2023 年，全球跨境投资流量下降 2%，发展中经济体引资下降 7%。面对严峻复杂的国际形势，中国实际利用外资金额同比有所下降，但仍然保持全球第二大外资流入国地位，引资规模处于历史高位，结构进一步优化，外资企业继续对中国市场充满信心。

1. 继续保持全球第二大外资流入国地位

2023 年，中国充分发挥超大规模市场、完备供应链体系、人力资本充足、创新应用场景丰富等综合优势，坚持扩大开放，超大经济体磁场效应持续显现。联合国贸发会议统计数据显示，2023 年中国吸收外国直接投资 1632.5 亿美元，占全球比重为 12.3%，继续保持全球第二大外资流入国地位，仅次于美国（3109.5 亿美元，占比 30.1%）。2020 年以来，中国实际利用外资在全球比重始终稳定在 12% 以上（见图 2–1）。中国仍然是世界上最受欢迎的投资目的地之一，为跨国公司全球业务发展提供重要支撑。

2. 引资规模处于历史高位

2023 年以来，受世界经济增速放缓、地缘政治风险上升、外需减弱等多重复杂因素交织，全球跨国直接投资不振，各国招商引资竞争更加激烈。联合国贸发会议发布的数据显示，2023 年全球外国直接投资流量为 1.33 万亿美元，比 2022 年减少 2%。如果排除少数"管道"经济体（即充当流向其他国家 FDI 的中介经济体）剧烈波动等影响，全球跨境投资流量实际下降 10% 以上。在全球最大的 20 个外资流入国中，有 10 个外资流量出现下滑[1]。在此背景下，2023 年，中国新设立外商投资企业 53766 家，同比增长 39.7%，

---

[1] UNCTAD，《2024 世界投资报告》。

处于历史第二高位；实际使用外资金额 1632 亿美元，同比下降 13.7%，但处于历史第三高位，仅低于比较特殊的 2021 年和 2022 年（见图 2-2）。

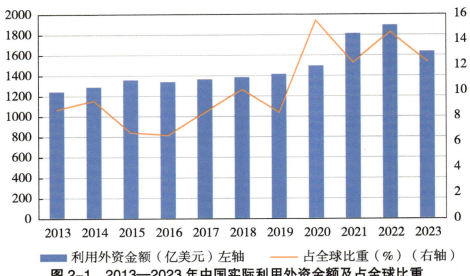

图 2-1　2013—2023 年中国实际利用外资金额及占全球比重

资料来源：2013—2022 年数据来自《中国外资统计公报 2023》，2023 年中国引资数据来自商务部，全球数据来自 UNCTAD《2024 世界投资报告》。

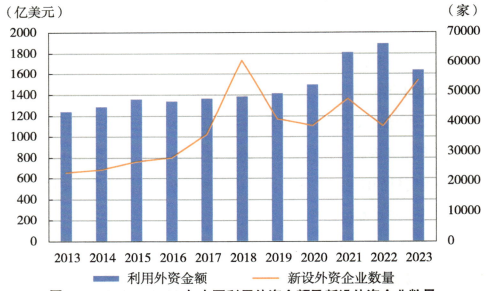

图 2-2　2013—2023 年中国利用外资金额及新设外资企业数量

资料来源：商务部。

3. 利用外资质量进一步优化

2023 年，中国高技术产业引资 4233.4 亿元人民币，增长 6.5%；占实际使用外资金额比重为 37.4%，较 2022 年全年提升 1.3 个百分点，创历史新高；制造业引资占比提升

1.6 个百分点，达到了 27.9%。从国别来看，法国、英国、荷兰、瑞士、澳大利亚等发达经济体实际对华投资分别增长 84.1%、81.0%、31.5%、21.4% 和 17.1%；欧盟、美国、日本在华新设外资企业数均实现增长。2024 年 1—4 月，外资规上工业企业利润总额增长 16.7%，高于全国平均水平（4.3%），表明外资企业经营状况有所改善。

4. 外资金融机构深度融入中国经济

在监管部门出台稳步取消外资股比限制、大幅降低外资准入门槛、扩大准入准营范围等一系列开放政策的推动下，外资金融机构通过收购股权、增资、成立分公司等方式不断加快布局中国市场的步伐。截至 2023 年底，30 家全球系统重要性银行均在华设立分支机构，全球最大的 40 家保险公司近半数进入了中国市场。截至 2024 年 5 月，已有 10 家外资控股证券公司、9 家外商独资基金管理公司、3 家外资控股期货公司获准在华开展业务[①]；1128 家境外机构进入中国债券市场，境外机构在中国债券市场的托管余额 4.27 万亿元（见表 2-2）。中国金融业对外开放持续扩大，双向开放的金融体系加速形成，有力支持了高质量发展。外资金融机构不断加快在华业务布局，持续加码中国市场，深度参与中国经济发展和金融市场运行，已经成为中国金融业一支非常重要的力量。

表 2-2　外资金融机构在华发展成就（截至 2023 年 12 月）

外资银行		外资保险公司	
法人银行	41 家	营业性机构	67 家
分行	116 家	代表处	70 家
代表处	132 家	资产总额	2.4 万亿元
营业性机构	888 家	占境内保险行业市场份额	10%
总资产	3.86 万亿元		

资料来源：2024 年 1 月 25 日，国务院新闻发布会，国家金融监管总局副局长肖远企答记者问，经作者整理。

5. 外资企业继续对中国市场充满信心

2023 年 6 月，中国贸促会发布的一项问卷调查结果显示，98.2% 的受访外资企业

---

① https://www.gov.cn/yaowen/shipin/202405/content_6950781.htm。

和外国商协会对中国经济发展前景有信心，表示将继续在华投资，分享中国发展红利。2024 年一季度，中国贸促会对超 600 家外资企业的营商环境调研[①]表明，受访外资企业对中国市场充满信心，七成以上企业看好未来 5 年中国市场发展前景，比 2023 年四季度提高约 3.8 个百分点；过半企业认为中国市场吸引力"上升"，比 2023 年四季度提高约 2.9 个百分点。受访企业对中国营商环境的满意度评价较高，所有指标"满意"及以上评价占比均较 2023 年四季度继续提升。

2024 年 2 月，中国美国商会发布的年度《中国商务环境调查报告》表明[②]，尽管仍然面临突出挑战，在华美企对中国商业环境信心较 2023 年普遍有所提升：约 40% 的受访企业对未来两年在华盈利潜力持乐观态度，高于 2023 年报告的 33%；44% 的受访企业表示对中国市场增长感觉良好；38% 的受访企业对中国经济复苏 / 增长感到乐观或较为乐观；一半受访企业将中国列为全球首选或前三位投资目的地。日本贸易振兴机构表示，近 90% 的受访日本企业将在中国维持或加大投资。中国欧盟商会的企业调查显示，77% 的受访企业有意扩大在华南地区的业务；中国德国商会的企业调查显示，一半以上德企计划在未来两年内增加在华投资[③]。

2024 年，联合国贸发会议对全球排名前 100 位跨国企业的跟踪研究表明[④]，2019 年以来，大型跨国企业从中国撤资的数量正在减少，跨国企业认识到在世界第二大经济体保持业务的战略重要性，这不仅是为了进入其广阔的市场，也是为了从中国先进的制造能力和完善的供应链中受益。

（二）对外投资合作平稳健康发展

2023 年，中国对外直接投资平稳健康发展，对外投资大国地位日益巩固，境外中资企业经营成效良好，制造业对外投资和对"一带一路"共建国家投资持续增长，金融业"走出去"成效显著，企业"走出去"能力和信心不断提升。

[①] https://www.ccpit.org/a/20240428/20240428ynnu.html，中国贸促会 2024 年 4 月例行新闻发布会。

[②] http://www.cacs.mofcom.gov.cn/article/gnwjmdt/sb/zm/202402/179540.html，中国贸易救济信息网，中国美国商会报告：美企乐观看待中国商业前景。

[③] 《中国发展改革报》：外贸实现"开门红"，外企看好中国未来，2024 年 3 月 30 日。

[④] UNCTAD，《2024 世界投资报告》。

1. 对外投资大国地位日益巩固

联合国贸发会议的数据显示，2023 年全球对外直接投资流量为 1.55 万亿美元，与 2022 年基本持平；中国实现对外投资稳中有进。据商务部、国家外汇局统计，2023 年中国对外直接投资流量为 1772.9 亿美元，比上年增长 8.7%。截至 2023 年底，中国 3.1 万家境内投资者在国（境）外共设立对外直接投资企业 4.8 万家，分布在全球 189 个国家（地区）。从全球来看，2023 年，中国对外直接投资流量居全球第三位 [1]，前两位分别为美国（4043.2 亿美元）和日本 1840.2 亿美元）。自 2012 年起，中国对外直接投资流量已连续 12 年在全球排名前三（见图 2-3）。

图 2-3　2013—2023 年中国对外投资金额及增速

资料来源：商务部、国家统计局、国家外汇管理局：《2023 年度中国对外直接投资统计公报》，中国商务出版社 2024 年版，经作者计算整理。

2. 境外中资企业经营成效良好

2023 年，境外中资企业总体经营情况良好，近七成企业盈利或持平，当年收益再投资 784.6 亿美元，为历史第三高值，占同期中国对外直接投资流量的 44.2%[2]。2023 年，

---

[1] UNCTAD，《2024 世界投资报告》。

[2] 商务部、国家统计局、国家外汇管理局：《2023 年度中国对外直接投资统计公报》，中国商务出版社 2024 年版。

境外企业向投资所在国家（地区）缴纳各种税金总额 753 亿美元，比上年增长 0.3%，年末境外企业从业员工总数 428.9 万人，其中雇用外方员工 257 万人，增加 7.7 万人，占比 59.9%[①]。

3. 四大领域占对外投资流量近八成

2023 年，中国对外直接投资涵盖了国民经济的 18 个行业大类，流向租赁和商务服务、批发和零售、制造业、金融业的投资均超过百亿美元。其中，制造业对外投资 273.4 亿美元，比上年增长 0.7%，占 15.4%。制造业对外投资主要流向汽车制造、其他制造、计算机/通信和其他电子设备制造、通用设备制造、有色金属冶炼和压延加工、非金属矿物制品、橡胶和塑料制品、医药制造、电气机械和器材制造、化学原料和化学制品、金属制品、专用设备制造等领域。流向租赁和商务服务、批发和零售、制造业、金融业的对外直接投资合计 1385.5 亿美元，占当年流量总额的 78.1%（见图 2-4）。

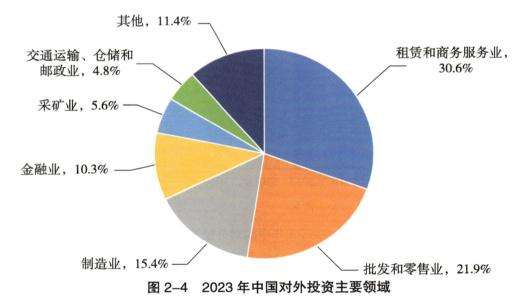

图 2-4　2023 年中国对外投资主要领域

资料来源：商务部、国家统计局、国家外汇管理局：《2023 年度中国对外直接投资统计公报》，中国商务出版社 2024 年版。

4. 对"一带一路"共建国家投资快速增长

根据《2023 年度中国对外直接投资统计公报》，2023 年，中国对亚洲投资 1416.0 亿美元，占当年对外直接投资流量的 79.9%，比上年增长 13.9%。对拉丁美洲投资 134.8 亿美

[①] 商务部、国家统计局、国家外汇管理局：《2023 年度中国对外直接投资统计公报》，中国商务出版社 2024 年版。

元，占当年对外直接投资流量的 7.6%，比上年下降 17.6%，主要流向开曼群岛、英属维尔京群岛、墨西哥、巴西、智利、哥伦比亚、厄瓜多尔、玻利维亚等国家（地区）。对欧洲投资 99.7 亿美元，占当年对外直接投资流量的 5.6%，比上年下降 3.6%，主要流向卢森堡、英国、荷兰、瑞典、德国、俄罗斯联邦、塞尔维亚、匈牙利、瑞士、爱尔兰、意大利、捷克、格鲁吉亚等国家。对北美洲投资 77.8 亿美元，占当年对外直接投资流量的 5.6%，比上年增长 7%。其中，对美国投资 69.1 亿美元，比上年下降 5.2%；对加拿大投资 3.5 亿美元，比上年增长 141%。2023 年，中国对"一带一路"共建国家直接投资 407.1 亿美元，较上年增长 31.5%，占当年对外直接投资流量的 23%。截至 2023 年末，中国企业对"一带一路"共建国家设立境外企业 1.7 万家，直接投资存量为 3348.4 亿美元，占中国对外直接投资存量的 11.3%，存量位列前十的国家是新加坡、印度尼西亚、卢森堡、越南、马来西亚、泰国、俄罗斯联邦、老挝、阿拉伯联合酋长国、柬埔寨。

5. 境外经贸合作区促进互利共赢、共同发展

境外经贸合作区是中国对外投资的方式创新和重要组成部分，是企业集群式走出去、与东道国开展互利共赢合作的重要平台。党的十八大以来，特别是共建"一带一路"倡议提出后，中国与有关国家积极开展合作区建设合作，取得积极成效。合作区快速发展，建设规模不断扩大，国别产业布局持续优化，集聚辐射效应持续放大，已成为高质量共建"一带一路"的生动实践、加强产业链供应链国际合作的有效载体、深化经贸关系的亮丽"名片"。截至 2024 年 6 月底，纳入商务部统计的境外经贸合作区分布在全球 46 个国家，涵盖了加工制造、资源利用、农业产业、商贸物流、科技研发等多种类型，累计投资近 800 亿美元，上缴东道国税费超 133 亿美元，为当地创造超过 55 万个就业岗位。埃及苏伊士经贸合作区、柬埔寨西哈努克港经济特区、泰国泰中罗勇工业园、匈牙利中欧商贸物流园等一批合作效果好、辐射效应大的合作区已成为各国开展互利合作的投资热土，携手共建境外经贸合作区已成为众多国家的共识。

6. 金融业"走出去"成效显著

中国金融机构"走出去"取得了显著成效，截至 2023 年 6 月，五大综合性商业银行[①]

---

① 中国工商银行、中国农业银行、中国银行、中国建设银行、交通银行。

在境外 67 个国家和地区设立经营性机构，覆盖了全球主要的国际性和区域性金融中心[①]，13 家中资银行在 50 个"一带一路"共建国家设立了 145 家一级机构；6 家中资保险机构在 8 个"一带一路"共建国家设立了 15 家境外分支机构。截至 2023 年 7 月，内地近 80 家证券期货基金经营机构在香港设立了子公司，跨境业务规模持续增长。近年来，人民币国际化稳步推进，为境内外经营主体提供更加多元化、便利化的币种选择，人民币的国际地位和全球影响力不断提升，目前已经成为全球第四大支付货币、第三大易融资货币和第五大外汇交易货币，已有 80 多个境外央行或货币当局将人民币纳入外汇储备[②]。

7. 企业"走出去"能力和信心不断提升

中国企业"走出去"跨国经营的能力稳步提升。2024 年 9 月，中国企业联合会、中国企业家协会发布 2024"中国 100 大跨国公司"名单及跨国指数[③]。上榜企业的平均跨国指数为 15.35%，较 2023 年下降 0.55 个百分点，同期世界跨国公司 100 大跨国指数下降 2.64 个百分点。中国 100 大跨国公司海外资产总额、海外员工总数分别比 2023 年提高 5.12%、6.90%；入围门槛为 198.40 亿元，较上年增加 19.31 亿元，提高 10.78%。2024 年 3 月，中国贸促会发布《中国企业对外投资现状及意向调查报告》[④]，2023 年中国企业对外投资平稳发展，超八成受访企业扩大和维持对外投资意向，较 2022 年增加近一成，超九成企业看好未来对外投资前景。

---

① 《金融时报》：我国金融机构"走出去"取得显著成效，2024 年 2 月 7 日。

② 《金融时报》：蹄疾步稳金融对外开放不断迈向更高水平，2024 年 7 月 16 日。

③ 新华网：https://www.xinhuanet.com/energy/20240912/a2c155504ce045148790b1f96cda4ceb/c.html.

④ 问卷调查覆盖国内 20 多个省份，共回收问卷 1118 份，涵盖各种类型、行业和规模企业，超六成问卷填答人属于企业管理层，能够反映中国企业对外投资的真实情况。

第三章 中国开放合作吸引力不断增强

在全球经济深度融合、中国经济高质量发展的背景下，中国吸引外资的主导优势正在从低成本要素优势向基于超大市场规模、全产业链和创新禀赋的综合优势转变。中国是全球超大规模且最有增长潜力的市场，拥有良好稳定的政策环境、全球最完备的产业体系，并且在全球创新体系中的地位不断上升、人力资本优势日益凸显，正在依托自身综合优势成为对全球要素资源的强大引力场，为各国投资者立足中国、面向全球、赢得未来提供更大空间。

一、超大规模市场带来广阔发展机遇

作为世界第二大经济体，中国经济的稳定发展，为全球经济复苏提供持续动力。随着中国经济高质量发展的深入推进，在先进制造业、消费结构升级、新型城镇化等方面将持续释放出巨大需求，成为吸引跨国企业来华投资的突出优势。

（一）为全球经济增长提供持续动力

2023 年，中国国内生产总值（GDP）达到 126.1 万亿元，增速 5.2%，人均 GDP 达到 1.27 万美元，比上年增长 5.4%。2024 年上半年，中国经济继续保持稳健增长势头，上半年 GDP 达到 61.7 万亿元、同比增长 5.0%，增速远高于全球平均水平。国际组织和市场机构纷纷上调了对 2024 年中国经济的增长预期。联合国、世界银行分别将 2024 年中国经济增速上调 0.1、0.3 个百分点至 4.8%，经合组织上调 0.2 个百分点至 4.9%，国际货币基金组织、高盛分别上调 0.2 至 0.4 个百分点至 5.0%，花旗银行上调 0.6 个百分点至 5.2%。中国美国商会、中国欧盟商会、中国日本商会等机构的调查显示，跨国企业对中国未来两年的商业前景预期明显改善，对各种经营指标表现出越来越乐观的态度，特别是在宏观经济、国内市场增长、盈利预期等方面，中国作为投资目的地的吸引力不断提升，50% 以上的受访企业仍将中国列为全球三大最优先投资目的地。[1] 中国的发展为全球经济增长提供持续动力，也为全球各国企业来华投资带来新的机遇（见图 3-1）。

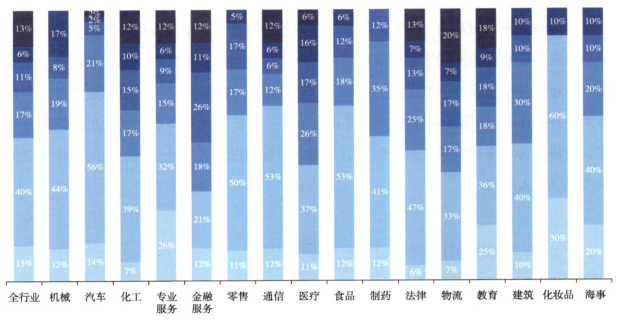

■ 首要投资目的地　■ 前3大投资目的地　■ 前5大投资目的地　■ 前10大投资目的地　■ 前10大投资目的地之外　■ 无计划投资

图 3-1　中国各行业在 2024 年全球投资计划的重要性

资料来源：中国欧盟商会《商业信心调查 2024》。

（二）在华跨国企业面临日益广阔的市场空间

中国拥有全球近五分之一的人口，近年居民收入水平稳步增长，中等收入群体规模不断扩大，让中国消费市场蕴藏的巨大潜力加速释放。根据国家统计局数据，2023 年中国居民人均可支配收入 39218 元，比上年增长 6.1%，中国中等收入人口（家庭年收入为 10 万 ~ 50 万元）占全国总人口的 47.2%[2]。作为全球第二大进口市场和第二大消费市场，2023 年中国社会消费品零售总额达到 47.2 万亿元，比上年增长 7.2%，最终消费支出对中国经济增长贡献率高达 82.5%。

---

[1] 详见中国美国商会（AmCham China）2024 年发布的《中国商务环境调查报告 2024》、中国欧盟商会（European Chamber of Commerce in China）2024 年发布的《商业信心调查 2024》和中国日本商会（Japanese Chamber Commerce and Industry in China）2024 年 5 月 14 日发布的《会员企业景气：事业环境认识问卷调查结果》。

[2] 2024 年 1 月 4 日，中国国际经济交流中心副理事长王一鸣接受央视新闻的采访。

超 14 亿人口的消费需求不断扩大和升级，为跨国公司提供了广阔的市场空间，越来越多的外企正在用实际行动深度扎根中国。调查显示，2023 年，在华美国企业的财务表现改善，盈利水平和息税前利润率均有所上升，尤其在消费和服务行业。近三分之一的受访企业预计其息税前利润率将超过 2022 年，其中资源和工业行业以及消费行业的息税前利润率将实现大幅增长。约 68% 的企业预计在华利润率将达到或超过全球平均水平（见图 3-2）。

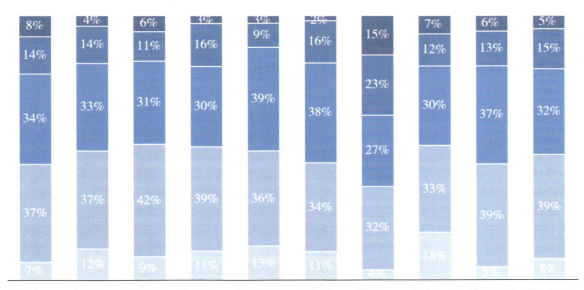

图 3-2　2022—2023 年美国在华公司财务表现

资料来源：中国美国商会《中国商务环境调查报告 2024》。

二、高效产业配套体系和良好投资环境全球领先

中国拥有全球最完备的产业配套体系，能为外商投资提供高效率、高可靠性的供应链支撑，有助于极大降低外资在华运作成本。同时，中国进一步扩大高水平对外开放，不断提升政策开放度和透明度，产业"硬配套"和政策"软环境"的结合为各国企业来华投资提供了全球最具竞争力的环境。

（一）保持全球最完备的产业链优势

跨国公司在华生产离不开本地配套体系的支撑，中国在产业配套方面拥有全球独

一无二的优势。按照联合国产业分类体系，中国拥有 41 个工业大类、207 个工业中类、666 个工业小类，是全世界产业门类最齐全、产业体系最完整、产业配套能力领先的国家，制造业规模连续 14 年居世界首位，培育了 45 个国家级先进制造业集群，建成了全球规模最大、技术领先的移动通信网络。这些因素为跨国公司在华开展制造业务提供了十分便利的条件，成为中国吸引外资的关键变量之一。根据汇丰银行发布的调研成果，73% 的企业预计未来三年将会增加其在中国的供应链布局，其中四分之一的企业预计将大幅增加；英国受访企业将增加中国供应链布局作为拓展中国业务的首要计划；东南亚企业对扩大其在中国市场的供应商网络尤其感兴趣，92% 的印尼企业、89% 的越南企业预计未来三年将扩大在中国的供应链布局[①]（见图 3-3）。

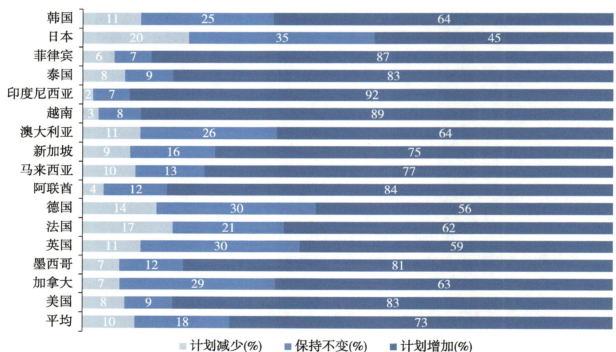

图 3-3　未来三年各受访市场的企业在中国供应链布局的计划
资料来源：汇丰银行《海外企业看中国 2023——数字化与可持续发展引领未来增长》。

从空间上看，中国中高端制造业高度集聚在长三角、大湾区、环渤海、成渝、长江中游城市群等地域，形成了许多富有活力的产业集群。以龙头企业为核心，产业链上下游配套企业形成了紧密的合作关系，极大提升了生产效率，形成了创新溢出效应，吸引

---

① 详见汇丰银行《海外企业看中国 2023——数字化与可持续发展引领未来增长》。

了大量外资企业集聚。其中，长三角城市群作为中国经济发展最活跃、开放程度最高、创新能力最强的区域之一，利用外资力度不断加大。2023 年江苏实际利用外资 253.4 亿美元，规模保持全国首位；上海实际利用外资突破 240 亿美元，居全国第二。粤港澳大湾区拥有完整的制造业链条和庞大的产业集群，为外商企业的研发制造提供完善的产业配套，2023 年制造业实际利用外资占全部外资比重回升到 30% 以上。各个城市群之间协同发展、产业互补，为外商来华投资兴业提供全方位的支持，让外资企业拥有广阔的发展空间、共享中国的发展红利。

专栏 3-1　富士康拟在郑州建设新事业总部

富士康是全球知名的代工制造企业，近几年正在加快推进"3+3"战略产业布局，即以"电动车、数字健康、机器人"三大新兴产业和"人工智能、半导体、新一代移动通信"三项新技术为发展重点。7 月 24 日，富士康科技集团同河南省政府签署了战略合作协议，拟在郑州建设新事业总部。项目一期选址位于郑东新区，建筑面积约 700 公亩，总投资约 10 亿元人民币。富士康表示，将充分发挥自身在智慧制造领域的技术和产业链优势，加快推动电动车整车、储能电池、数位健康和机器人产业落地，聚焦河南打造全球高端制造产业链和战略性新兴产业生态圈。

据报道，富士康新能源汽车试制中心项目将规划建设国际一流的新能源汽车高端化示范产线，打造向国内外知名汽车品牌提供制造服务的展示平台和整车领域的世界级灯塔工厂，为后续新能源汽车量产奠定坚实基础，目标是将郑州航空港建设成为富士康新能源汽车板块的核心生产基地。在固态电池项目方面，富士康将紧跟产业发展趋势，充分发挥公司长期积累的技术优势，秉承"整体规划、分步实施"原则，在郑州航空港布局发展固态电池产业，重点打造固态电解质、半固态及全固态电芯研发和生产制造项目。

资料来源：综合自《上海证券报》《每日经济新闻》等多家媒体报道。

（二）营造稳定透明可预期的投资环境

近年，中国全力营造市场化、法治化、国际化的一流投资环境，不断加大吸引外资力度，保障外资利益。鼓励外商投资方面，中国将《外商投资准入负面清单》项目从 2019 年版的 40 条，缩减到 2021 年版的 31 条；将《鼓励外商投资产业目录》范围从 2019 年版的 1108 条扩展到 2022 年版的 1474 条；2024 年 1 月修订《稳外贸稳外资税收政策指引》，提出了 51 项具体税收优惠措施，进一步提升中国作为投资目的地的吸引力和竞争力。中国注重加强对外资企业的合法权益保护，截至 2023 年底，国家级知识产权保护中心和快速维权中心总数达 112 家，比 2022 年底增长 15%，全年为 1500 余家外资企业提供调解服务。中国改善投资环境的举措得到了外资企业的积极肯定。

随着中国持续深化对外开放、不断优化营商环境，中国在全球投资格局中的吸引力和影响力进一步增强，尤其是在当前国际局势动荡不安的背景下，中国稳定的投资环境已经成为外商来华投资的重要考虑因素。欧盟受访企业中，认为其所处行业市场得到放开的受访企业比例显著增加（占 45%，同比上升 9 个百分点），认为其行业市场显著放开的受访企业比例（19%）同比上升 9 个百分点，达到 9 年来最高水平。受访企业中反映所处行业市场已全面开放的比例同比有小幅提升，处于历史最高水平（39%，同比上升 1 个百分点）。另有 10% 的受访企业预期两年内会实现重大开放，19% 的受访企业认为重大开放将出现在未来 2 至 5 年内[①]（见图 3-4）。

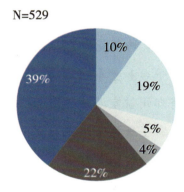

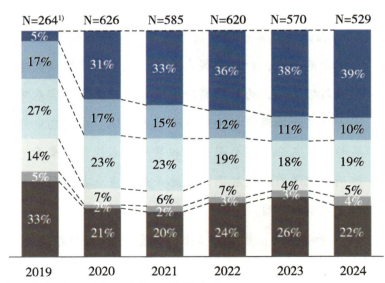

图 3-4　欧盟在华企业对中国市场开放的态度

资料来源：中国欧盟商会《商业信心调查 2024》。

---

① 详见中国欧盟商会《商业信心调查 2024》。

三、基于科技创新和人力资本的新型优势日益增强

中国高度重视科技创新在产业升级、高质量发展中的重要作用，坚持科技引领、创新驱动，加速创新、产业、资金、人才"四链"深度融合。在成为全球制造业大国的同时，中国正在成为"世界研发实验室"，在技术领域的实力受到海外企业的高度认可，投资中国、合作研发成为越来越多跨国企业发展全球竞争力的重要选择。

（一）为企业研发提供良好的创新生态

进入新时代，中国全面深化科技体制改革，不断完善市场导向的科技创新机制，着力优化调整重大科技任务组织实施方式，创建"揭榜挂帅""赛马"等新机制，明确科技成果转化的权利义务、分配方式、保障措施等。这些重要举措推动中国科技创新生态不断向好，推动科技资源配置效率有效提升，为跨国公司扩展在华研发业务提供了良好的生态。中国庞大的市场规模、旺盛的需求和研发成果快速商用等正向因素营造了一个极具活力的环境，鼓励跨国企业在华部署研发活动，以便更加接近客户，更有效地根据客户的需求进行创新，并可以进一步将研发成果输出到世界其他地区。中国吸引研发投资的计划取得了显著成效，越来越多的外资企业考虑增加在华研发投入，在信息技术、人工智能、医疗健康、食品和饮料以及能源等行业尤其明显，这表明中国已经成为这些行业的研发中心。

（二）创新场景开发和规模化应用优势凸显

信息技术、人工智能等领域的新应用、新产业在中国不断涌现。根据国家统计局数据，2023年中国高技术产业投资增长10.3%，增速比全部固定资产投资高7.3个百分点，其中，高技术制造业、高技术服务业投资分别增长9.9%和11.4%。以人工智能为例，中国科学技术信息研究所联合北京大学研制的《2023全球人工智能创新指数报告》显示，在全球人工智能发展上，中国的综合水平位列全球第二，人工智能企业数量和风险投资额也仅次于美国排名全球第二。中国在实现科技创新的高水平、规模化应用方面具有独特优势，成为吸引跨国公司来华开展相关业务的重要因素。越来越多的跨国企业正在将业务本地化，将在中国产生的利润在中国进行再投资。汇丰银行2023年对跨国企业的调

研显示，近九成（87%）的受访企业认为，中国在数字化等领域的快速发展正为它们带来新的投资机会。平均而言，各受访企业计划将其全球营业利润的 8% 投资于在华技术研发和业务数字化。美国企业尤其热衷于此：超过半数（52%）的美国受访企业计划将营业利润的 10% 甚至更多投资于在华技术研发和业务数字化。中国德国商会的调查结果显示，73% 的大型德企和 50% 的小型德企计划在未来两年增加对华投资。

（三）研发投入力度和整体创新能力不断提升

进入新时代，中国不断加大对研发的投入。根据国家统计局发布的《中华人民共和国 2023 年国民经济和社会发展统计公报》，2023 年中国研究与试验发展经费支出 33278 亿元，稳居全球第二，比上年增长 8.1%，研发经费投入强度达到 2.64%，已经跨过了创新型国家 2.5% 的基线（见图 3-5）。世界知识产权组织 2023 年 9 月发布的《全球创新指数（GII）2023》显示，中国创新能力综合排名由 2012 年的第 34 位提升至 2023 年的第 12 位，目前是前 30 名中唯一的中等收入经济体；中国目前拥有 24 个全球顶级科技集群，比 2022 年增加 3 个，是全球拥有科技集群数量最多的国家。在欧盟委员会的《欧洲创新记分牌》评价体系中，中国创新能力 2014 年总体水平仅相当于欧盟的 44%，而到 2023 年总体水平已达欧盟的 95%。在量子技术、集成电路、人工智能、生物医药、新能源等领域，中国都取得了一批重大原创成果。高效、大规模的研发投入显著提高了创新效能，推动了科技成果的商业化与产业化，为跨国公司在华开展创新业务提供了广阔空间。

图 3-5　2012—2023 年中国研发经费支出与研发经费投入强度

资料来源：国家统计局。

（四）大规模、高素质人才队伍为创新提供有力支撑

中国拥有全球规模最大的人才队伍，为跨国企业在华开展创新业务提供了坚实基础。根据国家统计局的数据，2023年中国具有大学文化程度人口超过2.5亿，人才资源总量、科技人力资源、研发人员总量均居全球首位。其中，研发人员已达660万人，同比增长3.8%。2023年，中国有1275人次入选"科睿唯安（Clarivate）[①]高被引科学家"榜单，占比从2018年的7.9%上升至17.9%；工程师数量也从2000年的约521万人，增长到2023年的约2059.2万人[②]。跨国企业表示，中国拥有众多的优秀人才，可以方便地招募并留住业务运营和技术研发所需的中国本土和外籍人才。此外，与高校和科研机构的合作在培养人才方面发挥了很好的作用，跨国企业经常通过合作培养中国研究人员、工程师并与他们建立联系，以便将他们纳入研发人才库。[③]高素质人才队伍已成为推动中国现代化产业体系建设、促进创新驱动发展的第一资源，是全球创新、合作研发不竭的动力源泉（见图3-6）。

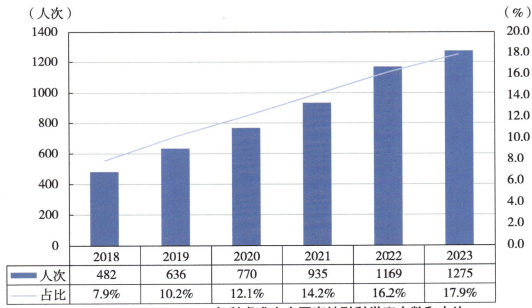

	2018	2019	2020	2021	2022	2023
人次	482	636	770	935	1169	1275
占比	7.9%	10.2%	12.1%	14.2%	16.2%	17.9%

图3-6　2018—2023年科睿唯安中国高被引科学家人数和占比

资料来源：科睿唯安"全球高被引科学家"名单。

[①] 全球数据分析服务公司，旗下拥有诸多业界知名品牌，包括Web of ScienceTM平台（含科学引文索引，即Science Citation IndexTM，简称SCI）、德温特世界专利索引（Derwent World Patents IndexTM，简称DWPI）以及TechstreetTM国际标准数据库等。

[②] 参见《人民政协报》：2024年1月30日，打造新时代卓越工程师队伍。

[③] 详见中国欧盟商会发布的《中国创新生态系统》、中国日本商会2024年5月14日发布的《会员企业景气：事业环境认识问卷调查结果》。

四、高水平开放平台的枢纽作用进一步凸显

中国以自贸试验区和自由贸易港、国家级经开区、大型国际会展等开放平台作为重要载体，不断提升对外开放水平。目前，自由贸易试验区、国家级经开区贡献全国外商直接投资总量的近四成。未来，高水平开放平台在外贸外资和制度创新中的重要作用将进一步加强。

（一）自贸试验区先行先试作用不断发挥

1. 自贸试验区开放创新成就显著

党的二十届三中全会提出，实施自由贸易试验区提升战略，鼓励首创性、集成式探索。自由贸易试验区是中国建设开放型经济新体制的重要基础、实践载体和行动平台。自 2013 年以来，中国分 7 批设立了 22 家自贸试验区，形成了覆盖东西南北中，统筹沿海、内陆、沿边的改革开放创新格局。自贸试验区坚持以高水平开放为引领，着力探索与国际经贸规则相衔接的制度体系，系统推进投资、贸易、金融、政府治理等领域改革创新，取得了一系列突破性、引领性的创新成果。例如，实施外商投资准入前国民待遇加负面清单管理模式，建立国际贸易"单一窗口"，实施跨境服务贸易负面清单，推动"证照分离"，探索自由贸易账户改革等。

自贸试验区以深化改革开放驱动产业创新发展，建成了一批世界领先的产业集群。例如，上海自贸试验区建立以"中国芯""创新药""智能造""蓝天梦""未来车""数据港"等六大产业为核心的现代化产业体系，天津自贸试验区成为全球第二大飞机租赁聚集地。浙江自贸试验区集聚油气企业上万家，保税燃料油加注规模居全球第五。2022 年，21 家自贸试验区以不到 4‰的国土面积，贡献了占全国 18.1% 的外商投资和 17.9% 的进出口贸易。2023 年，自贸试验区合计进出口 7.7 万亿元，增长 2.7%，占全国进出口总值的 18.4%，海南自由贸易港年度进出口连续 3 年保持两位数增长。

> ## 专栏 3-2 中国自贸试验区高水平改革开放的"五个率先"
>
> 一是率先实施外商投资准入前国民待遇加负面清单管理模式，推动投资管理体制实现历史性变革，积极推动实现外商投资管理由审批制到备案制的重大转变。

二是率先建立以国际贸易"单一窗口"为核心的贸易便利化模式，有力支撑贸易强国建设。上海自贸试验区上线全国首个国际贸易"单一窗口"，引领带动全国版"单一窗口"建设。

三是率先以跨境服务贸易负面清单管理模式为代表推进服务业综合开放，推动各类高端要素自由便捷流动。2021年，在海南推出首张跨境服务贸易负面清单，推动中国服务贸易管理与国际高标准经贸规则更好地进行对接。

四是率先实施"证照分离"等政府管理改革，促进营商环境改善和政府职能加速转变，着力解决"准入不准营"问题，促进商事基础制度改革。

五是率先在自贸试验区创设自由贸易账户，实现本外币一体化、账户内自由兑换，降低企业融资成本。各自贸试验区开展外资企业外汇资本金意愿结汇、跨境双向人民币资金池业务等金融服务创新。

2. 复制推广创新成果全国共享

2013年以来，率先试点并向全国推广了一批基础性、制度性改革成果，完善了投资、贸易、金融等领域基础管理制度，由点及面推动深化改革，探索实施一大批切口小、见效快的具体改革措施，带动各地开放发展。截至2023年7月，在国家层面已经总结七批自贸试验区改革试点经验、四批最佳实践案例，累计复制推广302项自贸试验区制度创新成果，各省区市自行推广复制超过2800项[①]。例如，在投资自由化便利化领域，企业设立、变更、经营、退出等领域的商事制度改革、工程建设项目审批制度改革等措施带动全国投资环境进一步优化。在贸易自由化便利化领域，从创新通关监管模式、优化税收机制到培育新业态新模式等贸易便利化制度，促进中国贸易高质量发展。在政府管理改革领域，从简化审批、强化监管到优化服务等一系列制度创新成果带动各地政府治理能力不断提升。在金融开放创新领域，从外汇管理便利化、跨境资本流动、人民币国际化到创新融资模式等一系列制度创新成果得到复制推广。

3. 海南自贸港高质量发展成型起势

2020年6月1日，《海南自由贸易港建设总体方案》对外发布，海南自由贸易港建

---

① 详见国务院新闻办公室官网 http://www.scio.gov.cn/live/2023/32694/tw/.

设加快推进。2021 年，全国人大常委会颁布《中华人民共和国海南自贸港法》，以法律形式固化自由贸易港建设相关政策。当前，海南自贸港以"贸易、投资、跨境资金流动、人员进出、运输来往自由便利和数据安全有序流动"为主框架的政策制度体系成型起势。海南自贸港坚持高水平制度型开放引领高质量发展，先行先试高标准经贸规则，制度型开放稳步扩大，根据 2024 年 8 月 5 日中共海南省委宣传方新闻发布会发布的相关数据，海南省先后推出制度集成创新案例 17 批 146 项，其中 11 项被国务院向全国复制推广。随着政策红利加速释放，海南成为投资热土，2018 年以来，海南新设外资企业以每年 65% 的增幅持续增长。2023 年，海南多项经济社会发展指标居全国前列。例如，GDP 增长 9.2%，规上工业增加值增长 18.5%，城乡居民人均可支配收入分别增长 6.3% 和 8.3%，体现自贸港经济形态的货物贸易、服务贸易分别增长 15.3%、29.6%。

（二）国家级经开区成为对外开放的重要抓手

1984 年，党中央、国务院作出设立国家级经济技术开发区的重大战略决策。40 年来，国家级经开区已发展成为中国产业最为聚集、开放型经济最为活跃、区域发展带动力最为强劲的园区之一，为中国深化改革、扩大开放，推动新型工业化、城市化作出了重要贡献。国家级经开区作为重要的开放平台和产业聚集区，以 3‰ 的国土面积，贡献了全国 1/10 的地区生产总值、1/5 的利用外资和外贸总额，在中国现代化产业体系建设和改革创新中发挥积极作用。从商务部对国家级经开区综合发展水平的最新考核评价结果来看[①]，国家级经开区的主要指标均保持增长，增速高于全国平均水平，占全国比重进一步提升（见表 3-1）。

1. 经济发展质量提升

2022 年，国家级经开区实现地区生产总值 14 万亿元，占国内生产总值的比重为 12%。截至 2022 年末，东部地区国家级经开区拥有主营业务收入 30 亿元以上、中西部地区国家级经开区拥有主营业务收入 15 亿元以上制造业企业共 1765 家，较前一年显著上升。

2. 开放带动作用提升

2022 年，国家级经开区实际使用外资金额 432 亿美元，占全国实际使用外资的比重

---

① 商务部每年 7—10 月对国家级经开区上一年度综合发展水平进行考核评价，当前最新考核评价结果为 2022 年。

为 23%。实现进出口总额 10.3 万亿元，占全国进出口总额的比重为 25%；其中高新技术产品进出口额 3 万亿元，占全国高新技术产品进出口额的比重为 27%。

3. 科技创新能力提升

截至 2022 年末，国家级经开区拥有国家级孵化器和众创空间 683 家，省级及以上研发机构 1.2 万家，高新技术企业 6.5 万家，较上年末均有明显提升。

4. 绿色低碳水平提升

2022 年，国家级经开区规模以上工业企业单位工业增加值能耗、水耗同比均显著下降，工业固体废物综合利用率较上年提高 2 个百分点。

5. 区域协调发展提升

截至 2022 年末，东部地区国家级经开区与中西部地区国家级经开区开展合作共建、国家级经开区对口援疆援藏援助边（跨）境合作区数量比上年增加 126 个。

表 3-1　2022 年 230 家国家级经开区考核评价部分指标

指标	数值	增速（%）	占全国比重（%）
地区生产总值	14 万亿元	5.6	12
实际利用外资	432 亿美元	11.5	23
进出口额	10.3 万亿元	15	25
高新技术产品进出口	3 万亿元	—	27

（三）大型国际会展带动作用增强

习近平主席在第五届中国国际进口博览会致辞中指出，要让"中国的市场成为世界的市场，世界的展商变成中国的投资商"[①]。进博会[②]、投洽会[③]等一系列国家级会展平台已经成为中国构建新发展格局的窗口、推动高水平开放的平台、全球共享的重要公共产品，为全球经济恢复发展积极贡献力量，也为扩大双边投资合作提供新的机遇。

进博会是全球第一个以进口为主题的国家级展会，是中国主动向世界开放市场的重大举措。2023 年 11 月，第六届进博会在上海举办，按年计意向成交创历届新高，金额

---

① 2022 年 11 月 4 日，习近平在第五届中国国际进口博览会开幕式上的致辞。

② 中国国际进口博览会。

③ 中国国际投资贸易洽谈会。

达 784.1 亿美元、比上届增长 6.7%。在第六届进博会上，154 个国家、地区和国际组织的代表参展，72 个国家和国际组织亮相国家展，其中，中国馆以"中国式现代化新成就为世界发展提供新机遇"为主题，聚焦自贸试验区建设十周年成就，重点展示推进高水平开放和高质量发展的最新成果，向世界讲述"中国好，世界会更好"的精彩故事。各参展国共举办近 200 场丰富多彩的展台活动，使国家展成为不同发展水平国家促进合作、互利共赢的重要平台。本届进博会共有 128 个国家和地区的 3486 家企业参加企业展，集中展示了 442 项代表性首发新产品、新技术、新服务。创新孵化专区吸引来自 39 个国家的超过 300 个创新项目参展。举办 5 年多来，进博会累计意向成交额近 3500 亿美元，"展商变投资商"溢出效应明显，持续释放开放红利。

投洽会已成功举办 23 届，双向投资促进、权威信息发布、投资趋势研究等三大功能不断强化，已成为最具影响力的国际投资盛会和中国双向投资的重要促进平台。2023 年 9 月，第 23 届投洽会在厦门举办，共吸引来自 100 多个国家和地区、1000 多个工商经贸团组、近 8 万名境内外客商参会 [1]。联合国贸发会议、联合国工发组织、上海合作组织、经合组织等 12 个国际组织参与相关活动。638 个项目在大会期间达成合作协议，计划总投资额 4845.7 亿元，参会机构数量和协议总投资额均创下 5 年来新高。

此外，中国进出口商品交易会、中国国际服务贸易交易会、中国国际高新技术成果交易会、中国—东盟博览会、中国西部国际博览会等一系列展会，也对中国与世界各国的贸易投资合作发挥了巨大的促进作用。

---

[1] https://www.gov.cn/yaowen/liebiao/202309/content_6903371.htm.

第四章　中国双向投资促进与世界互利共赢

开放是中国式现代化的鲜明标识。中国稳步扩大制度型开放，持续深化外商投资和对外投资管理体制改革，实现了双向投资互利共赢。外资企业看好中国市场巨大机遇、在华业务为全球业务发展提供重要支撑。中国企业对外投资不断提升长期发展能力、与东道国各方共享发展成果。通过双向投资合作，中国为全球经济注入更多确定性和增长新动力。

一、外资企业和中国市场双向奔赴、合作共赢

在中国改革开放 40 多年的历史进程中，跨国公司作为重要参与者、见证者、受益者，发挥了重要作用，也分享了中国市场开放的重大机遇和巨大红利。

（一）外资企业在中国市场发展良好

通过充分利用中国改革开放带来的政策红利和市场红利，在华外资企业获得快速发展。2013 年以来，外商投资规模以上工业企业利润总额稳中有增，盈利水平始终保持在7% 左右。2021 年、2022 年，外商投资规模以上工业企业利润总额分别为 2.28 万亿元人民币和 2 万亿元人民币，分别处于外商投资规模以上工业企业利润总额的第一、第二高位。2023 年，外商及港澳台商投资企业营业收入 27.2 万亿元，利润总额 1.8 万亿元，营业收入利润率为 6.6%，比全国规模以上工业企业总体盈利水平（5.76%）高出近 1 个百分点[1]（见图 4–1）。

2023 年，众多在华外资企业实现较高增长。例如，欧莱雅、博世集团在华销售额增长均超 5%；苹果公司大中华区营收约占公司总营收 1/5；默沙东在华销售额达 67.1 亿美元，同比增长 32%[2]；丰田汽车在中国市场销量超 190 万辆，占全球总销量 17%。中国日

---

[1] 2023 年数据来自：https://www.gov.cn/lianbo/bumen/202401/content_6928596.htm，2013—2022 年数据来自《中国外资统计公报 2023》。

[2] https://www.gov.cn/yaowen/liebiao/202403/content_6939076.htm.

本商会 2024 年 7 月发布的《中国经济与日本企业 2024 年白皮书》认为，中国为外资企业提供了巨大的市场机遇，成为众多外资企业盈利的重要来源，中国与外资企业已建立起双赢关系。

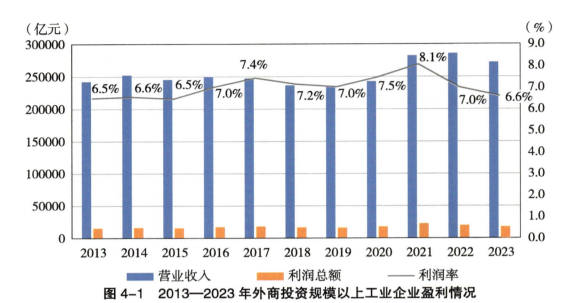

图 4-1　2013—2023 年外商投资规模以上工业企业盈利情况

资料来源：《中国外资统计公报 2023》，经课题组计算整理。

（二）外资企业为中国经济和社会发展作出重要贡献

外资企业是参与中国式现代化建设、推动中国经济与世界经济共同繁荣发展的重要力量。当前，外资企业占中国市场主体数量不到 2%，带动了超过 8% 的就业，贡献了 1/6 的税收和 1/3 的进出口额，为中国经济和社会发展作出重要贡献。

自改革开放以来，外资企业在中国货物贸易中所占比重逐步上升。2006 年外资企业占全国货物贸易进出口比重达 58.9%，为历史最高纪录[①]。此后，随着中国本土企业的成长与壮大，以及外资企业向产业链上游布局，外资企业在中国货物贸易中的占比有所下降，但仍保持重要地位。2023 年，外资企业占中国货物进出口比重保持在 30% 以上，为中国外贸稳定发展提供了重要支撑。2006 年和 2009 年外资企业缴税额占中国税收收入比重最高，均为 22.9%[②]，自 2013 年以来占比有所下降，但仍保持在 17% 以上，是中国

---

① 2012—2022 年数据来自《中国外资统计公报 2023》。2023 年数据来源：2024 年 1 月 12 日，国务院新闻办公室举行新闻发布会，海关总署副署长王令浚介绍情况。

② 《中国外资统计公报 2023》。

税收收入的重要来源（见图 4-2）。

图 4-2 外资企业对中国税收收入的贡献

资料来源：《中国外资统计公报 2023》，经课题组计算整理。

与中国市场共同成长的过程中，外资企业在技术、管理、创新等方面对本土企业产生了明显的外溢效应，带动了本土企业参与国际市场竞争合作，为本土企业深入融入全球产业链、供应链、价值链，加快产业转型升级和提升国际竞争力发挥了重要的推动作用。

（三）外资企业坚定携手中国，共创美好未来

数字、绿色、创新等成为中国市场的新机遇。2023 年以来，多个行业的跨国领军企业用加大投资力度表达对中国市场的信任、对与中国开放合作的高度重视。例如，特斯拉首个美国本土之外的储能超级工厂落户上海；大众汽车集团（中国）宣布投资 25 亿欧元，建立最大的海外研发中心；埃克森美孚在大亚湾石化区建设的惠州乙烯一期项目追加投资 100 亿元。2024 年 2 月，中国美国商会发布调查报告显示，中国市场对在华美国企业具有重要意义，近半数会员企业预计 2023 年将实现盈利[1]，半数会员企业仍将中国列为全球前三大投资目的地，比 2022 年增长了 5 个百分点。

---

[1] 该调查报告数据收集时间为 2023 年 11 月。

二、中国对外投资提升东道国经济社会发展能力

近年来，中国企业对外投资与国际化运营能力不断提升，在开展对外投资经营的过程中，也为东道国作出了重要贡献，如促进了当地基础设施完善，提升了当地就业和税收，为当地培育了技术人才等，为东道国经济社会发展作出积极贡献，与东道国各方共享发展成果。

（一）中国境外企业总体经营良好

2023 年，近七成中国境外企业盈利或持平，当年收益再投资 784.6 亿美元，为历史第三高值，占同期中国对外直接投资流量的 44.2%[1]。从成效看，2024 年 3 月，中国贸促会发布的《中国企业对外投资现状及意向调查报告》显示，超半数企业对外投资收益率增加或保持稳定，超三成企业对外投资利润率增加。欧盟中国商会的调查也表明[2]，尽管受到外部不利环境影响，受访中企对在欧长期经营仍持积极态度，约 90% 的受访企业反馈在欧营收实现增长，显著高于前一年的 70%；58% 的受访企业预计 2023 年营收将"略有增长"或"显著增长"；83% 的受访企业已制定进一步在欧增加投入、持续深耕欧洲市场的计划。美国中国总商会的调查也表明，尽管形势紧张导致忧虑情绪蔓延，但大部分在美中资企业仍然决定保持或扩大对美国市场的投资；在对未来收入走势的预期上，将保持当前投资水平和继续增加投资的企业占比近九成[3]。

（二）助力东道国完善基础设施，提升长期发展能力

中国企业在交通运输、水利电力设施、数字基础设施等领域具有综合优势，为东道国完善基础设施建设、加快提升工业发展水平、促进经济和社会长期发展提供了重要支撑。例如，在交通运输领域，中国企业建设的阿尔及利亚东西高速公路全长 1216 公里，

---

[1] 商务部、国家统计局、国家外汇管理局：《2023 年度中国对外直接投资统计公报》，中国商务出版社 2024 年版。

[2] 欧盟中国商会：《共筑互信之路，共创中欧繁荣——中国企业在欧盟发展报告 2023/2024》，2023 年 11 月 14 日。

[3] 美国中国总商会：《在美中资企业年度商业调查报告》，2024 年 6 月。

连接该国北部 17 个省，使交通时间由原来的 3 天缩短为 10 小时[1]，被媒体誉为阿"运输之路、旅游之路、发展之路、希望之路"。在水利电力设施领域，中国企业与老挝开展合作，助力老挝建设水电站和跨境输电网络，使电力出口占到老挝出口总额约 30%[2]，实现"东南亚蓄电池"的发展定位，大幅提升长期发展能力。

除了开展大型基础设施建设外，中国企业还在境外打造了一批"小而美"的民生项目，受到东道国民众欢迎。例如，在中老铁路建设过程中，中国企业为铁路沿线迁改供电线路 65 公里，新建改扩建便道 743 公里，搭建便桥 34 座，平整宅基地 14 万平方米，修建水渠 272 公里、水井 15 口。在非洲，中国企业建设了"鲁班工坊"、坦桑尼亚"村村通电"工程项目。这些项目接地气、惠民生、聚人心，切实改善了当地民众生活条件，提升了东道国的长期发展能力。

（三）创造就业和增加税收，助力东道国经济增长

中国企业在海外开展投资与运营，创造了大量就业岗位、缴纳各种税金，为东道国经济和社会发展作出直接贡献。党的十八大以来，中国累计对外直接投资达 1.68 万亿美元，相当于 2023 年存量规模的 57%，连续 8 年占全球份额超过一成，在投资所在国（地区）累计缴纳各种税金 5185 亿美元，年均提供超过 200 万个就业岗位[3]。2023 年，中国境外企业向投资所在国（地区）缴纳各种税金总额 753 亿美元，比上年增长 0.3%；年末境外企业从业员工总数 428.9 万人，其中雇用外方员工 257 万人，增加 7.7 万人（见表 4–1）。以在法国的中资企业为例[4]，截至 2023 年，中国已连续 3 年成为对法国投资和创造就业的第一大亚洲国家，2023 年中国投资者投资超过 900 家法国企业，为法国创造了超过 5 万个就业岗位。

---

① 《人民日报》：见证中阿高质量共建"一带一路"丰硕成果，2024 年 7 月 23 日。
② 《日本经济新闻》：中国企业加大对老挝电力基础设施的投入，2024 年 3 月 12 日。
③ 商务部、国家统计局、国家外汇管理局：《2023 年度中国对外直接投资统计公报》，中国商务出版社 2024 年版。
④ 《人民日报》：中法经贸合作互利共赢，2024 年 1 月 29 日。

表 4-1　2017—2023 年境外中资企业境外雇用外方员工人数

年份	2017	2018	2019	2020	2021	2022	2023
雇用外方员工（万人）	171	187.7	226.6	218.8	239	249.3	257

资料来源：商务部、国家统计局、国家外汇管理局：《2023 年度中国对外直接投资统计公报》，中国商务出版社 2024 年版。

（四）增加数字化与绿色发展投资，助力东道国创新转型

中国企业发挥数字经济、绿色发展领域的优势，在对外投资中为东道国带去数字技术、绿色技术，助力东道国数字化和绿色转型。例如，南非德阿风电场是中国企业在非洲第一个集投资、建设、运营为一体的风电项目，自 2017 年投入运行以来，每年供电约 7.6 亿千瓦时，满足 30 万户居民用电需求，每年减排二氧化碳超过 60 万吨。中国企业承建的肯尼亚东北部加里萨光伏发电站能够满足当地 7 万户家庭用电需求，每年减排数万吨二氧化碳，肯尼亚前总统乌胡鲁·肯雅塔赞许该电站为肯尼亚实现绿色发展、推动能源转型发挥积极作用[1]。欧盟是中国企业在发达经济体中投资存量最高的目的地，中国企业在德国、爱尔兰、比利时和匈牙利等多国建立研发中心、数据中心、网络安全中心和电池工厂等，为欧盟本地经济发展、就业市场和研发创新作出贡献[2]。

（五）提供技术援助，助力东道国培育人才

中国企业在对发展中国家投资合作过程中，不仅注重技术投资合作，还积极帮助东道国培训企业管理与技术人才。例如，中国企业在建设阿尔及利亚东西高速公路的过程中，在当地建起一所大型项目管理学院和一所国家质量控制中心，先后培养了超过 1.6 万名当地基建技术人员。中国企业在沙特建立海外培训中心，以健康、安全、环境管理体系和钻井技术培训为重点，自 2008 年成立以来，共举办各类培训班 1000 余期，培训沙特员工 4 万人次，为当地建立了完备的石油工程技术人员梯队，助力东道国提升自主

---

[1] 肯尼亚广播公司（KBC）网站新闻，中国：非洲绿色美好未来的可靠伙伴，2024 年 5 月 23 日。

[2] 欧盟中国商会：《共筑互信之路，共创中欧繁荣——中国企业在欧盟发展报告 2023/2024》，2023 年 11 月 14 日。

开采和冶炼石油的能力[1]。

三、中国双向投资为全球经济注入更多确定性和增长新动力

在全球经济增长放缓、地缘政治冲突加剧、各国产业政策深度调整的大背景下，中国以开放的大市场、完备高效的工业体系和强大的创新能力，为在华跨国企业带来巨大机遇，为全球经济增长作出新贡献。

（一）开放的中国大市场为全球经济复苏注入新动能

市场是最稀缺的资源，中国超大规模市场优势与市场化、法治化、国际化一流营商环境叠加，为各国企业提供了广阔的市场空间和合作机遇。近年来，中国经济保持平稳增长且充满韧性活力，对全球经济增长的贡献率保持在 30% 左右。中国扩大优质消费品、先进技术、重要设备、关键零部件进口，增加能源资源产品和国内紧缺农产品进口，发挥好进博会等重要展会平台作用，拓展多元化的进口渠道，提升进口贸易的便利化水平，培育国家进口贸易促进创新示范区，把中国超大规模市场打造成为世界共享的大市场，为全球经济复苏注入新动能。

2024 年 7 月，国际货币基金组织发布更新后的《世界经济展望报告》，预计 2024 年中国经济增长 5%，较 4 月报告上调 0.4 个百分点。中国德国商会的调查表明，大多数受访德企认为中国经济将在 5 年内恢复强劲增长，在电子、机械 / 工业设备、塑料 / 金属制品和汽车行业，都有超过 60% 的企业预计中国经济将在 3 年内恢复强劲增长[2]。中国日本商会发布的《中国经济与日本企业 2024 年白皮书》指出，超过 50% 的日本企业看好中国经济发展，将中国视为最重要或三大重要市场之一。《纽约时报》援引全球知名金融信息公司 FactSet（慧甚）的预测，虽然标普 500 指数中的美国上市公司近 60% 收入来自美国国内，但其最大的海外销售来源是中国，"许多美国大公司的很大一部分收入依赖中国"。据新华社报道，摩根大通亚太区首席执行官明确表示，中国经济的影响力已不容忽

---

[1] 《中国纪检监察报》：中国企业积极参与高质量共建"一带一路"以基础设施"硬联通"推动共画同心圆，2023 年 10 月 18 日。

[2] 中国德国商会：《2023|2024 年度商业信心调查报告》，2024 年 1 月。

视，对投资者而言，中国是一个无法回避的市场。

（二）完善高效的产业体系提升全球产业链的稳定性

作为拥有全球最完整、规模最大的产业体系和最为完善配套能力的全球价值链三大枢纽之一，中国坚持对外开放的基本国策，坚定奉行互利共赢的开放战略，为稳定全球产业链和供应链作出积极贡献。

例如，空中客车在中国成立的首家飞机全生命周期服务中心于 2024 年 1 月正式投入运营，标志着空中客车在中国的产业布局覆盖了从研发、零部件生产、飞机总装、技术支持和服务到循环利用的全产业链。空客中国相关负责人表示，在全球供应链紧张的大背景下，中国合作伙伴凭借独特的产业优势，在稳定供应链方面发挥了关键作用，展现了极强的韧性和竞争力。又如，2024 年 3 月，跨国生物制药巨头阿斯利康签约，将在无锡建设从制剂到包装的全产业链工厂。该工厂将加入阿斯利康全球生产供应基地，向国内外市场提供"中国制造"的优质创新药品，让"中国制造"充分发挥全球价值。

（三）不断增强的科技创新与产业化能力为全球创新发展与技术进步注入新活力

当前，新一轮科技革命和产业变革深入发展，中国加快建设科技强国，不断开辟新领域新赛道。2023 年，中国研发（R&D）经费支出 33278 亿元，比上年增长 8.1%，与国内生产总值之比为 2.64%，在全球处于较高水平；中国有效发明专利数量达 401.5 万件，较上一年增长 22.4%，成为世界上首个突破 400 万件的国家，其中高价值发明专利所占比重达到四成以上。中国发明专利申请量、通过《专利合作条约》提交的国际专利申请量多年蝉联世界第一[①]。

中国科技创新能力快速提升，不仅提高了本土企业的全球竞争力，也为跨国企业的科技创新提供了快速产业化的应用场景、注入了竞争力提升的新活力。中国支持外商投资在华设立研发中心，与国内企业联合开展技术研发和产业化应用，鼓励外商投资企业及其设立的研发中心承担重大科研攻关项目，为全球企业提供了良好的创新生态环境。截至 2024 年 6 月底，上海跨国公司地区总部累计认定达到 985 家，外资研发中心累计认

---

① 《人民日报》：勇担时代重任加快建设科技强国，2024 年 7 月 31 日，科学技术部党组。

定达到 575 家，继续成为中国内地跨国公司地区总部最为集中的城市 [①]。多家知名跨国企业已将规模庞大的研发中心、创新中心布局在中国。不少外资企业高管认为，中国拥有开放的创新体系、富有远见的人才培养战略和对产业发展的政策支持，将成为塑造未来技术与创新趋势的主要推动力量。中国强大的科技创新能力、持续优化的营商环境与完善的产业链供应链基础相叠加，将释放巨大发展动能，为跨国企业整合全球资源、深化产业链供应链合作提供广阔空间，也将继续为全球经济稳定发展提供重要支撑。

[①] https://www.jingan.gov.cn/rmtzx/003008/003008004/20240726/93db4e5d-d300-4b99-886e-d7c8ab58ac2a.html?type=2，上海市静安区人民政府网站：上海跨国公司地区总部累计达 985 家，外资将持续加大在华投资。

第五章 投资链接世界 机遇惠及全球

开放是中国式现代化的鲜明标识。中国坚持对外开放基本国策，坚持以开放促改革，依托超大规模市场优势，在扩大国际合作中提升开放能力，建设更高水平开放型经济新体制。未来中国将继续加强国际投资合作，以互利共赢促进全球双向投资稳定发展，为促进全球产业链供应链合作、推动数字化绿色化转型发展提供支撑，为世界经济持续增长注入新动能，推动落实全球发展倡议，推动经济全球化朝着更加开放、包容、普惠、均衡的方向发展。

一、推动全球跨境投资稳定发展与世界经济持续复苏

当前，国际形势动荡多变、全球经济持续低迷，一段时期内外国直接投资增长仍面临重重挑战。当前比以往任何时候都更需要国际合作与开放共享，只有坚持互利共赢，深度参与全球产业分工与合作，才能促进共同发展、可持续发展；营造开放包容的国际投资环境至关重要、势在必行，需要多方共同努力。未来，尽管全球贸易投资保护主义抬头、国际环境不确定不稳定因素增多，但中国将坚持推进高水平对外开放，稳步推进制度型开放，坚持以开放促改革，主动对接国际高标准经贸规则，打造高水平开放平台，建设透明、稳定、可预期的制度环境以及市场化、法治化、国际化的一流营商环境，更大力度吸引和利用外资，做好"投资中国"品牌，以切实巨大的市场机遇、合作机遇，为跨国公司在华投资提供新的空间、吸引国际人才来华工作，增强对华投资信心、拓宽外商投资渠道，为全球跨境投资发展注入新动能。中国将坚持高水平走出去，完善促进和保障对外投资体制机制，健全对外投资管理服务体系，进一步提高对外投资的便利化水平，促进共建"一带一路"高质量投资合作，鼓励中国企业在生产制造、研发合作、数字与绿色合作等方面提升国际化综合能力，为东道国提供更多就业岗位、经济增长新助力，增进合作共赢。

二、提升全球产业链供应链的效率与韧性

近年来，经济全球化遭遇逆流，当前世界经济复苏艰难，正如习近平主席指出，维护全球产业链供应链韧性和稳定是推动世界经济发展的重要保障。李强总理强调，巩固和加强全球产业链供应链合作，是各方的利益所系和迫切期盼。为维护产业链稳定与效率，促进供应链、产业链与创新链的深度融合，各国需要开放合作，避免排他的、封闭的产业链格局引发国际投资与供应链的地缘割裂。中国既是全球产业链供应链合作的参与者、受益者，也是坚定的维护者、建设者。未来，中国立足亚太地区供应链枢纽地位，依托完整的工业体系和完善的基础设施等综合优势，坚持推动产业链供应链开放合作，共同构筑安全稳定、畅通高效、开放包容、互利共赢的产业链供应链。同时，中国将支持全球跨国公司借助在华生产制造的规模优势、成本优势、科技优势，对全球供需变化作出快速响应；将支持跨国公司在华设立区域总部、研发中心等功能机构，为跨国公司拓展全球业务空间提供有力支撑；将坚持促进贸易投资自由化便利化，扩大面向全球的高标准自由贸易区网络，以高水平投资合作助力推进高质量共建"一带一路"，为各国企业来华投资兴业提供更多便利、更好保障，为促进东道国产业升级提供助力，为促进全球产业链供应链稳定高效运转作出新的贡献。

三、为数字化、绿色化转型发展提供支撑

数字和绿色等新兴领域发展是推动世界经济增长与转型的新动能。习近平主席在第四届中国国际进口博览会开幕式上表示，"中国将深度参与绿色低碳、数字经济等国际合作"。在数字化领域，作为数字经济大国，未来中国对内将进一步扩大数字领域市场准入，通过分类分级管理改善数字领域监管、提升数据跨境流动便利化水平，促进人工智能和数字领域国际投资合作；对外将坚持积极商签落实多双边数字经济投资合作制度性安排，积极促进数字贸易发展，推动消费端平台和国内产业端平台协同，鼓励电商平台带动智慧物流、移动支付等产业链上下游出海，为全球数字化发展提供新动力。在绿色领域，全球绿色投资空间巨大也面临诸多挑战。一方面，全球绿色投资缺口巨大，据中金公司 2021 年发布《碳中和经济学》报告测算，全球绿色投资需求总缺口约为 121.7 万

亿美元。中国是全球绿色投资的重要投资来源，据 2024 年 7 月国际能源署报告，中国将继续维持全球最大清洁能源投资国地位，清洁能源投资总额预计将达 6750 亿美元，接近美国（3150 亿美元）、欧盟（3700 亿美元）投资额之和。中国坚持绿色发展理念，加快推进绿色转型、鼓励清洁能源投资进入中国市场，将为全球先进的绿色技术提供广泛的应用场景、为全球绿色转型提供坚实支撑。同时，中国将继续坚持把绿色理念贯穿对外投资合作过程，发挥在新能源汽车、动力电池、光伏等领域的技术与产业优势，积极支持太阳能、风能、核能、生物质能等清洁能源领域对外投资，为弥补发展中国家电力短缺、绿色投资缺口贡献力量。

四、为推动落实全球发展倡议、推进可持续发展议程提供重要支撑

发展承载着人民对美好生活的向往，是解决一切问题的总钥匙，也是人类社会的永恒主题。可持续增长，是全球发展中国家的普遍诉求。2021 年 9 月，习近平主席提出全球发展倡议，为推动国际社会破解发展赤字贡献了中国方案。近年来，中国提出推动落实全球发展倡议的 32 项重大举措，相继举办全球共享发展行动论坛首届和第二届高级别会议，发布《共创未来行动计划》，涵盖包括技术援助、基础设施建设、人才培养等在内的 50 项成果，致力于推动实现更加强劲、绿色、健康的全球发展，有助于增强各国自主发展能力，也为推动跨境投资高质量发展提供了新的空间和机遇。2015 年 9 月，联合国发展峰会正式批准通过了 2030 年可持续发展议程，这是一个重要的世界发展规划。未来，中国将推动持续凝聚全球发展共识，继续推动落实全球发展倡议，帮助发展中国家加速落实全球 2030 可持续发展议程，利用多边开发银行的专业知识动员投资，倡议各国加大对全球发展合作的投入，拿出务实举措增加发展资源，积极推动以跨境投资"授人以鱼"和"授人以渔"，帮助广大发展中国家加快工业化转型和提高自主发展能力；共同做大并坚持互利共赢原则分好经济全球化的"蛋糕"；推动经济全球化朝着更加开放、包容、普惠、均衡的方向发展，用中国双向投资链接全球、惠及世界！

地区篇

第六章　上海市利用外资报告 [①]

利用外资是我国对外开放基本国策的重要内容。习近平主席多次强调，中国开放的大门只会越开越大。上海作为改革开放的排头兵和创新发展的先行者，始终把吸引外资作为扩大开放重中之重的工作，率先探索准入前国民待遇加负面清单管理制度，持续提升投资贸易自由化便利化水平。上海已经成为全球最富吸引力的外商投资热土之一，成为跨国公司产业链、供应链、创新链全球布局的首选地之一。

一、外商投资的进展与成效

上海是世界观察中国的窗口，也是外商投资进军中国市场的桥头堡，一大批外资外企在这里集聚发展，成为推动上海发展、中国发展的一支重要力量。

一是利用外资规模稳步增长。2023年，上海新设外资企业6017家，同比增长38.3%；实际使用外资240.87亿美元，再创历史新高，连续4年超过200亿美元。至2023年底，上海累计设立外商投资企业超过12万家，存量外商投资企业超过7.5万家，实际吸引外资金额超过3500亿美元。

二是利用外资结构持续优化。上海逐步形成以服务业和高技术产业为主的引资格局。2023年，服务业实际使用外资占比90.0%，主要投向信息服务、商务服务、科技

---

① 上海市商务委供稿。

服务、房地产、批发零售和金融服务六大行业；制造业实际使用外资占比 10.0%，主要投向电子元件制造、新能源汽车及汽车零部件、医药及医疗器械、通用设备、非金属矿物制造及食品制造等领域。高技术产业引资能力持续增强，实际使用外资 105.6 亿美元，同比增长 9.4%，占比达到 43.8%。

三是利用外资能级不断提升。地区总部和研发中心是上海利用外资的亮点和特色。2023 年，上海新增跨国公司地区总部 65 家，外资研发中心 30 家。截至 2023 年底，累计设立跨国公司地区总部 956 家，外资研发中心 561 家，继续保持中国内地跨国公司地区总部最集中的城市地位。总部项目能级不断提升，大中华区及以上级别的地区总部占 18%、世界 500 强企业设立的研发中心约占 1/4。

四是主要外资来源地保持稳定。2023 年，上海主要外资来源地为中国香港地区、新加坡、欧洲、日本、美国、韩国，合计实际投资占比超过 95%。RCEP 成员国合计对沪实际投资 31.9 亿美元，同比增长 27.5%，占比 13.3%。"一带一路"共建国家合计对沪实际投资 24.3 亿美元，同比增长 1.4%，占比 10.1%。

五是外商投资企业贡献突出。央企、上海国企、外企、民营企业约各占上海经济的 1/4。其中，外资企业贡献了全市超过 1/4 的 GDP、约 1/3 的税收、近 2/3 外贸进出口、约 1/5 的就业人数，以及超过 1/2 的规模以上工业总产值和 2/5 的规模以上工业企业研发投入。外资已经成为上海促进经济增长的重要引擎、调整产业结构的重要支撑、推动科技创新的重要主体和提升城市功能的重要力量。

二、重点亮点举措和发挥的作用

上海市委、市政府始终高度重视吸引和利用外资工作，认真贯彻落实习近平总书记对上海工作的重要指示精神，坚定推动全方位对外开放，以更大力度拥抱外资、引进外资、服务外资。

（一）以落实国家战略为牵引，推进高水平对外开放

坚持把扩大开放和吸收外资放在突出位置，率先落实国家各项开放举措。

推动更宽领域更深层次开放。深入落实外商投资准入前国民待遇加负面清单管理制度，实施国家最新版负面清单和鼓励外商投资产业目录，推进服务业扩大开放综合试点，先后出台"稳外资24条""加大吸引和利用外资20条"等政策措施，推动外商在更多新开放领域投资。全国首家外资独资券商、首批外商独资公募基金、外资控股合资理财公司、外商独资职业技能培训机构等一批首创性外资项目落户，国内首单外资班轮船公司"外贸集装箱沿海捎带"业务在洋山港正式落地。

深化自贸试验区高水平制度型开放。出台落实《全面对接国际高标准经贸规则推进中国（上海）自由贸易试验区高水平制度型开放总体方案》实施细则117条，进一步在服务贸易、货物贸易、数字贸易和边境后规则等领域加大压力测试力度。落实国务院《关于在有条件的自由贸易试验区和自由贸易港试点对接国际高标准推进制度型开放若干措施的通知》，沃尔沃建筑设备成为全国首家成功开展重点行业再制造产品进口试点业务的企业。自上海首个自贸试验区设立以来，一大批制度创新试点成果在全国复制推广，在国家层面复制推广的300多项自贸试验区制度创新成果中，源自上海首创或同步先行先试的事项占比近一半。

发挥进博会开放平台作用。连续5年在进博会期间举办上海城市推介大会，市委、市政府主要领导向全球发出邀约，开展近百场专题投资推介活动，推动更多参展商变为投资商，世界500强企业诺和诺德在进博会期间投资2亿元人民币，开展医药研发、成品进口及分销等业务；德国医药巨头勃林格殷格翰投资1.98亿美元，布局新药研发；乐高乐园主题度假区落户上海金山，总投资5.5

亿美元，将成为全球最大的乐高乐园度假区之一。举办进博会的 6 年里，上海共新增实际使用外资 1270 亿美元，占上海累计引进外资的 1/3 左右。

（二）围绕增强全球资源配置能力，大力发展总部经济

持续完善地区总部和外资研发中心政策，支持跨国公司在上海集聚业务、拓展功能、提升能级。

实施总部增能行动。修订出台《上海市鼓励跨国公司设立地区总部的规定》，新增跨国公司事业部总部，加大支持力度，符合条件的跨国公司地区总部可依法依规享受资助和奖励。完善配套政策，总部企业在资金运作与管理、贸易便利、科技创新、商事登记、人才引进、出入境便利等方面获得支持。近年来，上海跨国公司地区总部能级稳步提升，霍尼韦尔、汉高、福特汽车、沃尔沃建筑设备等设立了亚太区总部，康宁、松下电器机电等企业认定为事业部总部；总部功能不断拓展，95% 以上的跨国公司地区总部具有两种以上的功能，涵盖投资决策、资金运作、采购销售、贸易结算等功能，持续发挥资源集聚和辐射作用。

出台外资研发中心提升计划。上海始终坚持利用外资与提升自主创新能力相结合，积极鼓励外资企业在沪设立研发中心。修订完善外资研发中心支持政策，在原有"外资研发中心"认定标准上，增加了"全球研发中心"和"外资开放式创新平台"两个升级版。制定外资研发中心提升计划，涵盖支持外资研发中心加大研发投入、鼓励加强开放创新、优化科研物资通关和监管流程、支持研发数据依法跨境流动、提升知识产权保护水平、支持引才留才等 9 方面举措，让外资研发中心的资金、技术、人才等创新要素得以充分流动，为外资研发中心参与全球竞争提供有力支撑。2020 年底以来，已有迅达电梯、开利空调、锐珂医疗等 15 家企业获得全球研发中心的认定，其中德国福斯润滑油在上海设立的研发中心是集团全球三大研发

中心之一，东芝电梯设立的研发中心是日本总部以外规模最大的研发中心。开放式创新模式加快发展，强生、西门子医疗等跨国公司在上海设立了开放式创新平台。研发溢出效应增强，外资研发中心集聚了大量国际人才、资本、技术等创新要素，生物医药、信息技术、汽车及零部件等重点发展产业的外资研发中心占全市外资研发中心比重超过60%。

（三）加大投资促进力度，积极扩大外资流入

建立健全外商投资促进服务体系，全方位、全流程、全渠道加大投资促进力度。

强机制，制定出台《上海市统筹推进外商投资促进工作实施方案》，建立了由分管市领导担任召集人的"1+9+18+X"全市外商投资促进统筹调度机制，定期调度项目推进、投促活动和问题解决情况，统筹推进全市外商投资促进工作。出台《上海市促进外商投资全球伙伴计划》，发挥合作伙伴项目招引作用，不断拓展外商投资渠道。

抓活动，每年组织跨国公司地区总部和研发中心颁证仪式，在境内外举办各类投资促进活动数百场。加强海外招商，举办"投资上海·共享未来"海外行活动，市领导出席并发表主旨演讲推介上海投资环境，不断提升"投资上海"显示度和影响力。

建平台，建立上海外商投资促进服务平台，完善投资促进项目库、资源库和活动库，线上线下联动提供政策信息、项目配对、投资对接等服务，平台累计中英文访问量突破135万人次；每年编制《上海外商投资环境白皮书》、《上海外商投资指南》等宣传材料，集中展示上海外商投资环境。

搭网络，建立上海投资促进机构联席会议（SIPP），目前拥有约110家会员单位，涵盖了美、英、法、德、日、韩、澳、新加坡和中国香港地区等30多个上海主要

经贸合作伙伴国家和地区，为本市构建全球投资促进网络提供良好支撑。发挥海外办事处作用，组织线上线下经贸活动，加强信息交流和项目对接。

强队伍，聘任专业咨询机构、欧美日等商协会专业人才担任国际投资"促进大使"，会同各区和重点功能区聘用招商"服务大使"，举办"上海市外商投资促进能力提升培训班"，构建形成了一支专业化、国际化的投资促进队伍。

（四）强化企业服务，持续优化营商环境

坚持市区联动、部门联动、政企联动，营造安商稳商的良好氛围。

保障重大外资项目落地。建立全市重点外资项目清单，完善重点外资项目专班和专员服务机制，市区协同做好项目准入、规划、用地、用能、环保、外汇、人员出入境等事项，确保每个项目有跟进、有反馈、有进展；建立重点项目"绿色通道"，推动落地项目快开工、快投产、快见效。例如，特斯拉上海超级工厂2023年累计交付量达到94.7万辆，同比增长33%，在其全球产能中占比过半，零部件本土化率超过95%；2024年，特斯拉储能超级工厂项目正式开工建设，项目建成后，将形成特斯拉超大型商用储能电池1万台/年生产能力，储能规模近40GWh，显示出特斯拉对中国市场未来发展的信心。

深化政企沟通。上海自2019年起建立外商投资"政企沟通圆桌会议"常态化交流机制以来，市领导共主持召开了103场面向外资企业的政企圆桌会议，与外商投资企业和外国商协会代表面对面交流，宣讲最新政策，倾听困难建议，推进问题解决。5年来，近千家外资企业和外国商协会参加，共提出问题和建议上千个，解决率超过90%。圆桌会议已成为外资企业反映问题并推动问题解决的重要平台，也成为"上海服务"的闪亮品牌。

优化涉外服务水平。聚焦外籍人士在沪工作生活所

涉各类高频需求服务，新版上海国际服务门户（english.shanghai.gov.cn）于 2024 年 1 月 1 日上线运行，在三个海内外社交媒体平台（脸谱、x 平台、微信英文版）同时对外启用，从外籍人士视角和需求出发整合涉外政务服务、资讯服务和市场服务，打造英、日、德等 8 个语种上海国际服务门户，为来沪经商、工作、旅游、留学、购物等外籍人士提供权威的政策服务、精准的咨询服务和贴心的生活服务，打通了外籍人士在沪工作、生活全周期服务链条。

实施重点企业"服务包"制度。通过常态走访联系、专人服务对接、政策量身定制，帮助企业精准掌握政策、便利获取服务、高效办理需求。运用"政策速递""热点问答""总部信息直达机制"等多种方式开展政策解读，广泛宣介政策内涵、政策亮点、应用场景等内容，帮助企业用足用好各类政策。

（五）建立健全机制，依法保障外商投资合法权益

着力完善营商环境工作机制性安排，推进外商投资企业投诉工作机制建设，加大重难点问题解决力度。

强化法制保障。法治是最好的营商环境，是更高水平开放的有力保障，上海深入贯彻落实《中华人民共和国外商投资法》，2020 年率先出台全国首部地方外商投资条例，强调"全流程"国民待遇，加大外资企业享有准入后国民待遇的保障力度，在实施各项政策时平等对待外资企业。

加强权益保护。按照"一个机制、一个名称、一套机构、一个办法、一套流程、一个平台"的思路，成立外商投资投诉工作市级联席会议机制，出台《上海市外商投资企业投诉办法》，全市建立了"1+16+2"（1 个市级、16 个区、临港新片区和虹桥商务区）的外商投资企业投诉中心，畅通线上线下申请渠道，规范受理、办理、反馈等工作流程，实现外商投资企业权益保护工作制度化、规范化。

支持参与标准化工作。2024 年 4 月，上海成立了全

国首个外商投资企业标准化协作平台——上海市外商投资企业标准化协作平台，针对外商投资企业反映的不熟悉标准化政策、不了解参与路径、无法全面获取标准信息等问题，精准提供一站式服务，更加主动地倾听和回应企业关切，确保外商投资企业在标准化工作中的声音被听见、贡献被认可。目前，上海市共成立地方标准化技术委员会44个，其中，有外资企业代表作为委员的10余个，涉及疾病预防控制、电梯、新能源、建材、人力资源、智能交通、智能网联汽车、人工智能等标委会。

推进重难点问题解决。针对企业跨区迁移难，建立市级层面"三委三局"协调机制，设立服务专窗，优化办事流程，全口径税收1亿元以下企业可直接办理迁移。针对企业注销难，实行分类处置、同步办理、一次办结；推行简易注销程序，在企业信息公示系统中为企业注销提供公告服务。针对公平参与公共资源交易，外资企业可通过公共资源交易平台依法平等参与政府采购、招标投标、土地出让、产权交易等活动。针对外资企业维权难，编制《上海外商投资企业权益保护白皮书》，提供各部门政策和企业维权案例，为广大外资企业更好维护自身权益提供借鉴。

三、企业案例：强生"JLABS@上海"开放式创新平台

作为强生加速外部创新合作，建设开放式创新生态体系的重要一环，2019年6月，强生将全球最大、亚太首家创新孵化器JLABS安家在上海张江，由强生携手上海市政府、浦东新区人民政府和上海张江（集团）有限公司共同建立。总建筑面积4400余平方米的JLABS@上海，最多能容纳50家生命科学与医疗健康领域创新实体，涵盖了制药和医疗器械等领域。

JLABS@上海为初创企业提供拎包入驻服务，一站式高效灵活的创新平台，国际领先的实验空间和设备，科技、产业和融资领域专家指导，以及强大的强生内外部创

新网络支持，助其加速创新进程，提供优质的医疗健康解决方案，从而提高人类健康水平，攻克疾病，挽救生命，造福中国乃至全球的患者。

自启动以来，JLABS@上海共支持了93家企业，包括了57家已毕业企业和36家现驻企业。入驻企业来自全球各地，其中49%为中国本土公司，51%为国际公司，同时也有40%的企业为连续创业公司。入驻企业共获得估值达57亿美元的融资和战略合作，包括5家IPO、一家收购以及156项交易，其中超过1/3的企业目前与强生集团或JLABS公司至少合作过一次。

2020年12月1日，《上海市鼓励设立和发展外资研发中心的规定》施行以来，强生成为首家获得上海市政府认定的外资开放式创新平台，在强化全球资源配置、全力做强创新引擎上继续发挥行业领军作用。

开放式创新平台这种新模式的发展，进一步推动外资研发中心嵌入上海的产业链和创新链，并带动中小企业和团队的创新创业。

四、展望

上海将全面贯彻党的二十大和二十届二中、三中全会精神，坚定不移扩大对外开放，着力营造国际一流营商环境，持续打造新时代外商投资首选地、高质量外资集聚地。

一是推进高水平对外开放。对标CPTPP、DEPA等国际高标准经贸规则，稳步扩大规则、规制、管理、标准等制度型开放，积极争取先行先试。落实好自贸试验区及临港新片区、浦东引领区、虹桥国际开放枢纽等国家战略，加快实施高水平制度型开放"80条"，用好用足扩大开放政策。深入实施服务业扩大开放综合试点，推进新一轮服务业扩大开放措施。充分发挥进口博览会的平台作用，利用市场优势，拓展上海对外开放的广度和深度。

二是加强投资促进服务。统筹推进外商投资促进工作，加大海外招商推介力度和频次，围绕"引进来"和"走出去"讲好上海故事，推进外资参与绿色发展和数字化转型，共享发展机遇。用好促进外商投资全球伙伴计划、总部关键决策人信息直达等机制，开展精准招商。挖掘设备更新市场引资新潜力，支持外资企业参与产业链上下游配套协作。完善重点外资项目专班和专员服务机制，在用地、能耗、环评、融资等方面加大要素保障力度。

三是促进总部经济增能提升。贯彻落实新一轮跨国公司地区总部支持政策，持续完善总部企业培育、增能、升级三张清单。重点围绕增数量、拓功能、提能级，在资金管理、研发、人才、出入境等方面争取政策创新和先行先试举措。落实上海外资研发中心提升计划，加大对外资研发和创新的支持力度。

四是不断优化外商投资环境。持续办好各层级、多领域政企沟通圆桌会议，落实重点企业"服务包"制度，开展重点外资项目全覆盖点对点服务，切实帮助企业解决问题。深化外资营商环境改革，加大外商投资合法权益保护力度。探索优化数据跨境流动管理措施，在安全可控的前提下，分级分类推动数据跨境流动。不断提升外籍人士在工作签证、出入境、支付、人才服务等方面的便利度，打造宜居、宜业的国际化营商环境。

第七章　浙江双向投资报告 [1]

2023 年是浙江省实施"八八战略"20 周年，全省坚持以习近平新时代中国特色社会主义思想为指引，主动适应新形势新要求，深入实施"八八战略"，大力实施"地瓜经济"提能升级"一号开放工程"，推进开放型经济水平、双循环战略枢纽地位、制度型开放体系再提升，放大高水平"走出去"与高质量"引进来"高效联动的裂变效应，为全国双向投资发展提供了有力支撑。

一、浙江双向投资进展与成效

（一）"引进来"量质齐升，利用外资逆势上扬

1. 外资总量全国排名稳居前列，规模增量和经济贡献突出

2023 年浙江外资规上企业 4281 家，以占全省 7.5% 的规上企业数量，贡献了全省规上企业 18.9% 的营业收入、25.2% 的利润总额、14.6% 的纳税总额、15.2% 的就业人数，在全省工业经济中发挥了重要作用。从规模看，2023 年浙江省实际使用外资金额达 202.3 亿美元，首次突破 200 亿美元大关；占全国份额的 12.4%，总量居全国第四，比 2022 年提升 1 位，是近 5 年来最好成绩。从增速看，高于全国 18.5 个百分点。

① 浙江省商务厅供稿。

2. 外资结构优化提升，呈现"两升两降"特点

"两升"即制造业外资占比提升、来自发达经济体投资占比提升。2023 年，在大力招引先进制造业外资的导向下，全省制造业实际使用外资 91 亿美元，同比增长 85.8%，占全省实际使用外资的 45.0%，较 2022 年同期提升 19.6 个百分点，突破了历年新高。来自发达经济体投资力度不断增强，如来自欧盟国家实际使用外资 37.7 亿美元，占全省的比重为 18.6%，较 2022 年提升 16.7 个百分点。"两降"即房地产业占比下降、港资占比下降。2023 年全省房地产业实际使用外资 12 亿美元，占全省的 5.9%，较 2022 年下降 1.3 个百分点。来自香港地区实际使用外资 124.7 亿美元，占全省的 61.6%，比 2022 年下降 16.7 个百分点。

3. 标志性大项目取得突破，对外资拉动作用进一步凸显

从签约落地看，在杭州、舟山、金华等地协同推进下，沙特阿美并购荣盛石化、斯泰兰蒂斯集团与零跑科技战略合作两大 10 亿美元以上外资项目成功落地；诺华核药、瑞士西卡等一批高质量制造业项目以及碧迪医疗大中华区创新中心、辉瑞智慧医疗创新中心等外资功能性机构接连落户。从实到外资看，全年实际使用外资 3000 万美元以上大项目 129 个，合计到资 143.7 亿美元，占全省的比重为 71%，较 2022 年提升 7.3 个百分点。其中实际使用外资 1 亿美元以上大项目 27 个。从重点项目看，2023 年，全省共 67 个项目列入全国重点外资项目清单，数量居全国第二（仅次于江苏），较 2022 年增加 16 个；省级层面梳理"重大外资项目盯引清单"，项目数稳定在 30 个左右，并进行动态管理，将作为下一步重点发力、推动签约到资的目标。

（二）"走出去"布局全球，境外投资稳健有序

1. 对外投资稳中有升，新兴领域对外投资发展迅速

2023 年对外实际投资额 172.73 亿美元，同比增长

21.10%，在全国的占比为 16.97%，居全国第 2 位。2023 年共完成对外承包工程营业额 69.4 亿美元，同比增长 8.4%，在全国的占比为 4.3%，居各省（市）第五，较上年上升一位；新签合同额 49.2 亿美元，同比增长 7.4%；在境外设立制造业企业 454 家，备案额 115.80 亿美元，占比为 68.81%。制造业对外投资有效带动全省中间品出口。新能矿、数字经济、生物医药、光伏等新兴领域对外投资发展迅速。其中，2023 年新能矿领域设立境外企业 14 家，备案额 35.92 亿美元，增长 1.13%；数字经济领域设立境外企业 85 家，备案额 8.11 亿美元，增长 331.38%；生物医药领域设立境外企业 49 家，备案额 4.15 亿美元，增长 40.68%；光伏领域设立境外企业 31 家，备案额 7.51 亿美元，增长 212.92%。

2. 对外投资方式不断创新，规模以上跨国并购有所增长

随着浙江企业的发展壮大，对外投资方式不断创新，从单纯的出资设企到跨国并购、境外经贸合作区等。一是绿地投资大幅增长。以绿地投资方式新设境外企业 1203 家，增长 77.17%，备案额 118.96 亿美元，同比增长 53.38%，占全省 70.69%。二是规模以上并购有所增长。1000 万美元以上的并购企业数 35 家，比上年增加 13 家，备案额 21.78 亿美元，占并购备案额比例为 90.90%。并购主要集中在新能源矿产开采加工、汽车零部件制造和医药研发等领域。三是境外经贸合作区布局稳步推进。2023 年新增省级境外经贸合作区 1 家，总数达 19 家。全省境外经贸合作区遍及全球 13 个国家，其中 15 家园区在"一带一路"共建国家，形成了以东南亚为主、辐射全球的格局，境外经贸合作区在国内国际双循环中的枢纽地位进一步凸显。截至 2023 年底，境外经贸合作区累计投资 207.70 亿美元，其中浙江企业投资额 117.66 亿美元，占比 56.65%；2023 年园区总产值 299.84 亿美元，带动我国进出口 213.33 亿美元，同比增长 27.79%。

3. 对外投资市场多元，国际合作空间进一步扩大

一是对"一带一路"共建国家投资大幅增长。全省企业在"一带一路"共建国家（含港澳台地区）对外投资备案额 108.88 亿美元，增长 38.70%，占全省比重 64.89%。在 RCEP 成员国家投资项目 577 个，同比增长 96.93%，中方投资备案额 98.58 亿美元，同比增长 56.80%。泰国、越南利用其劳动力成本优势和区位优势吸引国内部分中低端行业企业开展投资合作。二是对欧美地区投资热度回升。对欧洲的投资备案额 18.89 亿美元，增长 13.15%，企业投资欧洲主要是为了开拓欧洲市场。如英飞特集团成功收购德国欧司朗旗下照明数字系统事业部。对北美的投资备案额 23.50 亿美元，增长 79.56%，特别是对墨西哥投资备案额 8.56 亿美元，增长 14.90%。中国新能源汽车企业有强烈需求进入欧洲市场，相关产业配套企业纷纷投资匈牙利，2023 年，全省企业在匈牙利投资项目 29 个，境外直接投资备案额 4.77 亿美元，同比增长 9.06%。

4. 龙头企业带动作用明显，本土民营跨国公司实力不断壮大

2023 年全省民营企业在境外投资设立企业 1457 家，占全省 97.59%；对外投资备案额 163.39 亿美元，同比增长 29.46%，占全省比重 97.09%。2023 年认定 60 家民营跨国公司"领航企业"，其中有 34 家在境外投资设立了 68 家企业，备案额 40.66 亿美元，占全省 24.89%。截至目前，60 家"领航企业"在境外累计设立企业 504 家，累计备案额 353.60 亿美元，占全省同期总数的 27.76%。

二、已推出政策创新、重点亮点举措和发挥的作用

（一）政策创新情况

一是第一时间贯彻国务院政策文件精神，出台浙江省《关于进一步优化外商投资环境加大吸引外商投资力度的实施意见》，制定提高利用外资质量、保障外商投资企业

国民待遇、持续加强外商投资保护、提高投资运营便利化水平、加大财税支持力度、完善外商投资促进方式等6方面22条具有浙江特色的政策举措。

二是出台浙江省《更大力度吸引和利用外资工作若干措施》，充分发挥省级资金撬动、引导和放大作用，对先进制造业、重大服务业、世界500强总部项目等给予重点支持，切实吸引了艺康漂莱特等一批标志性制造业外资项目签约落地。

三是制定《关于鼓励设立和发展外资研发中心的指导意见》，通过超常规落地奖励扩大增量，通过科研激励、税收支持、人才服务、知识产权保护等举措盘活存量，按照"科学灵活、适度放宽"的原则制定认定标准，已首批认定大和热磁等20家省级外资研发中心。

四是制定《进一步做好以制造业为重点利用外资工作的若干举措》，实施"项目专员"跟踪服务和重大项目晾晒机制，加强项目要素保障。

五是出台《加快培育浙江民营跨国公司"丝路领航"行动计划》，充分发挥浙江省民营跨国公司领航企业示范引领作用，培育一批跨国经营指数高、综合竞争力强、国际影响力大的民营跨国公司，提升浙江企业在全球产业链中的协同能力和资源配置能力，促进全省产业向全球价值链中高端延伸，推动共建"一带一路"高质量发展。

（二）重点亮点举措

1. 有序扩大服务业对外开放，统筹内外资招商

一是加快推动杭州市国家服务业扩大开放综合试点落地，拓展现代服务业利用外资，持续开展跨国公司与浙江省各市县"两业融合"合作意向对接，围绕科技服务、专业服务和批发和零售服务等12大领域，深入推进服务业扩大开放试点各项任务。二是探索建立统筹全省内外资招引的工作机制，整合招商力量，保障重大外资项目服务，打造对外招商的整体形象，已形成了省商务厅1个投资

处 +1 个投促中心（驻外商务服务中心，7 个海外商务代表处）+90 个县市区 +117 个开发区（园区）的大招商格局。2023 年全省共招引落地 10 亿元以上省外内资制造业项目及 1 亿美元以上外资制造业项目 165 个，统筹内外资招大引强取得积极成效。

2. 深化展会招商，持续擦亮"投资浙里"招商主品牌

一是开展"投资浙里"全球大招商。编制《"投资浙里"招商项目汇编》《"投资浙里"全球大招商指引》和《"投资浙里"全省招商引资创新案例集》，为全省投促系统精准招商赋能。全年组织各地超 200 个团组赴 30 余个国家和地区开展招商，境内外举办各类投资推介会、招商洽谈会 360 余场，共签约合作项目 175 个，投资总额约 131.7 亿美元，其中包括瑞士西卡新材料、日本信越化学、韩国 LG 新能源等一批优质外资项目。二是开展展会招商，举办第二十四届浙洽会签约外资项目 62 个，包括世界 500 强和行业龙头企业项目 17 个。港澳·浙江周期间，全省与港澳共签约合作项目 77 个，总投资额约 80 亿美元。第六届进博会全省共签约外资项目 24 个，总签约额 38.38 亿美元。第二届数贸会现场签约外资项目 11 个，投资额 17 亿美元。

3. 整合提升招商资源，不断优化招商方式方法

一是深化基金招商。实施"投资浙里"基金招商伙伴专项行动，成立"投资浙里"基金招商联盟，联盟成员单位超百家。连续两年举办浙江基金招商活动，以产业为主题开展系列项目专场路演，帮助各市搭建资金与项目对接的平台。二是优化布局海外招商网络。探索构建全球海外招商网络体系，充分整合跨国企业、境外经贸合作区、浙商侨商等对外联络信息资源，积极拓展海外中介和平台招商渠道。

4. 培育本土跨国公司，持续实施民营跨国公司培育"丝路领航"行动

实施浙江民营跨国公司"丝路领航"行动计划，加强企业总部建设，培育一批具备较强国际竞争力、全球资源配置能力和全球产业链供应链协同能力的民营跨国公司。179 家民营企业纳入培育，其中 2023 年认定 60 家民营跨国公司"领航企业"，60 家企业平均跨国指数 25.7%，高于中国 100 大跨国公司平均指数 9.8 个百分点。

5. 强化枢纽建设，推动共建"一带一路"高质量发展

推进中欧（义新欧）班列提质增效，助力全国中欧班列集结中心示范工程创建，中欧（义新欧）班列全年开行量 2300 列。优化境外经贸合作园区布局，加大培育力度，持续优化境外园区公共服务能力，引导对外投资企业集聚。推进"联盟拓市"，推动对外承包工程与对外投资、贸易融合发展。强化境内外园区联动，探索建立省级层面"两地双园"，创新举办中国－中东欧国家博览会相关活动。

6. 做好服务保障，优化营商环境

一是打响"浙是你的家"外资企业服务品牌。2023 年全年走访 200 余家外资企业开展上门服务，推动政策精准直达。落实好外资企业圆桌会议制度，协调解决问题诉求 68 个，切实做好稳商留企工作。二是强化资源要素保障。落实重大外资项目要素保障协调机制，积极向上推荐浙江重点外资项目，争取国家层面要素保障。目前浙江纳入商务部全国重点外资项目清单数量居全国第二。同时充分发挥省发展改革委、省经信厅、省科技厅等职能部门优势，完善部门分工协同机制，按照产业分类推动、部门共同参与的方式开展项目招引。三是做好项目全流程跟踪服务。迭代完善"浙江投促在线"系统，对省级重点外资项目开展常态化跟踪服务。充分用好省级议事协调工作机制，协调解决生命健康龙头企业碧迪医疗、世界 500 强瑞士诺华核药等诉求，推动项目顺利落地。

三、企业从政策创新中受益的案例

案例 1：华海药业跨国并购，实现技术与市场齐飞。浙江华海药业股份有限公司（以下简称"华海药业"）创立于 1989 年，是一家集化学药、生物药、细胞治疗及贸

易流通为一体的医药企业，20C3 年上市后开始进军制剂国际市场，2004 年在海外设立首家分（子）公司，是国内制药企业中通过国际主流市场官方相关认证最多的企业之一，在制剂出口以及国际化发展领域走在国内制药行业前列。目前，华海药业通过并贩、联盟等方式进入到了美国、德国、日本等地，在全球拥有近 20 个海外办事处。在美国市场，现已形成包括自主销售、大批发商、终端连锁店和商业公司等多渠道的营销体系。在欧洲市场，12 个制剂产品在欧洲 28 个国家获得批准并上市。

通过跨国投资项目，华海药业成为国内首家制剂通过美国 FDA 认证、首家自主拥有 ANDA 制剂文号、首家实现制剂规模化出口美国市场、首家挑战美国原研专利的制药企业。同时生产区已通过中国及美国、欧盟、WHO、澳大利亚、日本、墨西哥等多个国际主流官方质量体系认证。公司原料药和制剂两大产业链日趋成熟，具有从原料药到制剂的垂直一体化产业优势。公司已形成年产 200 多亿片固体制剂生产能力，并已通过欧美 CGMP 认证，拥有抗肿瘤固体制剂车间、水针车间及冻干粉针车间。

项目经营经验。一是加强国际战略联盟。充分利用国内外各种优势资源，开展多种形式的战略联盟。因此，华海药业在开拓国际医药市场时，首先考虑与所进入市场的相关医药企业形成合作或联盟关系，通过打造国际战略联盟，逐步在国际市场站稳了脚跟，并拥有了一定的国际市场话语权。二是结合自身发展战略。华海药业通过"走出去"和"引进来"，加快技术吸收、转移以及信息互享，实现研发、销售、战略、文化等方面的深度融合，充分发挥协同效应，争取效率和效益的最大化。三是选择合适的投资项目。综合考虑创新研究能力、国际市场规模以及对华海可持续发展影响等因素。四是做好尽职调查。选择专业的中介机构开展全面的尽职调查，尤其是财务、法律、税务等方面，降低了华海的并购风险。

案例 2：东方日升海外输出"中国技术"和"中国方案"。东方日升新能源股份有限公司（以下简称"东方日升"）创立于 1986 年，主营业务为太阳能电池组件的研发、生产和销售，以及太阳能电站 EPC 与转让、光伏电站运营、灯具、储能业务产品、辅助光伏产品和晶体硅料等的生产和销售。东方日升在全球范围内设立办事处和分公司，并且建立起全球销售网络，目前拥有 22 个营销服务中心，如中国、德国、澳大利亚、墨西哥、印度、美国、日本等，旨在为全球提供绿色新能源。

主要跨国投资项目。2021 年东方日升在马来西亚投产建设"3GW 高效太阳能电池及组件"项目，投资金额约 3 亿美元。2022 年 5 月 15 日，马来基地首条组件产线正式贯通，首批 210 高效组件顺利下线。东方日升香港子公司携手合作伙伴——越南塔斯克公司，共同与越南电力集团签订 100MW、50MW 太阳能电站 EPC 总承包协议，合同金额 6600 万美元。东方日升还在越南当地先后承建过多个 EPC 项目。

项目经营经验。一是制定科学的市场策略。东方日升在越南进行项目投资的前期，就做好了相应的市场调研，制定了完善的业务发展战略，项目运行后根据市场变化，灵活调整市场策略。东方日升还建立起了主动、独立、灵活、可控的销售渠道和销售网络，以及一支高素质的销售队伍。聘用越南当地有经验的咨询公司、会计师、律师，做好市场风险评估调研，依法依规设立企业、启动和运作项目。二是做好各项风险防范。东方日升的项目注册地（最终目的地）在越南。在投资前，认真研究越南当地政治形势、法律制度和人文环境，特别关注反垄断法，以及越南政府对资本市场的管制和当地劳工法等内容。同时，为避免汇率等相关财务风险，东方日升利用各种金融工具进行防范。在跨国支付时，公司尽量选择用软币支付，用硬币结算。此外，还成立了专门的项目管理部门，加强项目管理，加强投资预决算监管，严格监控项目的实施情况。三是做好跨文化企业管理。密切关注了中越两国员工在管理理念和方式方法等方面存在差异，加强企业间文化整合，构建双方员工共同接受的企业文化，在文化整合和企业自主权的维护方面寻求平衡点。

四、展望

下一步，浙江将继续贯彻落实习近平总书记重要讲话精神和党中央、国务院相关决策部署，继续深化改革，深入实施"地瓜经济"提能升级"一号开放工程"，坚持"立足浙江发展浙江，跳出浙江发展浙江"，统筹推进内外资招大引强，扎实做好"优外资"文章，抓住招大引强"窗口期"，引导企业有序开展国际布局，在国际产业链供应链融合发展中提升浙江价值，推动双向投资高质量发展，为中国式现代化贡献"浙江力量"。

开放平台篇

第八章　海南省利用外资取得积极进展 [1]

一、海南省利用外资情况

（一）近年海南实际使用外资情况

近年来，海南省吸引和利用外资实现了规模和质量的双提升。2018—2023年，全省累计实际使用外资达161.2亿美元，超过建省前30年实际使用外资的总和（96.07亿美元），6年平均增速达46%。其中，2018—2020年利用外资规模连续3年"翻一番"；2021年、2022年在高位基础上均保持了同比15%以上的快速增长，2023年吸引外资规模仍处历史高位。引资结构不断优化，现代服务业成为促增长、优结构的主要动力，现代服务业实际使用外资占比由2018年的61%增长至2023年的83%。

近6年，在海南投资的国家和地区累计达149个，一大批国际知名企业落户海南。医疗领域，目前美国晖致医药、美国艾昆纬、美国默沙东等全球知名企业纷纷落地海南，并带动一批行业企业投资海南，做大做强产业链。高端消费品领域，法国路威酩轩集团、瑞士历峰集团、法国开云集团、法国欧莱雅集团等一大批企业加快布局海南，行业资源加速集聚，产业链条不断延伸，有效吸引境外消费回流。金融领域，瑞士瑞联银行在海口设立私募基金管理公司。艺术品拍卖领域，全球头部拍卖行英国苏富比落地。信息技术服务领域，世界著名商业决策信息和分析服务机构美国邓白氏、信息技术头部企业英特尔落地。高端

---

① 海南省商务厅供稿。

食品加工领域，新加坡丰益集团旗下益海嘉里在海南落地食用油综合加工及中央厨房项目。教育领域，德国比勒费尔德应用科技大学在海南独立办学，是中国境内第一所境外高校独立办学项目，也是德国公办高校首个在国外独立办学项目。英国爱丁堡大学、考文垂大学，美国密歇根州立大学、罗格斯大学等在海南开展合作办学。新能源汽车领域，美国特斯拉、日本丰田落地开展贸易、销售、出行服务等业务。商业地产和物业管理领域，成功引进英国太古集团、香港世茂集团、英国第一太平戴维斯等。物流领域，波洛莱物流已在海南投资建设区域配送中心。能源环保领域，全球最大水务公司法国苏伊士集团落地海南开展污水处理业务，德国欧绿保建设厨余垃圾处理厂开展城乡有机废弃物无害化处理和资源化利用。

（二）2023 年实际使用外资情况

2023 年海南省实际使用外资增速有所回落，但规模仍处历史高位，外商投资海南依然保持很高的活跃度。全省实际使用外资 227 亿元，同比下降 7.1%（同期全国实际使用外资同比下降 8%）；新设外商投资企业数 1736 家，同比增长 28.4%。

从国别地区看，来自中国香港地区（139 亿元、占比 61%）、英国（58.3 亿元、占比 25.7%）、英属维尔京群岛（8 亿元、占比 3.5%）、开曼群岛（5.7 亿元、占比 2.5%）、新加坡（5.3 亿元、占比 2.3%）的外资金额排名前五。来自欧洲国家的外资同比增长最快，实现 62.2 亿元，同比增长 142%。

从行业看，现代服务业实际使用外资 188 亿元，占全省实际使用外资比重达 83%。其中，租赁和商务服务业（占比 58.3%），信息传输、软件和信息技术服务业（占比 17.8%），科学研究和技术服务业（占比 10.8%），批发和零售业（占比 7.1%），金融业（占比 2.8%）排名前五。

从企业看，一批国际知名的、有显示度的企业纷纷落户海南。高端消费领域，美国泰佩思琦、法国酩悦轩尼诗、意大利宝格丽等一批消博会参展企业落户；医疗健康领域，美国默沙东、瑞士雀巢落户；金融领域，斯通伍德在海口设立私募基金管理公司；物流领域，波洛莱物流正在海南投资建设区域配送中心；信息技术服务领域，英特尔落户三亚。

二、重点引资举措

（一）优化引资政策环境

1. 落实国家稳外资相关政策

认真贯彻落实党中央稳外资决策部署和《国务院关于进一步优化外商投资环境加大吸引外商投资力度的意见》（以下简称"国发 11 号文件"）。一是加强组织领导，高位推动落实。省委书记冯飞、省长刘小明高度重视国发 11 号文件贯彻落实工作，分别作出批示并明确具体要求。省商务厅第一时间组织专班牵头起草《海南省进一步优化外商投资环境促进利用外资稳中提质若干措施》（以下简称《若干措施》），经省政府常务会议审议通过，于 2023 年 11 月 5 日以省政府办公厅名义印发实施。二是明确责任分工，制定落实措施。《若干措施》围绕提高利用外资质量、提升投资便利化水平、持续加强外商投资保护、优化外商投资促进方式 4 个方面提出 20 条措施，每条措施均明确相关部门职责分工并已列入省政府督查事项，将由职责部门定期向督查室报送进展情况。三是开展政策宣介，进一步增强外商投资信心。省商务厅面向 18 个市县商务主管部门、13 个重点园区开展国发 11 号文件的宣传解读，并联合省税务局、人行海南省分行面向 150 余名外商投资企业、外商投资促进机构工作人员解读国发 11 号文件政策内涵以及自贸港税收政策、投融资便利化政策等，通过政策宣介进一步稳定外商投资预期，增强外商投资信心。

2. 编制发布《2023 年海南自贸港投资指南》

全面展现海南自贸港建设优势、政策利好、产业机遇、投资亮点，以及法治化、国际化、便利化的营商环境，为全球投资者提供认识海南、了解海南的窗口，为企业在海南开展投资和经贸活动提供指引。

3. 推进外资地方立法

目前，省发改委、省商务厅正在联合制定《海南自由贸易港外商投资条例》，从法律层面加强外商投资的促进、保护和管理。比如，在扩大外资市场准入方面，推进重点领域扩大开放；在投资促进方面，支持发展总部经济等；在投资保护方面，依法保护外国投资者在海南自贸港内的合法权益。

（二）创新招商方式，实施精准招商

1. 借助国际展会论坛等平台扩大引资流量

利用 2023 年博鳌亚洲论坛年会平台，与英国阿斯利康集团、沙特基础工业公司、美国高盛集团等重点外资企业开展"一对一"商务洽谈；借助第三届消博会平台，精心谋划开展各类外资招商活动，推动参展商变投资商，引进法国酩悦轩尼诗、意大利宝格丽、美国雅诗兰黛等一批国际知名品牌和头部企业落地。借助商务部"投资中国年"平台，面向全球投资者开展海南自由贸易港政策优势和发展新机遇，推进对外交流与合作。

2. 实施国际大招商行动

一是用好出访招商。2023 年，省委、省政府领导先后率团出访英国、德国、瑞士、日本、阿联酋、中国香港等地，举办专场推介会、"一对一"商务洽谈等活动，广泛宣介海南自贸港政策优势，向国际释放海南自贸港高水平对外开放的信号。省领导已开展 11 批次境外出访活动，开展各类活动总计约 250 场，其中海南自贸港综合、专题推介会 19 场，"一对一"经贸洽谈活动约 80 场，对接欧瑞康、渣打银行、嘉里集团、瑞士洛桑酒店管理学院等一批知名外资企业（机构），务实推进交流与合作，收获丰硕成果。二是举办面向重点国别的专场推介活动。在瑞士苏黎世、英国伦敦、日本东京、迪拜分别举办专场推介会，邀请当地政府部门和企业负责人参会，宣介海南自贸港政策和投资机遇，吸引企业来琼投资。三是进一步深化与在华外国商协会交流合作。与日本贸易振兴机构等投资促进机构开展会面洽谈，进一步加深沟通对接，共同谋划合作活动；与德国工商联合会、美国中国商会等欧美商会机构建立更加紧密的合作关系，不断深化海南与各国企业商协会的紧密联系，扩大投资合作。

（三）用好平台，发挥引资聚集作用

1. 推进服务业扩大开放综合试点工作

聚焦科技、商业服务、教育、金融等领域，扎实推进试点工作进展，及时总结试点经验做法、典型案例和制度创新成果，放宽外国高层次人才参与科技项目限制、开通国际人才职称评审绿色通道等 6 项实践案例被纳入国家服务业扩大开放综合试点第二批示范案例。

2. 推进国家级经开区创新提升

组织做好海南洋浦经济开发区参加 2023 年国家级经开区综合发展水平考核评价工作。指导洋浦经开区在落实 RCEP 中发挥先行示范作用，发挥洋浦"自贸港样板间"与 RCEP 规则的叠加效应，用好 RCEP 原产地规则和自贸港加工增值税收优惠政策。

（四）强化服务保障，优化营商环境

1. 建立外资工作专班制度

组建省级促进外贸外资平稳发展工作专班，由分管省领导担任组长，决策、协调解决重点外贸外资企业的困难诉求和制约外贸外资发展的突出问题，推动外贸外资工作稳定发展。同时，指导海口、三亚、儋州等 9 个重点外资

市县成立由市县政府主要负责人担任组长的市县外资工作专班，主要任务是对本辖区已落地重点外资项目开展全流程服务，并建立相关服务重点外资项目台账。

2. 建立覆盖省市两级的外商投资企业投诉工作机制。编制发布

《海南省外商投资企业投诉工作办法》和《海南省外商投资企业投诉指南》。目前，全省已建立省市两级的外商投资企业投诉工作机构 19 个，覆盖 18 个市（县），分级受理外商投诉事项。2024 年以来，省商务厅组织开展两期面向市县商务部门和外商投诉工作人员的投诉工作培训交流活动，有效提升了各级人员投资服务能力水平。省商务厅通过对 186 家外资企业开展问卷调查了解，86% 的受访者对我省外资投诉服务工作表达了满意。

3. 建立外资企业圆桌会议制度

省商务厅制定《海南自由贸易港外资企业圆桌会议制度实施方案》。并会同海口、三亚、儋州、澄迈等市县政府举办了 5 场外资企业圆桌会议，邀请"省 – 市（县）"政府部门、园区和重点外资企业参会，通过跨区跨部门沟通协调机制，聚焦企业普遍关注的政策现场回应，高效解决企业反映的问题。会后，省商务厅会同市县政府建立清单台账，明确问题诉求的责任单位，加强跟踪督办，实现闭环服务。

三、企业落地案例

海南利用外资活力足，是海南建省办经济特区以来厚积薄发的结果，是海南自贸港建设直接推动的结果，也是当前海南政策优势凸显、营商环境改善、产业基础夯实、投资机会增多、平台助力发展、政策预期强化的结果。

（一）政策红利释放

海南自贸港建设以来，一系列优惠政策措施落地生效，政策红利不断释放。企业在落地和运营中，切实享受到不少优惠。

优惠政策为企业发展注入强大活力。以毕马威为例，在贸易投资领域，海南自贸港外商投资准入负面清单、跨境服务贸易负面清单出台，三张"零关税"清单落地实施等，使得大量企业关注并落地海南，为毕马威提供了大量市场合作机会；在财税金融领域，海南自贸港"两个15%"所得税优惠政策等出台，毕马威享受了相关税收优惠。此外，RCEP 生效实施与自贸港优惠政策的叠加也促进了毕马威发展。

率先开放政策初显成效。海南自贸港外商投资准入负面清单与我国现行自贸区版外资准入负面清单相比，在教育、增值电信、法律服务、采矿业 4 个领域率先开放。目前，中国境内首个境外高校独立办学项目海南比勒费尔德应用科学大学已开学。

离岛免税政策等不断优化。这些年来，海南离岛免税政策经历了多轮优化调整，有效激发市场活力，离岛免税购物活跃，不少外商投资企业从中受益。比如，2020 年 6 月起，离岛免税新政施行，对泰佩思琦销售额起到"翻番"的刺激效果，而以"即购即提"为代表的便利性措施也对市场发挥着积极影响。

（二）产业基础夯实

近年来，海南发挥自然资源丰富、地理区位独特以及背靠超大规模国内市场和腹地经济等优势，加快培育具有海南特色的合作竞争新优势，产业基础不断夯实，不少领域"链式招商"颇有成效，产业链、人才链等要素加速集聚。比如，华熙厚源生物科技（海南）有限公司落户海口高新区美安生态科技新城，一个重要原因是看中这里正在打造千亿级生物医药产业集群。泰佩思琦等企业看中海南在旅游业、现代服务业等领域的发展基础，积极利用海南离岛免税政策等优势，深挖中国大市场，有的开新店、首发新品，有的进行生产加工，有的建设区域总部等项目，集聚效应不断显现。

（三）营商环境优化

海南持续优化营商环境，加快政策落地，推进制度集成创新，同时在转变政府职能上下功夫，为企业提供精细化服务，积极解决企业发展中遇到的各种难题，提振了外商投资信心。

高效服务便利企业投资。加拿大客商投资的加绿巧食品制造业（海南）有限责任公司（以下简称"加绿巧海南公司"）在证照办理、生产厂房选址时，当地政府贴心、高效服务，使企业在极短时间内就投产营业。得益于相关部门、园区等的大力支持，欧绿保海南公司仅用6个月时间，就完成了计划建设期为一年的海口市餐厨垃圾及粪便无害化处理扩建项目。

优惠政策吸引外籍人才。对于外籍人才，海南在政策体系、事业平台、营商环境等方面加大推进力度，努力搭建让外籍人才各尽其用、各展其才的舞台，吸引了不少外籍人才来琼创新创业和工作。海口不断优化外国人来华工作许可、居留许可审批服务，在推行"一窗通办"之外，构建"多点发力"的外籍人才服务网，为企事业单位引进外籍人才排忧解难。

（四）平台赋能合作

博鳌亚洲论坛年会、中国国际消费品博览会等平台，向中外嘉宾展示了海南开放形象，促成全球不少投资者投资海南，一批优质合作项目落地。消博会是加拿大绿色巧克力工厂有限公司了解中国市场的平台，该公司2021年参加首届消博会后，同年9月成立加绿巧海南公司。泰佩思琦因消博会坚定了投资海南自贸港的信心和决心，泰佩思琦中国旅游零售总部在首届消博会举行一年后高效落地。正大集团通过博鳌亚洲论坛年会、消博会等平台，深入对接海南，深化同海南多领域的合作。

四、下一步工作举措

下一步，全省将全面贯彻落实党中央、国务院稳外资决策部署，聚焦打造对外开放新高地，推进实施更大范围、更宽领域、更深层次对外开放，全力开创高质量吸收外资新局面。

（一）持续优化外商投资环境

一是优化外商投资政策环境。落实好国务院和海南省优化外商投资环境文件精神，密切跟踪相关部门配套政策措施出台情况，通过宣传解读，确保外资企业应知尽知。二是严格贯彻落实外商投资准入前国民待遇加负面清单管理制度，发挥《鼓励外商投资产业目录》导向作用，引导外资更多投向先进制造业和现代服务业。三是常态化开展内外资不合理差别待遇清理。对于外资企业反映的"大门开、小门不开""准入不准营"等问题，及时了解情况、疏通堵点，持续推动清理各类隐形壁垒，落实"非禁即入"要求。四是从国别、产业等结构深入分析外资企业境内再投资信息，更加准确、全面掌握存量外资企业的投资经营情况，为加强形势研判、出台精准引资政策提供支撑。

（二）继续开展好国际大招商行动

一是利用好出访招商机遇，锁定美国、法国、英国、德国、意大利、日本、韩国、阿联酋、新加坡、中国香港等重点地区，赴境外开展"面对面"商务洽谈、"综合推介会"等活动。建立与世界 500 强、知名跨国公司企业沟通联系机制，推动与重点企业的合作，为引入标志性、有影响力的外资项目打好基础。二是利用好平台招商，利用博鳌亚洲论坛年会、商务部"投资中国"峰会等国家级平台，开展综合性招商推介活动，对接国际高质量市场主体。进一步强化消博会平台的投资服务功能，扩大宣传推介、提升海南自贸港知名度和影响力。三是开展好产业链招商和以商招商，加强与产业链龙头企业对接，聚焦高新技术制造、新能源汽车、医疗健康等重点行业开展产业链招商，鼓励企业引进合作伙伴和上下游配套企业落户。四是开展好委托招商、中介招商，利用四大会计师事务所、知名咨询公司、中资金融机构境外网点等中介公司、金融机构的客户资源优势，宣传推介海南自贸港政策，引荐优质企业落户海南；与全国及各地外商投资企业协会，中国美国商会、中国欧盟商会、英中贸易协会等境内外知名国际商协会、海南同乡会密切交往，深化合作交流，不断拓宽外资招引渠道。五是开展好基金招商，加强与金融局等部门的协调联动，做好 QFLP 境外基金类招商工作，吸引优质境外资本流入，充分发挥海南自贸港跨境投融资便利优势吸引更多高质量外资项目。此外，在举办各类招商活动时，注重活动质量，促进项目对接，提高招商活动成果转化。

（三）强化企业（项目）服务保障

一是优化外资企业圆桌会议机制。继续用好圆桌会议机制，下沉市县（园区）分片区、分领域务实召开外资企业圆桌会议，适时请省领导主持召开，与企业面对面座谈交流，倾听企业意见建议，认真推动解决企业反映的问题诉求，不断增强企业获得感。二是争取更多重点外资项目纳入国家外贸外资服务协调机制保障范围。推荐一批符合海南自贸港产业发展导向的先进制造业、高新技术、现代服务业等产业领域重点外资项目纳入国家外贸外资服务协调机制保障范围，加快项目落地建设，强化项目要素保障。三是完善外资企业一站式服务平台。优化完善"企航自贸港"一站式服务平台，做好外资企业落地前、落地中和落地后全生命周期服务保障工作，提升投资便利化水平，持续优化外商投资营商环境。

第九章　国家服务业扩大开放综合示范区建设报告 [1]

2015 年，北京在全国率先启动服务业扩大开放综合试点，聚焦服务业重点领域，在全市域推行纵向改革开放，开辟了产业开放新模式。2020 年，在习近平总书记亲自关怀、亲自部署、亲自宣布下，"试点"正式升级为"示范区"，北京成为全国唯一的国家服务业扩大开放综合示范区（以下简称"示范区"）。北京市委、市政府高度重视，将示范区与中国（北京）自由贸易试验区建设统筹推进（简称"两区"建设），开启了首都改革开放新篇章。如今，示范区建设已进入迭代升级的 2.0 阶段，8 年间，北京始终坚持以开放促改革促发展，产业开放与园区开放并行发力、制度创新与项目落地双轮驱动，积极为形成更大范围、更宽领域、更深层次对外开放新格局提供地方实践，探索出一条以高水平开放促进高质量发展的北京路径。

一、持续深化示范区建设，打造对外开放新高地

（一）以政策创新引领高水平制度型开放

一是切合国家战略需要率先对接国际高标准，为国家高水平对外开放探路先行。以落实国务院批复方案为主线、争取一批国家事权突破，用 3 年时间完成国务院批复首轮示范区建设任务的 98%。在此基础上争取出台《支持

① 北京市商务局供稿。

北京深化国家服务业扩大开放综合示范区建设工作方案》（以下简称"示范区 2.0 方案"），推进示范区建设迭代升级，从投资、贸易、数字经济、金融服务、知识产权、争端解决、风险防控 7 个方面构建高水平服务业开放制度体系，有序对接《全面与进步跨太平洋伙伴关系协定》（CPTPP）和《数字经济伙伴关系协定》（DEPA）规则，相关对标举措达 70 余项，占整个试点任务的 40%。北京自贸试验区在全国首批开展对接国际高标准推进制度型开放试点，在货物贸易创新发展、服务贸易自由便利、优化营商环境、加强风险防控等方面先行先试，全面推进试点任务落地。

二是立足首都城市战略定位稳步扩大制度型开放，努力开创首都高水平开放发展新局面。在落实国家赋予试点任务基础上，围绕科技创新、数字经济、绿色金融、生物医药等符合首都城市战略定位且具有优势的领域，以及投资、贸易、人才、知识产权、国际收支等关键要素推动全产业链开放、全环节改革，首批制定实施 10 余个专项方案。同时，围绕离岸贸易、美丽健康、文化贸易、低空经济等"小而美"的细分领域开展政策"会诊"，支持区域特色产业发展；聚焦部分前瞻性强、综合性强的领域，以项目化管理方式推动集成式政策制度创新，首批推出外资企业和外国人场景化集成服务等 47 项创新任务，落地率近九成。

（二）发挥开放平台优势打造外资集聚磁场

一是坚持重点园区特色化差异化发展，塑造多元开放格局。在全市推出 21 个"两区"重点园区（组团），实施发展提升专项行动，指导各组团加快优势产业发展。丽泽金融商务区稳妥开展数字人民币试点，区内银河证券在全国率先落地证券行业首个数字人民币应用场景；全球跨境支付公司易付达中国总部入驻。北京中德经济技术合作先行示范区集聚奔驰、Ameco 等百余家德资企业，2023 年产业规模达 400 亿元。北京中日创新合作示范区设立首期规模 20 亿元的中日基金，累计落地外资企业 100 余家。

2023 年，21 个园区以占全市不到 2% 的面积，创造和贡献了超两成的规上收入和超 1/3 的税收收入。

二是实施自贸试验区提升行动，做强开放引领。以重要制度创新、重大平台、重点项目为抓手，塑造"创新、数智、绿色、便利、协同"五个自贸品牌，北京高博医院正式开业运营，加速医药研发成果转化；中国 – 新加坡首个全环节跨境贸易数字化实单试点落地；发布全国首个整合"标准认证 + 生产采购 + 金融扶持"功能的标准化碳链平台，支持北京绿色交易所建设全国统一的温室气体自愿减排交易中心；亦庄迎商中心 2.0 启动建设，打造全国首个"一站式入区服务集成平台"；推出京冀"自贸通办"模式，实现北京市级和通州区级 3600 余项政务服务事项在河北自贸试验区跨区域无差别办理。发挥自贸试验区在开放型经济发展中的主阵地作用，2023 年，北京自贸试验区以占全市 0.7% 的面积贡献了 19.3% 的实际使用外资规模。

三是高质量推进综合保税区建设，优化开放布局。全国首家空港型综合保税区——北京天竺综合保税区跨境贸易便利化标准化试点通过验收，在 2022 年度全国综合保税区发展绩效评估中位列 A 类，2023 年进出口规模实现史上首破千亿元，同比增长 41%。加速北京大兴国际机场综合保税区建设，开通跨境电商直邮出口模式，完善跨境电商产业链，保税公共服务平台、保税智能仓储中心及物流中心等项目投运。北京中关村综合保税区作为全国首个以研发创新为特色且首个取消物理围网的综合保税区成功获批，在全国率先探索智慧监管模式。

（三）为中外投资合作营造一流营商环境

一是发挥项目促进机制作用。把项目作为推进"两区"建设的落脚点，落实"两区"项目"一库四机制"（一库，即"两区"建设项目管理系统；四机制，包括预期目标管理工作机制、定期协调调度工作机制、政企对接机制和督查评价机制）。截至目前，累计入库 2.6 万余个项目，落地出库近 1.8 万个项目，涉及投资额超 3.6 万亿元。

二是加大力度吸引和利用外资。结合北京实际，落实国务院吸引外资"24 条"，发布《北京市关于进一步优化外商投资环境加大吸引外商投资力度的若干措施》，从提高利用外资质量、保障外商投资企业国民待遇、持续加强外商投资保护、加大财税支持力度等方面促进更大力度、更加有效吸引和利用外商投资；制定《北京市深化服务业扩大开放促进外商投资实施方案》，持续推进外商投资领域扩大开放。

三是完善外商投资服务体系。畅通政企常态化沟通渠道，召开市领导与在京国际商协会和世界 500 强企业座谈会，实施外资企业圆桌会议制度和"闭环式"企业诉求响应机制，实现政企沟通"时时可联系、月月有沟通、季季有对接"，为外资企业排忧解难。发布涵盖科技创新、数字经济等 10 个领域的中英双语招商引资政策服务包，依托"两区"全球联络站、"亲密伙伴计划"、投资北京全球合作伙伴工作机制、世界投资促进机构协会等渠道平台，开展"两区"政策宣介，助力外资企业用足用好政策。

四是健全法治保障体系。制定实施"两区"一条例一决定，确保重要改革创新于法有据，加速出台《北京市外商投资条例》，保护外商投资合法权益、规范外商投资服务管理；成立北京国际商事法庭、北京法院国际商事纠纷一站式多元解纷中心，推进国际商事仲裁中心建设，构建多元化纠纷解决机制。2020 年至 2023 年，北京实际使用外资规模近 590 亿美元，占全国的 8.8%，其中服务业实际使用外资占比超九成。

二、持续深化改革开放探索，激发高质量发展强劲动能

（一）与国际科技创新中心建设联动，为发展新质生产力营造开放共享的创新生态

一是促进资源要素融通，加强高水平国际科技合作。依托北京基础研究力量雄厚和金融资源集聚的优势，获批

建设中关村科创金融改革试验区，力争通过 5 年时间构建金融有效支持科技创新的体制机制，增强金融服务科创企业能力；在全国率先开展股权投资和创业投资份额转让试点，落地全国首个认股权综合服务试点，启动设立全国首只认股权策略创业投资基金，拓宽科创企业融资渠道；北京股权交易中心正式落地全国首批"专精特新"专板，支持优质专精特新企业加速挂牌、上市。推动国家重大科技基础设施开放共享，怀柔综合性国家科学中心初步形成国家重大科技基础设施平台集群，加快打造世界级原始创新承载区，布局的 37 个科技设施平台已有综合极端条件实验装置、地球系统数值模拟装置等 10 个科技设施平台实现全面开放。深度链接高水平国际化资源，全国首个国际科技组织总部集聚区落地，国际数字地球学会、国际智能制造联盟等 12 家国际科技组织实现入驻。

二是加速引入开放创新主体，助力重点产业链延链补链强链。推动外资企业参与国际科技合作、畅通链接全球创新资源渠道，出台支持外资研发中心一揽子措施。截至 2023 年底，累计认定空客、施耐德、ABB 等 107 家外资研发中心，引进丰田燃料电池研发与生产、GE 医疗高端产线、SMC 中国区总部、拜耳新建现代化生产线等一批标志性外资项目。

三是以改革释放发展动能，促进科技成果转化为现实生产力。全国率先启动高新技术企业"报备即批准"政策试点，在集成电路、人工智能、生物医药、关键材料等 4 个重点领域实行随申请、随认定、随报备，较常规流程压缩 80% 以上，累计试点企业 377 家；探索科技成果赋权改革，开展赋予科研人员职务科技成果所有权或长期使用权试点，9 家试点单位完成 59 个项目赋权；实施技术转让所得税优惠政策，已有 108 户企业享惠，减免税额 7.42 亿元。

（二）聚焦服务业重点领域开放，为服务和融入国内国际双循环相互促进的新发展格局提供北京实践

一是持续深化金融领域扩大开放。丰富金融市场主

体，全国首家外资独资新设券商——渣打证券、全球资管界著名机构贝莱德在北京新设全资子公司——磐琰投资、中信证券新设资产管理公司等一批标志性、重量级金融机构在京落地。支持金融机构拓宽业务范围，东方汇理全资子公司在北京首次增资并新增 QDLP 试点额度，汇丰保险经纪有限公司获批证券投资基金销售业务资格，宝马（中国）保险经纪有限公司和安顾方胜保险经纪有限公司获批经营保险经纪业务。厚植绿色金融底色，德意志银行（中国）有限公司、法国兴业银行（中国）有限公司成为首批纳入碳减排支持工具的外资银行；全国首批新能源 REITs 项目中航京能光伏 REIT 上市；中金公司、中信建投等券商获得碳排放权交易资格。支持北京证券交易所发展，联手港交所推出"北 +H"机制，支持符合条件的企业在京港两地上市，打造服务创新型中小企业主阵地，截至 2023 年底，北京证券交易所上市公司数量达 239 家，总市值增至近 4500 亿元。

二是深入推动医疗、专业服务等领域改革开放。健康医疗领域，在 30 家医疗机构开展研究型病房示范建设，在建及建成研究型床位 4800 张；出台支持美丽健康产业高质量发展若干措施，落地全国首个化妆品个性化服务体验中心；在昌平区和经开区挂牌设立"北京药品医疗器械创新服务站"，累计服务企业近 2800 家次。专业服务领域，率先落地证券、基金、期货"三位一体"金融领域国际职业资格认可机制；实施会计师事务所在自贸试验区设立分所试点。航空服务领域，全国首创保税物流供应链监管新模式；实现航空器材维修企业适用借助综合保税区通关实行增值税免抵退税办法；推进"空中丝绸之路"创新示范区建设，提升"双枢纽"国际功能。

（三）助力打造全球数字经济标杆城市，强化数字经济领域规则探索

一是培育发展数据要素市场。启动建设全国首个数

据基础制度先行区，发布创建方案和政策清单，打造数据基础制度综合改革试验田。加速激活数据交易，北京国际大数据交易所成立数据资产服务中心，围绕数据资产服务开展数据资产登记、评估、入表、融资服务等业务，数据交易规模超 20 亿元，数据交易联盟成员扩大至百余家；上线全国首个工业数据专区，为工业企业提供数据产品开发、数据资产交易等服务；在空间领域实现全国首次数据资产登记，完成全国首笔空间数据入场交易。探索新领域新业态知识产权保护规则，全国首批开展数据知识产权试点，是全国唯一全面完成规则制定、登记实践、保护案例、交易使用、数据资产入表等试点工作的试点城市，圆满审结涉数据知识产权登记证效力"第一案"。

二是依法有序推动数据跨境流动。获批全国首个数据出境安全评估案例，通过首例个人信息出境标准合同备案，实现数据出境合规"两个第一"，2023 年通过 38 个安全评估项目、27 个标准合同备案项目，率先实现民航、汽车、教育、医药、学术、人工智能等 6 大行业领域数据合规出境，数据出境通过率和申报场景数量居全国前列；打造全国首个服务跨境场景的数据托管服务平台，建成数据安全与治理公共服务平台，引入社会力量参与数据跨境流动治理。

三是赋能重点产业创新发展。建成全球首个网联云控式高级别自动驾驶示范区，推动 3.0 阶段 580 平方公里扩区工作，部署智能网联乘用车等 8 大场景 700 余台车辆在区内测试使用，千余台车辆在全市 6 个区内开展示范应用，累计提供出行、零售等服务超 700 万人次，日均订单量近 3000 张；发布全国首个基于真实场景的车路协同自动驾驶数据集和智能网联路侧操作系统、全国首个自动驾驶示范区数据安全管理办法和数据分类分级管理细则。2023 年，全市实现数字经济增加值超 1.8 万亿元，同比增长 8.5%，数字经济增加值占地区生产总值比重超四成。

（四）深化优势互补的区域联动，构建京津冀协同发展的高水平开放平台

一是共促协同创新。加强创新联动，签署《京津冀自贸试验区协同发展行动方案》，以贸易投资自由化便利化、港口互联互通、金融创新、产业发展、资源便捷流动等方面务实举措提升三地协同发展水平，联合发布京津冀自贸试验区"1+5+18"系列协同创新成果。建成全国首个综合类技术创新中心——京津冀国家技术创新中心，促进科技成果在区域内落地转化。建设全国首个基于互联网的涉企信用信息征信链平台"京津冀征信链"，实现工商、司法等多领域高质量涉企信用信息跨区域共享，上链产品调用总量近 2500 万笔，依托征信链支持放贷户数近 2000 万户，形成贷款发放总额超 1000 亿元。

二是共推互联互通。深化口岸合作，实现京津冀国际贸易"单一窗口"用户体系互认，推出"京津冀协同服务专区"，企业可登录三地任一"单一窗口"使用服务专区的办事功能。推进政务服务一体化，截至 2023 年底，共推出五批 203 项京津冀自贸试验区政务服务"同事同标"事项，实现"无差别受理、同标准办理"；发布 165 项互认清单，实现三地从业资质资格跨区域互认。

三、持续推动政策扩面增效，塑造"北京服务"品牌

一是促进投资自由便利。持续放宽外资准入，全国首家外资新设全资期货公司、全市首家外商投资职业技能培训机构、首家外资商业保理公司等一批标志性项目在京落地；保险中介市场对外开放有关措施实施后的全国首家外商独资保险经纪公司——汇丰保险经纪公司顺利在京开业，实现注册资本由 1000 万元至 11.08 亿元的数量级跨越，成为国内实缴注册资本最高保险中介法人机构。便利在京投资兴业，积极推动实施外商投资企业线上办理营业执照、涉税事项、银行开户等企业开办事项，降低兴业成本。

二是促进贸易自由便利。优化贸易监管模式，建成全国首家综合保税区内特殊物品公共查验平台，实现企业开箱一次完成"收货、发货、理货、查验"四个环节；设立进口药品通关抽样一体化平台，同步办理进口药品通关和抽样材料审核，实现 24 小时内完成进口药品通关备案和抽样工作，为企业提升效率、降低成本发挥积极作用。加快发展外贸新业态新模式，推出免税保税跨境电商相衔接、跨境电商进口医药产品、"保税＋消费升级"试点等新模式，发展离岸贸易等新型国际贸易，"京贸兴"成为全国首个跨区域提供服务的离岸贸易公共服务平台；国家对外文化贸易基地（北京）打造国家级文化贸易服务平台，培育境外艺术品保税修复等新业态，艺术品进口规模占全国的 1/3。

三是促进资金进出便利。加强资金统筹管理，在全国率先获批开展本外币跨境资金集中运营管理试点，形成"本外币一体化＋本外币跨境"资金池政策体系，惠及全市 100 余家跨国公司近 5000 家境内外成员单位。提高资金使用效率，在中关村示范区海淀园和北京自贸试验区开展外债一次性登记试点，试点登记额度超 1000 亿元；优质企业贸易外汇收支便利化持续扩容升级，将 140 家"专精特新"企业、医院、科研院所等机构纳入试点范围，试点主体突破 230 家，金额累计超 3600 亿美元；跨境融资便利化试点主体范围扩展至高新技术、"专精特新"和科技型中小企业；获批开展扩大跨境贸易投资高水平开放试点，便利更多经营主体合规办理跨境贸易投资业务。

四是促进人才进出境和执业便利。提升人才服务水平，外籍人才工作许可、工作类居留许可"两证联办"办理时限缩短至 5 个工作日，已有 4000 余名外籍人才及家属享受相应服务；开展外籍"高精尖缺"人才认定标准试点，扩充外国高端人才（A 类）和外国专业人才（B 类）认定范围，提供工作许可办理便利；启用中关村国际人才服务功能区，为外籍人才提供政务办理、生活保障、事业发展等3方面32类服务。促进外籍人才在京执业，持续升级"两个目录"，发布北京市境外职业资格认可目录3.0版，涵盖122项境外职业资格，筛选出ACM会士等7项高含金量境外职业资格形成急需紧缺目录；发布"两区"人力资源开发目录2023年版，包括130个重点开发方向和58个急需紧缺职业（工种）。

五是强化知识产权保护运用。积极稳妥发展知识产权融资，出台知识产权质押融资服务高质量发展政策，建立知识产权评估、质押登记信息在线查询、白名单双向推送、风险补偿等10项全链条服务机制，扩大知识产权质押融资普及度和普惠面，2022年以来专利和商标质押金额超278亿元，2023年度知识产权质押融资服务高质量发展专项资金项目的企业满意度超98%。创新知识产权保护模式，全国首创知识产权保险试点，累计支持近500家企业的4800余件专利投保国内专利执行险和被侵权损失险，保险保障金额约54亿元；全国率先开展知识产权海外纠纷法律费用保险试点，为17家企业提供保险保障金额1亿元。完善知识产权保护体系，推进专利侵权纠纷行政裁决示范建设，累计结案300余件，专利侵权纠纷"先行裁驳、另行请求模式"向全国推广。健全服务体系，完善知识产权保护分中心模式，在全国率先实现地市级综合性知识产权公共服务机构全覆盖；建成北京市海外知识产权公共服务信息库数据，数据量突破10万件，提供信息服务3.7万次。

四、展望

党的二十届三中全会指出，开放是中国式现代化的鲜明标识，要坚持以开放促改革，建设更高水平开放型经济新体制。全会精神为首都开放指明了方向。下一步，示范区建设将以习近平总书记关于高水平对外开放重要论述和对北京系列重要指示精神为根本遵循，全面贯彻落实党的二十大和二十届二中、三中全会精神，准确把握新形势新要求，立足深层次改革需要、高质量发展需要、开放合作需要，打造具有首都特色的高水平开放样板，在新起点上展现首都更大担当作为，为助力建设更高水平开放型经济新体制贡献力量。

一是坚持稳步扩大制度型开放。以国家需求为导向，发挥示范区范围大、行业全、样本多的优势，精准对接国际高标准经贸规则，稳步扩大规则、规制、管理、标准等制度型开放，在推动示范区 2.0 方案落地见效的同时，同步谋划 3.0 方案，为我国积极推进加入高标准经贸协定积累地方实践，为构建高标准服务业开放制度体系提供支撑。

二是持续助力现代化产业体系建设。坚持系统观念与目标导向，围绕数字经济、金融、健康医疗等重点领域以及人才、知识产权等关键要素持续深化全链条、全环节改革开放，优化产业发展生态；聚焦生物医药、增值电信、自动驾驶等重点领域开展开放压力测试。探索干细胞、基因诊断及治疗技术开发与应用开放发展新模式，实施关键核心技术攻关、临床转化能力提升等重大工程，加快打造世界级产业集群。

三是构建多元开放格局。强化重点园区（组团）、综合保税区等平台开放承载，坚持特色化差异化探索，加快创新成果提炼和推广，形成更多创新性强、实用性好的经验做法向全国复制推广。

四是加大吸引外资力度。用好"投资北京全球合作伙伴""两区"全球联络站等渠道平台，打造"政策直通车"，借助服贸会、进博会等国际性展会，面向企业开展"两区"宣介，充分调动经营主体和社会各界积极性，助力各类企业用足用好政策，推动已落地政策扩面增效。

五是统筹好开放与安全。坚持高质量发展与高水平安全良性互动，推动发展与安全深度融合，落实好外商投资安全审查、出口管制、文化产品进口内容审查、反垄断审查等各项管理措施，加强重点领域安全能力建设，细化风险评估、预防预警、管理处置等机制，构建制度、管理和技术衔接配套的安全防护体系，为示范区更高水平开放保驾护航。

第十章　投洽会：着力打造新一轮高水平对外开放的重要平台①

中国国际投资贸易洽谈会（简称"投洽会"）是经中华人民共和国国务院批准，由中华人民共和国商务部主办，联合国贸发会议（UNCTAD）、联合国工发组织（UNIDO）、经济合作与发展组织（OECD）、世界银行国际金融公司（IFC）、世界投资促进机构协会（WAIPA）和中国国际投资促进会（CCIIP）参与协办，福建省人民政府、厦门市人民政府、商务部投资促进事务局承办，中国大陆31个省、自治区、直辖市，香港特别行政区、澳门特别行政区、部分计划单列市、国家有关部门和部分全国性商协会作为成员单位参与组织工作并组团参展参会。

投洽会是中国目前唯一以促进双向投资为目的的全国性国际投资促进活动，也是目前全球规模最大的国际投资促进盛会。投洽会以"引进来"和"走出去"为主题，通过展览展示、项目对接洽谈，为中外投资合作提供平台。围绕中国吸收利用外资政策导向和鼓励中国企业"走出去"政策导向，举办"国际投资论坛"和数十场投资热点问题研讨会。投洽会还广泛邀请境外政府机构、商协会、企业前来宣传介绍其吸收外资政策、投资环境，展示市场商机，为国际双边、多边的投资合作提供平台。投洽会自1997年起，每年9月8日至11日在厦门举行。它的前身是已经成功在厦门举办了十届的福建投资贸易洽谈会。投

① 投洽（厦门）会展有限公司总经理陈文水供稿。

洽会开创了全新的国际投资促进模式，已经发展成为世界上最具影响力的投资促进平台，有力地推动了中国利用外资工作和对外开放战略的实施，带动了投资洽谈类展览会的蓬勃发展。投洽会还大力推进了中国与发展中国家的投资合作，充分展示中国政府促进共同发展与繁荣的诚意，有效推动两岸经贸交流与合作，很好地宣传和展示了中国坚持改革开放、通过扩大投资合作谋求共同发展繁荣的良好形象，有力地提升了中国的国际地位。

2018 年，习近平主席向第 20 届中国国际投资贸易洽谈会致贺信，希望投洽会以双向投资促进为主题，精耕细作，打造国际化、专业化、品牌化的精品，办成新一轮高水平对外开放的重要平台，为推动形成全面开放新格局、建设开放型世界经济发挥积极作用。

一、投洽会的发展历程及其开放的战略价值

（一）投洽会发展历程

投洽会的发展历史，是中国改革开放进程的浓缩和折射。2024 年 9 月 8 日迎来第二十四届投洽会开幕，如果加上 10 年福建投资贸易洽谈会的历史，投洽会已经走过了 34 年的辉煌历程。40 多年来，根据中国对外开放大政方针，投洽会励精图治，努力顺应国内外经济形势变化，适时调整办会主题和内容，逐步从最初的区域性经贸活动发展成为当今全球最具影响力的国际投资促进盛会。

福建是习近平新时代中国特色社会主义思想的重要孕育地和实践地。投洽会是习近平总书记在闽工作期间参与创办和精心培育的重要展会，蕴含了习近平总书记在经济领域探索对外开放的思想和实践。1987 年，厦门市人民政府创办"闽南三角区外商投资贸易洽谈会"，习近平总书记时任厦门市委常委、副市长，亲自参与了展会创办工作，为投洽会奠定了重要基础；1988 年，洽谈会改由福建省人民政府主办，更名为"福建投资贸易洽谈会"；1997

年经商务部（原外经贸部）批准，升格为"中国投资贸易洽谈会"，商务部作为唯一主办单位；2005年再次升级更名为"中国国际投资贸易洽谈会"。2014年中央统筹国家领导人出席涉外机制性展会，调整投洽会为每两年举办一届（逢双数年举办）。

习近平总书记高度重视、关心关爱投洽会发展，1999至2002年连续担任四届投洽会组委会主任，多次提出并亲自推动投洽会向"国际投资博览会"目标发展；2010年，习近平总书记时任中央政治局常委、国家副主席，莅临厦门出席第十四届投洽会及第二届世界投资论坛，发表主旨演讲，并亲自启动"金钥匙"为投洽会开馆。2018年，在投洽会举办20届的重要节点，习近平主席向大会致贺信，为进一步办好投洽会指明了方向。他指出，20多年来，投洽会致力于打造双向投资促进、权威信息发布和投资趋势研讨三大平台，已发展成全球最具影响力的国际投资盛会之一，为我国改革开放和社会主义现代化建设作出了积极贡献。

经过30多年的探索与发展，投洽会形成独具特色的办会模式，逐步确立以投资促进为主线，采取投资与贸易相结合、展览展示与项目洽谈相结合、项目推介与政策咨询相结合、政策研讨与信息发布相结合的方式，推动投资与合作朝双向、多元化发展，为与会者提供全方位的服务。如今，投洽会作为世界投资博览会的品牌魅力进一步彰显，并发展成为一个重要的国际投资促进平台。

（二）投洽会在推动对外开放中发挥了重要作用

作为国内最早的投资贸易洽谈会，从创办之初以引进外资为主，到"引进来"和"走出去"并举，再到主动融入和引领高水平开放发展，投洽会折射了我国全面改革开放的不凡历程，体现了全面改革开放的进取精神，见证了全面改革开放的巨大成就，是经贸投资领域服务和落实国家发展战略的重要平台。

一是打造全球最具影响力的双向投资促进平台。投资是当今世界各国最为关注的热点之一，投资对带动各国经济增长的贡献率在 40% 以上。投洽会把招商引资作为主题，既适应国际经济的发展趋势，也符合中国对外开放的总体部署。投洽会每年都结合各地引进外资的总体目标，精心组织和筛选一大批引资项目，安排了层次不等、形式多样的双向交流、投资项目对接洽谈活动，为国内外投资者和引资者进行投资洽谈合作创造条件。投洽会为国际资本进入中国、中国企业走向世界提供了高效便捷的对接平台。每届投洽会，各省、自治区、直辖市集中组团参展参会，促成了一大批项目签约落地；境外国家设展招商，举办投资说明会、推介会等活动，深入中国市场，寻求合作商机。通过投洽会，境内外客商可一站式了解中国各地及其他国家和地区的投资环境和投资资讯，选择合适的投资项目与合作伙伴。投洽会举办 23 届以来，展览规模从首届 2.8 万平方米增加到 12 万平方米，成员单位从 37 个增加到 57 个，累计超过 200 个国家和地区、30 多万名境外客商、1000 多个工商社团、超 450 家世界 500 强企业参展参会，3 万多个项目在大会上签约，3400 多亿美元资金从投洽会进入中国，一大批中国企业从投洽会走向世界。

二是坚定有效服务我国经济外交大局。联合国贸发会议、联合国工发组织、世界贸易组织、经济合作与发展组织、世界银行国际金融公司、世界投资促进机构协会等六大国际组织加盟联合主办，发布投资报告、研讨投资趋势、协调投资机制，使投洽会成为链接国际经济组织、助力经济外交的重要平台。近年来，面对复杂多变的国际政治经济形势，投洽会敏锐捕捉投资市场动向，以活动的权威性、前瞻性和针对性，有力展示了我国高水平对外开放的决心和能力，助力维护经济全球化。

三是推动国际经贸领域多双边务实合作。历届投洽会都紧紧围绕中国吸引外资的产业政策，大力宣传和展示利用外资的成绩及对国民经济发展的促进作用，宣传各地投资环境和投资政策，推介各地投资重点项目，使投洽会能最为集中地提供大量的投资相关信息，方便投资者对投资中国进行"一站式"的投资选择。近年来，我国全面拓展对外开放的广度和深度，加速形成全方位、多层次、宽领域的全面开放新格局，通过"一带一路"共建、金砖合作和 RCEP 签署实施等一系列多双边经贸合作，变经济全球化进程的参与者为推动者和引领者。在新一轮高水平对外开放的浪潮中，投洽会深耕"一带一路"，与共建国家共商共享投资发展新机遇；努力拓展金砖国家合作新领域，助力金砖国家在经贸、投资、产业领域的务实合作；服务高质量实施 RCEP，为国内外机构和企业共享区域合作红利搭建交流平台，为深化经贸领域多双边务实合作、推动投资贸易自由化便利化，较好地发挥了投资促进"窗口"和"平台"作用。

（三）投洽会在服务国家战略中发挥了积极作用

不仅在对外开放方面，投洽会更是确认了"突出全国性和国际性，突出投资洽谈和投资政策宣传，突出国家区域经济协调发展，突出对台经贸交流"四大特色，有力配合了国家经济发展战略的实施，促进区域经济协调发展。

一是服务国家经济高质量发展需求。30 多年来，投洽会服务国民经济发展的现实需要和对外开放的总体部署，推出了一系列反映当代中国投资热点的项目：例如，西部大开发、振兴东北老工业基地、中部崛起、"一带一路"、自由贸易试验区建设、国企改革、服务贸易、数字经济、科技发展等重大主题，以及专利技术转让、产权交易、金融不良资产转让等合作需求，不遗余力将这些投资热点推向投资领域的前沿，引导国内外资本进行投资合作，大大拓展了投资的增长空间。

二是结合海西经济区建设促进两岸融合发展。投洽会选在与台湾仅一水相隔的厦门每年定期举行，有效推动两岸经贸交流与合作，展示祖国大陆改革开放取得的经济成就和巨大的发展潜力，有效推动两岸经贸交流与合作，推动一大批台资企业落户大陆。每年在投洽会期间举办两岸经贸合作与发展论坛、海峡两岸农产品采购订货会等经贸活动，有力促进两岸工商界常态化、多渠道、深层次交流，拓展两岸产业合作空间。

三是带动了境内外投资促进展会活动蓬勃发展。投洽会历经 30 多年的经验积累，在实践中不断完善了办会体制和运作模式，即由政府部门组织全国性的招商展会，通过项目推介、产品展示、政策发布、专题研讨等方式，为海内外客商提供全面的集中的投资洽谈和咨询机会。这种模式是投洽会首创的，也是投洽会的独有特色，获得了各界的充分肯定和积极评价。英国原首相戈登·布朗曾这样说道："我很高兴英国已与这个盛大的投资贸易洽谈会建立了长期的合作关系。英国将一如既往地借助投洽会这个平台举办一系列推介活动，并期望进一步推动双方之间的双向投资。"世界贸易组织原总干事帕斯卡尔·拉米曾这样盛赞："我早就听说过投洽会。我认为它展示了中国改革开放的形象，表达了世界经济合作、和谐发展的愿望，有利于世界各经济体制之间的互相开放和发展。这也是为什么这么多的国际经济组织参与投洽会的原因。"联合国贸易与发展会议原秘书长素帕猜在参加投洽会后也留下感言："在过去的 10 多年时间里，投洽会硕果累累，特别是近几届参会境外客商人数的不断攀升，使越来越多来自全球各地的客商能在这个平台上共享商机。这个投洽会办得非常高效圆满。联合国贸发会议作为投洽会的协办单位，今后将一如既往地支持这一国际盛会，为中国全面发展经济提供强有力的支持。"从国内的实践看，投洽会开创了全新的国际招商模式，带动了投资洽谈类展览会的蓬勃发展。

二、投洽会在新一轮高水平对外开放中的成效

近年来，投洽会深入贯彻落实习近平主席贺信精神，积极融入国家发展战略，前瞻引领全球投资趋势，努力打造国际投资公共平台，不断提质增效、创新发展。

（一）努力打造"三化"精品

1. 突出国际化

近年来，投洽会努力克服疫情影响，以更加开阔包容的国际视野，贯彻践行全球发展倡议，助力扩大高水平对外开放。2021—2023 年均有超过 40 个境外国家和地区线下设展或举办招商推介会、专场对接会。第 23 届投洽会深入贯彻全球发展倡议，推动"一带一路"倡议、金砖合作、区域全面经济伙伴关系协定（RCEP）深化融合，国际化特点更加鲜明突出。

2. 坚持专业化

秉持做专做精、做出特色的理念，打造展、谈、会精品项目。在展览展示方面，同期举办金砖国家新工业革命展，培育了工业互联网展、绿色创新技术产品展、投资服务暨金融展、中国外资企业展等一批产业属性鲜明的展览。在产业项目对接方面，紧扣投洽会投资属性，创新设置"项目资本对接馆"，打造新兴产业项目路演和投融资服务平台，促进产业项目与资本、人才、园区等同台撮合。在数字化方面，建设"云上投洽会"APP、小程序、官网多元线上矩阵，打造数字化、常态化的投资促进新平台。

3. 提升品牌化

持续培育形成了"丝路海运"国际合作论坛、两岸经贸合作与发展论坛、世界商业领袖圆桌会议、中国国际绿色创新发展大会等 10 多个固定品牌；近年来培育了"鼓浪屿论坛"新品牌，邀请外国驻华使节、国际投资促进机构和商协会负责人、跨国公司高管等，围绕落实习近平主席提出的全球发展倡议，共谋国际投资、共促全球发展。推出领航中国新兴产业投融资合作大会、中外投资促进机

构工作会、"走出去"发展系列活动、绿色低碳产业国际合作系列活动、中国投资热点城市展区系列活动，进一步形成了投洽会的品牌体系。

（二）持续做优"三大平台"

1. 做优双向投资促进平台

围绕"引进来"和"走出去"两大主题深耕细作，每年邀请90多个国家和地区参展参会，不断扩大"一带一路"、金砖国家和RCEP成员国"朋友圈"，举办"丝路海运"国际合作论坛、金砖国家可持续投资论坛、RCEP国际合作论坛等品牌活动，促进越来越多的国家之间，特别是发展中国家之间扩大相互开放和投资，推动投资与合作朝双向、多元方向发展。

2. 做优权威信息发布平台

近年来，投洽会围绕引进外资和对外投资、国际投资和全球发展，积极邀请国际组织、国家部委、知名研究机构发布营商环境、投资环境及投资指数，以及一系列投资信息、政策和报告。包括：《世界投资报告（中文版）》《金砖国家投资报告》《中国外商投资指引》《中国外资统计公报》《中国外商投资报告》《中资企业国别发展报告》等投资领域的公共产品，指引跨国投资和全球合作。

3. 做优投资趋势研讨平台

投洽会以国际投资论坛为核心，带动提升系列高端会议论坛研讨活动，紧扣全球投资和国际合作，构建国际政、商、学界共议世界经济重大前沿问题、研究全球投资趋势、促进世界经济增长的权威平台。2021年第21届投洽会以"新发展格局下国际投资新机遇"为主题，在全球疫情起伏、经济艰难复苏的形势下，释放出我国进一步扩大开放的积极信号。2022年第22届投洽会以"全球发展：共享数字机遇 投资绿色未来"为主题，紧紧围绕高水平开放和国际投资合作，持续传播中国投资好声音，努力打造国际投资公共平台。2023年第23届投洽会以"开放·融合 引领高质量发展"为年度主题，围绕共商港航合作、共建丝路通道、共享经贸繁荣的愿景，举办"一带一路"发展高层论坛、"丝路海运"国际合作论坛、海丝中央法务区论坛、"丝路电商"政企对话会等一系列活动，持续深化国际投资务实合作。

（三）传递中国投资"好声音"

新冠疫情前，每届投洽会都集聚了大量的国内外重要来宾，包括政府官员、国际组织负责人、国内外知名企业家等，使投洽会成为一个重要的高级公关场所。从第六届投洽会开始，国外来宾人数皆突破 1 万人，国内来宾保持在 4 万人以上。每届投洽会期间，中央政府及各相关主管部委的负责人，各省、自治区、直辖市主管对外经济合作的副省长、副主席、副市长以及中国国有大企业的负责人和有关专家、海内外近 300 家权威媒体的 1200 多名记者云集投洽会现场，各种高层会晤洽谈频频，大量宣传报道从投洽会会场飞向世界各地，起到了良好的公关及新闻效应，给与会境内外企业开展高级公关活动，展示企业形象提供极佳机会。

鉴于目前国际上以投资促进为主题的大型活动很少，中国已成为全球吸引外资最多的国家之一，加上连续近四十年成功举办投洽会，投洽会的国际影响力和美誉度逐年提高。随着办会水平的提高和国际影响力的增强，投洽会每年吸引了大量国际政要、知名学者和跨国公司总裁前来参会，并有众多境内外媒体通过报刊、电视、网络等各种媒介向全世界报道和宣传中国的发展状况、消费市场和日趋完善的投资环境，进一步加强了外部世界对中国的认识。中国和平发展，不仅为中国带来了繁荣和进步，也为世界经济的发展作出了贡献。在这个过程中，肩负投资促进功能的投洽会，在世界经济的发展和国际资本流动中，都发挥了重要的作用。

三、未来投洽会致力打造国际投资公共平台

立足新发展阶段，投洽会要以习近平新时代中国特色社会主义思想为指导，深入贯彻落实习近平主席致投洽会贺信精神，以吸引优质外资、推动对外投资、便利国际投资为主要内容，围绕"三化三平台"深耕细作，持续传播中国投资好声音，拓展国际投资新机遇，致力打造国际投资公共平台，推动更多国家之间扩大相互开放和投资，努力发展成为我国在经贸领域推动落实习近平主席提出的"全球发展倡议"的首选展会，以鲜明特色主题和务实行动支持全球合作和共同发展，推动建设开放型世界经济，服务构建人类命运共同体。

（一）强化新时代投洽会国家战略平台的使命担当

面对百年变局和世纪疫情，开放合作是推动世界经济稳定复苏的现实要求。当前，全球经济和跨国投资复苏比以往更加需要开放合作的国际投资公共平台。我们要充分挖掘投洽会在双向投资促进领域的差异定位和独特优势，进一步明确新发展阶段的使命担当，为世界各国搭建持续、稳定的国际经贸合作平台，不仅为中国搭台唱戏，还为其他更多国家间的双向投资搭台唱戏，不仅让中国有收获，也让参会其他国家都有收获，以经贸合作促进共同发展。

一是提升国际投资权威公共平台功能，推动更多国家通过投洽会平台扩大相互开放和投资，努力推动经济全球化与投资自由化、便利化，彰显我国与世界各国分享投资机遇、推动全球合作和共同发展的大国担当。

二是打造深化多双边务实合作的枢纽平台，重点围绕"一带一路"共建、高质量实施 RCEP 与促进金砖新工业革命合作等重要活动，充分挖掘投洽会在实施区域经济战略中的独特作用，进一步固化与相关国家地区交流合作机制。积极发挥投洽会在促进两岸经济融合上的"窗口"作用，进一步促进两岸工商界常态化、多渠道、深层次交流，以密切经贸合作加速两岸实质融合。

三是深化全球务实合作。积极搭建广阔平台，以实际

行动推动全球发展倡议走深走实。中心展区展示全球发展倡议的中国实践成就；国家国际发展合作署全球发展促进中心举办全球发展倡议对话会，进一步推动全球各国对话交流；举办全球特殊经济区联盟，发起国际机构联袂设展；商务部举办世贸组织投资便利化内部交流活动，组织各国代表探讨更好地落实世界贸易组织《促进发展的投资便利化协定》。

四是凸显高质量引进外资。按照中央有关决策部署，持续打造"投资中国"主题活动。策划举办外资企业圆桌会、跨国投资对话等活动，发布吸引外资的多项权威报告，邀请更多跨国企业、境外投资商共享中国发展红利，提振外资企业投资中国的信心。同时围绕国家级经开区设立 40 周年以来的发展成就进行综合展示并组织对接交流活动，突出国家级经开区在推动高水平开放、高质量发展方面的重大贡献。

（二）在国际化上寻求新突破

投洽会的整体价值定位是国际投资公共平台，应以全球领先、时代前沿、行业尖端为理念，在高质量"引进来"和高水平"走出去"中积极参与全球事务治理，充当国际投资关键驱动力，助推经济全球化和共同发展。

积极拓宽全球视野。以"全球投资、共谋发展"为主线，以打造国际投资公共平台为目标，以服务建设开放型世界经济为使命，完善以合作共赢为中心的国际高层对话机制，关注世界经济中的前瞻性、全面性问题，设计可持续发展相关议题和倡议，重点探讨全球经济治理体系新思路，区域经济协调发展新举措，以及投资贸易的自由化和便利化等经济全球化面临的重要问题，进一步提升投洽会作为经贸领域贯彻落实"全球发展倡议"重要平台的战略地位，为改善全球经济治理贡献中国智慧。

挖掘汇聚高端资源。全面加强与国际组织、国际机构及重点地区的合作，围绕"一带一路"共建、金砖国家、中东国家、东南亚国家、RCEP、上合组织、中非合作等多双边合作机制和热点区域，设计多双边投资研讨和对接活动，共享投资发展机遇。比如：推动六大联合主办机构每年轮流在投洽会上举办自己的品牌活动、发布权威投资报告；挖掘上合组织从安全领域合作向经贸领域延伸的契机，推动其在投洽会上举办以经贸合作为主题的展览和论坛等活动；依托金砖创新基地建设，持续办好金砖国家可持续投资论坛、金砖国家数字经济对话会等活动，助力金砖经贸、投资、产业等领域的务实合作；围绕区域协调发展和多双边务实合作，策划举办"一带一路"互联互通投融资研讨会、RCEP 投资合作高峰论坛等活动，充分发挥多双边合作工作机制、境外商（协）会联席会等机制作用，动员机制成员及合作伙伴组织参会。

（三）紧扣展会投资属性，在专业化上实现新提升

当前全球范围内商品贸易类展览众多，但知名的投资类展览几乎没有。在专业化水平提升上，投洽会应积极开辟金融投资新领域，坚持投洽会作为我国投资领域最重要展会平台的发展定位，同时因应当前国际投资的新模式、新特点，将展会所呈现的投资渠道进一步向金融投资领域拓展，策划 2024 国际投资论坛及金融资本对接等活动，邀请我国金融监管部门和境内外大型金融投资机构共论深化金融领域改革、防范化解金融风险、促进金融资本服务实体经济的途径和举措，助力金融市场高水平对外开放。

在展览展示方面，以全球产业科技创新为核心展示内容，以项目路演和对接洽谈作为主要形式，配套组织投资机遇和投资服务展，同时强化展、谈、会一体化融合，重点打造具有国际影响力的全球产业科技创新展，围绕新质生产力、新能源、新材料、新型显示、集成电路、人工智能等全球前沿产业和重点领域，邀请世界 500 强、跨国公司、龙头企业、行业领军企业、科创企业、研发机构发布展示新产品、新技术。同时，可充分借助国际知名展览机构在中国扩展市场的契机，利用自身的平台效应与其品牌

优势合作，共同策划精品主题展览。

在投资洽谈方面，进一步做优做强"项目资本对接"平台，举办更多类似"领航中国·新兴产业投融合作大会"、中国外资企业展等展洽深度融合的对接活动，促进初创项目、产业园区、产业人才、投融资服务机构等投资促进关键要素有效对接，打造新兴产业项目路演和投融资服务平台，加大对国内外专业参会客商、参展展商、观展观众的邀请力度，提高投引资、投融资双方交流对接成效。

在投资服务方面，持续优化提升投资服务暨金融展，邀请投行、咨询、金融、证券、保险、律所、会计师事务所等投融资服务机构设展，展示、推介与投资相关的产品和服务，有效发挥展会的投资服务功能。创新设置投资热点领域展，把握未来投资风口产业，就热点投资领域开展专题展览，例如新能源、智联网、元宇宙等。

（四）聚焦提质增效，在品牌化上打造新亮点

坚持传承与创新并举，对标进博会、服贸会、广交会、消博会等国家级展会，在国际投资促进领域打造国家级品牌，突出投洽会在经贸领域服务"全球发展倡议"、促进国际双向投资的重要定位。在品牌打造上，以做优做强国际投资论坛为核心，既要沉淀固化已有品牌，又要精心培育创新品牌，形成投洽会的品牌体系和独特魅力。

做优国际投资论坛。下大力气将其打造成为贯彻践行"全球发展倡议"的国际高端平台。论坛形式进一步固化，采取"一个主旨论坛＋若干分论坛"的模式，充分烘托主旨主题，继而引领带动其他专业会议凝聚高端资源；论坛主题紧扣全球共同发展和国际投资新机遇，突出国际性、前沿性和专业性；加大力度邀请外国政界要员、国际经济组织负责人、知名经济学家和大型跨国公司等重要人士莅会演讲，研讨全球经济发展和国际投资重大前沿问题。

精心培育"鼓浪屿论坛"。在 2022 年首次举办"鼓浪屿论坛"的基础上，继续优化提升、深度培育，充分挖掘

"历史国际社区"多元文化交融并蓄的深厚底蕴，与新时代全球发展理念深度融合。每年固定邀请 98 位高层次嘉宾参会，特别是各国驻华大使、国际投资促进机构和商协会负责人、跨国公司高管等，以更加新颖、轻松的方式开展交流探讨，将其打造成促进国际投资、服务全球发展、深化各方交流与合作的高端平台。

聚焦供应链合作。首次设置全国供应链创新展区，同期举办 2024 供应链合作创新大会、第五届中国供应链管理年会及供应链大赛，汇聚境内外供应链头部企业及专家学者，围绕供应链可持续发展、韧性与安全、创新与应用、管理策略及市场趋势等前沿热点发表前瞻性演讲，深入互动交流，充分彰显投洽会在加强供应链国际合作、维护供应链安全稳定方面的积极作为。

策划推出特色项目。梳理整合国家部委、国际组织、专家智库等合作机构的资源，争取外交部、国家发展改革委、联合国贸发组织、世界银行、WTO 等的更大支持。比如：积极争取与世界银行开展合作，推动其在投洽会上举办"全球营商环境大会"；争取联合世界经济论坛组委会在厦举办夏季达沃斯论坛；主动加强与国家发展改革委的沟通，推动其在投洽会上发布营商环境报告；与国务院发展研究中心对外经济研究部等国家高端智库合作，于 2023 年发布投洽会首份旗舰报告《中国双向投资报告》；拓展与中国国际发展知识中心等"全球发展倡议"智库机构的合作，策划或引进契合国际投资合作和全球共同发展主题的活动，发布相关权威信息、重量级研究报告或行动计划。

优化提升既有品牌。商务部每年举办"外资企业圆桌会"，邀请世界 500 强企业和知名跨国公司深度参与，服务高质量引进外资；持续办好"丝路海运"国际合作论坛，高水平推进"海丝核心区"建设，服务高质量共建"一带一路"；持续培育提升领航中国·新兴产业投融资合作大会、绿色中国·低碳产业国际合作高峰论坛、"走出去"绿色发展系列活动等一系列特色品牌项目。

协会篇

第十一章　跨国公司在华投资趋势的新观察 [1]

过去 30 多年，经济全球化为跨国公司在中国的发展创造了有利条件。跨国公司深度参与了中国经济社会的发展，成为中国高质量发展的重要支撑和深度融入全球产业链供应链的重要纽带。当下，全球政治、经济格局发生重大变化，我们观察到，在华经营的跨国公司正在探索新的投资策略和模式。

一、合资企业数量显著增加

改革开放初期，受中国外资产业政策的限制，部分行业的跨国公司必须以中外合资的形式，才能进入中国。随着中国 2001 年入世，市场准入的逐步放开，合资企业的占比逐渐减少，外商独资企业占比接近 90%。近年来，我们看到合资企业数量明显有所回升。跨国企业以更加主动的姿态与本土企业融合发展，打造开放型生态圈，从而实现互惠共赢。

形成这一趋势的主要原因：一是一批具有国际竞争力的中国本土企业逐渐形成，这对外资形成了竞争的态势，也促使它们更多与本土企业合作发展。二是外资越来越强调本土化运营，和中国本土企业合作可以形成优势互补。三是合资可以与中国企业共担风险。

案例 1：丰田与比亚迪合资设立纯电动车研发公司。

---

① 上海市外商投资协会黄峰、丁隧亮，上海外商投资咨询有限公司邹妍琪、万天南供稿。

在汽车行业电动化、网联化、智能化和共享化"新四化"产业变革下，通过全球产业链抱团合作以寻求降本增效，相继成为各大跨国公司的重点应对方案。2020 年 4 月，丰田与比亚迪合资的纯电动车研发公司——比亚迪丰田电动车科技有限公司正式成立，双方各出资 50%，主要业务包括纯电动车及该车辆所用平台、零件的设计、研发等。未来丰田将基于比亚迪在天津的 e 平台生产基地生产电动车，充分使用比亚迪现有的电动平台技术及电动零部件体系，并融入丰田的品质及安全控制标准要求。此次合作，区别于丰田与一汽、广汽的合作模式，是丰田首次同中国汽车品牌开展"技术对等"的整车开发合作，共同开发纯电动车和动力电池。比亚迪和丰田联合，能够填补丰田在纯电动车领域的技术短板，解决丰田在中国市场缺少适销对路电动汽车产品的问题，对行业格局，对加快全球电动车技术发展和普及意义重大。

案例 2：中国医疗器械有限公司与 GE 医疗设立合资企业。在生物医药领域，跨国企业加强与本土企业深度合资合作，成为企业本土化战略的一大趋势。2023 年 2 月，国药集团国药控股旗下中国医疗器械有限公司与 GE 医疗中国在北京签署协议，在中国成立医疗设备合资公司。该合资公司初期将主要为中国的基层医疗和广阔市场提供包括 CT 和超声等在内的普惠型医疗设备。未来，双方将共同推进高端医疗装备领域合资合作，重点布局高端医疗影像设备产业。国药器械与 GE 医疗中国的合作，不仅推动了国际领先医药装备企业与国资央企合作模式的创新，还有利于加强医疗领域的国际合作，对打造全面国产化的高端医疗设备工业平台具有重要实践和标志性意义。

案例 3：博格华纳与陕西法士特汽车传动集团成立合资公司。跨国公司通过与国内企业的合作，实现研发能力与产品线的互补，高效整合资源。2023 年 1 月，博格华纳与专注于变速箱和传动系统的陕西法士特汽车传动集团达成一致，将成立合资公司，共同研发适用于重型卡车和工程车辆等商用车辆的控制器应用，以继续扩大其在纯电动和混动领域的商用车产品组合。博格华纳在汽车控制器领域具有深厚的技术底蕴、强大的研发能力和供应链整合能力；而法士特集团是中国领先的商用车变速器和高品质汽车传动系统及高端智能制造装备综合解决方案供应商。通过共同研发适用于重型卡车和工程车辆等商用车辆的控制器应用，该合资企业将支持双方在电动商用车市场的功率电子产品线业务的增长，将高效的控制器产品投入市场，也将为中国商用车市场提供更加丰富、优质、稳定、安全的电控产品及驱动传动系统解决方案。

案例 4：江森自控与飞旋科技成立合资公司。跨国公司通过与国内企业合作，加强智能制造的运用和绿色低碳转型。2024 年 1 月，江森自控与中国磁悬浮高速旋转机械整体解决方案提供商飞旋科技成立合资公司，该公司将专注推动暖通空调行业的创新发展和节能减排。江森自控与飞旋科技的合作将推动无油磁悬浮机组的发展，它将有效减少零部件运动损耗，提升产品能效，延长机组的使用寿命。江森自控依托在建筑领域的创新经验，以及在华近30 年的创新实践，携手飞旋科技拓展技术创新、整机集成等方面的合作广度，探索品质管理、运营体系等方面的深度，为中国市场更多行业量身定制智能、高效、环保的解决方案，为行业转型升级和可持续发展目标的达成增加推动力，对于暖通空调行业的绿色发展具有里程碑意义。

案例 5：捷豹路虎与奇瑞汽车战略合作。跨国公司与本土企业的合作，也有利于本土企业出海。2024 年 6 月，捷豹路虎与奇瑞汽车携手宣布战略合作，奇瑞捷豹路虎将推出全新电动汽车产品线，该产品线将搭载奇瑞纯电平台，并使用捷豹路虎授权的"Freelander 神行者"品牌。这一品牌曾是路虎旗下的热销车型，拥有深厚的市场基础和消费者口碑，如今在奇瑞捷豹路虎的平台上得以重生，将焕发新的活力。通过整合奇瑞在中国汽车市场的领先地位和捷豹路虎的全球品牌与设计实力，双方将共同打造具有竞争力的电动产品，满足消费者对高品质、高性能电动汽车的需求。据悉，"Freelander 神行者"电动产品线将先期通过特定网络在中国市场进行销售，未来还将实现海外出口。这一战略举措不仅将加强奇瑞捷豹路虎在中国市场的竞争力，也将进一步提升其在全球市场的地位。随着电动化时代的到来，汽车产业的竞争格局正在发生深刻变化。捷豹路虎与奇瑞汽车的此次合作，无疑将为双方带来新的发展机遇，同时也将为中国乃至全球的汽车产业注入新的活力。

二、企业风险投资（CVC）开始流行

企业风险投资（CVC）是指跨国公司开展的风险投资。相比于传统的风险投资机构（IVC），CVC 具有更为突出的行业资源整合能力和战略目的。CVC 通常设立的战略目标更多的是配合母公司的长期战略，以投资方式驱动创新与模式扩张，并依托母公司的业务优势为被投创新企业提供独特的增值服务。

近年来，跨国公司在中国的 CVC 投资活动日益活跃。随着中国经济的快速增长和创业生态的日益完善，越来越多的跨国公司开始通过 CVC 投资来参与产业链上下游，并以此巩固自己行业的优势地位。

跨国公司在中国的 CVC 投资主要有两种模式：一是直接投资，大公司设立独立的投向中国创业企业的创投基金或机构。这种模式使得跨国公司能够直接参与到被投企业的管理和决策中，对创业企业拥有更强的控制力，更容易实现公司创业投资的战略性目标。二是间接投资，大公司向投资公司（或基金）投资，由这些投资公司或基金再去投资中国的创业企业。虽然这种模式相对于直接投资来说，对创业企业的控制力较弱，但它能够利用专业投资公司的资源和经验，降低投资风险。

直接投资的典型案例包括：

案例 6：2018 年，博世集团在中国正式落地其创投

机构——博世（上海）创业投资有限公司，加快在中国的创投团队建设与投资速度。2021 年，博世集团又成立了在我国的第一个具有本土独立决策过程的市场化投资平台——博原资本，博世集团在其中持股 50%，发起设立博世中国成长基金 I 期。如今，博世的创投机构已成为在国内比较活跃的跨国企业创业投资机构，例如，2021 年联合领投了自动驾驶公司 Momenta 的 C 轮融资。博世在中国的创业投资也为集团在中国的智能汽车业务带来了助力，2024 年 8 月，其参与投资的黑芝麻智能公司成功在香港交易所主板完成挂牌上市，成为"中国智能汽车 AI 芯片第一股"。

案例 7：2022 年，欧莱雅在上海成立了首家投资公司——上海美次方投资有限公司，致力于投资创新美妆科技，并于 9 月对中国本土高端香水香氛品牌闻献 DOCUMENTS 进行股权投资。2024 年 1 月，上海美次方再次对第二个中国香水香氛品牌观夏（to summer）进行少数股权投资，进一步走进中国香氛市场。

间接投资的典型案例包括：

案例 8：赢创的风险投资部门以有限合伙人（LP）的身份参与了多支中国创投基金。2015 年，赢创在中国投资了富华天使投资三期基金（GRC SinoGreen Fund III）。2021 年，赢创再次注资了两支中国基金：富华天使投资五期基金（GRC SinoGreen Fund V）和沃衍资本三期创投基金（Richland VC Fund III）。主要投资行业包括循环经济、合成生物学、碳材料、数字制造等新兴产业。这两支创投基金的投资领域与赢创在中国重点关注的增长行业高度相关。

案例 9：雀巢集团出资 3000 万美元，首次投资于中国本土 VC 基金，成为天图投资 VC 美元基金一期基金的基石投资者。

案例 10：2020 年，星巴克与红杉中国达成战略合作，在中国开展战略投资，在新生代餐饮和零售科技方面进行商业合作，并落地了一家创投企业，由星巴克出资 5000

万元，红杉资本担任执行事务合伙人（GP）。

跨国公司在中国的 CVC 投资活动对于促进中国创业生态的健康发展、推动技术创新和产业升级具有重要意义。随着中国政府对创业投资的支持力度不断加大和创业生态的日益完善，跨国公司在中国的 CVC 投资也将面临更多的机遇。

三、投资建设运营产业园区

产业园区作为促进跨国经济合作、优化资源配置、推动产业升级的重要平台，得到了国家以及各地政府的大力支持。近年来，各地政府在财政扶持、金融支持、人才引进等多个方面，出台了一系列政策措施，为产业园区的发展提供了有力的政策保障。然而，在快速发展的同时，产业园区也面临着融资渠道狭窄、投资回报期长等多重瓶颈，以及客户对绿色低碳、数字化的新要求。

近年来，引入跨国企业直接参与产业园区的投资建设、招商引资或运营管理，成为推动产业园区高质量建设的重要解决方案。跨国企业可以从拓宽融资渠道、促进国际合作、加强顶层设计、强化团队服务和提升品牌影响力等多方面，为国际合作产业园区注入新的活力。例如，

案例 11：2022 年 2 月，法国埃顿集团旗下的 NXpark 在埃顿西安高端汽车零部件产业基地中为法国佛吉亚搭建高端汽车座椅研发生产基地，该厂房荣膺"绿色能源与环境设计先锋奖（LEED）"认证金奖。埃顿西安高端汽车零部件产业基地位于西安市高新区草堂区域，园区总占地面积 161 亩，总建筑面积 82142.55 平方米，项目总价值达 20 亿元人民币。园区内建有汽车产业核心部件生产所需的厂房、办公楼、职工公寓及配套设施等，满足企业的多元化需求，为周边龙头企业提供汽车零部件制造服务。目前，法国佛吉亚高端汽车座椅研发生产线已入驻园区开始投产。该项目也被评为央视财经 2024"投资中国"年度十大优秀案例。

案例 12：2023 年 7 月，法国埃顿集团在中法（无锡）产业合作园投资 1.5 亿美元建设法国施耐德电气集团绿色智慧产业园。中法（无锡）产业合作园位于无锡高新区，是国家发展改革委、法国总领馆共同指导推动，由中国法国工商会授牌的中国第一家"中法合作示范区"。合作园由法国埃顿集团投资建设、招商引资和运营管理，核心区项目计划总投资 5 亿美元，分两期建设：一期为智能制造产业化基地，预计 2024 年底交付使用；二期规划建设中法创新中心、商业办公等，预计 2025 年 6 月交付使用。园区整体建成后将成为集生产、销售和研发于一体，数字化、集成化水平更高的新一代"超级工厂"。作为中法产业合作园核心区率先启动、分量最重的"压舱石"，施耐德电气绿色智慧产业园总投资 1.5 亿美元，以绿色、低碳、智能为目标，充分体现"绿色＋智慧"特色，引入 5G 通讯、人工智能等前沿技术，打造成为集绿色可持续发展理念、数字化工厂与创新中心为一体的综合性园区。

跨国公司在投资建设运营产业园区的过程中，不仅促进了当地经济的增长和产业升级，还加强了国际经济交流与合作。通过引入先进的技术和管理经验，跨国公司帮助园区内的企业提升了竞争力，推动了整个产业链的协同发展。

四、探索非股权安排投资

跨国公司参与国际生产体系的方式不仅包含直接投资和贸易，还包含非股权经营模式。非股权经营模式包括合约制造、服务外包、订单农业、特许经营、许可经营、管理合约及其他类型的合约关系，跨国公司通过这些关系协调其在全球价值链的活动并影响东道国公司的管理，而并不拥有其股份。

在生物医药行业，非股权经营模式被越来越多地采用。近年来，跨国药企（MNC）纷纷将产品交由本土药企销售。在创新药领域，跨国药企与中国本土企业的授权合作也持续活跃。在 2023 年中国医药 BD 交易中，License out 事件数为 53 件，交易金额达 425.9 亿美元，占比 84.2%，交易数量、交易金额较往年都显著增加，项目受让方大部分为在华跨国药企。

License in 的典型案例包括：

案例 13：2022 年 3 月，礼来和信达生物共同宣布并达成两项合作协议：礼来授予信达生物在中国大陆进口、销售、推广和分销希冉择（雷莫西尤单抗）和塞普替尼（Retsevmo）获批后独家商业化权利，以及授予信达生物享有 Pirtobrutinib 未来在中国大陆商业化权利的优先谈判权，实际上这已经是双方的第五次合作。

License out 的典型案例包括：

案例 14：2023 年 12 月，葛兰素史克（GSK）公司与国内老牌药企翰森制药共同宣布，双方就翰森制药自主研发的 ADC 新药 HS-20093 达成独家许可协议，GSK 将获授予全球独占许可（不含中国大陆、香港、澳门及台湾地区），包括首付款与里程碑付款在内的交易总金额超过 17 亿美元。

案例 15：2023 年 12 月，百利天恒发布公告：其全资子公司 SystImmune 与百时美施贵宝就一款 EGFR x HER 3 双抗 ADC（BL-B01D1）达成独家许可和合作协议。

案例 16：2024 年 1 月，宜联生物宣布已与罗氏达成全球合作和许可协议。双方将合作开发靶向间质表皮转化因子（c-MET）的下一代抗体偶联药物候选产品 YL211（c-MET ADC），用于治疗实体瘤。根据协议条款，罗氏将获得宜联生物 YL211 项目在全球范围内的开发、制造和商业化的独家权益。

五、结语

全球政治、经济格局变化促使跨国公司调整在华投资策略，使得跨国公司在华投资呈现多元化、本土化、合作化和灵活化的趋势。跨国公司通过与中国本土企业建立广泛的合作关系、进行 CVC 投资、参与建设运营产业园区、采用非股权安排等措施，积极应对全球变化并寻求长期发展。这些新策略不仅促进了跨国公司在华业务的持续增长，实现了跨国公司与中国市场的深度融合，也为中国经济的高质量发展提供了重要支撑。

第十二章　新加坡中资企业投资与发展 [1]

在中资企业全球化的浪潮中，东南亚市场以其庞大的体量、经济韧性、人口红利和文化相似性，吸引了大批中资企业的目光。其中，新加坡凭借其独特的地理位置、友好的贸易政策和优越的商业环境，成为中资企业进军东南亚的理想门户。随着中国与东盟以及新加坡的经贸合作不断加深，《区域全面经济伙伴关系协定》（RCEP）的红利持续释放，以及中国加入《数字经济伙伴关系协定》（DEPA）谈判的推进，都极大地促进了中资企业在新加坡及东南亚的贸易和投资。

本章旨在通过研究 2023 年至 2024 年上半年中新之间的贸易与投资活动，分析中资企业在新加坡的发展情况、投资亮点及对当地经济的贡献，并结合具体企业案例，以期为有意拓展东南亚及新加坡市场的中资企业提供参考和借鉴。

一、中新经贸合作关系发展现状

（一）中国连续 11 年成为新加坡最大贸易伙伴，而新加坡也连续 11 年是中国新增投资的最大来源国

自 2008 年起，中新之间的自由贸易协定不断升级加深。2023 年 4 月，中国与新加坡宣布实质性完成自贸协定升级后续谈判，并签署了谅解备忘录。双方在原协定基

---

[1] 中资企业（新加坡）协会、德勤中国／德勤东南亚供稿。

础上，进一步提高服务贸易和投资开放承诺水平，新增电信章节，并纳入国民待遇、市场准入、透明度、数字经济等高水平经贸规则。新加坡在环境保护、海运等多个中方重点关注领域作出了高水平开放承诺，为中资企业进一步开拓新方市场创造了更大机遇。中国则对制造业领域限制总体"清零"，并在货物运输、陆上石油开采、分销以及医疗等广泛领域作出更开放承诺[①]。中国与新加坡双边货物进出口总额 2023 年达到 1083.9 亿美元，同比下降 2.6%。其中，中国出口额为 769.6 亿美元，同比下降 1.1%；进口额为 314.3 亿美元，同比下降 6%[②]（见图 12-1）。

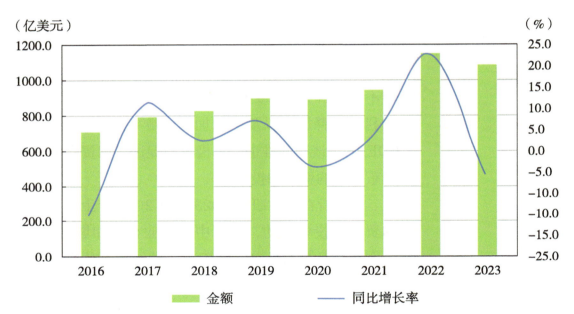

（亿美元）　　　　　　　　　　　　　　　　　　　　（%）

图 12-1　2015—2023 年中国与新加坡双边货物进出口额及同比增长率

资料来源：中国国家统计局、外交部、德勤研究。

　　新加坡 2013 年起是中国最大的新增投资来源国。2022 年 4 月，新加坡首次超越日本，成为累计最大外资来源国。过去几年，中新之间的直接投资额稳步提升。截至 2023 年底，新加坡累计在华实际投资 1412.3 亿美元，中国累计对新加坡投资 896.3 亿美元[③]（见图 12-2）。

① 中国商务部，"商务部国际司负责人解读中新自由贸易协定进一步升级议定书"，2023 年 12 月。
② 中国外交部，"中国同新加坡的关系"，2024 年 4 月更新。
③ 中国外交部，"中国同新加坡的关系"，2024 年 4 月更新。

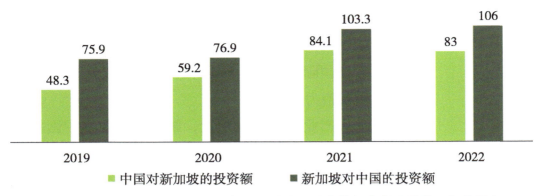

图 12-2　2019—2022 年中国与新加坡的双边直接投资额（单位：亿美元）

资料来源：中国国家统计局、外交部、德勤研究。

（二）中新之间贸易依存度高，产业合作基础深厚

新加坡的高端制造和商业服务具有优势，在与中国的贸易合作上已有所体现。新加坡不仅是与中国双边贸易规模最大的东盟国家，也是唯一长期保持对华服务贸易顺差的东盟国家。在商品贸易层面，新加坡在半导体和精密设备等产品方面一直对中国保持了大量的出口，2022 年对华出口集成电路和制造半导体材料的机器与装置分别达到 70.8 亿和 43.9 亿美元。而新加坡成品油市场高度依赖进口，为中国最大的成品油出口目的地，2022 年出口额达到 96.2 亿美元[①]。同时，新加坡也是中国集成电路主要出口国之一，2022 年出口额达到 58 亿美元。在服务贸易层面，新加坡对华主要出口类别为：运输、其他商业服务和金融，2022 年占比分别达到 34.3%、28.7% 和 13.7%[②]。

● 商品贸易特点：一是中国的出口比较优势主要体现在工业制成品上，且主要集中于劳动密集型产品，而新加坡的出口比较优势主要体现在资本密集型和资源密集型的工业品上。二是新加坡出口对中国市场依赖相对较高（2022 年占比达 15.8%），中新双边商品贸易互补性较强。

---

① 《新加坡贸易指南（2023 年）》。

② 中国商务部，《对外投资合作国别（地区）指南——新加坡（2023 年版）》，2024 年 4 月。

● 服务贸易特点：新加坡服务贸易总体竞争力水平高于中国，并在运输、金融、商业服务等现代服务业领域具有较强国际竞争力，预计未来两国在服务贸易领域具有较大增长潜力。

从产业合作角度来看，新加坡企业在中国扎根多年，合作基础深厚，未来科技创新潜能不可小觑。2022 年前三季度，新加坡对中国江苏省投资高达 21 亿美元（28.3 亿新元），超过 2021 年全年的 14 亿美元，为近 3 年来最高水平。两方合作领域涵盖绿色和可持续发展，包括先进制造业以及生物医学方面的探索。2021 年，新加坡胜科工业以 33 亿人民币收购中国风能太阳能资产，凯德地产公司（CapitaLand Development）与三菱地所株式会社（Mitsubishi Estate）成立合资公司，斥资 15 亿元人民币在苏州高新区开发商业园区[①]。

（三）RCEP 实施两年后，中国与东盟之间的贸易便利化和投资自由化水平不断提升

自 2022 年 RCEP 正式生效起，成员国家的货物贸易便利度显著提升，投资环境得到持续优化，互联互通水平不断提高，提升了中小企业的国际竞争力，推动东盟跨境电商的发展。据中国海关统计，2023 年中国与 RCEP 其他成员进出口总额达 12.6 万亿元，占中国外贸总额的 30.2%，相较协定生效前 2021 年增长 5.3%。截至 2023 年 7 月，中国同东盟国家累计双向投资额超过 3800 亿美元，在东盟设立直接投资企业超 6500 家[②]。

根据中资企业（新加坡）协会行业于 2024 年 6 月至 7 月发起的调研（调研详情参见文末"关于本调研"章节），65% 的中资企业认为《区域全面经济伙伴关系协定》扩大出口市场、增加贸易机会。65% 的企业认可 RCEP 带

---

① 中华人民共和国驻新加坡共和国大使馆经济商务处，"新加坡对华投资"。
② 中华人民共和国驻东盟使团，"RCEP 生效实施满两年 持续释放政策红利 为区域经济注入活力"，2024 年 1 月。

来的贸易便利化、关税减免等政策红利。42%的企业表示，该协议会加剧国际竞争，38%的企业认为该协议能够创造有利的电子商务环境（见图12-3）。

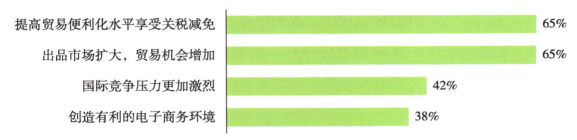

图12-3　《区域全面经济伙伴关系协定》（RCEP）对在新中资企业带来的影响

资料来源：中资企业（新加坡）协会行业企业调研，德勤研究。

中国于2021年正式申请加入DEPA并持续推动谈判磋商。目前中国在区域贸易协定层面就数字贸易治理所作的最高承诺主要体现在RCEP中，中国将立足于RCEP的基础上申请加入DEPA。中国加入DEPA不仅可加强同DEPA成员的数字经贸合作，还为中国数字经济出海创造更多机会，有助于增强国内数字技术的对外输出，壮大中国数字贸易规模，让中国企业走出去。根据调研，超过2/3的中资企业认为中国加入DEPA将促进贸易便利化、完善网络安全并优化信任环境，使跨境数据流动更加便利（见图12-4）。

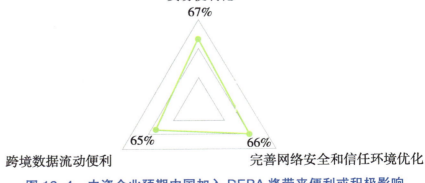

图12-4　中资企业预期中国加入DEPA将带来便利或积极影响

资料来源：中资企业（新加坡）协会行业企业调研，德勤研究。

二、中资企业在新投资现状与展望

（一）中资企业赴新加坡投资持续升温，并购稳步回升

伴随中资企业出海的浪潮，新加坡凭借其优越的地理及区位优势，成为中资企业"走出去"的首选地之一。据中国商务部统计，从累计投资金额来看，中国对新加坡投资主要集中于金融保险业、建筑业和贸易业。2023年，在新加坡中资企业数量约 8500 家[①]。

随着亚太区域经济一体化的加强，中资企业在新加坡的投资持续升温。超过半数的在新中资企业计划在新加坡扩大投资，有六成的受访企业计划扩大在新加坡之外的东南亚地区的投资。不少中资企业看重的是 6 亿多人的东南亚市场，通过新加坡这一枢纽有效管理和扩展其在东南亚业务。除了科技互联网之外，能源化工、基础建设、金融科技、物流等领域也都有中国企业的足迹。调研显示，受访企业对未来在新加坡的投资持乐观态度，74%的受访企业预计中资企业在新加坡的投资将会呈上升趋势，25%的企业认为将保持平稳，高于 2021/2022 年度调研[②]的 19%，仅 1%的企业预测会出现下行（见图 12-5）。

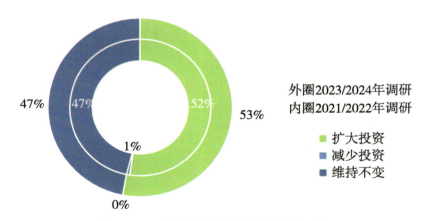

外圈2023/2024年调研
内圈2021/2022年调研

- 扩大投资
- 减少投资
- 维持不变

图 12-5　受访企业对新加坡的投资意向

资料来源：中资企业（新加坡）协会行业企业调研，德勤研究。

① 中国商务部，《对外投资合作国别（地区）指南——新加坡（2023 年版）》，2024 年 4 月。

② 中资企业（新加坡）协会，《2021-2022 中资企业年度发展报告》，2023 年 7 月。

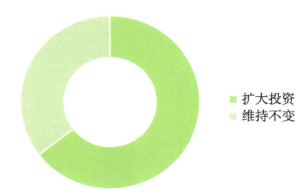

图 12-6　2024 年中资企业在东南亚地区（新加坡以外）的投资意向

资料来源：中资企业（新加坡）协会行业企业调研，德勤研究。

图 12-7　受访企业对未来中资企业来新加坡投资发展的预测

资料来源：中资企业（新加坡）协会行业企业调研，德勤研究。

　　新加坡也是中资企业境外并购的重要目的地。2018 年至 2024 上半年，中资企业对新加坡的并购交易次数占到中资在东南亚地区总并购交易的一半，累计达到 118 笔。越南和印度尼西亚也是中资企业并购的活跃国家，分别累计达 36 笔。虽然 2023 年中资企业在东南亚的并购活跃度仍未恢复到疫情前水平，但全年交易次数较 2022 年的低谷反弹了 48%。从行业分布来看，金融、制造、批发零售和医疗健康领域受到中资企业的高度关注。

　　从"产品出海"到"产业链出海"的趋势推动了中国企业对跨境投融资金融服务的需求不断增加。中资券商纷纷布局资产管理和投资银行业务，推动境内外业务协同发展，支持更多中国企业走向海外。2024 年 4 月，中国银河证券旗下"银河海外"品牌正式亮相，标志着其国际

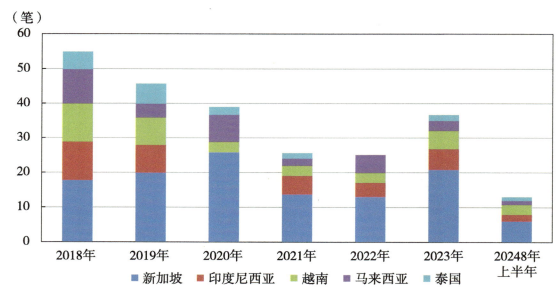

图 12-8　2018 年至 2024 年上半年中资企业在新加坡及东南亚地区的
并购交易事件 – 地区分布

资料来源：投中网 CVsource，德勤研究。

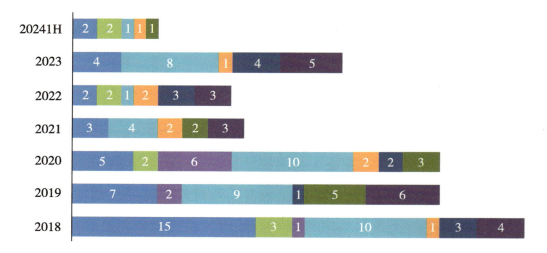

图 12-9　2018 年至 2024 年上半年中资企业在新加坡及东南亚地区的
并购交易事件 – 行业分布（单位：笔）

资料来源：投中网 CVsource，德勤研究。

化从合资模式转变为 100% 控股的中资券商模式。早在
2018 年，中国银河证券收购了马来西亚联昌集团的证券
业务，成立合资公司银河 – 联昌。到 2023 年 12 月，中
国银河证券实现了对银河 – 联昌的全资控股，并将其更名
为银河海外。在财富管理领域，新加坡的资产管理规模于
2023 年首次超越中国香港，成为亚洲最大的金融中心及

全球第三大金融中心。财富的持续涌入推动金融机构不断加强在新加坡的财富管理业务。同年，中信证券在新加坡设立了财富管理平台，华泰国际在新加坡开展了证券交易及企业融资业务，国泰君安国际则对其新加坡子公司进行了增资。

（二）营商环境以及独特的区位优势是吸引中资企业长期投资的主要因素

调研显示，高达 67% 的中资企业认为新加坡营商环境优秀。新加坡营商环境多年位居全球前列，受到中资企业的高度认可。2023 年，认为新加坡营商环境优秀的企业高达 67%，而认为良好的企业则有 33%，认为环境一般的企业仅有 1%，较 2021/2022 年上一轮调研下降 2%（见图 12-10）。

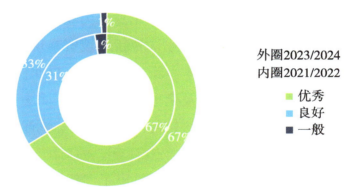

外圈2023/2024
内圈2021/2022

- 优秀
- 良好
- 一般

图 12-10　中资企业对新加坡营商环境的总体评价
资料来源：中资企业（新加坡）协会行业企业调研，德勤研究。

政府公共服务、税收制度、国际贸易便捷度是新加坡营商环境最吸引中资企业的前三大因素，分别达到 78%、53% 和 49%。与 2021/2022 年度调研相比，企业对税收制度、金融服务与资本市场、劳动力及人才的支持率有显著提升（见图 12-11）。根据瑞士洛桑国际管理发展学院（IMD）发表的《2024 年全球竞争力年报》，新加坡在 2020 年至 2023 年短暂跌出榜首后，时隔 4 年再次登顶，成为全球最具竞争力的经济体。便利商业活动的政策与新加坡开放创新的氛围，为企业和个人提供了良好的发展平台，吸引了包括中国企业在内的大量国际企业在此设立区域总部。

图 12-11　新加坡营商环境优势吸引企业的主要方面

资料来源：中资企业（新加坡）协会行业企业调研，德勤研究。

受访企业将新加坡的独特区位优势作为其加码投资的主要原因。91% 的企业认为新加坡可联动东南亚市场，78% 的企业认为新加坡企业身份有助于海外拓展，46% 的企业认为新加坡资本市场可触达到美国、香港外的国际资本。新加坡长期被企业视为拓展东南亚市场的理想门户以及全球化的实验室。此外，还有国际化高端人才可得性高、科技创新环境优秀、高净值人群服务需求巨大等原因。

2021 年，面对国际产业链重组和重塑的新趋势，新加坡适时推出了"新加坡 +1"战略，吸引了包括中国企业在内的大批国际资本。"新加坡 +1"战略由新加坡贸易和工业部下属的经济发展局（Economic Development Board of Singapore）牵头制定。该战略结合了新加坡作为全球商业中心和创新生态的优势，以及马来西亚、印尼、越南的制造业优势，实现 1+1>2 的效应，帮助制造企业快速拓展区域市场，打造多元化供应链和区域化新格局。

许多中国企业已通过"新加坡 +1"战略成功进入东南亚市场，包括药明康德、比亚迪、蔚来汽车、万国数据、领益智造等。随着新加坡制造业 2030 愿景和制造业 ITM 逐步落实，加上数字经济的支持，越来越多的中国制造业公司能够利用"新加坡+1"发展模式，实现东盟区域的协同发展。

以新加坡为起点，辐射东南亚

区域总部	利用新加坡的亲商环境、国际贸易的便捷度、具有竞争力的税收与人才市场、在东南亚的战略位置开拓和管理区域新业务
创新中心	利用新加坡蓬勃的创新和研发生态、高校资源和全球领先的知识产权保护框架来开发新产品
物流供应链中心	利用新加坡在马六甲海峡的战略位置、物流枢纽和清关效率
制造控制塔	新加坡距离东南亚的各大制造基地仅需6小时飞行时间。企业可申请新加坡政府推出的东南亚制造联盟项目

图 12-12　"新加坡+1"战略为企业提供独特的区域协同机遇
资料来源：新加坡经济发展局《把握东南亚制造业新机遇》。

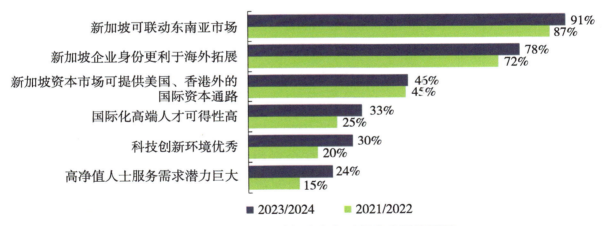

图 12-13　中资企业选择在新加坡投资发展的原因
资料来源：中资企业（新加坡）协会行业企业调研，德勤研究。

（三）中资企业投资热点聚焦科技与软件、新兴金融服务和生物科技三大行业

科技与软件、新兴金融服务和生物科技是中资企业认为增长最快的三个行业，突出科技赋能作为主要增长驱动力。此外，交通运输与物流、智能制造和电子商务行业也被部分企业视为未来的高增长领域，而基础设施建设行业的增长潜力则相对较小。

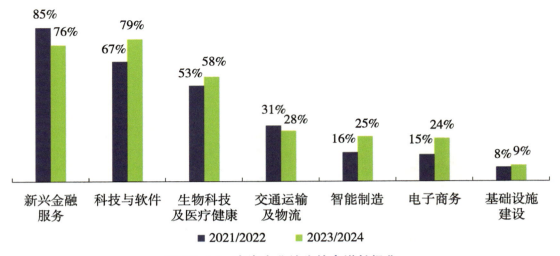

图 12-14　中资企业认为的高增长行业

资料来源：中资企业（新加坡）协会行业企业调研，德勤研究。

新加坡及东南亚市场的金融科技、软件服务、生物科技等科技赋能领域展现出长期的发展潜力。

金融科技行业蓬勃发展。作为亚洲最领先的金融科技市场，新冠疫情的暴发催化了新加坡金融科技市场的高速发展，网上银行、数字支付和电子商务等数字服务的需求激增。随着支付和借贷市场规模的扩大和业务生态的成熟，金融科技领域的新进入者正在财富管理、资本市场、保险科技、监管科技和数据分析等多个领域探索市场空间。而新加坡在金融科技的领导地位与基础设施为这些初创公司提供了有利创新空间。

B2B 产业成为科技新蓝海。后疫情时代，东南亚市场的数字化转型为 B2B 产业带来了巨大商业机会。新加坡是许多全球性科技公司的所在地，这样丰富的产业生态为科技公司之间的合作以及与终端应用公司共同开发解决方案提供了广阔的市场空间。B2B 赛道中，工业 4.0 科技、企业服务软件、B2B2C 物流解决方案为较具前景的领域。不少 B2B 公司先在新加坡打磨技术和验证商业模式，并选择将数据中心设在新加坡，作为进入东南亚市场的地区总部。

生物医药企业国际新基地。东南亚医药市场的规模和速度、高人口密度、与中国较小的人种差异等市场因素吸引中国生物医药企业加速在新加坡的布局。在拥有强大制造基础、高效连接的交通和物流网络的前提下，新加坡已成为全球国际生物医药企业的新基地，引得中资生物医药企业来新加坡进行并购与建厂。新加坡在生物医药领域的科技创新能力和创新成果居世界前列，并拥有健全的知识产权保护框架，为生物医药企业的研发成果提供了保障，激励了企业的健康发展。2023 年以来，BioNTech、Moderna 等全球 mRNA 疫苗巨头及君实生物、药明康德、金斯瑞生物、复星医药等国内生物医药企业相继进驻新加坡。

三、中资企业对本地经济发展的贡献

（一）中资企业增加了新加坡本地的就业机会，尤其在数字科技和金融行业

中资企业在新加坡的投资不仅促进了经济发展，还推动了本地就业。目前，中资企业在新加坡雇用本地员工的比例呈现出多样化的分布，新加坡本地员工占比超 60% 的中资企业达 54%（见图 12-15）。中资企业持续深化与当地商业伙伴的互信合作，探索更为高效、切实的可持续发展之路。这不仅增加了当地人的就业机会，而且推动了贸易、金融、航运、物流、房地产等多个行业全方位的创新发展。

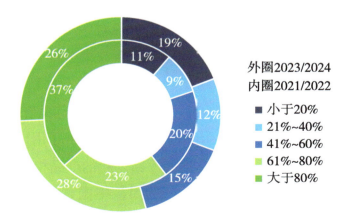

图 12-15　中资企业雇用新加坡本地员工占比情况分布

资料来源：中资企业（新加坡）协会行业企业调研，德勤研究。

（二）中资企业在产品及服务等五大领域的创新发展

中资企业对新加坡的贡献突出表现在产品及服务创新领域，整体发展注重提升客户价值和战略支撑。根据调研，高达 58% 的企业反馈了新加坡子公司在技术及服务创新领域的成果，40% 的企业反馈了在绿色发展创新方面的进展，较上一轮 2021-2022 年调研提升 9%。此外，中资企业还对新加坡的商业模式创新、技术创新和管理创新方面有所突破，占比在 20%~30% 之间（见图 12-16）。

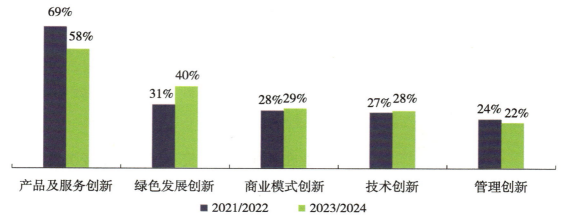

图 12-16　中资企业为新加坡作出创新发展的领域

资料来源：中资企业（新加坡）协会行业企业调研，德勤研究。

为深入了解新加坡中资企业在创新发展方面的成果，2024 年 7 月中旬，中资企业（新加坡）协会集中开展为期 2 周的视频访谈调研，近 20 家企业负责人结合企业的经营情况，对中资企业参与新加坡经济社会发展，在五大领域的创新成果进行分享。

1. 产品及服务创新

中资企业在新加坡的发展为各行业带来了创新的产品和服务，显著提升了用户体验并创造了持久的市场影响力。通过不断创新的产品和服务，这些企业引领了市场的发展。

例如，中国建筑作为践行国际化的先行者，于 1992 年在新加坡组建成立中国建筑（南洋）发展有限公司（简称"中建南洋"）。作为新加坡建筑行业领军企业之一，中建南洋已扎根新加坡 30 个年头，迄今已打造遍及教育、商业、酒店、医疗和交通等领域的 214 个优质工程，获得奖项 223 个。近年来，中建南洋积极助力新加坡政府倡导的建筑业转型蓝图，在创新业务领域进行多方面探索，持续提高生产效率。中建南洋始终关注行业技术应用前沿，提升建筑工业化程度和水平，减少现场作业工序。公司保持敏锐行业洞察力，持续推动数字化建造，采用 BIM 和虚拟建造技术来增强施工的精确度，探索智慧工地建设，提高管理效率。响应"双碳"要求，中建南洋探索绿色低碳产业方向，使用新型建筑材料，并加强产学研互动以推动创新技术研究。自 2016 年以来，中建南洋积极辐射新加坡周边市场，已成功布局马来西亚，承接了吉隆坡生态城和新山宜家等重点项目，品牌效益初显。

2. 绿色发展创新

在绿色发展创新领域，中资企业的贡献主要体现在通过采用环保机制和绿色技术实现节能减排。此外，中资企业在社会责任，绿色技术的先进性、实用性及推广性方面也取得了显著进展，与 2023 年相比有所提升。然而，在绿色创新科技基础研究方面仍有不足。

例如，中冶新加坡公司隶属于中国五矿旗下中冶集团建筑研究总院有限公司，是其海外区域性公司。自 1996 年进入新加坡市场以来，该公司实现了四次产业升级，现已发展成为城市建设全产业链一体化企业，其承建的多项工程获得了新加坡绿色建筑认证。中冶新加坡公司先后在新加坡完成了多个有影响力的项目，如新加坡会展中心、新加坡环球影城、圣淘沙海事博物馆等。其中，由中冶新加坡建设的新加坡万礼热带雨林生态主题公园项目，是推动减排降温、绿色发展的典型案例。2020 年 5 月，中冶新加坡克服疫情影响，中标了新加坡万礼热带雨林公园项目的设计施工总承包工程。该项目是新加坡政府致力于建立、管理世界级动物园和野生动植物生态体验的大型绿色生态文旅项目，旨在通过结合动物园和各种游览设施，将万礼打造成集自然与野生动物、植物为一体的自然主题公园，为游客提供前所未有且令人难忘的自然环境与野生动物园体验。这也是世界上首个以热带雨林为主题的公园，使得万礼成为新加坡集动植物保护、教育科研、文化旅游为一体的典型项目。项目一期北园将于 2024 年底完成，二期南园预计于 2025 年底全部落成，届时新加坡万礼生态区的年访客人数将超过 1000 万人次。

中国建设银行于 1993 年在新加坡设立代表处，1998 年成立分行，并于 2020 年获得全面牌照，成为新加坡 10 家全牌照银行之一。中国建设银行新加坡分行利用其强大的客户网络，为中国、新加坡以及"一带一路"和"陆海新通道"的客户提供全面的金融服务。建行新加坡分行积极推动绿色熊猫债的落地，并与新加坡金管局绿色足迹平台达成合作意向，探索形成客观、量化和可比的 ESG 评价结果，帮助中国和 RCEP 区域的中小企业获得更有针对性的绿色融资服务，促进区域可持续发展。此外，建行新加坡分行通过牵头或参与绿色融资项目，支持绿色经济发展，协助新加坡建屋局发行绿色债券，并为本地公共建筑屋顶太阳能项目提供绿色贷款。

3. 商业模式创新

在商业模式创新领域，中资企业作出的贡献主要在提高客户价值，为客户提供性价比更高的产品服务，提供深度客户服务和追踪调查。尽管中资企业在商业模式上有一定的竞争优势，但由于进入东南亚市场时间较短，在商业模式的韧性及稳定性、行业促进、价值重构、财务价值四个方面仍有提升空间。

例如，中国人寿保险新加坡有限公司是中国人寿设立的第一家海外子公司，在 2015 年进入新加坡市场。新加坡已跻身世界第三大金融中心，在金融保险方面已经是发达成熟的市场。新加坡寿险市场竞争激烈，无论从总量规模还是市场开拓来看，都已经进入红海状态。中国人寿新加坡作为后来者，坚持产品差异化、服务数字化和销售精细化，并定位对中国人寿产品比较认同的华人高净值客户。从这几年的业务数据来看，与本地市场平均值和头部公司相比，中国人寿新加坡子公司在跟中国市场的连接以及在东南亚客户的开拓上有超过市场平均增长率的表现。

4. 前沿技术创新

在技术创新领域，中资企业作出的贡献主要是领先的技术创新战略，以行业领先作为技术创新目标，而非快速跟进或模仿技术。中资企业凭借在中国广阔且竞争激烈的市场中锤炼的前沿技术，以及应用成功案例，较容易在东南亚找到相近的应用场景。

例如，中国联通新加坡公司在推广5G、数据存储、安全、机房和AI应用等前沿技术方面业务增长迅猛。从2020年到2023年，收入和利润都实现了规模性增长。这主要得益于联网通信类产品的增长，特别是IDC产品、数据中心、云计算和云应用等新兴创新型应用产品。中国联通新加坡公司通过与新加坡本地的一些商协会组织，如中小企业协会、制造商企业协会等，开展交流活动。把中国成功的5G场景化应用案例带到新加坡市场和园区，达到双赢。公司还提升了研发实力与投入，设立研发机构、研发支出高于行业平均，并参与创新联盟。在算网数智领域，中国联通新加坡也在尝试和拓展新的应用。作为国内5G网络的应用专家，基于很多应用场景，在区域开展了多个成功案例。例如，在泰国，联通实现了长城汽车工业园区和美的工厂的无人化连接，提供高端的信息化服务，如灯塔工厂和无人工厂的应用。通过这些成熟的案例，中国联通推动区域内各个行业的数字化转型。

5. 管理模式创新

在管理创新领域，中资企业作出的贡献主要体现在企业管理的特定方面（如组织与管控、信息管理、供应链管理）采用优于同行的理念和做法。比如，并购是中资企业出海的主要方式之一，有效的并购后整合需要中资企业迅速搭建一套适用当地市场的管理体系。中资企业在管理成效方面也作出了显著贡献，创新管理理念获得市场认可。

例如，中国石油国际事业新加坡公司于 2000 年在新加坡成立，初期主要从事国内成品油的出口和东南亚区域销售。2009 年，中石油新加坡公司收购了新加坡石油公司（SPC），获得上游资产和生产业务，包括炼油厂、樟宜机场飞机加油业务和船舶加油业务。通过业务整合，中石油新加坡公司在上游、炼油和销售业务的管理上取得了显著进展。收购后，公司注重企业文化建设，尊重新加坡的多元文化、语言和风俗习惯，坚持多元文化融合。与 SPC 的业务整合效果超预期，中石油新加坡公司在 2023 年的贸易利润和贸易量达到了历史最高水平。

四、结语

中资企业在新加坡的投资和创新发展取得了显著成果，推动了中新之间的经贸合作与双向投资。在绿色发展、科技创新和城市建设等领域，中资企业不仅展示了强大的竞争力和适应能力，也为新加坡的经济和社会发展注入了新活力。

随着《区域全面经济伙伴关系协定》（RCEP）和《数字经济伙伴关系协定》（DEPA）的进一步推进，中资企业在新加坡乃至整个东南亚市场的机会将持续增加。新加坡凭借其独特的地理优势和优越的商业环境，继续吸引着大批中资企业前来投资和拓展业务。

未来，中新双方应继续深化合作，共同探索更多双赢的投资机会。通过不断优化贸易政策和商业环境，双方必将实现更加紧密的经济联系，为区域经济的繁荣发展作出更大贡献。希望能为有意进入东南亚及新加坡市场的中资企业提供有价值的参考和借鉴，助力其在全球化的浪潮中扬帆远航。

关于本调研

为深入了解中资企业在新加坡的投资现状，中资企业（新加坡）协会于 2024 年 6 月至 7 月发起了 2023/2024

年度发展报告调研问卷，并收到了协会企业的百余份有效回复。从行业分布来看，首先是基础设施及建筑、金融行业和国际贸易分别占比14%，其次是交通运输、通信科技以及能源。从所有制分布来看，央企、民企与地方国企分别占比44%、28%与14%。它们在新加坡的机构类型主要是区域总部和区域销售中心，少数为区域物流管理中心和区域制造及生产中心（见图12-17）。

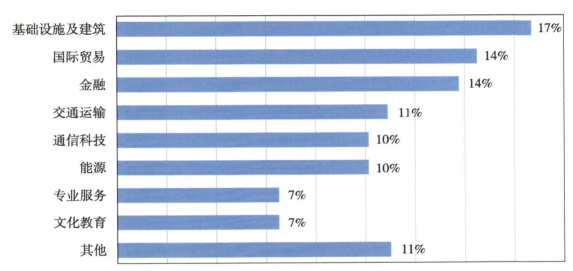

图 12-17 调研企业的行业分布

资料来源：中资企业（新加坡）协会行业企业调研，德勤研究。

注：其他行业包括先进制造、生物科技及医疗健康、消费品生产及零售。

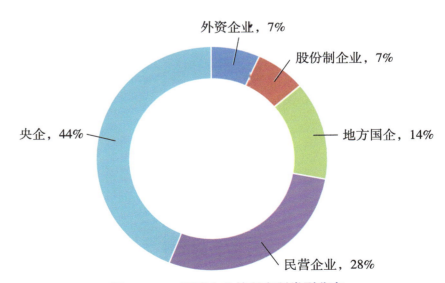

图 12-18 调研企业的所有制类型分布

资料来源：中资企业（新加坡）协会行业企业调研，德勤研究。

产业篇

第十三章 金融高水平开放的新成效 [1]

作为中国高水平开放的重要组成部分，党的十八大以来金融开放步伐明显加速。通过大幅放宽金融业市场准入、扩大外资金融机构业务范围、推动资本市场双向互联互通等一系列制度性举措，中国金融开放程度实现了显著提升与深化。2023年，面对新冠疫情恢复期、俄乌冲突、主要国家货币政策分化及中美利差倒挂等多重挑战，中国依然坚定不移地推进金融领域制度型开放，不断完善跨境金融交易与跨境金融服务体系，深化金融市场互联互通，稳步提升人民币国际货币功能；继续推动上海、香港国际金融中心建设，其国际竞争力和规则影响力持续提升。展望未来，中国金融高水平开放将更好地统筹开放与安全、"引进来"与"走出去"，助力构建更高水平开放型经济新体制。

一、持续扩大金融领域制度型开放

2018年以来，中国从给予外资机构国民待遇、取消外资持股比例限制、扩大业务范围、优化管理规则等方面，全面推进金融业制度型开放。2023年10月，中央金融工作会议进一步提出"稳步扩大金融领域制度型开放"，旨在继续优化市场规则，着力提升金融开放的深度与广度。

（一）持续放宽外资机构准入门槛

当前，中国已经取消银行、证券、基金管理等领域外

---

① 国务院发展研究中心金融研究所张丽平、孙飞供稿。

资机构持股比例限制，极大降低了外资机构设立金融机构的门槛。银行业方面，2019年底前取消银行持股比例限制、外国银行来华设立外资法人银行和分行的总资产要求。截至2023年底，外资银行在华已设立41家法人银行、116家外国及港澳台银行分行和132家代表处，营业性机构总数量达到888家，总资产达3.86万亿元。证券期货业方面，2023年1月渣打证券获批设立，成为2020年4月1日证券公司外资股比限制正式取消后首家获批设立的外商全资控股券商。截至2023年末，共有17家外资参控股证券公司获批设立，总资产超6500亿元，实现营业收入超275亿元。保险业方面，2020年底前，取消人身险公司外资持股比例、经营年限要求等准入条件；2022年9月，取消外资保险公司持股比例上限。截至2023年末，境外保险机构在境内已经设立了67家营业性机构和70家代表处，外资保险公司总资产达到2.4万亿元，在境内保险市场份额达10%。此外，中国还在支付、评级、企业征信等领域给予外资机构国民待遇。2023年11月，万事达在华合资银行卡清算机构万事网联获批开业。

（二）不断拓展外资机构准营业务范围

在放宽准入门槛的同时，进一步拓展外资机构的业务资质，不断优化营商环境。2023年1月，渣打银行（中国）获批参与国债期货交易，成为首家获准参与国债期货交易的在华外资银行。交易商协会发布公告显示，根据2023年非金融企业债务融资工具承销业务相关会员申请从事承销相关业务市场评价结果，新增汇丰银行、渣打银行和东方汇理银行为非金融企业债务融资工具一般主承销商；新增摩根大通银行、瑞穗银行、三菱日联银行为境外非金融企业债务融资工具专项主承销商；新增东亚银行、富邦华一银行、三井住友银行、星展银行为非金融企业债务融资工具承销商。此外，中国金融主管部门在开展新业务试点时，对中外资机构一视同仁、平等对待，如人民银行碳减排支持工具的金融机构目前已纳入德意志银行、法国兴业银行、汇丰银行等 13 家外资银行。

（三）进一步优化市场规则

在金融领域制度型开放的过程中，根据市场的新变化和市场主体的新需求，不断优化市场规则，更好地促进金融市场的公平竞争与创新发展，提升金融开放深度。资本市场方面，2023 年 2 月，中国证监会、香港证监会开放因不满足结算安排而关闭的沪深港通交易日，优化沪深港通交易日历；中国证监会发布《境内企业境外发行证券和上市管理试行办法》及 5 项配套指引，支持企业依法合规到境外上市。外汇管理方面，2023 年 11 月，人民银行、国家外汇管理局对《境外机构投资者境内证券期货投资资金管理规定》进行修订并发布征求意见稿，进一步简化登记手续、优化账户管理、简化汇兑管理、便利外汇风险管理，拟取消 QFII/RQFII 在外汇局办理资金登记的行政许可要求。

（四）加快实施特定区域金融开放政策

特定区域金融开放政策是推动金融领域制度型开放的重要举措。优化这些区域的金融市场准入、资本流动、金融服务等方面的规则，不仅可以吸引更多国内外金融机构和投资者进入，促进金融资源的高效配置和市场的深度融合，进而带动区域经济的高质量开放，而且能够通过发挥先行先试作用降低改革风险，积累可复制可推广的经验，加快中国金融领域的开放进程。近年来，特别注重对标国际高标准经贸协议中金融领域相关规则，在重点区域出台一揽子金融创新政策。2023 年 2 月，人民银行、银保监会、证监会、外汇局、广东省人民政府联合印发《关于金融支持横琴粤澳深度合作区建设的意见》和《关于金融支持前海深港现代服务业合作区全面深化改革开放的意见》，分别提出了三十条金融改革创新举措。横琴新政策鼓励通过发展跨境金融业务，为粤澳两地的经济合作提供更为便捷的金融支持；前海新政策鼓励合作区内的金融机构进行产品和服务的创新，以满足现代服务业的多元化金融需求。

二、不断完善跨境金融服务体系

完善跨境金融服务体系是金融开放进程中的重要一环。近年来，中国不断完善跨境金融服务体系，不仅更好地满足了企业和个人对跨境投融资等金融服务的需求，还进一步促进了金融市场的互联互通，推动金融开放向更深层次、更广领域发展。

（一）不断优化跨境投融资支持政策

一方面，在近年来持续出台跨境贸易投资便利化措施的基础上，2023 年 12 月，外汇局发布《关于进一步深化改革促进跨境贸易投资便利化的通知》，从推进贸易外汇收支便利化、扩大资本项目便利化、优化资本项目外汇管理三大方面，推出 9 项贸易和投融资便利化政策。《通知》从主体范围、试点地区、试点额度等方面对跨境融资便利化政策进行了升级，特别是将科技型中小企业纳入试点主体，政策覆盖范围从此前的 17 个省（市）扩展至全国，将此前 17 个省（市）的便利化额度提高至等值 1000 万美元，体现了金融开放对具有技术优势和一定发展潜力的科技企业的支持。

另一方面，持续加大对科技创新和中小企业的外汇支持力度。针对中小微高新技术和"专精特新"企业等净资产规模较小的企业，开展跨境融资便利化试点，允许企业在等值 1000 万美元或 500 万美元额度内自主借用外债。根据外汇局资料，目前试点区域已覆盖全国约 80%、28万家高新技术和"专精特新"企业。通过搭建跨境金融服务平台，推出 8 个融资类应用场景和 3 个便利化类应用场景，助力以中小企业为主的近 20 万家涉外企业累计获得融资金额超 2900 亿美元、付汇金额超 1.2 万亿美元。

（二）中资机构积极拓展全球业务

中资金融机构通过自身"走出去"拓展全球业务，为服务企业"走出去"提供保障。2023 年，中资金融机构"走出去"步伐加快。银行业方面，通过增设海外分行充分发挥国际经贸往来的窗口和桥梁作用，为服务企业"走出去"提供保障。截至 2023 年 6 月末，中资银行在境外 71 个国家和地区设立了 295 家一级机构，在支持中国企业增强海外竞争能力上发挥了重要作用。其中，五大行已在境外 67 个国家和地区设立了经营性机构，基本覆盖了主要国际性、区域性金融中心。在发达国家布局的同时，银行业还注重围绕中国外经贸重点国家和地区设立境外机构，不断扩大对"一带一路"共建国家的金融服务覆盖面。2023 年下半年以来，中国银行于 7 月、9 月分别在巴基斯坦伊斯兰堡和沙特阿拉伯利雅得新设分行；中国建设银行于 2023 年 11 月在马来西亚槟城开设分行。

保险业方面，根据金融监管总局数据，截至 2023 年 6 月末，中资保险机构在 17 个国家和地区设立了 74 家分支机构，为走出去中资企业和共建"一带一路"提供了优质金融服务。如截至 2023 年底，中再产险公司已为数百个共建"一带一路"项目提供超千亿元风险保障，为 1 万余列中欧班列、超 80 万标准箱跨境贸易货物提供风险保障。

三、继续深化金融市场互联互通

近年来，通过积极推动金融市场双向开放，我国已初步形成涵盖股票市场、债券市场、外汇市场、衍生品市场的开放格局，"沪港通""深港通""债券通""互换通"等已经成为国内外投资者积极参与的金融市场互联互通方式。截至 2023 年底，"深港通"累计交易金额超过 75.43 万亿元；跨境理财通个人投资者已达 6.92 万人，跨境理财通市值余额达到 51 亿元。2023 年，债券通"北向通"交易量增长 24%，全年成交 9.97 万亿元人民币。从 2023 年的新亮点来看，突出表现为以下几个方面。

（一）债券市场互通深度和广度进一步拓展

2023 年全年外资净增持境内债券 230 亿美元。截至 2023 年末，共有 1124 家境外投资者进入中国债券市场，涵盖 70 多个国家和地区的主权类和商业类投资者，持有中国债券总量为 3.7 万亿元。截至 2023 年 12 月底，境外投资者连续 11 个月净买入中国债券，其中 2023 年 11 月境外投资者净买入中国债券约 3600 亿元，增持约 2500 亿元，创历史新高。根据人民银行数据，截至 2023 年底，境外机构持有银行间市场债券约达 3.67 万亿元。此外，2023 年熊猫债发行量创历史新高，全年发行规模首次突破 1500 亿元。

（二）利率互换市场互联互通正式启动

为帮助境外投资者更好管理利率风险，2023 年 5 月，内地与香港利率互换市场互联互通合作（"互换通"）正式上线。境内外投资者可经由内地与香港金融市场基础设施机构在交易、清算、结算等方面互联互通的机制安排，在不改变交易习惯、有效遵从两地市场法律法规的前提下，便捷地完成人民币利率互换交易和集中清算。截至 2023 年 12 月末，共有境内报价商 20 家，境外投资者 51 家，累计成交 2000 多笔，名义本金超 9000 亿元。

（三）ETF 互通产品不断丰富

自 2022 年 ETF 纳入内地与香港股票市场交易互联互通机制开通以来，深股通 ETF 持续扩容。2023 年新增 25 只 ETF 纳入深股通名单，持续丰富境外投资者 A 股投资工具。另外，深新 ETF 互通合作也不断深化。截至 2023

年底，沪股通 ETF 共 76 只，深股通 ETF 共 55 只，港股通 ETF 共 8 只，互联互通 ETF 数量共计 139 只，相较于首批沪深港通 ETF 产品数量增加 60%。此外，深新互通产品银河富国中证 1000ETF 于 2023 年 11 月在新加坡交易所上市，为新加坡投资者提供了配置 A 股的新工具[①]。

四、稳步提升人民币国际货币功能

（一）人民币在跨境贸易中的使用增多

为更好地满足外经贸企业交易结算、投融资、风险管理等需求，2023 年 1 月，人民银行会同商务部发布《关于进一步支持外经贸企业扩大人民币跨境使用促进贸易投资便利化的通知》。2023 年，银行代客人民币跨境收付金额为 52.3 万亿元，同比增长 24.2%，人民币成为中国跨境收付第一大结算币种。其中，货物贸易跨境人民币收付金额合计 10.7 万亿元，占同期货物贸易本外币跨境收付总额的比重为 25%，较 2022 年上升 7 个百分点，保持较高水平。环球银行金融电信协会（SWIFT）的数据显示，2023 年 11 月，人民币支付金额在全球货币支付总金额中的占比为 4.61%，超过日元位列全球第四位支付货币。据中国人民银行统计，2023 年，经常项下跨境人民币结算金额为 14.03 万亿元，其中货物贸易、服务贸易及其他经常项目分别为 10.69 万亿元、3.34 万亿元；直接投资跨境人民币结算金额为 7.6 万亿元，其中对外直接投资、外商直接投资分别为 2.6 万亿元、5 万亿元。

（二）人民币跨境支付的便利化程度加深

外国居民在中国跨境支付便利化程度大大增强。2023 年，国务院办公厅印发的《关于释放旅游消费潜力推动旅

[①] 资料来源：https://baijiahao.baidu.com/s?id=1788506878680186396&wfr=spider&for=pc。

游业高质量发展的若干措施》提出，提高入境游客使用境外银行卡和各类电子支付方式便捷程度以及外币兑换便利性。自 2023 年以来，支付宝、财付通携手商业银行、清算机构、卡组织陆续落地系列优化举措，一方面推动"外卡内绑"，境外银行卡可绑定支付宝或微信在国内商户消费；另一方面支持"外包内用"，更多的境外电子钱包被允许在国内使用。支付宝和微信外卡支付均已实现将外籍来华人员使用移动支付的单笔交易限额由 1000 美元提高到 5000 美元、年累计交易限额由 1 万美元提高到 5 万美元。[①]。

中国居民跨境支付便利度持续提升。人民币跨境支付系统（CIPS）服务区域扩大、服务水平提升，2023 年国庆、中秋假期首次实现长假"不打烊"，持续为境内外客户提供跨境人民币支付清算服务，充分发挥跨境支付主渠道作用。截至 2023 年末，CIPS 共有直接参与者 139 家，间接参与者 1345 家，业务范围覆盖全球 182 个国家和地区的 4442 家法人银行机构。

（三）人民币使用的国际化网络更加完善

2023 年，中国人民银行与沙特、阿联酋等国央行新签或续签双边本币互换协议，目前有效双边本币互换协议共 31 份；在巴西、柬埔寨、塞尔维亚等国新设人民币清算行，目前已在 31 个国家和地区授权了 33 家人民币清算行，覆盖主要国际金融中心。

五、有序推进国际金融中心建设

习近平总书记在省部级主要领导干部推动金融高质量发展专题研讨班开班式上的重要讲话中明确指出，强大的国际金融中心是金融强国关键核心金融要素之一。近年

---

① 资料来源：https://baijiahao.baidu.com/s?id=1794221409212700185&wfr=spider&for=pc。

来，上海、香港国际金融中心立足于各自的国际竞争优势，全球资源配置能力不断增强，国际影响力稳步提升，在推动金融强国建设中发挥着重要作用。

（一）上海国际金融中心稳步发展

受发展历史、国情等因素影响，国际金融中心各具特色，但从其共性特征看，均在某些领域拥有强大的国际竞争优势。上海的突出优势在于其建设国际金融中心是党中央、国务院从中国改革开放和社会主义现代化建设全局高度提出的一项重大国家战略。1992 年党的十四大首次提出把上海建成国际金融中心，2009 年国务院 19 号文进一步明确了上海建设国际金融中心的目标和主要任务。上海以此为引领在跨境人民币结算、资本市场互联互通等方面深化改革，成为中国金融领域改革开放的重要窗口，2020年基本建成了与中国经济实力以及人民币国际地位相适应的国际金融中心。2021 年以来，上海迈入能级全面提升的新阶段。在继续完善股票、债券、货币、黄金、外汇、商品期货、金融期货、保交所、票交所等金融要素市场的基础上，以上海数据交易所为载体探索金融数据流动，依托上海环境能源交易所推进碳金融发展，形成了较其他国际金融中心更为齐全的市场功能。

近年来，上海国际金融中心资源聚集效应进一步显现，同时积极发挥辐射作用和带动作用。依托自贸试验区及临港新片区金融开放创新先行先试优势，上海深入开展跨境贸易投资高水平开放试点，便利境外机构投资者投资在中国资本市场上公平交易。金融机构方面，2023 年上海持牌金融机构总数 1771 家，其中外资金融机构占比接近三分之一；总部设在上海的外资法人银行、合资基金管理公司、外资保险公司均占内地总数的一半左右；上海在银行、投资、保险等多个子业务排名进入全球前 5。资金管理方面，上海资管规模已占全国近 30%，其中公募、私募和保险资管位居全国首位。金融人才方面，上海金融从业人员约 50 万人，其中浦东新区金融业人才占总就业人口的比例接近 9%，居全球前列。

（二）香港国际金融中心发挥重要作用

香港一直都是众多国际知名银行、保险公司、证券公司等金融机构的亚洲总部所在地，也是全球重要的财富管理市场，作为国际金融中心继续发挥着全球引领作用。截至 2023 年底，香港金融市场管理的资产总值年化增长 2.1%，总额跃升至 31.19 万亿港元[1]，主要为私人银行和私人财务管理业务；持牌证券机构共 3257 家，上市公司 2609 家，总市值 4.0 万亿美元；香港是亚洲最大国际债券发行中心，2023 年新发行国际债券 1754 亿美元，是全球最大离岸人民币市场，拥有最大离岸人民币资金池，2024 年 1 月，人民币存款余额 9547 亿元[2]。

香港的竞争优势主要体现在以普通法为基础的法律框架，覆盖会计、审计、法律、咨询等领域的专业服务体系，较低的税率以及跨境资金的自由流动等方面，这些优势为香港巩固提升国际金融中心地位奠定了基础。

六、中国金融高水平开放展望

在党的二十届三中全会作出进一步全面深化改革决定的大背景下，中国将继续深化金融领域制度型开放，以更优良的营商环境、更高效的资源配置、更完善的市场体系、更专业的人才队伍，进一步提升金融业开放质效。但同时也要看到，面对复杂的国际形势以及国内外金融市场的不确定性，中国金融开放面临诸多挑战。随着中国金融开放进入深水区，在更加开放的过程中如何更好地构建金融安全机制，积极参与国际金融治理，提升中国金融体系

---

[1] 香港证监会，《2023 年资产及财富管理活动调查》，https://baijiahao.baidu.com/s?id=1805356594368225398&wfr=spider&for=pc，2024-7-23。

[2] 搜狐网，香港与新加坡领先优势大对比，谁是国际金融中心第三城，https://www.sohu.com/a/789674319_121304879。

的国际竞争力成为中国金融开放的重要议题。

一方面，更好地统筹金融开放和安全。通过积极参与国际金融治理与合作，进一步深化国际金融合作，推进全球宏观经济金融政策协调。近年来，中国已在规则、制度、管理、标准等多个方面，主动与高标准国际规则接轨，发起成立"一带一路"银行间常态化合作机制（BRBR）、"一带一路"绿色投资原则（GIP）等。未来将继续与高标准国际规则接轨，积极参与国际金融标准的制定与修订，不断提升金融业的国际化水平。同时，还将通过中美、中欧金融工作组等机制，进一步推动金融领域的对话与交流，共同探索金融开放的新路径，促进全球金融市场的稳定与发展。

另一方面，更好地统筹"引进来"与"走出去"。2023年10月，中央金融工作会议再次明确"坚持'引进来'和'走出去'并重"。在"引进来"方面，未来将继续扩大外资金融机构业务范围，进一步优化营商环境。在"走出去"方面，随着中国企业"走出去"步伐的加快，金融机构将积极拓展海外市场，参与国际金融合作与竞争，提升国际竞争力。

第十四章　在华跨国公司积极投身 ESG 实践 [1]

　　跨国公司积极履行绿色责任，对中国绿色发展产生重要示范作用。根据净零排放追踪器的统计，全球最大的 2000 家上市公司中已经有 1142 家制定了净零目标，是 2020 年 417 家的 2.7 倍。跨国公司的海外投资更加强调环境保护、社会责任及公司治理（ESG）要求，更加注重结合东道国比较优势推动当地绿色产业发展。在中国加快绿色转型的背景下，在华跨国企业也积极投身 ESG 实践，进一步提升可持续目标。同时，发挥绿色技术优势带动供应链上下游企业共同提升 ESG 能力和水平。中国外商投资企业协会投资性公司工作委员会，选取了五家跨国公司 ESG 实践案例，展示了不同领域和行业的成功经验和创新实践。

案例 1：福特汽车的可持续发展战略

　　福特汽车全球的可持续发展战略旨在加大对社会和环境的正面影响，公司对气候变化、能源使用、材料、水、废弃物、人权、员工等分别制定了详细策略和目标，发布了 2050 年碳中和的承诺，并且根据科学降碳目标倡议（SBTi）制定了中长期减碳目标，致力于同利益相关方建立直接、开放、透明和频繁的联系和互动。

　　福特汽车在中国的工厂努力将战略和目标转变为实践活动：

　　在可再生能源使用方面，福特中国采取积极举措推进

---

① 中国外商投资企业协会投资性公司工作委员会供稿。

可再生能源使用和碳中和工作；福特在中国的工厂安装了总容量超过 110MWp 的屋顶和停车场太阳能光伏板，大幅度减少了碳排放，年发电量超过 8 千万度。

在水资源方面，福特全球最新的水资源管理策略中除了继续致力于提高用水效率，让每个人都拥有清洁的水资源。福特在中国的制造工厂分别采用先进的节水工艺，如涂装车间前处理电泳工艺采用旋转浸涂工艺、干式喷房、废水深度处理和中水回用系统，回用水用于涂装工艺补水、雨水灌溉绿化、深挖冷却塔潜力、管网补漏改造等措施，确保生产制造过程中的用水量持续降低。

福特中国持续努力推进废弃物的减量、回收和再利用。从 2021 年开始，福特在中国的工厂全部实现了废弃物"零填埋"，工厂产生的所有废弃物都不再填埋处理，而是回收再利用，或者经由焚烧发电。2021 年 9 月，长安福特杭州工厂获得由杭州市人民政府颁发的"无废工厂"称号，以此来表彰杭州工厂在废弃物管理、实现废弃物零填埋、推进工业和生活垃圾分类以及减少污泥、漆渣和一般固废方面的工作和成绩。杭州工厂成为杭州"无废城市"建设的重要组成部分。

长安福特重庆工厂致力于改善生产流程，减少挥发性有机物 VOCs 排放，工厂涂装工艺产生的废弃回收溶剂经由深度处理后回用到生产线，实现了循环经济。江铃汽车富山工厂，为涂装安装了全线的 VOC 废气处理设施，该工厂成为全球最低的 VOCs 排放工厂之一。

福特中国成功入选"2023 企业 ESG 杰出社会责任实践案例"。2023 年，长安福特重庆工厂被评选为国家级绿色工厂认证。

案例 2：拜耳"拥抱绿色"项目

拥抱绿色活动持续开展 5 年（2019-2023 年），彰显了拜耳作物科学在华不辍深耕、积极推进农业生产方式绿色转型和农业高质量发展的长足愿景、坚定决心、踏实行动。

"拥抱绿色"系列公益活动全称为"拥抱绿色·共赢未来——绿色发展能力提升行动计划",是由拜耳作物科学和全国农业技术推广服务中心联合主办的大型公益性培训项目和中德农业合作的亮点,旨在通过提供专业、丰富的绿色发展专业技能培训,为中国农业绿色发展和高质量发展提供有力的人才支撑。

"拥抱绿色"项目实施的 5 年中,先后在江苏、山东、广东、云南、西藏、河南、内蒙古、上海等 18 个省、自治区、直辖市举办 15 场线下培训活动及 12 场线上直播,打造 12 种作物共 22 块示范田。1000 多个县市的 2600 余名线下学员通过现场观摩、专家授课、案例分享、决策研讨等多种形式参加培训,直播培训超过 32 万人次。这一公益培训项目传播了高质量发展、绿色防控、农药减施增效等新技术、新理念,为广大学员的知识更新、行动优化和能力提升提供了很好的契机和平台。

案例 3:宜家打造可持续消费

中国是宜家全球发展最快也最为重要的市场之一,也是拥有完整价值链的市场,业务涉及产品设计、测试、生产、采购、仓储及配送、零售、商业地产等领域。宜家将可持续理念融入整个价值链。

1. 产品开发

宜家在产品开发阶段就遵循可持续的理念。已有4000多种可持续性尤为突出的产品，如节能、节水、由环保或可回收材料制成、有可持续认证、植物基食品等。

以地毯产品为例，宜家全球每年约使用 3 万吨的丙纶制造地毯。丙纶是以从石油中提炼出的丙烯为原材料制成的，这也意味着宜家每年需消耗约 12 万吨原油。宜家正尝试使用回收丙纶来代替原生丙纶。市面上广泛应用的再生回收涤纶纱线主要由塑料瓶制成，而宜家合作伙伴研发出可对纺织品制造过程中产生的涤纶废料进行回收再造的技术，可将废料重新制成涤纶纱线并再次用于生产。 得益于该技术的突破，宜家实现了涤纶纺织品的循环闭环。目前，此项技术已应用到床品、家用纺织品、地毯等新产品的开发中。 2030 年，宜家的目标是：在开发阶段，定义所有产品的生命周期，所生产的产品只使用可再生或可回收材料。

2. 循环市集

目前，全国所有 35 家宜家商场均设有"可持续循环市集"。循环市集售卖的产品主要为商场陈列的样品、运输包装破损的产品等。产品在上架前经过修复，在确保产品功能及安全性后才会进行售卖，价格较为实惠。循环市集作为卖场中的重要组成部分，既能启发消费者注重绿色

循环的生活方式，又将产品赋予了二次生命，是很好的消费者宣传教育空间。

3. 绿色可持续生活产品专区

宜家在卖场内设有专门的空间，陈列符合绿色可持续家居生活理念的产品，如节水龙头、LED 灯、食品密封袋等。"绿色可持续生活产品专区"能够向消费者可视化地展示节约资源、节约用水、减少浪费、重复使用等多个维度的可持续产品，有助于提高大众对可持续生活方式的认识。

4. 绿色动线（门店 100% 落地实施）

可持续发展需要来自整个社会的协同努力。因此，宜家积极利用多样的平台与渠道扩大绿色影响力。面向消费者，宜家通过优化商场视觉设计，在商场中特别设计有可持续绿色动线，展示产品中的可持续亮点，激励更多消费者探索可持续的生活方式。通过加强店内宣传，宜家以更直接、更贴近本地的方式分享对可持续发展的见解。

案例 4：绿色供应链——施耐德电气的实践

根据全球环境信息研究中心（CDP）测算，企业供应链生态所产生的碳排放往往是其企业运营范围碳排放的5.5 倍。不少企业已经推动绿色供应链，如施耐德电气联手合作伙伴共同推进碳中和，既是可持续的践行者，也是赋能者。

在供应链可持续发展方面，施耐德电气通过借力数字化技术，打造了涵盖绿色设计、绿色采购、绿色生产、绿色交付、绿色运维的端到端绿色供应链。

施耐德电气把可持续发展目标融入主业，并借力技术，联手合作伙伴共同推进碳中和。在中国，施耐德电气有 15 家工厂已经成为工信部认证的"绿色工厂"，同时还拥有 19 家"零碳工厂"和 12 家"碳中和"工厂，源源不断为中国和全球市场提供绿色创新产品。到 2025 年，施耐德电气计划帮助全球客户节约和避免二氧化碳排放量达到 8 亿吨。

基于在可持续发展方面的持续优秀表现，施耐德电气连续 12 次登上企业爵士（Corporate Knights）评选出的年度"全球可持续发展百强企业"榜单，同时也成为业界唯一一家连续 11 年跻身碳排放披露项目（CDP）"A 级名录"的公司。

可持续发展需要全社会的共同努力。现阶段，大量企业缺少减碳的整体思路和能力，急需经验分享和技术支持，先行者的赋能对于减碳和可持续发展具有重要意义。作为可持续发展的赋能者，为应对系统性难题，施耐德电气搭建了覆盖广泛的减碳生态圈，以经验和技术持续为供应商赋能。

为推动供应商减碳，施耐德电气于 2021 年发起供应商"零碳计划"，旨在通过提供技术指导、咨询服务等方式，帮助全球前 1000 位供应商 2025 年减碳 50%，其中包括中国的 230 家核心供应商。到 2023 年底，该计划实现了碳排放平均减少 27%。

具体举措包括：

1. 深化对供应商的绿色培训

施耐德电气为供应商提供碳足迹分析和碳轨迹定义等技术培训和脱碳解决方案，以及领先的数字化解决方案，帮助其发展减碳能力，增效减排，实现绿色转型。

2. 分享领先经验

通过举办施耐德电气智慧工厂、智慧物流中心现场参观活动和减碳相关的探索研讨会，为供应商减排提供建议和支持，集生态圈的力量共同实现整个价值链的碳排放目标。

3. 建立平台跟进减碳进程

在减碳 50% 的框架内，施耐德电气建立了针对供应商的零碳项目平台，将协助各个供应商设定各自的减碳目标，并监控项目进度，加强供应商系统内的减碳报告分析，同时保持内外部沟通，分享晟佳实践。

天津津荣天宇精密机械股份有限公司（以下简称"津荣天宇"）正是施耐德电气供应链上的减碳标杆之一。自 2021 年参与施耐德电气供应商"零碳计划"后，津荣天宇建立了自身可持续发展顶层规划和远期目标，计划到 2025 年实现较基准年（2019 年）减碳 50%。津荣天宇基于施耐德电气 EcoStruxure 架构融入多项节能减碳技术，其中仅铺设自有光伏这一项，预计每年就可减碳 1100 吨。到 2022 年底，津荣天宇每亿元销售额的碳减排量降幅已达 22.2%。

案例 5：ABB 厦门工业中心践行"零排放愿景"

作为电气与自动化领域的技术领导企业，ABB 是推动能源转型的核心力量之一，支持全球各地客户实现能效倍增、电气化和脱碳化，帮助客户保持竞争力，降低碳足迹，让交通、生产、工作和生活方式更加可持续。ABB 长期关注并多角度布局 ESG，目前已获得国际权威指数机构 MSCI 在 ESG 领域的最高 AAA 评级。

为实现 ABB2030 与 2050 科学净零目标，ABB 在中国积极推进可持续发展，支持中国加快绿色低碳转型，通过开发和推广高效节能产品和解决方案，帮助工业、交通、建筑、数据中心等各领域的客户提升能源效率，减少碳排放，降低对环境的影响。

积极部署可持续发展战略，致力于迈向净零未来

ABB 2030与2050科学净零目标

ABB 厦门工业中心，占地面积为 42.5 万平方米，员工数量达 3000 人，通过践行 ABB 全球"零排放愿景计划"，预计每年可减少 13400 吨碳排放，清楚展示了 ABB 智能数字技术如何将脱碳和减排（用电间接排放）的愿景变为现实。作为"碳中和"园区和可持续智能制造的示范基地，ABB 厦门工业中心采用创新的能源调控系统，集成新能源发电和储能系统的应用，大幅降低碳排放和提高用能效率，擘画出可复制可扩展的低碳蓝图。

ABB 厦门工业中心拥有先进的中压、低压开关柜和断路器生产线，通过安装 100000 平方米的屋顶光伏，实现了 50% 的绿电替代。通过多策略精准柔性调控技术，实现清洁能源的更大化本地消纳，源荷储协同提高能源使用效率。该智慧能源解决方案配置发电预测和负荷预测 AI 算法，通过预测发电和用电的情况，部署调控策略，实现用电低碳化和经济性之间的平衡。

项目部署 ABB Ability™ ZEE600 智慧能源管理平台对园区的"源－网－荷－储"进行精准调控。该平台接入光伏、储能、配电、暖通空调、照明、充电桩等能源设施，实现对整个园区的优化能源管理。其中，eStorage 智

慧储能小屋解决方案，涵盖配电和控制设备，通过与智慧能源管理系统 ZEE600 调控管理，有效平衡光伏波动，提高光伏的本地消纳率；其中构建的直流微电网为光储直柔技术的广泛应用提供有效示范。

ABB 厦门工业中心的电力系统对接至国网厦门供电公司虚拟电厂平台，通过能源管理系统自主调控的需求侧响应，形成"源荷互动"，有力支持新型电力系统建设。

分布式屋顶光伏配电模块、智慧储能模块、楼宇负荷和充电桩有序充电管理等均为模块化的解决方案。这使得 ABB 厦门工业中心的解决方案易于在其他场地复制，减少了安装时间和项目复杂性。这些打包解决方案和中低压配电设备皆为中国本地生产。

第十五章　中国电子信息产业对外投资报告 [1]

电子信息产业是中国重要的支柱产业。2023 年，面对复杂的国内外环境和低迷的市场周期压力，电子信息产业生产恢复向好，出口降幅收窄。与此同时，电子信息产业加快"出海"步伐，2023 年中国电子信息产业对外绿地投资为 408.5 亿美元，比 2022 年增长了 132.8%；电子信息产业跨境并购金额为 180.7 亿美元，比 2022 年增长了 38.8%。

一、2023 年中国电子信息产业对外开放推进情况

（一）生产和效益稳步回升，夯实对外开放合作基础

2023 年，中国规模以上电子信息制造业增加值同比增长 3.4%。2022-2023 两年同期平均增长 5.5%，信息传输、软件和信息技术服务业增加值增长 11.9%，两年同期平均增长 12%，生产稳步恢复。2023 年，电子信息产业收入规模比上年增长 4.5%。软件和信息技术服务业累计完成业务收入 12.3 万亿元，同比增长 13.4%；软件业利润总额 1.5 万亿元，同比增长 13.6%，增速较上年同期提高 7.9 个百分点，主营业务利润率提高 0.1 个百分点至 9.2%，行业效益逐步增长。中国电子信息产业生产和效益逐步恢复，为企业"走出去"奠定了坚实的产业基础。

---

① 中国电子信息产业发展研究院关兵、陈禄平、杨济菡、高雅供稿。

（二）构建现代化产业体系，提升产业国际竞争力

2023 年，中国电子信息产业的产业结构进一步优化，推动关键原材料、核心零部件和高端设备的发展，促进产业链上中下游融通创新、贯通发展，提升产业链供应链韧性。2023 年，手机产量 15.7 亿台，同比增长 6.9%；集成电路产量 3514 亿块，同比增长 6.9%；软件产品收入 2.9 万亿元，同比增长 11.1%；信息技术服务收入 8.1 万亿元，同比增长 14.7%，其中，云服务、大数据服务共实现收入 1.2 万亿元，同比增长 15.4%；集成电路设计收入 3069 亿元，同比增长 6.4%；电子商务平台技术服务收入 1.2 万亿元，同比增长 9.6%。电子信息产业体系持续优化，对提升产业国际竞争力、推动产业对外合作具有重要意义。

（三）"走出去"步伐加快，全球化布局能力提升

一方面，电子信息产业出口仍然低迷。受国际复杂形势以及产业周期影响，2023 年，规模以上电子信息制造业出口交货值同比下降 6.3%，比同期工业降幅大 2.4 个百分点；软件业务出口小幅下滑，2023 年软件业务出口 514.2 亿美元，同比下降 3.6%。其中，软件外包服务出口同比增长 5.4%。另一方面，电子信息产业加快"出海"步伐。2023 年，中国电子信息企业对外绿地投资为 408.5 亿美元，比 2022 年增长了 132.8%；电子信息产业跨境并购金额为 180.7 亿美元，比 2022 年增长了 38.8%。

（四）政策护航产业稳增长，推进对外开放深化

电子信息制造业规模总量大、产业链条长、涉及领域广，是稳定工业经济增长的重要领域。2023 年工业和信息化部等部门出台《电子信息制造业 2023-2024 年稳增长行动方案》，提出"稳住外贸基本盘，提升行业开放合作水平"。一方面，稳定出口市场，从优化出口产品结构、打造品牌国际竞争力、开展跨境电商业务等方面提出具体

措施，深挖国际市场潜力。另一方面，积极开展国际交流合作，鼓励外资企业在我国扩大电子信息领域投资，建立与有关国家（地区）间常态化交流合作机制，推动国际产能和应用合作进程。

二、2023 年中国电子信息产业对外投资基本情况

（一）电子信息产业 [①] 对外绿地投资情况

一是从总体上看，2023 年，面对国内外复杂的经济形势，中国电子信息企业积极"走出去"，通过全球化布局推动产业发展。据 fDI markets 数据库的数据分析，2023 年中国电子信息产业对外绿地投资为 408.5 亿美元。

二是从区域分布看，绿地投资集中度较高，主要投向新兴经济体。2023 年中国对外绿地投资最大目的地是越南，其次是摩洛哥、沙特、土耳其、马来西亚等国家。数据统计显示，前十大投资目的地占中国电子信息产业对外绿地投资额的 87.0%，表明中国电子信息产业绿地投资目的地具有较高的集中度，主要集中在新兴市场和发展中国家。

三是从投资领域和企业看，2023 年中国电子信息产业对外绿地投资领域涵盖了终端产品、电子零组件等十个领域。从投资企业看，中国电子信息产业对外绿地投资主体也较为集中在少数大型企业。前十大对外绿地投资企业占总投资额的 63.4%，大型企业在推动产业国际化方面发挥着主导作用。

（二）2023 年电子信息产业跨境并购情况

2023 年，电子信息产业跨境并购保持较快增长态势。根据 Orbis M&A 数据库计算，2023 年，中国电子信息产

[①] 根据 fDI markets 数据库分类进行归纳，电子信息产业包括电子组件、半导体、通信产品、消费电子、软件和 IT 服务业五类。

业跨境并购金额为 180.7 亿美元。从区域分布看，中国电子信息企业的跨境并购活动集中在少数经济体，如开曼群岛、新加坡等经济体。前五大目标国的并购金额超过 170 亿美元，占中国企业跨境并购总金额的 92%。从产业分布看，信息服务业是跨境并购的首选领域，2023 年跨国并购金额为 168.3 亿美元，占总并购金额的比重为 93.1%，其他电子信息产品的比重不足 7%，呈现行业高度集中态势。

三、中国电子信息产业对外投资模式和典型经验

（一）通过产品和模式创新，积极拓展全球市场

一是以成熟的产品为基础，通过收购提升品牌打开海外市场。拥有成熟的产品是企业出海参与国际市场竞争的前提。2017 年 8 月海外上线之前，TikTok 的原型"抖音"已在国内市场上线运行一年多，通过"敏捷开发、小步快跑"的迭代风格，逐渐形成了相对领先的技术架构和精细化的运营体系，是一款性能稳定、用户体验流畅的成熟产品。2018 年，字节跳动通过收购 Musical.ly 帮助 TikTok 快速进入北美市场，加速国际扩展。收购之后，TikTok 通过将 Musical.ly 品牌与自身品牌相结合，进一步提升了其在全球范围内的品牌认知度。整合 Musical.ly 的技术和内容，丰富了 TikTok 平台上的内容库，增强用户黏性，并吸引更多用户加入。截至 2024 年 4 月，TikTok 全球下载量已超过 49.2 亿次，月活跃用户数达 15.82 亿人，成为全球最受欢迎的短视频平台之一。

二是复制成熟的发展路径，打造 C2M 模式聚焦海外市场。2022 年 9 月创立至今，拼多多集团的海外分支 Temu 已经将业务版图拓展至全球 50 多个国家和地区。一方面，Temu 的成功很大程度上源于拼多多在国内电商市场成功经验的复制，核心是采取低价战略。与拼多多相似，Temu 也主打性价比战略，其商品定价集中在

0.09~20 美元之间，部分商品价格甚至低至 1 美分，提供免费退货服务，29 美元及以上的订单提供免费送货服务。另一方面，Temu 打造的 C2M（客户对制造商）模式，创新了电商零售的商业和营销模式，极大限度减少中间环节。在海外，像亚马逊、eBay 等电商巨头，其商品大多来自第三方卖家或经销商，Temu 的 C2M 模式绕过经销商这个中间商，让中国的供应商能直接面对海外消费者。平台承担从推广、仓储、物流到配送和售后的所有环节，极大减轻了商家的运营负担，保障制造商轻松出海。

（二）通过供应链出海与品牌提升，实现全球化布局

一是从产品出海到供应链出海。中国家电出海，已经从最初追求出口订单和贴牌生产的时代，跨越到部分企业实现海外本土化生产和运营的时代，正在逐步成为全球家电产业的引领者。例如，美的集团在全球化布局中逐渐从传统的"中国供全球，海外做补充"的模式演化成"中国供全球，区域供区域"的全球发展模式。这种出海模式的特征是在管理模式和人才培养上进行对外输出，在海外制造基地大力推广国内精益制造体系和培育海外精益人才，制造端不再依靠国内。目前，美的在海外设有 20 个研发中心和 18 个主要生产基地，海外员工约 3 万人，结算货币达 22 种。再如，创维集团旗下的海外业务已实现本地化人员配置、供应链、生产制造、测试品控、销售供应、售后服务的全流程标准化，形成了全球可管可控的专业服务能力。

二是多品牌、多板块进行全球化布局。多品牌建设、多板块发展在企业全球化战略中具有重要意义，有利于企业适应不同市场需求，分散风险，提升竞争力，推动创新。在 50 多年的发展历程中，美的集团通过整合全球资源，已形成东芝、美的、Comfee 三个全品类品牌，以及开利、Eureka 等 13 个细分品类专业品牌。业务除针对消费者的智能家居及各类家电外，还包括智能家居、工业技

术、楼宇科技、机器人与自动化、数字化创新五大板块。海尔智家在2005年开启全球化品牌战略以来，实现"海尔、卡萨帝、Leader、GE Appliances、Fisher&Paykel、AQUA、Candy"七大世界级品牌布局与全球化运营，业务涵盖六大洲共200多个国家和地区，在全球建立十大研发中心。在品牌全球化拓展道路上，中国企业也逐渐向产业链高端延伸，以创新科技实力及引用户。例如，海信自主研发、在南非率先上市的"生活链接"智能控制平台，通过集合人工智能及物联网等相关技术，为用户提供更智能、便捷、节能的家电产品和解决方案。

（三）通过本地化合作，与海外市场共创共赢

一是积极与本地政府和非政府组织合作，推动人才培养，开展数字基础设施建设。一方面，企业在出海过程中，积极与当地合作进行人才培养。例如，中兴与埃塞俄比亚政府合作，建立了多个通信技术培训中心，为当地培养了大量的通信技术人才；中兴与印度多个IT分校合作，成立了联合培训和研究项目，专注于通信技术的研究与人才培养，为中兴通讯在印度市场培养了一大批技术人才。另一方面，企业积极与非政府部门合作进行网信基础设施建设，推动互联网普及应用。例如，中兴通讯与泰国运营商合作，建设了东南亚最大的5G网络；与巴西多家电信运营商合作，参与了巴西全国范围内的4G网络建设；华为支持南非建成非洲首个5G商用网络。

二是与当地企业建立广泛的合作关系，实现互利共赢。一方面，通过建立合资公司实现资源共享、优势互补。光伏企业在出海过程中，通过与本地企业建立合资公司，以更好地适应当地市场。例如，晶科能源的子公司晶科中东与沙特阿拉伯公共投资基金PIF的子公司RELC以及VI在沙特阿拉伯总投资约9.35亿美元，共同成立了一家合资企业，用于建设10GW高效电池及组件项目。这种合作模式有助于光伏企业在中东市场建立更稳固的立

足点，并推动该地区可再生能源行业的发展。另一方面，与当地企业合作，共同推广本土文化和品牌。例如，Tik Tok 与美国全国零售联合会（NRF）合作推出了品牌专区，与零售商合作展示它们的产品和品牌故事。通过跨境电商和内容平台，字节跳动帮助当地中小企业和个体商户拓展了市场，增加了企业收入和就业机会。欧洲牛津经济学院的报告显示，欧洲包括法国、德国等五国的大量中小企业通过 Tik Tok 进行市场拓展，2023 年为欧洲经济贡献了 48 亿欧元，并支撑了 5.1 万个就业岗位。

（四）通过深耕当地市场，强化海外业务拓展

一是充分尊重与适配当地文化。OPPO 在出海时不强调国家属性，而是充分尊重和适配当地市场文化。一方面，在团队方面进行本地化配置，聘用海外本土市场的高管及员工。OPPO 在印尼和泰国市场的品牌运营管理人员、旗舰店工作人员以及工厂员工都是本地人，以此来确保运营方式的有效性。另一方面，在产品侧进行本土化设计创新。在东南亚市场，OPPO 针对年轻人热爱自拍且擅长社交的特性对产品设计和宣传进行了调整；在印度市场，OPPO 对 ColorOS 7 进行了本土化改进，将其与印度的 DigiLocker 平台结合，以方便用户在出行时使用手机进行身份验证；在欧洲市场，针对用户喜欢使用后置摄像头的习惯，对产品进行了适配性调整，专注提升后置摄像头的使用体验，推出了首个具备物理级防抖功能的摄像头，使手机在运动等特殊场景下也能保持稳定表现，以便更快适应当地市场。

二是深度推进本土化创新，构建良好生态系统。坚持本土化创新是传音控股成功的关键。传音控股在进入非洲市场时，深入了解当地用户的需求和偏好，例如，推出了专门针对非洲市场的手机，配备了较大容量的电池和多 SIM 卡槽，以应对非洲电力供应不稳定和多运营商使用的情况；进行防水防腐设计，开发针对黑肤色优化的相机

技术，增强照片效果等。传音控股在加速非洲智能手机普及的过程中，也积极构建良好的生态，围绕非洲主流操作系统传音 OS 开发了应用商店、广告分发平台、大数据服务平台以及手机管家等应用程序，还同国内互联网公司网易、腾讯等进行出海战略合作，孵化移动互联网产品。

四、中国电子信息产业对外投资合作趋势展望

一是从"制造"到"智造"，企业出海力量趋于多元。中国企业出海正在经历从消费电子等劳动密集型产品出口，逐步转向光伏、锂电池等技术密集型产品的升级之路，资金和技术含量日益提升，实现向全球输出"中国制造"转向"中国智造"。

二是从制造业企业到互联网企业，企业出海生态趋于多元。中国企业出海正从手机、笔记本等智能终端设备产品加工，逐步转向从产品向服务体验、跨境电商、本地化体验的提升转变，持续提升"中国体验"和"中国品牌"价值。产业出海也正从单独行动逐步向产业链上下游企业"抱团"出海转变。

三是从欧美市场到"一带一路"共建国家，企业出海市场趋于多元。东南亚等周边国家是电子信息企业出海的首选地区，是中国主要的投资伙伴。随着国内外形势的变化，企业出海的市场日益多元化，一方面为规避贸易壁垒，北美、欧洲等发达市场正成为大企业出海的重要目的地；另一方面，为获得更多市场和资源，南美、非洲、中东地区也正在成为中国企业出海的"新蓝海"。

四是从"出海产品化"到"出海数字化"，平台和市场趋于多元化。随着新一轮科技革命和产业变革的推进，新技术逐步向制造业渗透应用，"新业态""新模式""新产品"不断涌现，推动中国企业出海形式从单纯制造型逐渐向数字化、融合型迈进。工业互联网、物联网、人工智能等新兴技术与消费电子、移动游戏、跨境电商等领域的融合，将为企业出海注入更多新动能。

第十六章　商贸流通业对外投资实现提质升级 [①]

近年来，全球投资环境发生深刻变化，投资保护主义抬头，全球产业链和供应链遭受冲击。中国商贸流通业积极应对挑战，紧抓全球投资发展机遇，发挥流通产业服务优势作用，积极稳妥推进对外投资，不断优化投资结构、提高对外投资质量，对畅通国内循环和国际循环，构建新发展格局形成有力支撑。

一、中国商贸流通业对外投资情况

商贸流通业是指商品流通和为商品流通提供服务的产业，按国民经济行业分类，主要包括批发和零售业，住宿和餐饮业，交通运输、仓储和邮政业。中国商贸流通业对外投资情况如下。

（一）对外投资规模稳步增长

从投资存量看（见图 16-1），中国商贸流通业对外投资存量自 2013 年的 1208.23 亿美元，增长到 2023 年的 5300.10 亿美元，年均增速达到 17.86%。商贸流通业对外投资存量在全行业中的占比较为稳定，2020—2023 年，占比在 16% 左右。

从投资流量看（见图 16-2），我国商贸流通业对外投资流量自 2013 年的 180.36 亿美元，增长到 2023 年的 482.10 亿美元，年均增速为 11.54%。商贸流通业对外投资流量自 2018 年以来呈现稳步回升态势，2023 年达到近

---

① 国务院发展研究中心市场经济研究所黄千员供稿。

年来的峰值，2023 年商贸流通业对外投资相对于 2022 年增长约 120 亿美元，增长 33.1%。

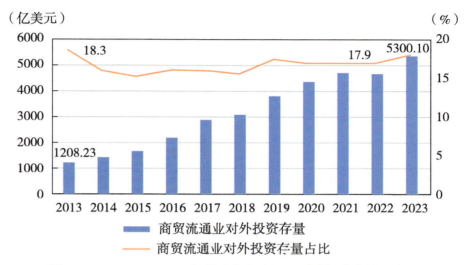

图 16-1　2013—2023 年我国商贸流通业对外投资存量及占比

资料来源：商务部、国家统计局、国家外汇管理局：《2023 年度中国对外直接投资统计公报》，中国商务出版社 2024 年版。

图 16-2　2013—2023 年我国商贸流通业对外投资流量及占比

资料来源：商务部、国家统计局、国家外汇管理局：《2023 年度中国对外直接投资统计公报》，中国商务出版社 2024 年版。

（二）对外投资流向较为集中

中国商贸流通业对外直接投资目的地较为集中，2023 年批发和零售业对外直接投资主要投向中国香港、东盟、欧盟和美国，占比分别为 70.71%、12.39%、4.46%、3.17%（见图 16-3）。

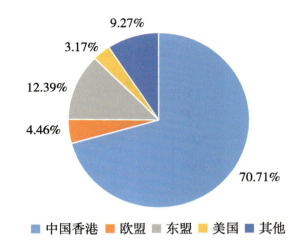

图 16-3　2023 年批发和零售业对外投资流向分布

资料来源：商务部、国家统计局、国家外汇管理局：《2023 年度中国对外直接投资统计公报》，中国商务出版社 2024 年版。

2023 年交通运输、仓储和邮政业对中国香港、东盟、美国的投资占比分别为 65.02%、16.49%、1.39%（见图 16-4）。

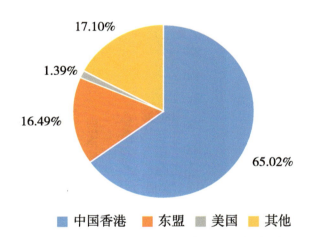

图 16-4　2023 年交通运输、仓储和邮政业对外投资流向分布

资料来源：商务部、国家统计局、国家外汇管理局：《2023 年度中国对外直接投资统计公报》，中国商务出版社 2024 年版。

（三）批发和零售业对外投资规模大，占比高，增速放缓

从全行业对外投资存量看，批发和零售业对外投资规模大，仅次于租赁和商务服务业，位居第二位。2013 年到 2023 年，批发和零售业对外投资存量自 876.48 亿美

元,增长到 4214 亿美元,在商贸流通业对外投资存量中的占比,自 72.54% 增长到 79.51%。从流量看,批发和零售业对外投资自 2013 年的 146.47 亿美元增加到 2023 年的 388.20 亿美元,年均增速 11.44%,投资流量在商贸流通业中的占比在 2023 年恢复至 80.52%(见表 16-1)。

表 16-1 2013—2023 年批发和零售业对外投资存量、流量及占比

年份	投资存量		投资流量	
	金额（亿美元）	占比（%）	金额（亿美元）	占比（%）
2013	876.48	72.54	146.47	81.21
2014	1029.57	74.10	182.91	81.21
2015	1219.41	74.32	192.18	80.54
2016	1691.68	78.76	208.94	84.78
2017	2264.27	79.53	263.11	86.35
2018	2326.93	76.65	122.38	83.28
2019	2955.39	78.39	194.71	65.26
2020	3453.16	80.12	229.98	81.28
2021	3695.82	79.27	281.52	78.36
2022	3615.93	78.22	211.69	69.26
2023	4214.00	79.51	388.2	80.52
年均增速（%）	19.06	1.02	11.44	−0.09

资料来源:商务部、国家统计局、国家外汇管理局:《2023 年度中国对外直接投资统计公报》,中国商务出版社 2024 年版。

(四)交通运输、仓储和邮政业对外投资稳中有降

交通运输、仓储和邮政业对外投资主要分布在水上运输、多式联运和运输代理、航空运输、管道运输等领域。从投资存量看,交通运输、仓储和邮政业对外投资仅次于批发和零售业,对外投资存量自 2013 年的 322.28 亿美元,增长到 2023 年的 1042.60 亿美元,占比自 2013 年的 26.67% 下降到 2023 年的 19.67%,年均占比下降

3.33%。从投资流量看，近年来，交通运输、仓储和邮政业对外投资有所波动，2022 年投资流量达到了 2013 年以来的最高水平，投资金额达到 150.38 亿美元，在商贸流通业中的占比达到了 30.08%，但 2023 年对外投资额为 84.40 亿元，相对于 2022 年下降了 43.88%，投资占比下降到 17.51%（见表 16-2）。

表 16-2　2013—2023 年交通运输、仓储和邮政业对外投资存量、流量及占比

年份	投资存量		投资流量	
	金额（亿美元）	占比（%）	金额（亿美元）	占比（%）
2013	322.28	26.67	33.07	18.34
2014	346.82	24.96	41.75	18.34
2015	399.06	24.32	27.27	18.38
2016	414.22	19.29	16.79	12.03
2017	547.68	19.24	54.68	6.94
2018	665.00	21.90	51.61	17.31
2019	765.34	20.30	38.80	27.52
2020	807.76	18.74	62.33	16.20
2021	917.23	19.67	122.26	21.24
2022	968.40	20.95	150.38	30.08
2023	1042.60	19.67	84.40	17.51
年均增速（%）	13.93	-3.33	10.97	-0.51

资料来源：商务部、国家统计局、国家外汇管理局：《2023 年度中国对外直接投资统计公报》，中国商务出版社 2024 年版。

（五）住宿和餐饮业对外投资规模和占比相对较小，目前对外投资有所恢复

2016 年以来，住宿和餐饮业对外投资存量保持在 40 亿～50 亿美元，投资存量占比最高不超过 2%。从投资存量看，住宿和餐饮业对外投资流量波动性较高，2023 年，

住宿和餐饮业对外投资 9.5 亿美元，相对于 2022 年大幅增长，在商贸流通业中的投资占比自 2022 年 0.66% 增长到 2023 年的 1.97%。2023 年住宿和餐饮业对外投资存量增长到 43.50 亿美元（见表 16-3）。

表 16-3 2013—2023 年住宿和餐饮业对外投资存量、流量及占比

年份	投资存量		投资流量	
	金额（亿美元）	占比（%）	金额（亿美元）	占比（%）
2013	9.47	0.78	0.82	0.08
2014	13.07	0.94	2.45	0.46
2015	22.33	1.36	7.23	1.08
2016	41.94	1.95	16.25	3.19
2017	35.13	1.23	−1.85	6.72
2018	44.04	1.45	13.54	−0.59
2019	49.20	1.31	6.04	7.22
2020	49.26	1.14	1.18	2.52
2021	49.10	1.05	2.69	0.40
2022	38.32	0.83	0.14	0.66
2023	43.50	0.82	9.5	1.97
年均增速（%）	18.45	0.51	31.26	43.54

资料来源：商务部、国家统计局、国家外汇管理局：《2023 年度中国对外直接投资统计公报》，中国商务出版社 2024 年版。

二、商贸流通业对外投资主要特征

（一）对外投资结构不断优化，投资质量提升

批发和零售业对外投资占比稍有下降，目前占比保持在 80% 左右；交通运输、仓储和邮政业近十年对外投资波动起伏，目前投资占比在 17% 左右；住宿和餐饮对外投资占比大幅提升，从 2013 年的 0.08% 提升到 2023 年

的 1.97%（见图 16-5）。商贸流通业各子行业对外投资结构持续调整。相对于 2022 年，2023 年批发和零售业在中国香港、欧盟、美国的投资占比在上升，而在东盟的投资占比则下降了 7.5 个百分点。2023 年，交通运输、仓储和邮政业对中国香港投资占比虽依然位居首位，但相对于 2022 年的 81.01% 下降了 15.61 个百分点；对东盟投资占比，则从 2022 年的不到 1%，上升到 2023 年的 16.59%，2023 年对欧盟投资占比呈现负增长（见表 16-4）。

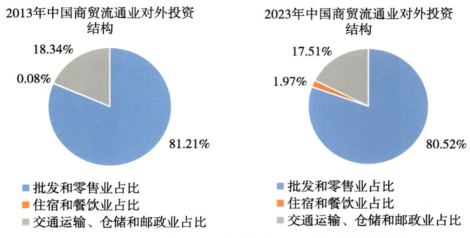

图 16-5　2013 年与 2023 年商贸流通业对外投资结构变化

资料来源：根据历年《中国对外直接投资统计公报》整理。

表 16-4　2022 年与 2023 年商贸流通业投资流向占比变化

	批发零售投资流向占比		交通运输、仓储和邮政投资流向占比	
	2023 年	2022 年	2023 年	2022 年
中国香港	70.71%	64.14%	65.40%	81.01%
欧盟	4.46%	3.05%	−0.62%	1.49%
东盟	12.39%	19.84%	16.59%	0.99%
美国	3.17%	2.78%	1.40%	1.80%
其他	9.27%	10.19%	17.20%	14.71%

资料来源：商务部、国家统计局、国家外汇管理局：《2023 年度中国对外直接投资统计公报》，中国商务出版社 2024 年版。

（二）海外物流基础设施投资与运营并重

我国商贸流通企业在全球范围内加强港口、航空枢纽等海外物流基础设施投资建设，并加强相关设施运营活动。以招商局、中远海运为代表的中央企业拓展到全球100多个国家和地区，覆盖全球主要区域近2000个港口，年度货运量超过13亿吨。按照权益吞吐量计算，招商港口和中远海运港口在全球集装箱码头运营商中，分别排名第二位和第三位，两家企业在全球集装箱码头市场中的占有率达到12.6%（见表16-5）。

表 16-5 2023 年全球集装箱码头运营商排名

运营商	权益吞吐量（百万TEU）	增长率（%）	全球市场占有率（%）
PSA 国际	62.6	4.6	7.2
招商港口	55.0	8.7	6.4
中远海运港口	53.8	1.4	6.2
APMT	48.9	−1.2	5.6
DP world	44.3	−4.7	5.1
和记港口	43.0	−4.6	5.0
MSC	42.3	10.3	4.9

资料来源：德鲁里《全球集装箱码头运营商年度回顾与预测》（2024/25）。

（三）跨境电商＋海外仓新模式发展迅速，全球化端到端配送物流体系不断完善

跨境电商成为我国外贸增长的新引擎，海外仓作为跨境电商海外物流重要节点，投资建设进入"快车道"。商务部数据显示，目前我国已建设海外仓超2500个、面积超3000万平方米，其中，专注于服务跨境电商的海外仓超1800个，面积超2200万平方米。海外仓建设投资打通跨境电商"最后一公里"，提高了物流服务效率。例如，

物流平台菜鸟网络在全球 18 个国家及地区运营了超 80 万平方米海外仓，广泛覆盖欧洲、亚太地区及北美，配送时效实现海外仓所在国 3 日达、泛欧洲 7 日达，美国 3—7 日达。海外仓提供仓储、联动配送等本土化服务外，同时也具有营销、市场数据采集、海外消费市场洞察等综合功能，为中国企业更好服务全球消费市场提供支撑。

（四）形成一批国际流通战略支点城市

围绕构建新发展格局，推动形成内畅外联的现代流通网络，一批流通发展基础好、辐射带动能力强的城市，成为高效衔接国内外市场的国际流通战略支点城市。在 102 个现代流通战略支点城市布局建设名单中，北京、上海、天津、广州、深圳、厦门等 24 个城市，被列为综合型流通支点城市。例如，福建省厦门市，充分利用经济特区、海上合作战略支点城市以及综合改革试点等优势政策，持续深化改革开放，将供应链服务产业打造为支柱型产业之一，外贸进出口占福建省近一半，外贸综合竞争力居全国第 11 位、福建首位。厦门拥有供应链服务企业超 2.3 万家，3 家龙头供应链服务企业 2023 年总营收超过 1.5 万亿元。2023 年，厦门市进口大宗商品规模增长 33.7%，高于全国 18.5 个百分点，煤炭、花岗岩等进口规模全国第一，国外进口粮食、外销粮食年均增长率均达 15%，成为重要的大宗商品配置中心。2023 年，厦门对台海运快件量达1585 万件，增长 1.7 倍；新批台资项目数、实际使用台资分别增长 64% 和 408%，成为对台物流枢纽和经贸中心。

（五）流通业国际竞争力不断增强

从流通企业国际竞争力看，在 2024 年《财富》世界500 强中，中国大陆有 16 家流通企业上榜，其中京东集团、阿里巴巴、中国邮政、厦门建发进入前 100 名（见表16-6）。上榜商贸流通企业总营收达到 1.2 万亿美元。从物流运输能力看，海运作为世界贸易主要运输方式，我国海运运力位居世界前列。截至 2022 年底，我国海运船队运力规模达 3.7 亿载重吨，较十年前增长一倍，船队规模跃居世界第二。从流通品牌国际影响力看，在英国品牌评估机构"品牌金融"（Brand Finance）发布的 2024 "全球物流品牌价值 25 强"排行榜中，顺丰集团、中国邮政、京东物流等上榜，分别位列第 7 位、第 8 位和第 16 位。

表 16-6 2024 世界 500 强中国大陆流通企业名单

企业名称	排名	营收（百万美元）	行业
京东集团	47	153217.4	零售
阿里巴巴	70	131337.9	零售
中国邮政	83	112778.5	邮政业
厦门建发	85	110665.6	贸易
中粮集团	106	97765.1	贸易
厦门国贸	142	85818.8	贸易
物产中大	150	81952.4	贸易
厦门象屿	187	69286.9	贸易
中远海运	267	53929.6	运输及物流
浙江交通集团	330	45772	运输及物流
美团	384	39092.5	零售
山东高速集团	412	36502.4	运输及物流
顺丰控股	415	36502.4	运输及物流
海亮集团	429	39286.9	贸易
拼多多	442	34981.1	零售
中国航油	483	32984.2	贸易

资料来源：2024 年《财富》世界 500 强排行榜。

三、趋势展望

（一）产业间协同走出去

稳定、高效的流通体系是畅通国内国际双循环、推动对外投资合作高质量发展的重要基础。随着我国制造业、采矿业、跨境电商等行业加快国际化布局，商贸流通作为生产性服务业，进一步加强与农业、制造业、跨境电商等产业深度融合，以服务产业国际化，充分发挥行业间、行业内比较优势，在对外投资中实现协作共赢。例如，随着新能源产业发展，一些商贸物流企业积极打造国际资源供应链，实现"商贸物流业＋矿业"深度融合，提供全流程供应链服务。

（二）完善国际商贸物流网络

充分发挥商贸流通链接国内外市场的作用，通过加强对外投资合作，实现补短板、强弱项，不断提升国际流通效率，持续优化国际商贸流通网络布局，增强商贸流通业国际化服务能力。加快"两沿十廊"国际物流大通道建设，对接区域全面经济伙伴关系协定（RCEP）等，强化服务共建"一带一路"的多元化国际物流通道辐射能力。大力发展铁海联运、江海联运、国际铁路快线等运输模式，完善全球陆海联运通道体系。构建互联互通的全球大宗商品物流运输体系，加强全球物流运输合作，完善大宗商品端到端全程物流服务体系，提升服务于资源开采、仓储、运输、通关等多个环节的能力，完善大宗商品国际物流运输走廊。围绕东南亚、非洲、南美等重点区域市场，加强重点港口、仓储等交通枢纽建设，提升海外属地化服务保障能力。

（三）扩大商贸流通数字领域对外投资合作

提升商贸流通业数字化水平，通过并购、参股、增资等方式，增强流通新技术对外投资，提升东道国商贸流通数字基础设施互联互通水平，助力东道国商贸流通数字化转型。增强对海外消费市场洞察能力，培育发展国际商贸流通新技术新业态新模式，更好满足国际市场消费需求，带动促进我国对外贸易高质量发展。对全球贸易多元化基础设施、供应链流程实施数字化升级改造，提升国际商流、物流数字化水平，进一步推广和普及电子提单，提升国际贸易效率。推动出海消费端平台和国内产业端平台协同，通过新建、并购、参股、增资等方式建立海外分销中心、展示中心，加强对跨境电子商务综合服务平台投资建设，鼓励电商平台带动智慧物流、移动支付等产业链上下游出海。

（四）持续增强绿色低碳领域对外投资

商贸流通业作为先导性与基础性产业，其绿色低碳转型不仅直接影响经济社会全面绿色转型的成效，对整个产业链供应链绿色低碳转型具有重要作用。商贸流通业在对外投资中，紧抓全球绿色低碳转型机遇，加强绿色低碳领域相关布局，持续增强商贸流通业国际竞争力。加强绿色航运投资，在清洁能源和高效能技术领域增强对外投资合作。对海外运营的船舶、港口实施绿色化改造投资，在全球范围内积极推广和建设零碳智慧港口，提升商贸流通业基础设施绿色化水平，打造国际绿色物流走廊。加大对绿色产品和技术国际投资，并在全球范围内推广应用，增强绿色采购、绿色包装投资，协同推进绿色供应链管理。

后 记

　　《中国双向投资报告2024》是在国务院发展研究中心隆国强副主任指导下，由中国国际投资贸易洽谈会组织委员会、国务院发展研究中心信息中心与对外经济研究部联合撰写。其中，第一章由全球经济特区联盟主席、世界投资大会执委会主席詹晓宁和南开大学葛顺奇教授共同撰写，第二至五章由国务院发展研究中心团队撰写。感谢南京大学自贸区综合研究院李锋研究员等专家给予的研究支持。第六至十章（地区篇和开放平台篇），我们选取在双向投资中成效显著、具有特色的地区和开放平台，由上海市商务委、浙江省商务厅、海南省商务厅、北京市商务局、投洽（厦门）会展有限公司供稿。第十一、十二章（协会篇），我们邀请上海市外商投资协会、上海外商投资咨询有限公司、中资企业（新加坡）协会和德勤中国/德勤东南亚等分别就跨国公司在华投资新趋势、中国企业在新加坡投资分享双向投资合作共赢的企业与国别案例。第十三至十六章（产业篇），我们邀请国务院发展研究中心金融研究所、中国外商投资企业协会投资性公司工作委员会、中国电子信息产业发展研究院、国务院发展研究中心市场经济研究所的专家学者，分别就金融高水平开放、在华跨国公司积极投身ESG实践、中国电子信息产业对外投资、商贸流通业对外投资等方面最新进展进行深入分析。感谢商务部外国投资管理司、对外投资和经济合作司、投资促进事务局等单位给予的研究支持！感谢中国商务出版社的支持！我们对为此报告编写、校对、出版等付出辛勤努力的所有专家和工作人员表示诚挚感谢！由于水平有限，报告难免有不足之处，敬请读者指正。

2024 年 9 月

China Two-way Investment Report 2024

China International Fair for Investment and Trade Organizing Committee

Information Center of the Development Research Center of the State Council

Department of Foreign Economic Research at the Development Research Center of the State Council

Translator:

Zhang Gaoping   Chen Xu   et al

General Report

Chapter 1　Global FDI Trends and Prospects

Due to factors such as the pandemic crisis, global economic downturn, geopolitical tensions, ongoing regional conflicts, and trade disputes, international investment....globally has remained sluggish in recent years, exhibiting seven major characteristics. In the short term, global cross-border investment will remain at relatively low levels. Fromthe medium-to long-term perspective, the global industrial chain is significantly adjusted, with international investment and production expected to shift in ten key directions. Meanwhile, sustainable investment, digital transformation, the rise of emerging markets, strengthened regional cooperation, and increased industrial resilience and innovation will present new opportunities for countries worldwide.

I. Global FDI Trends

There are seven major characteristics of global foreign direct investment (FDI) in 2023-2024.

A. Persistent Low Levels in Investment Volume

In 2023, global FDI flows experienced an decline of 10%, dropping to USD 1.3 trillion. Even with the significant reversals in the three major transit FDI countries (the Netherlands, Luxembourg, and Ireland) factored into the global total, global FDI still decreased by 2% compared to 2022, reaching nearly the lowest level in a decade. As of now, global FDI growth in 2024 is sluggish and remains at a low level (see Figure 1-1).

B. FDI in Developed Economies at Historical Lows

In 2023, FDI inflows into developed economies increased by 9%, representing only a modest rebound after a sharp decline and constituting non-substantial growth. This increase was primarily driven by significant reversals in the three major transit FDI countries, where net inflows shifted from a negative USD 106 billion to a positive USD 16 billion. Notably, the European Union's FDI inflows dropped from USD 627 billion in 2019 to outflows of USD 85 billion. In 2023, European Union's FDI inflows reached USD 58 billion, which was comparable to Africa's total and only around 10% of Asia's FDI and one-third of China's (see Figure 1-2). Meanwhile, U.S.'s FDI inflows fell by 6% to USD 311 billion, with cross-border mergers and acquisitions plummet by 40% to USD 81 billion, only half the average level of the past decade.

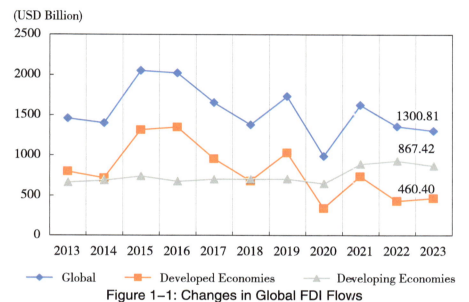

Figure 1–1: Changes in Global FDI Flows

Source: UNCTAD FDI database.

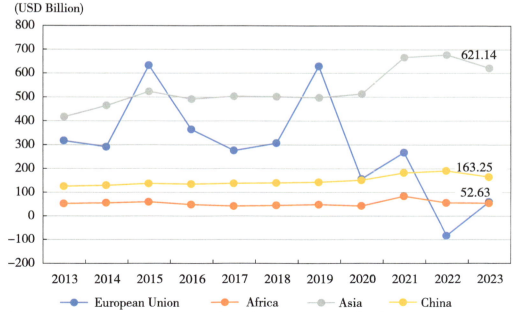

Figure 1–2: Changes in FDI Inflows by Major Global Regions, 2013—2023

Source: UNCTAD FDI database.

C. Weakening Growth Momentum in Developing Economies' FDI

FDI in developing economies decreased by 7% to USD 867 billion, reversing the growth trend of the past few years. Asia, as the main driver of FDI growth in developing countries, saw FDI decline by 8%. Similarly, FDI in Africa and Latin America dropped by 3% and 1%, respectively.

D. Recovery of Manufacturing FDI

FDI in the manufacturing sector has increased, reversing the stagnation of the past decade. This growth was mainly driven by geopolitical factors, particularly"nearshoring" and "friend-shoring". Additionally, FDI driven by technology applications contributed to this trend, including spillover effects from artificial intelligence-related technologies.

E. Significant Shifts in Sectoral FDI

According to the *Financial Times* FDI Intelligence report, global FDI in 2023 and the first half of 2024 was primarily driven by large capital-intensive businesses, especially in renewable energy, battery, and metal industries. Conversely, momentum in software and IT services weakened, dropping from 6th place in 2022 to 11th place in 2023. This marks the first time since 2013 that this sector has did not rank among the top ten FDI sectors (See Figure 1-3).

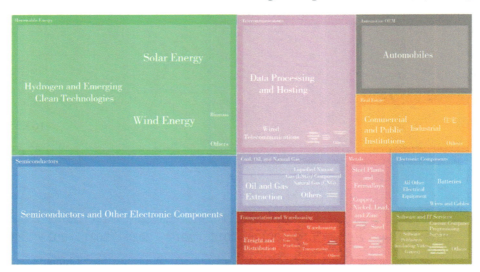

Figure 1-3: Sectoral Investment Matrix

Source: *Financial Times* FDI Intelligence.

F. Service Sector FDI Continues to Lead Global FDI Growth

The growth of cross-border investments in the service sector has been a long-term trend. Since 1990, FDI in the service sector has grown significantly every decade, increasing fivefold by 2000, fourfold by 2010, and over 50% by 2020. The growth rate of tertiary sector FDI far exceeds that of the secondary and primary sectors. Currently, service sector investments account for 72% of total FDI, while the service sector's share of global GDP is 67% (see Figure 1-4).

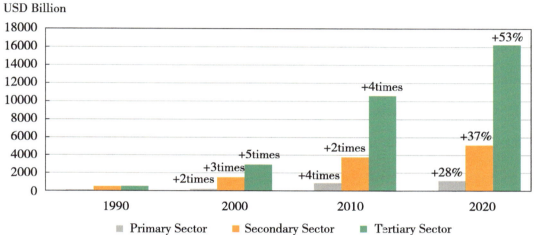

Figure 1–4: Evolution of FDI Trends in Key Sectors Over the Past 30 Years (USD billions and %)

Source: James X. Zhan, based on UNCTAD data.

G. Sovereign Funds as a New Source of FDI

The assets of public pension funds (PPFs) have surged from USD 18 trillion in 2018 to USD 23 trillion in 2023. Similarly, the assets of sovereign wealth funds (SWFs) have grown from USD 7 trillion to USD 11 trillion, bringing the total assets under management of these both types of funds to USD 34 trillion. Sovereign investors, including PPFs and SWFs, are increasingly investing in infrastructure, energy, real estate, and manufacturing.

II. Challenges and Opportunities Facing Global FDI

A. Challenges

1. Geopolitical tensions

Ongoing regional conflicts and trade disputes, particularly those involving major economies, created uncertainty and risks, making investors more cautious.

2. Economic uncertainty

Macroeconomic conditions characterized by"three highs" (high interest rates, high debt levels, and high inflation) and "three lows" (low GDP growth, low trade flows, and low productivity), along with highly volatile financial markets, present challenges to the economic environment. These factors significantly increase investment costs and reduce the attractiveness of cross-border investments.

3. Regulatory changes

Stricter regulations on foreign investment, particularly in sensitive sectors like technology and infrastructure, in major countries have complicated the investment process and increased policy risks. Additionally, policy uncertainty(stemming from elections and post-election policy adjustments in over 70 global economies) poses greater challenges for long-term investments.

4. Supply chain disruptions

Global supply chains continue to face disruptions, raising costs and logistical obstacles for companies involved in outward investment. Key global transit points in supply chains are highly vulnerable to climate change and geopolitical conflicts. Disruptions in critical shipping routes, such as the Suez Canal, Panama Canal, and the Black Sea Strait, have posed unprecedented challenges to global trade, affecting millions of people across regions. Attacks on shipping in the Red Sea have severely impacted transit through the Suez Canal, reshaping global trade routes.

5. Technological adaptation

Rapidly changing technologies require substantial investments in new technologies and skills, which could pose significant challenges, particularly for certain regions and developing countries.

B. Opportunities

1. Sustainable investment

Increasing attention to sustainable and green investments is creating significant opportunities. Governments worldwide are providing incentives for renewable energy, sustainable infrastructure, and environmentally friendly technology projects. The United Nations' coordination of the implementation of Sustainable Development Goals (SDGs) globally has also expanded the space for international investments.

2. Digital transformation

Investments in digital infrastructure, artificial intelligence, and other advanced technologies are expected to grow, with a growing trend toward continued digital transformation of enterprises.

3. Emerging markets

Regions such as Asia, Latin America, and Africa continue to attract FDI due to their growth potential and expanding consumer markets. These areas offer substantial opportunities for investors seeking to enter new markets.

4. Regional cooperation

Increasing regional cooperation and trade agreements are creating more integrated markets, reducing barriers to cross-border investments, and making it easier for investors to operate across multiple countries.

5. Resilience and innovation

Businesses are increasingly looking for investments that can enhance their resilience and innovation capabilities, including investments in automation, advanced manufacturing, and technologies that improve operational efficiency.

Overall, advances in technology, government policies, and growing global demand are expected to drive significant growth in renewable energy and digital infrastructure sectors. Addressing challenges while seizing these opportunities is crucial for countries and companies aiming to attract and benefit from FDI in the coming years. Investors should closely monitor global developments and adjust their strategies accordingly.

III. Prospects for Global FDI

A. Global FDI to Remain Sluggish in the Short Term

Global economic growth in 2024 is expected to reach 2.6%, remaining below the pre-pandemic average of 3.2% (2015-2019) for the three consecutive year (see Figure 1-5). Global trade and investment are also expected to stagnate at low levels. According to WTO data, global merchandise trade volume is projected to grow by 2.6% in 2024 (see Figure 1-6). For the past four years, global cross-border investment has lingered at low levels. Against this backdrop, global international direct investment is anticipated to remain subdued in 2024. From 2025 to 2026, global international investment is likely to rebound, but this will mainly be a restorative recovery and structural adjustment rather than expansive growth. It is unlikely to return to pre-pandemic peak levels.

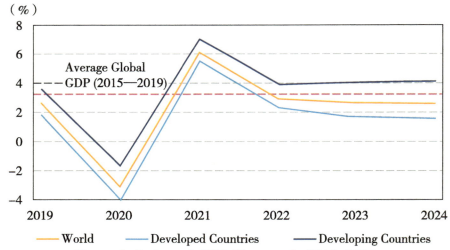

Figure 1–5: Annual GDP Changes in 2019–2024

Source: UNCTAD.

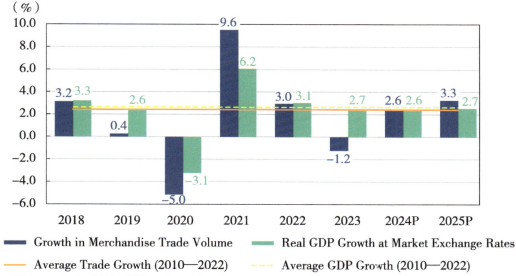

Figure 1–6: Global Merchandise Trade Volume and GDP Growth in 2018–2025

Source: WTO.

Note: Figures for 2024 and 2025 are projections. From 2010 to 2023, merchandise trade grew at an average annual rate of 2.5%, while GDP grew at an average rate of 2.7%.

B. Industries with Promising FDI Prospects

Despite global FDI remaining at low levels overall, the following industries are poised to become investment highlights, offering significant opportunities for investors seeking to capitalize on emerging trends and technologies.

1. Renewable energy

Renewable energy projects, including solar, wind, and hydropower, are expected to attract substantial FDI as the global push for sustainable development continues. This sector is critical for achieving climate goals and reducing carbon emissions.

2. Technology and digital economy

Investments in technology, particularly in fields such as artificial intelligence, cybersecurity, and digital infrastructure, are projected to grow steadily. The digital transformation of enterprises and their increasing reliance on technology are driving this trend.

3. Healthcare and biotechnology

The healthcare sector, including biotechnology and pharmaceuticals, continues to attract FDI due to ongoing advancements in medical research, drug development, and increasing demand for medical services.

4. Infrastructure

Investments in infrastructure projects, such as those in transportation, communications, and urban development, remain a priority. These investments are essential for economic growth and improving connectivity.

5. Carbon capture, utilization, and storage (CCUS)

As efforts to reduce carbon emissions intensify, the CCUS sector is becoming a significant destination for FDI. This industry offers opportunities for both environmental impact and economic development.

IV. Major Transformation of the Global Industrial Chain: Reallocation of Trade and Investment

In the medium to long term, global industrial chains are undergoing substantial structural adjustments and reorganization, influenced by three major factors: technological innovation and industrial revolutions, the wave of sustainable development, and geopolitical and economic dynamics. International investment and production are expected to shift in the following ten directions (see Table 1-1).

A. Ten Directions of Global Industrial Chain Transformation

Table 1-1: Ten Directions of Global Industrial Chain Evolution

Key Aspects	Ten Directions
Industrial Chain Reshaping	Regionalization of industrial chains
	Clustering of industries
	Digitalization and asset-light industrial chains
	Internationalization of services and integration of manufacturing
	Resilience-and security-driven diversification of industrial chains

Key Aspects	Ten Directions
Changes in Investment and Trade Models	Decline in global efficiency-driven FDI, increase in regional market-driven FDI
	Rising downward pressure on intermediate goods trade
	Transition from mass production to customized production
	Growth in FDI in infrastructure and public services
	Focus on green, blue, and circular economy investments

Source: ① Zhan J. X., Qi, F., & Wu, Q.Q. (2024). Trends and Policy Outlook for International Direct Investment Amid Global Changes, *International Economic Review*, 2024 No.2 pp.1-24.

② Zhan J. X., "GVC Transformation and a New Investment Landscape in the 2020s: Driving Forces, Directions, and a Forward-looking Research and Policy Agenda", *Journal of International Business Studies*, 69(4): 206-220, 2021. Zhan, J. X. (詹晓宁) (2021). "GVC Transformation and a New Investment Landscape in the 2020s: Driving Forces, Directions, and a Forward-looking Research and Policy Agenda. " *Journal of International Business Studies* , 2021, 69(4): 206-220.

1. Regionalization of industrial chains

Multinational corporations are reorganizing their global production networks into multiple regional and sub-regional production hubs, leading to the regionalization of global industrial chains. Regional value chains will play an increasingly prominent role in the global production system, with localized production leveraging regional resource advantages. However, regional value chains are neither closed nor exclusive, as international investments, including those from outside the region, will remain key drivers. Cooperation among regional value chains through trade and investment will continue.

2. Clustering of industries

Modern manufacturing global value chains are increasingly inclined to simplify steps and localize processes, resulting in shorter, less fragmented value chains with more concentrated value-added components, forming industrial clusters. The shortening of value chains is influenced by both regionalization and the reshoring efforts of developed economies. At the same time, distributed manufacturing, an innovative value chain model, enables globally efficient production while maintaining activity concentration. The widespread application of 3D printing and industrial digitization allows broader distribution of production while concentrating value-added activities in specific locations.

3. Digitalization and asset—light industrial chains

Large digital multinational corporations will provide digital infrastructure by digitizing the global industrial chains, leading to an asset-light industrial chain model. Furthermore, digital platforms provided by these corporations will replace traditional multinational governance models, enabling a value chain governance system driven by multiple digital platforms.

4. Internationalization of services and integration of manufacturing

Enhanced digital technologies are significantly impacting the service sector, particularly high-value-added services such as professional and business services, finance, engineering, and related marketing activities. These services will play an increasingly important role in global value chains. Driven by labor cost arbitrage, digital technologies make the service sector the new frontier for offshore outsourcing, facilitating its globalization. Traditional mid- and high-value-added services will increasingly be provided remotely from overseas. Additionally, the servicification of manufacturing also deserves attention. The interplay between services and digitization will increasingly lead to the integration of manufacturing with digital services.

5. Resilience—and security—driven diversification of industrial chains

Geopolitical and economic factors have altered perceptions of global economic integration and interdependence. Cost and efficiency are no longer the top priorities for international investment and production layouts. Meanwhile, digital technologies facilitate industrial chain diversification, though this comes at the expense of some economies of scale. Localization through reshoring, friend-shoring, and the establishment of comprehensive industrial systems are key features of current industrial chain diversification.

6. Decline in Global Efficiency—Driven FDI, Increase in Regional Market—Driven FDI

Vertical specialization within value chains has historically attracted efficiency-seeking FDI. However, with the development of technology, the erosion of labor cost advantages and the shift in digital multinational corporations' focus from fixed to intangible assets, multinationals are emphasizing market-seeking investments. These investments replicate production processes across regions to enhance market access and industrial chain resilience, driving a shift from efficiency-seeking to market-seeking FDI.

7. Rising downward pressure on intermediate goods trade

The near-shoring and localization of global industrial chains, along with geographically concentrated production processes and value-added activities, reduce cross-border trade in intermediate goods, especially cross-regional trade, which has already begun to decline and will continue to increase. With the shift from efficiency-oriented to market-oriented investments, multinational corporations will directly serve the consumer market.

8. Transition from mass production to customized production

Emerging production technologies such as 3D printing enable small-scale, localized production close to markets, reshaping traditional international production models. Advanced manufacturing supports distributed production, shifting from mass production and economies of scale to customized production and economies of scope. Additionally, the servicification of manufacturing advances customization, with manufacturers offering advanced customization services as a key component of customer-centric global value chains. Supported by big data and the Internet of Things, manufacturing servicification will have profound implications for the future trade and investment of multinational corporations.

9. Growth in FDI in infrastructure and public services

Sustainable development, global industrial chain restructuring, and the digital economy have increased demand for infrastructure investments, countries around the world are all striving to promote infrastructure investment. Policies increasingly favor foreign investment in public services such as healthcare, education, utilities, and digital infrastructure, creating new opportunities for FDI in these sectors.

10. Focus on green, blue, and circular economy investments

Global sustainable development is imperative, with green, blue, and circular economies holding significant potential for international investment. Multinational corporations are increasingly aligning their investment decisions, production processes, products, and services with sustainable development goals (SDGs). Unified ESG standards and enhanced corporate accountability are driving multinational corporations and their global supply networks to integrate sustainability into investment decisions. SDGs are becoming mainstream in investment policymaking, with strategies for investment promotion and facilitation being reoriented toward sustainable development. As these priorities gain prominence on political agendas, they will benefit from greater policy support.

B. Future International Production Landscape

Although the current trend of global industrial chains is moving toward regionalization, it does not signify the disintegration of global industrial chains. Instead, it represents a new layout at the regional level, which will significantly impact the future international investment landscape. From the recent trends in FDI flows among major global economies and regions, the following characteristics of the future international production structure can be identified:

1. Triangular dominance of China, the United States, and Europe in the global production landscape

American multinational enterprises will remain upstream in the global industrial chain in fields such as the manufacturing of computers, electronics, optical products, and high-end equipment. These enterprises will continue to decompose production stages across countries or regions, but under U.S. policy support, many stages may return to domestic or nearshore markets, strengthening control over value chains in key industries. Similarly, European multinational enterprises deeply engage in the global industrial division of labor, focusing on high-end manufacturing and services. Although foreign direct investment (FDI) inflows and outflows in Europe have declined in recent years, its participation in the global industrial chain remains among the highest worldwide. China, as the world's largest manufacturing power, possesses the most comprehensive industrial chains and strategic industrial clusters globally, continually advancing toward higher-value-added segments in global value chains and international divisions of labor. Geopolitically induced reshoring, nearshoring, and friend-shoring have exerted significant pressure and influence on China, but it remains a crucial destination for international investments, especially in high-tech sectors. In the future international production system, the three major economies—China, the United States, and the European Union—will continue to occupy core positions in the global industrial division of labor and dominate the flow of international investments.

2. Expansion of industrial chain division systems in East Asia, North America, and Western Europe

In the coming years, significant adjustments in global FDI flows will persist. Firstly, in East Asia, especially Northeast Asia (China, Japan, and South Korea), capital and traditional production capacity will shift southward, expanding into Southeast and South Asia, with a noticeable increase in FDI inflows into Association of Southeast Asian Nations (ASEAN) countries. Secondly, in North America, funds and production capacity will transfer or return from other regions to Central America and the Caribbean, forming new export-oriented industrial clusters, with Mexico as a representative example. Lastly, in Europe, the flow of capital, which had long expanded from west to east, is now reversing from east to west and extending southward to the Mediterranean coast.

In conclusion, global foreign direct investment remained subdued in 2023 and is expected to hover at low levels in 2024. A rebound in 2025—2026 is anticipated, though it will likely be a restorative recovery and structural adjustment rather than expansive growth, falling short of pre-pandemic peaks. Over the medium to long term, the global industrial chain structure will continue to undergo significant adjustments, trending toward regionalization and multipolarity, eventually forming a"triangular dominance" of China, the United States, and Europe as the three major global production systems.

Chapter 2   New Developments in China's Two-Way Investment

In recent years, despite the challenging and complex international environment and the global decline in cross-border direct investment, China has adhered to a balanced approach of "introducing FDI" and "going global". The country has made "strengthening efforts to attract and utilize foreign capital" one of the key tasks determined at the 2023 Central Economic Work Conference, continuously enhancing the facilitation of two-way investment. In 2023, China maintained its position as the world's second-largest recipient of foreign direct investment (FDI) and ramled the third globally in outbound direct investment (ODI). Two-way investment achieved steady growth in both volume and quality, with highlights.

I. Continuous Improvement of Two-Way Investment Policies

A. Introduction of Policies with Greater Efforts to Attract Foreign Investment

Utilizing foreign capital is an important aspect of China's basic national policy of opening-up. In building a new development pattern, foreign-invested enterprises play a unique bridging role in linking domestic and international dual circulation and optimizing resource allocation. At the end of 2022, the Central Economic Work Conference identified "strengthening efforts to attract and utilize foreign capital" as one of the key tasks for the year. Since 2023, China has successively launched a series of high-level opening-up and investment promotion initiatives, unprecedented in scale. These measures have further lowered the thresholds for foreign investment, enhanced the facilitation of cross-border resource flows, deepened the opening-up of the financial sector, hosted roundtable meetings for foreign-invested enterprises, and established the "Invest China" brand. These practical measures have accelerated the formation of a world-class business environment that is market-oriented, law-based, and internationalized.

1. Solid promotion of high-level opening-up

Since 2023, based on the *Foreign Investment Law of the People's Republic of China*, China has continually expanded high-standard institutional opening-up, improved the foreign investment management system, and introduced a series of policies to enhance the business environment. These include measures to expand foreign investment market access, stabilize foreign investment in manufacturing, ensure fair treatment for foreign investors, open up the service sector, encourage the establishment of research and development (R&D) centers, and align with international high-standard economic and trade rules (see Table 2-1).

The two "24 Measures" for attracting foreign investment have drawn great attention and welcome from multinational corporations. In August 2023, China's State Council has issued a statement *Regarding Further Optimizing the Foreign Investment Environment and Intensifying Efforts to Attract Foreign Investments* ("24 Measures" to Attract Foreign Investment), proposing six initiatives: enhancing the quality of foreign investment, ensuring national treatment for foreign-invested enterprises, strengthening the protection of foreign investments, improving investment facilitation, increasing fiscal and tax support, and improving foreign investment promotion methods. These initiatives aim to create a world-class business environment that is market-oriented, law-based, and internationalized, further attracting foreign investment and promoting high-level opening-up. Local governments are also encouraged to formulate supplementary measures tailored to local conditions to enhance the synergy of policies. In March 2024, the General Office of the State Council issued the *Action Plan for Steadily Advancing High-Level Opening-up and Making Greater Efforts to Attract and Utilize Foreign Investment* ("24 New Measures" to Attract Foreign Investment). While expanding market access, the plan proposes optimizing a fair competition environment, improving services for foreign-invested enterprises, and ensuring the effective implementation of related policies. It includes issuing fair competition review rules in the bidding and tendering field to eliminate local protectionism and ownership discrimination and introducing national product standards for government procurement to ensure equal treatment for products produced by both domestic and foreign-invested enterprises that meet the standards.

Accelerating the Construction of a System Aligned with International High-Standard Economic and Trade Rules. In June 2023, the State Council published an official document titled *Notice Regarding the Implementation of Several Measures to Promote Institutionalized Opening-up of Qualified Free Trade Pilot Zones and Free Trade Port in Accordance with International High Standards*. These measures propose a series of institutional innovations in six areas: promoting innovative development in goods trade, facilitating free and convenient services trade, simplifying temporary entry for business personnel, fostering the healthy development of digital trade, improving the business environment, and establishing comprehensive risk prevention and control mechanisms. These pilot measures have now been fully implemented, yielding a number of leading achievements. In December 2023, the State Council released the *General Plan for Advancing Institutional Opening-up of China (Shanghai) Pilot Free Trade Zone in Alignment with High-Standard International Economic and Trade Rules*, supporting the Shanghai Pilot Free Trade Zone in leading high-standard alignments with economic and trade rules in areas such as service trade, financial openness, and digital trade. Relevant measures are being implemented at an accelerated pace, with positive progress achieved in some fields.

Encouraging Foreign Investment in Technology Innovation Cooperation: A Key Focus of China's New Era Policies to Attract Foreign Investment. In January 2023, the General Office of the State Council forwarded the *Several Measures on Further Encouraging Foreign Investment to Establish Research and Development Centers* issued by the Ministry of Commerce and the Ministry of Science and Technology. The measures outlined 16 initiatives, including improving financial support for technological innovation, facilitating access to government projects, supporting the lawful cross-border flow of R&D data, and enhancing intellectual property enforcement. Highlights include supporting foreign investment R&D

centers in using large-scale scientific research instruments and improving the convenience of work permits for foreign personnel, creating a favorable development environment for foreign investment R&D centers to better leverage their unique advantages in global innovation resource allocation.

Table 2-1: Comprehensive Policies Issued Since 2023 to Encourage Foreign Investment in China

Publication Date	Policy Title	Issuing Authority	Key Content
July 2024	*Opinions on Strengthening Business-Finance Synergy and Making Greater Efforts to Support the High-quality Development of Cross-border Trade and Investment*	Ministry of Commerce and other departments	Stabilizing foreign trade and investment, deepening Belt and Road Initiative economic and investment cooperation
April 2024	*Three-Year Action Plan for Digital Commerce (2024—2026)*	Ministry of Commerce	Promoting digital transformation across business sectors
March 2024	*Action Plan for Steadily Advancing High-level Opening up and Making Greater Efforts to Attract and Utilize Foreign Investment*	General Office of the State Council	24 new measures to enhance foreign investment
August 2023	*Regarding Further Optimizing the Foreign Investment Environment and Intensifying Efforts to Attract Foreign Investments*	State Council	24 measures to optimize the foreign investment environment and increase foreign investment
June 2023	*Notice by State Council Regarding the Implementation of Several Measures to Promote Institutionalized Opening-up of Qualified Free Trade Pilot Zones and Free Trade Port in Accordance with International High Standards of the State Council*	State Council	Aligning with high international standards and advancing institutional opening-up
March 2023	*Notice by 17 Departments Including the Ministry Of Commerce Regarding Several Measures for Serving the Establishment of a New Development Pattern and Promoting the High-Quality Development of Border (Cross-Border) Economic Cooperation Zones*	Ministry of Commerce and 17 departments	Deepening regional opening-up

Continued Table

Publication Date	Policy Title	Issuing Authority	Key Content
January 2023	*Notice of the General Office of the State Council forwards the Ministry of Commerce and the Ministry of Science and Technology on Several Measures on Further Encouraging Foreign Investment to Establish Research and Development Centers*	Ministry of Commerce and Ministry of Science and Technology	Supporting technological innovation

Source: Compiled from publicly available information.

2. Further expansion of market access for foreign investment

Since the 18th National Congress of the Communist Party of China, building on the pilot programs in free trade zones, *Foreign Investment Law of the People's Republic of China* has established a pre-establishment national treatment and negative list management system for foreign investment. By 2021, the negative lists for foreign investment in the pilot free trade zones and nationwide were reduced to 27 items and 31 items, respectively. Restrictions on manufacturing industries were "completely eliminated" in the pilot free trade zones, while sectors such as finance, transportation, commercial logistics, and professional services were progressively opened, providing foreign enterprises with broader market opportunities. In 2023, during the opening ceremony of the Third Belt and Road Forum for International Cooperation, President Xi Jinping announced the complete removal of foreign investment restrictions in the manufacturing sector, reaffirming China's determination to expand openness.

Gradual Relaxation of Foreign Investment Access Restrictions. In March 2024, the General Office of the State Council issued the *Action Plan for Steadily Advancing High-level Opening up and Making Greater Efforts to Attract and Utilize Foreign Investment*. This plan proposed significant measures to expand market access, such as reasonably reducing the negative list for foreign investment, piloting relaxed access for foreign investment in technological innovation, and expanding the market access for foreign financial institutions in the banking and insurance sectors. Key examples include: Complete removal of foreign investment restrictions in the manufacturing sector and continued opening-up in sectors such as telecommunications and healthcare. Allowing pilot free trade zones in Beijing, Shanghai, and Guangdong to expand access for foreign-invested enterprises in fields such as the development and application of gene diagnostics and treatment technologies. Supporting eligible foreign institutions in lawfully conducting bank card clearing operations under the premise of ensuring security, efficiency, and stability.

Expansion of Pilot Programs for opening-up of the Value-Added Telecommunications Sector. China's value-added telecommunications sector has garnered significant attention from foreign enterprises due to its immense market potential. In April 2024, the Ministry of Industry and Information Technology of the People's Republic of China issued the *Pilot Program to Expand Opening-up in Value-Added Telecom Services*. This program will first be implemented in the Beijing's National Comprehensive Demonstration Zone for Expanding opening-up in the Services Sector, the Lingang New Area of the Shanghai Pilot Free Trade Zone, the Hainan Free Trade Port, and the Shenzhen Special Economic Zone. It removes foreign equity restrictions on services such as Internet Data Centers (IDC), Content Delivery Networks (CDN), Internet Service Provider (ISP), online data processing and transaction processing (excluding Internet news and information, online publishing, online audio-visual and Internet cultural operation), and certain information protection and processing services, as well as the restrictions on the proportion of foreign shares. This marks a significant breakthrough in opening-up China's telecommunications market, attracting more foreign enterprises to engage in value-added telecommunications businesses in China.

Promoting the Establishment of a Unified Market and Fair Competition. In June 2023, the State Administration for Market Regulation, National Development and Reform Commission, Ministry of Finance, and Ministry of Commerce issued the *Notice on Conducting Policies and Measures Cleanup Work that Hinders Unified Market and Fair Competition*. The notice aims to eliminate policies that obstruct market access and withdrawal and hinder the free flow of goods and factors. It fosters a more open, transparent, and orderly competitive market environment, providing a solid institutional guarantee for foreign enterprises to expand their presence in China.

3. Deepening financial sector opening-up

The opening-up of the financial sector is a critical component of high-level opening-up and is pivotal for multinational corporations' long-term strategic layouts in China. Since 2018, China has consistently advanced high-level financial opening-up, with the People's Bank of China and other financial regulatory authorities introducing more than 50 policies to open the financial sector to foreign investment. These measures have created a market-oriented, law-based, and internationalized world-class business environment, attracting more foreign investment and long-term capital to establish and expand operations in China.

The 2023 Central Financial Work Conference further emphasized advancing high-level financial opening-up, ensuring national financial and economic security, and maintaining a balance between "introducing FDI" and "going global". The conference highlighted the need to steadily expand institutional opening-up in the financial sector, improve cross-border investment and financing facilitation, and attract more foreign financial institutions and long-term capital to develop in China.

Currently, China's financial opening-up is advancing in an orderly manner across multiple areas. On the one hand, Expanding Openness in Financial Services: Restrictions on foreign ownership in banking, securities, fund management, futures, and life insurance have been completely removed. Foreign institutions are granted national treatment in areas such as credit reporting, ratings, and payments. Requirements related to shareholders' qualifications, such as asset scale and years of operation, have been relaxed. Foreign institutions' business scope has been significantly expanded, and they receive equal treatment with domestic institutions in pilot projects, such as tools supporting carbon emissions reduction. On the other hand, Orderly Opening of Capital Markets: Bond, stock, and financial derivatives markets are gradually opening to foreign participation. Mechanisms like Shanghai-Shenzhen-Hong Kong Stock Connect Programs, Mutual Recognition of Funds, Bond Connect, Shanghai-London Stock Connect, and Swap Connect have been established and continuously improved.

The QFII and RQFII quota limits have been fully removed, and the Cross-Boundary Wealth Management Connect in the Guangdong-Hong Kong-Macao Greater Bay Area has been optimized. These measures have significantly enhanced the ease of foreign participation in China's financial markets. According to the People's Bank of China, as of the end of September 2023, the total value of domestic RMB financial assets held by foreign institutions, including stocks and bonds, reached CNY 9.3 trillion. In March 2024, the *Action Plan for Steadily Advancing High-level Opening up and Making Greater Efforts to Attract and Utilize Foreign Investment* explicitly proposed expanding access for foreign financial institutions in the banking and insurance sectors, broadening their scope of participation in the domestic bond market, and advancing the Qualified Foreign Limited Partner (QFLP) pilot program for domestic investment.

4. Promoting safe and orderly cross—border data flows

With the ongoing wave of openness and innovation in the digital economy, ensuring safe and orderly cross-border data flows has become a focal point for multinational corporations. *Provisions on Regulating and Promoting Cross-Border Data Flows (Draft for Comments)* released in September 2023, the *Provisions on Promoting and Regulating Cross-Border Data Flows were published by the Cyberspace Administration of China* in March 2024. These provisions aim to promote lawful, orderly, and free cross-border data flows while ensuring data security. Key measures include: (1) Defining standards for applying for security assessments for exporting important data. (2) Specifying conditions for exemption from applying for security assessments, signing standard contracts for personal information export, and achieving personal information protection certification for data export activities. (3) Establishing a negative list system for free trade pilot zones. (4) Adjusting conditions for applying for security assessments, signing standard contracts, and achieving certification for data export activities. (5) Extending the validity period of security assessment results for data exports and allowing data processors to apply for extensions. Overall, these measures have significantly enhanced the convenience of cross-border data flows, helping reduce compliance costs for enterprises, expanding high-level openness, and receiving positive recognition from multinational corporations.

5. Continuing to build the "Invest China" brand

In the current global context of slowing economic growth, rising geopolitical risks, and intensifying competition among nations to attract investment, the complexity, severity, and uncertainty of the external environment pose challenges to China's ability to attract foreign investment. Since March 2023, the Ministry of Commerce has launched the "Investment in China Year" series of events, coordinating resources to promote regular, serialized, and diversified investment attraction initiatives. On the one hand, efforts to "Introducing FDI" investors have included comprehensive activities such as keynote forums, provincial-level promotional events, and initiatives like "CIIE Going Local" and "Multinational Corporations Visiting Local Areas. " These platforms and channels showcase investment opportunities across Chinese provinces and cities, solidifying the "Invest China" brand. On the other hand, efforts to "go global" have involved leveraging exhibition platforms, overseas commercial offices, and investment promotion agencies to support Chinese provinces and enterprises in conducting targeted promotions in overseas markets. These multi-level and multi-format activities create bridges for domestic and international investment matchmaking. Under the "Invest China" brand, provinces and cities across the country have organized a series of complementary activities tailored to their geographic advantages, resource endowments, and industrial characteristics, forming a unified national investment promotion strategy. This series of activities demonstrates China's commitment to expanding market access and creating a high-level business environment. It also highlights the potential and vitality of China as the world's second-largest consumer market, bolstering the confidence of foreign enterprises in investing in China.

Column 2-1: Establishing a Roundtable Meeting Mechanism for Foreign-Invested Enterprises

Since July 2023, the Ministry of Commerce has established a roundtable meeting mechanism for foreign-invested enterprises, regularly convening meetings to listen to the challenges, issues, and suggestions raised by foreign enterprises. The roundtable meeting encourages open dialogue, with some issues resolved on the spot. For unresolved common or complex issues, a work log is created, and in-depth discussions are conducted with relevant departments to formulate practical solutions.

1. Resolving Key Issues Promptly. The Ministry of Commerce, in collaboration with the Ministry of Finance and the State Taxation Administration, continued to refund value-added tax in full for domestic equipment purchases by foreign R&D centers. The Ministry of Finance and the State Taxation Administration extended the personal income tax policies for allowances for foreign individuals until the end of 2027. The National Development and Reform Commission clarified green power trading rules. The State Administration for Market Regulation issued the *Ten Questions and Answers on the Participation of Foreign-Invested Enterprises in China's Standardization Work*, supporting their equal participation in standard-setting processes.

2. Improving and Refining Policy Provisions. Under the impetus of the roundtable meeting mechanism for foreign-funded enterprises, the Ministry of Foreign Affairs released a new version of the visa application form for foreigners coming to China, making it easier for foreign personnel to enter the country. The National Immigration Administration introduced a new permanent residence ID card for foreigners, simplifying their work, study, and life in China. The State Administration for Market Regulation revised the *Administrative Measures for the Registration of Formula Food for Special Medical Purposes*, improving the management of such products.

3. Addressing Hot Topics of Concern. The roundtable meetings facilitated dialogue with major foreign chambers of commerce, including the American Chamber of Commerce in China, the European Union Chamber of Commerce in China, and the Japan Chamber of Commerce and Industry in China. These discussions focused on data cross-border flows, export controls, the anti-espionage law, and the latest foreign investment policies. The "face-to-face" approach enhanced mutual trust between the government and enterprises, significantly improving policy transparency and predictability.

As of the end of January 2024, the Ministry of Commerce had convened 16 roundtable meetings, with over 400 foreign enterprises and foreign chambers of commerce participating, and resolved more than 300 issues raised during the meetings. At the provincial level, over 140 roundtables were held, involving more than 2,200 foreign enterprises and chambers of commerce, resolving over 900 issues.

6. Facilitating work and life for foreigners in China

Since 2023, China has introduced more than 20 policy measures to facilitate the travel and business activities of foreign personnel, stabilize their development expectations in China, and create a world-class business and investment environment.[①] Firstly, optimizing Policies for Foreign Personnel Coming to China. In August 2023, China extended the implementation of personal income tax preferential policies for allowances for foreign personnel. For foreign nationals holding ordinary passports who urgently need to travel to China for business cooperation, visits, investment, entrepreneurship, or tourism, port visa facilitation has been provided. Secondly, providing Visa Facilitation for International Business Personnel. The range of visa-free countries has been expanded. For instance, trial unilateral visa-free policies were introduced for nationals of France, Germany, Italy, the Netherlands, Spain, and Malaysia, later extended to Switzerland. By July 2024, 41 open ports across 19 provinces, autonomous regions, and municipalities in China offered 72-hour or 144-hour visa-free transit policies for nationals from 54 countries. For foreign personnel engaged in business cooperation and investment activities in China who need to make multiple return trips for valid reasons, multiple-entry visas valid for up to five years can be issued, with options for convenient visa extension, replacement, or reissuance. Thirdly, enhancing Immigration and Exit-Entry Services. Multi-language government websites and new media platforms for administrative services have been launched, providing timely updates on policies for foreigners coming to China and visa application requirements.

---

① http://www. scio. gov. cn/live/2024/33491/tw/, Jia Tongbin, the head of the Foreigners Management Division of the National Immigration Administration, answered reporters' questions.

B. Gradual Improvement of Outbound Investment Policies

Outbound investment is a critical means of integrating global innovation resources, optimizing resource allocation, promoting domestic industrial upgrading, and facilitating domestic and international dual circulation. China adheres to the principles of "government guidance, enterprise leadership, and market-based operations", encouraging and supporting enterprises to carry out outbound investment prudently and orderly. This enables deep participation in global industrial division and cooperation. China continues to improve its outbound investment management and service system, advancing investment facilitation, enhancing pre-, during, and post-investment supervision, guiding enterprises to enhance compliance standards, and supporting outbound investment cooperation in digital economy and green development fields, thereby improving the quality and level of outbound investment.

1. Improving the policy system for outbound investment management and services

China has been optimizing its outbound investment management mechanisms and gradually establishing a policy and service system centered on regulatory policies, supportive policies, and service promotion. (1) Enhancing Investment Management. China has established a full-cycle, all-process management system for pre-, during, and post-investment activities. Based on the *Measures for Overseas Investment Management*, a "record-based approach complemented by approval" is adopted to manage outbound investment filings (approvals), ensuring the authenticity and compliance of outbound investments. The "double random and one open" inspection mechanism is implemented for outbound investments, urging enterprises to comply with regulatory requirements. Pre-reporting of overseas mergers and acquisitions and risk alerts during the filing and approval process are conducted to guide enterprises in managing outbound investment risks. (2) Improving Investment Promotion. China has facilitated outbound investment by implementing paperless management of filings (approvals) and promoting the use of electronic licenses for outbound investments. Over 30,000 electronic licenses have been issued, significantly improving administrative efficiency. Major trade fairs such as the CIIE, Canton Fair, CIFTIS, CIFIT, and Hainan Expo have been leveraged to provide platforms for enterprises to explore outbound investment cooperation, aiding their global expansion efforts. (3) Safeguarding Rights and Interests. China has actively promoted the establishment of bilateral and multilateral investment cooperation working groups. It has signed bilateral investment protection agreements with over 130 countries and regions, 22 free trade agreements with 29 countries and regions, and established over 70 bilateral investment cooperation working groups with more than 60 countries, creating a favorable external environment for enterprises engaging in outbound investment cooperation. (4) Strengthening Comprehensive Overseas Services. The Ministry of Commerce has established and improved the "going global" Public Service Platform, providing one-stop universal public services such as policy consultation, business handling, and information sharing for enterprises. It regularly publishes the *Guide for Countries and Regions on Overseas Investment and Cooperation*, covering over 170 countries and regions. The guide offers information and services on investment environments, legal regulations, and industrial developments to support outbound enterprises. (5) Enhancing the Management of Foreign Contracted Projects. Foreign contracted projects have played a significant role in promoting the global expansion of Chinese products, technologies, and services, contributing to the new development paradigm and fostering mutually beneficial cooperation with related countries. In May 2024, the Ministry of Commerce issued the *Administrative Measures for the Filing and Approval of Foreign Contracted Projects (source)*[1], further optimizing regulatory processes.

2. Promoting digital and green development in outbound investment cooperation

Digital and green transitions are new drivers of global economic growth. China has consistently been a proactive advocate and participant in international cooperation in digital and green fields. At the fourth China International Import Expo (CIIE) opening ceremony in 2021, President Xi Jinping stated that "China will actively engage in international cooperation on green, low-carbon, and digital economies". In October 2023, during the Belt and Road Forum for International Cooperation Trade Connectivity Subforum, China and relevant countries jointly released the *Initiative on International Trade and Economic Cooperation Framework for Digital Economy and Green Development*. This framework comprises four

---

[1] http://www. mofcom. gov. cn/article/xwfb/xwsjfzr/202405/20240503510979. shtml

parts: digital trade cooperation, green development cooperation, capacity building, and implementation and outlook. It focuses on seven pillars, including: Creating an open and secure environment, Enhancing trade facilitation, Bridging the digital divide, Strengthening consumer trust, Promoting a policy environment for green development, Strengthening trade cooperation for sustainable and green development, Encouraging the exchange and investment in green technologies and services. The first batch of 35 countries confirmed participation in this initiative[1]. International organizations such as UNCTAD, UNIDO, and the International Trade Centre have expressed support. This framework has taken root, delivering tangible benefits to participating parties. China is actively guiding enterprises to implement the *Green Development Guidelines for Overseas Investment and Cooperation* and the *Guidelines for Outbound Investment and Cooperation on Digital Economy*. It has signed 76 agreements with 44 countries in digital, green, and blue economy sectors, fostering bilateral investment cooperation and creating new momentum for outbound investment cooperation.

3. Enhancing financial services for "Going Global" enterprises

First, improving support policies for overseas financing. In October 2023, the Ministry of Finance issued the *Debt Sustainability Framework for Market Access Countries of the Belt and Road Initiative*, complementing the 2019 version *Debt Sustainability Framework for Low-Income Countries of the Belt and Road Initiative*. Together, these frameworks cover low- and middle-income countries participating in the Belt and Road Initiative, providing guidance for Chinese enterprises involved in Belt and Road investments and financing. In July 2023, the State Administration of Foreign Exchange released the *Collection of Exchange Rate Risk Scenarios and Applications of Foreign Exchange Derivatives*. Through real-world cases, the collection helps enterprises understand the importance of exchange rate risk hedging and its practical application, supporting outbound investment enterprises in managing exchange rate risks. Second, promoting financial institutions' own "going global" expansion. China's major

---

① Including Afghanistan, Argentina, Belarus, Brunei, Cambodia, Cameroon, Central African Republic, Chile, China, Cook Islands, Côte d'Ivoire, Ethiopia, Hungary, Iran, Kenya, Kyrgyzstan, Laos, Mongolia, Mozambique, Myanmar, Nicaragua, Nigeria, Niue, Pakistan, Papua New Guinea, the Philippines, Serbia, Sierra Leone, Sri Lanka, Tajikistan, Tanzania, Thailand, Turkmenistan, Uzbekistan, and Zambia

banks have steadily expanded overseas, providing robust support for outbound enterprises. By June 2023, according to the Bank of China Research Institute, the top five Chinese banks had established operational entities in 67 countries and regions, covering major international and regional financial centers. Third, financial institutions innovate products and services continuously based on the actual needs of enterprises "going global". Financial institutions like the China Development Bank and the Export-Import Bank of China leverage policy-based finance to support enterprises' "going global" efforts, such as the high-quality development of the China-Europe Railway Express. Fourth, optimizing financial infrastructure for cross-border payments. The Cross-Border Interbank Payment System (CIPS) has significantly enhanced its operations, facilitating convenient fund settlements for outbound enterprises. According to the *Payment System Report 2023* released by the People's Bank of China, the Cross-Border Interbank Payment System (CIPS) processed 6.6133 million transactions in 2023, with a total value of CNY 123.06 trillion, representing year-on-year increases of 50.29% and 27.27%, respectively.

4. Improving safety management systems for overseas institutions and personnel

On November 7, 2023, during the Roundtable on High-Quality Development of Cross-Border Investment at the sixth China International Import Expo, the Ministry of Commerce and the China International Contractors Association jointly released the third edition of the *Regulation on the Safety Management of Overseas Chinese-funded Enterprises, Institutions and Personnel*. As the first guidance document addressing safety risk management for Chinese enterprises abroad, the Guidelines were initially released in 2012 and have since undergone continuous updates and improvements. The latest version systematically addresses various risks faced by overseas Chinese enterprises and personnel and summarizes relevant risk management principles. It covers seven dimensions, including risk identification, assessment and early warning, safety control, and emergency response, providing practical and effective references for Chinese enterprises engaged in cross-border investment activities.

5. Continuing to deepen belt and road cooperation mechanisms

In October 2023, during the High-Level Forum on Green Development at the third Belt and Road Forum for International Cooperation, the Green Development Investment and

Financing Partnership was launched. It was included in the Chairman's Statement and the list of multilateral cooperation outcomes of the forum. Jointly initiated by the Belt and Road International Green Development Coalition and its domestic and international partners, the partnership adheres to the principles of openness, inclusiveness, mutual benefit, and market-based operations. Its objectives include: Leveraging the professional strengths of partners to promote green development investment and financing cooperation, exploring green investment and financing models and project evaluation methods. Improving ESG evaluation and management of projects, and the partnership aims to address bottlenecks in financing for green Belt and Road projects by establishing a communication and cooperation platform and providing practical solutions.

II. Sustained Improvement in the Quality and Efficiency of Two−Way Investment

A. Utilization of Foreign Capital at Historic Highs, Maintaining Second Place Globally

In 2023, global cross-border investment flows decreased by 2%, and foreign investment in developing economies dropped by 7%. In the context of challenging and complex international environment, the amount of foreign capital actually utilized by China was decreased year-on-year, but the position as the world's second-largest recipient of foreign direct investment (FDI) was still remained. The scale of foreign investment reached historic highs, with further optimization in its structure. Foreign-invested enterprises remain confident in the Chinese market.

1. Maintaining the position as the World's second largest recipient of FDI

In 2023, China capitalized on its super-large-scale market, complete supply chain system, abundant human capital, and rich innovation scenarios, adhering to the principle of expanding opening up and demonstrating its strong economic attraction. According to statistics from the UN Trade and Development (UNCTAD), China absorbed USD 163.25 billion in foreign direct investment in 2023, accounting for 12.3% of global FDI inflows. This positions China as the world's second-largest recipient of FDI, following the United States (USD 310.95 billion, accounting for

30.1%). Since 2020, China's share of global FDI has remained consistently above 12% (see Figure 2-1). China continues to be one of the most popular investment destinations globally, providing critical support for the global business development of multinational corporations.

2. Foreign investment scale at historic highs

Since 2023, global FDI has been sluggish due to multiple complex factors, including the slowdown in global economic growth, rising geopolitical risks, and weakening external demand. According to UNCTAD, global FDI flows totaled USD 1.33 trillion in 2023, a 2% decrease from 2022. Excluding fluctuations caused by "conduit" economies that act as intermediaries for FDI flows to other countries, global cross-border investment flows declined by over 10% in real terms. Among the world's 20 largest FDI recipient countries, 10 experienced a decline in FDI inflows[1]. In this context, China recorded 53,766 newly established foreign-invested enterprises in 2023, a year-on-year increase of 39.7%, marking the second-highest figure in history. The actual utilization of foreign capital reached USD 163.3 billion, an 13.7% year-on-year decline, but still ranked as the third highest in history, following the exceptionally high figures in 2021 and 2022 (see Figure 2-2).

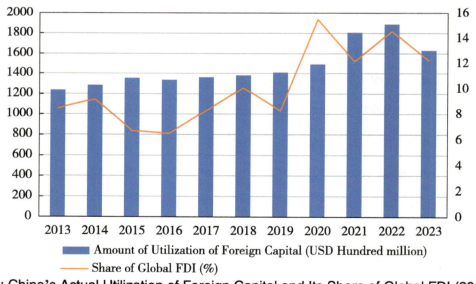

Figure 2–1: China's Actual Utilization of Foreign Capital and Its Share of Global FDI (2013—2023)

Source: Data for 2013—2022 are from the *Statistical Bulletin of FDI in China 2023*; 2023 China investment data are from the Ministry of Commerce, and global data are from the UNCTAD *World Investment Report 2024*.

---

[1] UNCTAD, *World Investment Report* 2024.

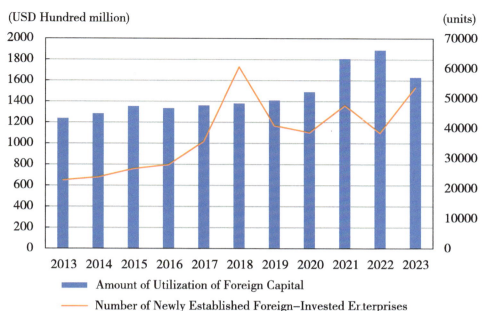

Figure 2–2: China's Utilization of Foreign Capital and Number of NewlyEstablished Foreign-Invested Enterprises (2013—2023)

Source: Ministry of Commerce.

3. Further optimization of foreign capital utilization quality

In 2023, China attracted CNY 423.34 billion in foreign investment to high-tech industries, a 6.5% increase year-on-year. This accounted for 37.4% of the total utilized foreign capital, up 1.3 percentage points from 2022, reaching a record high. The proportion of foreign investment in manufacturing rose by 1.6 percentage points to 27.9%. By country, actual investment in China from developed economies such as France, the United Kingdom, the Netherlands, Switzerland, and Australia grew by 84.1%, 81.0%, 31.5%, 21.4%, and 17.1%, respectively. The number of newly established foreign-invested enterprises from the EU, the United States, and Japan in China also increased. In the first four months of 2024, the total profits of foreign-invested industrial enterprises above a designated size grew by 16.7%, surpassing the national average of 4.3%, indicating an improvement in the operational performance of foreign enterprises.

4. Deep Integration of foreign financial institutions into the Chinese economy

Driven by regulatory policies such as the gradual removal of foreign equity restrictions, significant reductions in foreign investment thresholds, and expanded market access, foreign financial institutions have accelerated their presence in the Chinese market through equity acquisitions, capital increases, and the establishment of branches. As of the end of 2023, all 30 globally systemically important banks had established branches in China, and nearly half of the world's top 40 insurance companies had entered the Chinese market. By May 2024, there were 10 foreign-controlled securities companies, 9 wholly foreign-owned fund management companies, and 3 foreign-controlled futures companies approved to operate in China[1]. Additionally, 1,128 overseas institutions had entered China's bond market, with a total custodial balance of CNY 4.27 trillion (see Table 2-2). China's ongoing financial opening-up and the accelerated formation of a two-way open financial system strongly support high-quality development. Foreign financial institutions are increasingly active in expanding their operations in China, deeply integrating into the China's economic development and financial markets, and becoming a vital force in China's financial industry.

Table 2-2: Achievements of Foreign Financial Institutions in China (As of December 2023)

Foreign Banks		Foreign Insurance Companies	
Legal Entity Banks	41 units	Operating Institutions	67 units
Branches	116 units	Representative Offices	70 units
Representative Offices	132 units	Total Assets	CNY 2.4 trillion
Operating Institutions	888 units	Market Share of the Domestic Insurance Industry	10%
Total Assets	CNY 3.86 trillion		

Source: January 25, 2024, State Council press conference, based on statements by Xiao Yuanqi, Deputy Director of the National Financial Regulatory Administration, and compiled by the author.

5. Foreign enterprises remain confident in the Chinese market

In June 2023, a survey conducted by the China Council for the Promotion of International Trade (CCPIT) revealed that 98.2% of surveyed foreign enterprises and chambers of commerce were confident in China's economic prospects and expressed intentions to continue investing in China to share in its development dividends. In Q1 2024, a CCPIT survey of

---

[1] https://www. gov. cn/yaowen/shipin/202405/content_6950781. htm

over 600 foreign enterprises[1] indicated that foreign enterprises remain optimistic about the Chinese market. Over 70% of respondents were optimistic about the market's prospects over the next five years, an increase of approximately 3.8 percentage points from Q4 2023. More than half of the enterprises noted an "increased" attractiveness of the Chinese market, up 2.9 percentage points from Q4 2023. Additionally, satisfaction with China's business environment was high, with all indicators showing an increase in "satisfied" or above ratings compared to Q4 2023.

In February 2024, the American Chamber of Commerce in China released its annual *China Business Climate Survey Report*[2] Despite facing challenges, American companies reported improved confidence in China's business environment compared to 2023: Approximately 40% of surveyed companies expressed optimism about their profitability potential in China over the next two years, up from 33% in the previous report. 44% felt positive about market growth in China, and 38% were optimistic or relatively optimistic about China's economic recovery/growth. Half of the respondents ranked China among their preferred or top three global investment destinations. The Japan External Trade Organization (JETRO) reported that nearly 90% of surveyed Japanese companies planned to maintain or increase their investments in China. The European Union Chamber of Commerce in China found that 77% of surveyed companies intended to expand their operations in South China. Similarly, a survey by the German Chamber of Commerce in China showed that more than half of German companies planned to increase their investments in China within the next two years[3].

A UNCTAD study in 2024 tracking[4] the top 100 global multinational enterprises

---

① https://www. ccpit. org/a/20240428/20240428ynnu. html, CCPIT April 2024 regular press conference.

② http://www. cacs. mofcom. gov. cn/article/gnwjmdt/sb/zm/202402/179540. html, China Trade Remedies Network: American Chamber of Commerce Report-U.S. Companies Remain Optimistic About China's Business Prospects.

③ *China Development and Reform News*, "A Strong Start for Foreign Trade: Foreign Enterprises Optimistic About China's Future, " March 30, 2024.

④ UNCTAD, *World Investment Report 2024.*

found that since 2019, the number of divestments from China has decreased. Multinational corporations recognize the strategic importance of maintaining operations in the world's second-largest economy, not only to access its vast market but also to benefit from its advanced manufacturing capabilities and robust supply chains.

B. Stable and Healthy Development of Outbound Investment Cooperation

In 2023, China's outbound direct investment (ODI) maintained stable and healthy growth, solidifying its position as a major global investor. Chinese enterprises operating overseas achieved favorable results, with continued growth in manufacturing investments and investments in Belt and Road partner countries. The financial sector's international expansion yielded significant results, and enterprises' capability and confidence in "going global" continued to improve.

1. Strengthened position as a leading global investor

According to UNCTAD, global outbound direct investment flows totaled USD 1.55 trillion in 2023, remaining stable compared to 2022. China achieved steady progress in outbound investment. Data from the Ministry of Commerce and the State Administration of Foreign Exchange (SAFE) show that China's outbound direct investment reached USD 177.29 billion in 2023, an 8.7% increase year-on-year. By the end of 2023, 31,000 domestic investors from China had established 48, 000 outbound direct investment enterprises across 189 countries and regions. Globally, China ranked as the third-largest outbound investor[1], following the United States (USD 404.32 billion) and Japan (USD 184.02 billion). Since 2012, China's ODI flows have consistently ranked among the top three globally for 12 consecutive years (see Figure 2-3).

---

[1] UNCTAD, *World Investment Report* 2024.

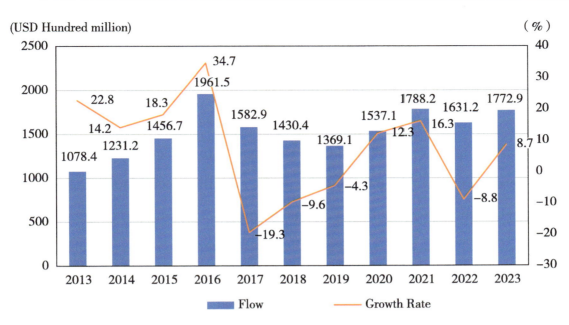

Figure 2-3: China's Outbound Investment Amount and Growth Rate (2013—2023)

Source: Ministry of Commerce, National Bureau of Statistics, and State Administration of Foreign Exchange, *2023 Statistical Bulletin of China's Outward Foreign Direct Investment*, China Commerce and Trade Press, 2024 Edition. Compiled and calculated by the author.

2. Strong performance of overseas Chinese enterprises

In 2023, Chinese enterprises operating overseas achieved good overall results, with nearly 70% reporting profits or breaking even. Reinvestment of earnings for the year totaled USD 78.46 billion, the third-highest amount in history, accounting for 44.2% of China's outbound direct investment (ODI) flows during the same period[①]. Overseas enterprises paid USD 75.3 billion in taxes to host countries/regions, a 0.3% increase year-on-year. By the end of the year, overseas enterprises employed a total of 4.289 million people, including 2.57 million local employees, up 77, 000 from the previous year, accounting for 59.9% of total employment[②].

---

① Ministry of Commerce, National Bureau of Statistics, and State Administration of Foreign Exchange: *2023 Statistical Bulletin of China's Outward Foreign Direct Investment*, China Commerce and Trade Press, 2024 Edition.

② Ministry of Commerce, National Bureau of Statistics, and State Administration of Foreign Exchange: *2023 Statistical Bulletin of China's Outward Foreign Direct Investment*, China Commerce and Trade Press, 2024 Edition.

3. Four key sectors accounted for nearly 80% of outbound investment

In 2023, China's ODI covered 18 major economic sectors. Investments exceeding USD 10 billion were made in leasing and business services, wholesale and retail, manufacturing, and finance. Manufacturing investments reached USD 27.34 billion, a 0.7% year-on-year increase, accounting for 15.4% of total ODI. Key areas of manufacturing investment included: automobile manufacturing, other manufacturing activities, computers/communications, and other electronic manufacturing, general equipment manufacturing, smelting and processing of non-ferrous metals, non-metallic mineral products, rubber and plastic products, pharmaceuticals manufacturing, electrical machinery and equipment manufacturing, chemical raw materials and chemical products, metal products, specialized equipment manufacturing. Combined ODI in leasing and business services, wholesale and retail, manufacturing, and finance totaled USD 138.55 billion, accounting for 78.1% of total ODI flows (see Figure 2-4).

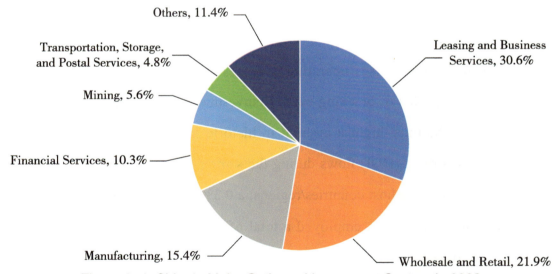

Figure 2–4: China's Major Outbound Investment Sectors in 2023

Source: Ministry of Commerce, National Bureau of Statistics, State Administration of Foreign Exchange, *2023 Statistical Bulletin of China's Outward Foreign Direct Investment*, China Commerce and Trade Press, 2024 Edition.

4. Rapid growth of investment in Belt and Road partner countries

In 2023, China invested USD 141.6 billion in Asia, accounting for 79.9% of ODI flows, a 13.9% increase year-on-year. Investment in Latin America reached USD 13.48 billion (7.6% of ODI flows), a

17.6% decrease year-on-year, primarily targeting countries such as the Cayman Islands, British Virgin Islands, Mexico, Brazil, Chile, Colombia, Ecuador, and Bolivia. Investment in Europe totaled USD 9.97 billion (5.6% of ODI flows), a 3.6% decrease year-on-year, primarily targeting countries such as Luxembourg, the United Kingdom, the Netherlands, Sweden, Germany, Russia, Serbia, Hungary, Switzerland, Ireland, Italy, the Czech Republic, and Georgia. Investment in North America amounted to USD 7.78 billion (5.6% of ODI flows), a 7% increase year-on-year. Investment in the U.S. dropped by 5.2% to USD 6.91 billion, while investment in Canada grew by 141% to USD 350 million. China's direct investment in Belt and Road partner countries grew significantly, reaching USD 40.71 billion, a 31.5% increase year-on-year, accounting for 23% of total ODI flows. By the end of 2023, Chinese enterprises had established 17,000 overseas entities in Belt and Road partner countries, with an ODI stock of USD 334.84 billion, representing 11.3% of China's total ODI stock. The top ten recipient countries were Singapore, Indonesia, Luxembourg, Vietnam, Malaysia, Thailand, Russia, Laos, the UAE, and Cambodia.

5. Overseas economic and trade cooperation zones foster mutual growth

Overseas economic and trade cooperation zones represent an innovative model for outbound investment, serving as platforms for enterprises to engage in mutually beneficial cooperation with host countries. Since the 18th National Congress of the CPC, especially after the launch of the Belt and Road Initiative, China has actively developed cooperation zones, achieving significant results. With rapid development, continuous expansion of construction scale, continuous optimization of national industrial layout, and continuous amplification of agglomeration and spread, the cooperation zones have become a vivid practice of high-quality joint construction of the Belt and Road, an effective carrier for strengthening international cooperation in the industrial and supply chains, and a shining "business card" for deepening economic and trade relations. As of June 2024, 46 countries host economic and trade cooperation zones covered in the Ministry of Commerce statistics. These zones focus on manufacturing, resource utilization, agriculture, trade and logistics, and R&D. Cumulative investments have exceeded USD 80 billion, with taxes paid to host countries surpassing USD

13.3 billion and over 550,000 jobs created locally. Notable zones include China-Egypt Suez Economic and Trade Cooperation Zone, Cambodia Sihanoukville Special Economic Zone, Thailand-China Rayong Industrial Park, Hungary's Central European Trade and Logistics Park. These zones have become attractive hubs for cooperation, reinforcing the consensus among participating countries on the value of developing overseas economic and trade cooperation zones.

6. Significant achievements of "Going Global" in the financial sector

Chinese financial institutions have achieved significant results in their "going global" efforts. By June 2023, the five major comprehensive commercial banks[1] had established operational institutions in 67 countries and regions, covering major international and regional financial centers[2]. In addition, 13 Chinese banks had set up 145 primary institutions in 50 Belt and Road partner countries, while six Chinese insurance institutions had established 15 overseas branches in eight Belt and Road partner countries. As of July 2023, nearly 80 securities, futures, and fund management firms from mainland China had set up subsidiaries in Hong Kong, with the scale of cross-border business continuing to grow. In recent years, the internationalization of the RMB has progressed steadily, providing domestic and international market participants with a more diversified and convenient currency choice. The international status and global influence of the RMB have steadily increased, making it the fourth most-used payment currency, the third most-used financing currency, and the fifth most-traded foreign exchange currency globally. Over 80 foreign central banks or monetary authorities have included the RMB in their foreign exchange reserves[3].

7. Enhanced capability and confidence of enterprises in "Going Global"

Chinese enterprises have steadily improved their cross-border operations. In September

---

[1] Industrial and Commercial Bank of China, Agricultural Bank of China, Bank of China, China Construction Bank, and Bank of Communications.

[2] *Financial Times*: "China's Financial Institutions Achieve Significant Results in 'going global'", February 7, 2024.

[3] *Financial Times*: "Steady and Rapid Progress in China's Financial opening-up", July 16, 2024.

2024, the China Enterprise Confederation and the China Entrepreneurs Association released the 2024 List of "China's Top 100 Multinational Companies"[1]. The average transnationality index of listed enterprises was 15.35%, a slight decline of 0.55 percentage points from 2023, but still outperforming the 2.64 percentage-point decline in the global top 100. Total overseas assets and employees increased by 5.12% and 6.90%, respectively. The entry threshold is CNY 19.84 billion, an increase of CNY 1.931 billion from the previous year, representing a rise of 10.78%. In March 2024, the CCPIT published the *Survey on Current Conditions and Intention of Outbound Investment by Chinese Enterprises*. Over 80% of surveyed enterprises expressed[2] intentions to expand or maintain their overseas investments, an increase of nearly 10% from 2022. More than 90% of enterprises remained optimistic about the prospects of outbound investment.

---

[1] Xinhuanet, https://www.xinhuanet.com/energy/20240912/a2c155504c3045148790b1f96cda4ceb/c.html.

[2] The survey covered more than 20 provinces in China, with 1,118 questionnaires collected. It included enterprises of various types, industries, and sizes, with over 60% of respondents being members of corporate management, reflecting the true status of Chinese enterprises' outbound investment.

Chapter 3　China's Growing Appeal for Opening-up and Cooperation

Amid the deep integration of the global economy and China's pursuit of high-quality development, the country's comparative advantage in attracting foreign investment is shifting from low-cost factors to comprehensive advantages based on a very large markets, a complete industrial chain, and innovation capabilities. As a massive and fast-growing market, China offers a stable policy environment, the world's most complete industrial system, and an increasingly prominent position in the global innovation landscape, backed by its human capital advantage. These comprehensive strengths make China a strong magnet for global resources, offering international investors greater opportunities to bosed, expand globally, and secure future growth.

I. A Super-Sized Market Offering Broad Development Opportunities

As the world's second-largest economy, China's steady development provides ongoing momentum for global economic recovery. With the advancement of high-quality development, areas such as advanced manufacturing, consumption upgrades, and new urbanization will continue to generate enormous demand, making China a highly attractive destination for multinational companies.

A. Providing Sustained Momentum for Global Economic Growth

In 2023, China's gross domestic product (GDP) reached CNY 126.1 trillion, growing by 5.2%, with per capita GDP increasing by 5.4% to USD 12,700. In the first half of 2024, China maintained steady growth, with GDP reaching CNY 61.7 trillion, a year-on-year increase of 5.0%, significantly outpacing the global average growth rate. International organizations and market institutions have raised their forecasts for China's economic growth in 2024. For instance: The United Nations and the World Bank raised their growth forecasts by 0.1 and 0.3 percentage points, respectively, to 4.8%. The OECD adjusted its forecast by 0.2 percentage points to 4.9%. The IMF and Goldman Sachs raised their projections by 0.2~0.4 percentage points to 5.0%. Citibank increased its forecast by 0.6 percentage points to 5.2%. Surveys conducted by organizations such as the American Chamber of Commerce in China (AmCham China), the European Chamber of Commerce in China, and the Japanese Chamber of Commerce and Industry in China reveal that multinational companies have significantly improved their expectations for China's business prospects over the next two years. They exhibit growing optimism about key performance indicators, particularly in areas such as macroeconomic stability, domestic market growth, and profitability forecasts. More than 50% of surveyed companies continue to rank China among their top three global investment destinations.[①] China's development provides sustained momentum for global economic growth and presents new opportunities for international companies to invest in China (see Figure 3.1).

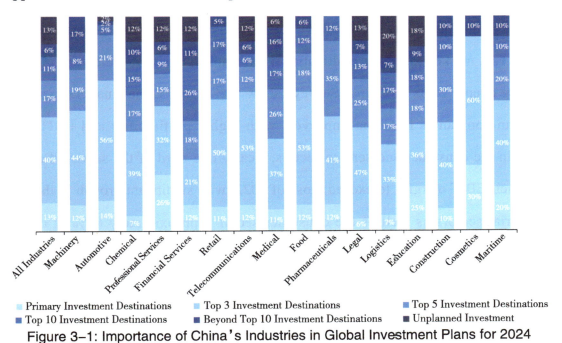

Figure 3–1: Importance of China's Industries in Global Investment Plans for 2024

Source: *Business Confidence Survey* 2024, European Chamber of Commerce in China

---

① For details, see the *China Business Climate Survey* 2024 issued by AmCham China, the *Business Confidence Survey* 2024 issued by the European Chamber of Commerce in China, and the *Member Company Business Climate: Business Environment Perception Survey Results* issued by the Japanese Chamber of Commerce and Industry in China on May 14, 2024.

B. Multinational Enterprises in China Face an Expanding Market Space

China accounts for nearly one-fifth of the world's population. In recent years, income levels have steadily increased, and the size of the middle-income population has expanded, rapidly unleashing the enormous potential of China's consumer market. According to data from the National Bureau of Statistics, China's per capita disposable income in 2023 was CNY 39,218, a 6.1% increase year-on-year. The middle-income population (household annual income of CNY 100, 000~500, 000) accounted for 47.2% of the total population[①]. As the world's second-largest import and consumer market, China's total retail sales of consumer goods reached CNY 47.2 trillion in 2023, a 7.2% increase year-on-year. Final consumption expenditure contributed as much as 82.5% to China's economic growth.

With a population of over 1.4 billion, the expanding and upgrading consumer demand provides a vast market space for multinational companies, many of which are increasingly establishing deeper roots in China. Surveys show that in 2023, the financial performance of American companies in China improved, with higher profitability and EBIT margins, especially in the consumer and service sectors. Nearly one-third of the surveyed companies expected their EBIT margins to exceed those of 2022, with significant growth in the resource and industrial sectors as well as the consumer sector. Approximately 68% of companies anticipated their profit margins in China would meet or exceed the global average (see Figure 3-2).

[①] On January 4, 2024, Wang Yiming, Vice President of the China Center for International Economic Exchanges, was interviewed by CCTV News.

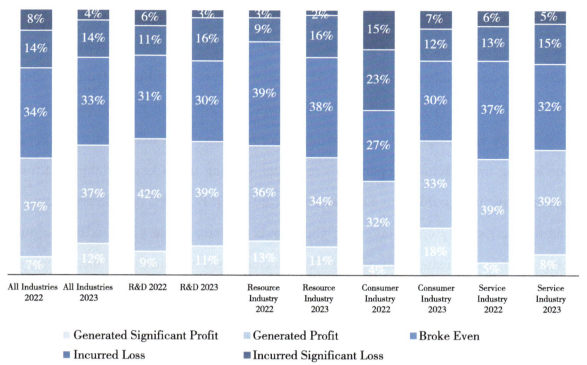

Figure 3–2: Financial Performance of American Companies n China, 2022—2023

Source: *China Business Climate Survey* 2024, American Chamber of Commerce in China

II. Globally Leading Industrial Support System and Investment Environment

China possesses the world's most comprehensive industrial support system, providing foreign investors with high-efficiency and highly reliable supply chain support, significantly reducing operating costs for foreign enterprises in China. A: the same time, by further expanding high-level openness, improving policy openness and transparency, and combining robust industrial infrastructure with a favorable policy environment, China offers one of the most competitive investment environments globally.

A. Maintaining the Advantage of the World's Most Complete Industrial Chain

The production activities of multinational corporations in China rely heavily on the local support system, and China possesses unparalleled advantages in industrial support. According to the United Nations Industrial Classification System, China has 41 industrial categories,

207 industrial subcategories, and 666 industrial subclasses, making it the most complete industrial system in the world. For 14 consecutive years, China has maintained the largest manufacturing scale globally, developed 45 national-level advanced manufacturing clusters, and built the world's largest and most technologically advanced mobile communication network. These factors provide multinational corporations with exceptional convenience for conducting manufacturing operations in China, making this a key variable in attracting foreign investment. According to a survey conducted by HSBC, 73% of enterprises anticipate expanding their supply chain layout in China over the next three years, with one-quarter planning significant increases. Among them: British enterprises rank increasing their supply chain presence in China as their top priority for expanding business in the country. Southeast Asian enterprises, particularly those from Indonesia (92%) and Vietnam (89%), are especially interested in expanding their supplier networks in China within the next three years[1] (see Figure 3-3).

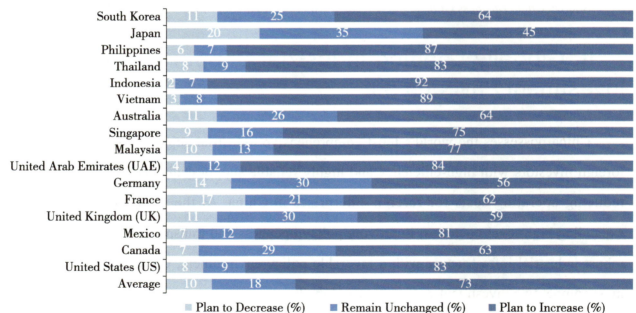

Figure 3–3: Plans for Supply Chain Layout in China by Enterprises from Surveyed Markets over the Next Three Years

Source: HSBC's report: *Overseas Businesses View China 2023—Digitalization and Sustainability Driving Future Growth.*

---

[1] For more details, see HSBC's report: *Overseas Businesses View China 2023-Digitalization and Sustainability Driving Future Growth.*

From a spatial perspective, China's mid-to-high-end manufacturing industry is highly concentrated in regions such as the Yangtze River Delta, the Greater Bay Area, the Bohai Economic Rim, the Chengdu-Chongqing area, and the urban city clusters in the middle reaches of the Yangtze River. These regions have developed vibrant industrial clusters centered around leading enterprises, with tightly integrated upstream and downstream supply chain businesses. This integration significantly boosts production efficiency, generates spillover effects in innovation, and attracts a large number of foreign-funded enterprises. The Yangtze River Delta urban agglomeration, as one of the most dynamic, open, and innovative regions in China, has seen continued growth in foreign investment. In 2023, Jiangsu Province utilized USD 25.34 billion in foreign investment, ranking first nationwide, while Shanghai utilized over USD 24 billion, ranking second. The Guangdong-Hong Kong-Macao Greater Bay Area, with its complete manufacturing chain and large industrial clusters, provides comprehensive industrial support for foreign enterprises' R&D and manufacturing. In 2023, the proportion of disbursement of foreign investment in the manufacturing sector in the Greater Bay Area rebounded to over 30%. The collaborative development and industrial complementarity among urban agglomerations provide foreign investors with all-around support, offering them vast development opportunities and allowing them to share in the dividends of China's growth.

Column 3-1: Foxconn's Plan to Establish a New Business Headquarters in Zhengzhou

Foxconn, a globally renowned contract manufacturer, has accelerated its"3+3" strategic industrial layout in recent years. This strategy focuses on three emerging industries—electric vehicles, digital health, and robotics—and three key technologies—artificial intelligence, semiconductors, and next-generation mobile communications. On July 24, Foxconn Technology Group signed a strategic cooperation agreement with the People's Government of Henan Province to establish a new business headquarters in Zhengzhou. The first phase of the project will be located in Zhengdong New District, covering a construction area of approximately 700 hectares, with a total investment of about CNY 1 billion. Foxconn plans to leverage its expertise in intelligent manufacturing and its supply chain advantages to advance industries such as complete electric vehicles, energy storage batteries, digital health, and robotics, aiming to transform Henan into a global high-end manufacturing hub and a strategic emerging industry ecosystem.

Reports indicate that Foxconn's new energy vehicle (NEV) trial production center will include the construction of a world-class demonstration production line for high-end NEVs. It aims to create a manufacturing service platform for renowned domestic and international automobile brands and a world-class "lighthouse factory" for complete vehicle production, laying a solid foundation for mass NEV production. The goal is to build Henan Zhengzhou Airport Economy Zone into the core production base of Foxconn's NEV sector. For the solid-state battery project, Foxconn plans to follow industry trends, utilize its technological expertise, and adhere to a "comprehensive planning and phased implementation" principle. It will focus on advancing the solid-state battery industry in the Zhengzhou Airport Economy Zone, developing R&D and manufacturing projects for solid-state electrolytes, semi-solid and fully solid state battery cells.

Source: Compiled from reports by *Shanghai Securities News*, *National Business Daily*, and other media outlets.

B. Creating a Stable, Transparent, and Predictable Investment Environment

In recent years, China has worked to create a world-class investment environment characterized by marketization, rule of law, and internationalization. Efforts to attract foreign investment have been intensified, ensuring the protection of foreign investors' rights and interests. In terms of encouraging foreign investment, China has reduced the number of items on the *Negative List of Foreign Investment Access* from 40 in the 2019 version to 31 in the 2021 version. And, expanded the *Catalogue of Encouraged Industries for Foreign Investment* from 1,108 items in the 2019 version to 1,474 items in the 2022 version. Also, China has revised the *Stabilizing Foreign Trade and Foreign Investment Tax Policy Guidelines* in January 2024, proposing 51 specific tax incentive measures to enhance China's attractiveness and competitiveness as an investment destination. China has also strengthened the protection of foreign enterprises' legal rights. By the end of 2023, the total number of national-level intellectual property protection centers and rapid rights protection centers reached 112, a 15% increase from the end of 2022. Throughout the year, over 1,500 foreign-funded enterprises received mediation services. These measures to improve the investment environment have been widely recognized and appreciated by foreign enterprises.

As China continues to deepen its opening-up and optimize its business environment, its attractiveness and influence in the global investment landscape have further strengthened. In the context of current global instability, China's stable investment environment has become a key factor for foreign businesses investing in the country. Among surveyed EU companies, the proportion of respondents reporting that their sector has opened up increased significantly (45%, up 9 percentage points year-on-year). The proportion of respondents stating that their sector has seen significant opening-up (19%) also rose by 9 percentage points year-on-year, reaching the highest level in nine years. Additionally, the proportion of respondents reporting that their sector is fully open saw a slight year-on-year increase, reaching a historic high (39%, up 1 percentage point). Furthermore, 10% of respondents expect significant opening-up within the next two years, while 19% foresee major opening-up within two to five years[1] (see Figure 3-4).

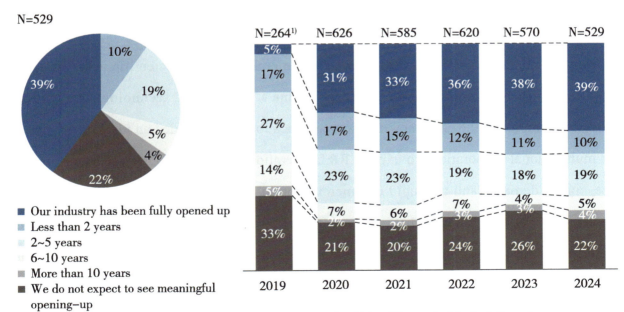

Figure 3–4: Attitudes of EU Enterprises in China Towards Market Opening

Source: European Chamber of Commerce in China, *Business Confidence Survey* 2024.

---

[1] Source: European Chamber of Commerce in China, *Business Confidence Survey* 2024.

III. Strengthening New Advantages Based on Technological Innovation and Human Capital

China places great importance on the role of technological innovation in industrial upgrading and high-quality development. By adhering to science-led and innovation-driven strategies, China has accelerated the deep integration of the "four chains"—innovation, industry, capital, and talent. While being a global manufacturing powerhouse, China is also evolving into a "global R&D laboratory". Its technological prowess is widely recognized by international enterprises, with investing in China and engaging in collaborative R&D becoming crucial strategies for multinational corporations seeking global competitiveness.

A. Providing a Favorable Innovation Ecosystem for R&D

In this new era, China has comprehensively deepened reform of its science and technology system, continuously improving market-oriented mechanisms for technological innovation. Major reforms include optimizing the organization and implementation of key scientific and technological tasks and introducing new mechanisms such as "leaderboards" and competitive "horse races". These initiatives clearly define the rights, obligations, distribution methods, and safeguards for the commercialization of scientific achievements. Such measures have significantly enhanced China's science and technology innovation ecosystem, improved the efficiency of resource allocation, and provided an ideal environment for multinational corporations to expand R&D operations in China. China's massive market size, robust demand, and the rapid commercialization of R&D outcomes create a dynamic environment, encouraging multinational corporations to conduct R&D activities closer to their customers, tailor innovations to customer needs, and export these R&D results to other regions worldwide. China's R&D investment attraction strategies have yielded remarkable results, with an increasing number of foreign-funded enterprises planning to boost R&D spending in the country. This trend is particularly evident in sectors like information technology, artificial intelligence, healthcare, food and beverages, and energy, demonstrating that China has become a key R&D hub for these industries.

B. Highlighting Innovation Scenario Development and Scaled Applications

New applications and industries in fields such as information technology and artificial intelligence are rapidly emerging in China. According to the National Bureau of Statistics, China's investment in high-tech industries grew by 10.3% in 2023, outpacing total fixed asset investment growth by 7.3 percentage points. Specifically, investment in high-tech manufacturing and high-tech services grew by 9.9% and 11.4%, respectively. For instance, in artificial intelligence, the *2023 Global Artificial Intelligence Innovation Index*, jointly produced by the Institute of Scientific and Technical Information of China and Peking University, shows that China ranks second globally in AI development. China is also second only to the United States in the number of AI enterprises and venture capital investment in the sector. China's ability to achieve high-level and large-scale applications of technological innovations gives it a unique advantage in attracting multinational corporations. Increasingly, these corporations are localizing their operations, reinvesting profits generated in China back into the country. According to an HSBC survey of multinational corporations in 2023, 87% of respondents believe China's rapid advancements in areas like digitalization are creating new investment opportunities. On average, surveyed enterprises plan to invest 8% of their global operating profits in technology R&D and digitalization efforts in China. American companies are particularly enthusiastic, with over half (52%) planning to allocate 10% or more of their operating profits toward R&D and digitalization in China. Survey results from the German Chamber of Commerce in China reveal that 73% of large German enterprises and 50% of small German enterprises plan to increase investment in China over the next two years.

C. Increased R&D Investment and Enhanced Overall Innovation Capacity

Entering a new era, China has continued to increase its investment in research and development (R&D). According to the *Statistical Communiqué of the People's Republic of China on the 2023 National Economic and Social Development* published by the National Bureau of Statistics, China's R&D expenditure in 2023 reached CNY 3.3278 trillion, ranking second globally, with an 8.1% year-on-year growth. The intensity of R&D investment reached 2.64%, surpassing the 2.5% baseline for innovative economies (see Figure 3-5). The *Global Innovation Index (GII) 2023*, released by the World Intellectual Property Organization in September 2023, showed that China's overall innovation capability ranking improved from 34th in 2012 to 12th in 2023, making it the only middle-income economy among the top 30. Currently, China has 24 global top-tier technology clusters, three more than in 2022, making it the country with the most technology clusters worldwide. In the European Commission's *European Innovation Scoreboard*, China's innovation capacity was only 44% of the EU's level in 2014, but by 2023, it had reached 95%. China has achieved significant original breakthroughs in fields such as quantum technology, integrated circuits, artificial intelligence, biomedicine, and new energy. Efficient and large-scale R&D investments have significantly boosted innovation performance, advancing the commercialization and industrialization of technological achievements. This provides multinational corporations with extensive opportunities to engage in innovative business operations in China.

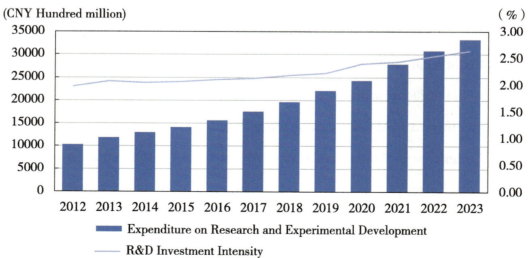

Figure 3–5: China's R&D Expenditure and R&D Investment Intensity, 2012—2023

Source: National Bureau of Statistics

D. Providing Strong Support for Innovation via A Large, High-Quality Talent Pool

China boasts the largest talent pool in the world, providing a solid foundation for multinational corporations to carry out innovative business operations within the country. According to data from the National Bureau of Statistics, in 2023, China had over 250 million people with a university-level education, and the total amount of talent resources, scientific and technological human resources, and R&D personnel ranked first globally. Among them, R&D personnel totaled 6.6 million, representing a 3.8% year-on-year increase. In 2023, 1,275 individuals from China were included in the Clarivate[1]Highly Cited Researchers list, with China's share rising from 7.9% in 2018 to 17.9%. Additionally, the number of engineers grew from approximately 5.21 million in 2000 to about 20.59 million[2]in 2023. Multinational corporations have noted that China offers access to numerous exceptional talents, making it convenient to recruit and retain both domestic and foreign professionals for business operations and technical R&D. Moreover, partnerships with universities and research institutions play a crucial role in talent cultivation. Multinational corporations often collaborate with these institutions to train Chinese researchers and engineers, building connections to incorporate them into their R&D talent pool. This high-quality talent pool has become the primary resource driving the development of China's modern industrial system and promoting innovation-driven growth[3]. It serves as a powerful and inexhaustible source of momentum for global innovation and collaborative R&D (see Figure 3-6).

---

[1] A global data analytics company that owns several renowned industry brands, including the Web of Science™ platform (featuring the Science Citation Index™, abbreviated as SCI), the Derwent World Patents Index™ (abbreviated as DWPI), and the Techstreet™ International Standards Database.

[2] Source: *CPPCC DAILY*, January 30, 2024: Building an Outstanding Team of Engineers for the New Era.

[3] References: *China's Innovation Ecosystem*, published by the European Chamber of Commerce in China, and *Survey on Members' Business Climate: Perceptions of the Business Environment*, published by the Japanese Chamber of Commerce and Industry in China on May 14, 2024.

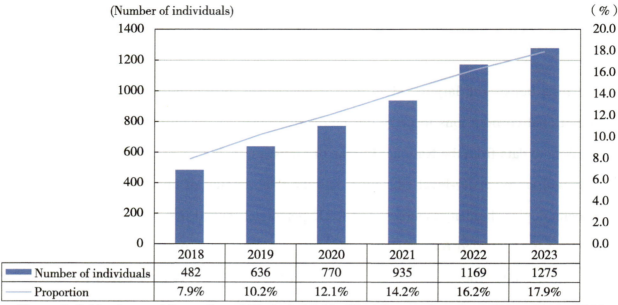

Figure 3-6: Number and Proportion of Clarivate Highly Cited Researchers from China, 2018—2023

Source: Clarivate Highly Cited Researchers List, Clarivate.

IV. Strengthened Role of High-Level Opening-up Platforms

China leverages platforms such as pilot free trade zones (FTZs), free trade ports, national economic development zones, and major international exhibitions as key drivers for enhancing its level of openness. Currently, pilot FTZs and national economic development zones contribute nearly 40% of the China's total foreign direct investment (FDI). In the future, the significant role of these high-level platforms in foreign trade, FDI, and institutional innovation will continue to expand.

A. Continuous Advancement of Pilot FTZs as Testing Grounds

1. Significant achievements in openness and innovation of pilot FTZs

The Third Plenary Session of the 20th CPC Central Committee proposed implementing a strategy to enhance pilot FTZs, encouraging original and integrated explorations. Pilot FTZs serve as vital foundations, practical platforms, and operational tools for building China's new open economy system. Since 2013, China has established 22 pilot FTZs in seven phases, creating a reform and opening-up landscape that integrates coastal, inland, and border areas across eastern, southern, western, northern, and central regions. Guided by high-level openness, these zones explore institutional systems aligned with international trade and economic rules. They systematically promote reforms and innovations in investment, trade, finance, and government governance, achieving a series of groundbreaking and leading innovations. Examples of these innovations include implementing a pre-establishment national treatment and negative list management model for foreign investment, establishing a "single-window" system for international trade, applying a negative list for cross-border service trade, streamlining the separation of permits and licenses, and experimenting with reforms in free trade accounts.

Pilot FTZs have driven industrial innovation and development through deepened reform and openness, building world-class industrial clusters. For instance: Shanghai Pilot FTZ has developed a modern industrial system centered around six industries: "China Chips", "Innovative Medicine", "Smart Manufacturing", "Blue Sky Dreams", "Future Cars", and "Data Ports". Tianjin Pilot FTZ has become the world's second-largest aircraft leasing hub. Zhejiang Pilot FTZ has attracted over 10, 000 oil and gas companies, ranking fifth globally in bonded fuel oil refueling volume. In 2022, the 21 pilot FTZs, occupying less than 4% of China's land area, contributed 18.1% of the nation's FDI and 17.9% of import-export trade. In 2023, their total import-export volume reached CNY 7.7 trillion, a 2.7% increase, accounting for 18.4% of China's total trade. Hainan Free Trade Port maintained double-digit annual import-export growth for three consecutive years.

Column 3-2: "Five Initiatives" for High-Level Reform and Opening Up in China's Pilot Free Trade Zones

First, leading in implementing the national treatment with pre-investment foreign investment access and negative list management model: This initiative aims to promote a historic transformation in the investment management system, actively facilitating a significant shift from an approval-based to a registration-based foreign investment management approach.

Second, leading in establishing a trade facilitation model centered on the international trade "single window": This model strongly supports the construction of a trading power. The Shanghai Free Trade Zone launched the first national International Trade "Single Window", setting a precedent for the nationwide implementation of the "Single Window" system.

Third, leading in promoting comprehensive opening up of the service sector with a negative list management model for cross-border service trade: This initiative supports the free and convenient flow of various high-end factors. In 2021, Hainan introduced the first negative list for cross-border trade in services, aligning China's service trade management more closely with international high-standard economic and trade rules.

Forth, pioneering government management reforms such as "separation of permits and licenses". This reform has improved the business environment and accelerated the transformation of government functions. It addresses the "entry without operational permission" issue and advances the reform of foundational commercial systems.

Fifth, pioneering the establishment of free trade accounts in pilot FTZs. These accounts integrate domestic and foreign currency operations and allow free exchange within the accounts, reducing corporate financing costs. Pilot Free Trade Zones have also innovated financial services, such as voluntary foreign exchange settlement for foreign-invested enterprises and cross-border two-way RMB fund pooling.

2. Nationwide replication and sharing of innovations

Since 2013, a series of foundational and institutional reforms piloted in FTZs have been replicated and promoted nationwide, improving basic management systems in investment, trade, and finance. These initiatives have advanced reforms from specific zones to broader regions by implementing targeted and effective measures with quick results, driving openness and development across the country. As of July 2023, seven batches of pilot FTZ reform experiences and four batches of best practices have been summarized at the national level, resulting in the replication and promotion of 302 institutional innovation achievements from FTZs. Local governments have independently replicated and promoted over 2,800 innovations[1]. Examples include: investment liberalization and facilitation, reforms in business registration, changes, operations, and exits, as well as engineering project approval systems, which have enhanced the national investment environment. Trade liberalization and facilitation: innovations in customs supervision models, optimized taxation mechanisms, and the cultivation of new trade formats and models have promoted high-quality trade development. Government management reforms: Simplified approvals, strengthened regulation, and improved services have enhanced governance capabilities across local governments. Financial openness and innovation: measures such as foreign exchange management facilitation, cross-border capital flows, RMB internationalization, and innovative financing models have been replicated and promoted nationwide.

3. High-quality development of Hainan free trade port taking shape

On June 1, 2020, the *Overall Plan for the Construction of Hainan Free Trade Port* was officially released, accelerating the construction of Hainan Free Trade Port. In 2021, the Standing Committee of the National People's Congress enacted the *Hainan Free Trade Port Law of the People's Republic of China*, which legally codified policies related to the port's development. At present, Hainan Free Trade Port has established a policy framework with a primary focus on trade, investment, cross-border capital flows, personnel mobility, transportation freedom and convenience, and the secure and orderly flow of data. By adhering to high-level institutional openness as a guide, Hainan has pioneered the implementation of high-standard economic and trade rules, steadily expanding institutional openness. To date, 16 batches of 140 institutional innovation cases have been issued, of which 11 cases have been replicated and promoted nationwide by the State Council. As policy dividends accelerate, Hainan has become a hotspot for investment. Since 2018, the number of newly established foreign enterprises in Hainan has grown by 65% annually. In 2023, Hainan led the country in

---

[1] Please refer to the official website of the State Council Information Office: http://www. scio. gov. cn/ live/2023/32694/tw/.

various economic and social indicators. Notable achievements include a 9.2% GDP growth, an 18.5% increase in industrial added value above designated size, and 6.3% and 8.3% growth in per capita disposable income for urban and rural residents, respectively. Reflecting the unique economic model of the free trade port, goods trade increased by 15.3%, while service trade grew by 29.6%.

B. National Economic and Technological Development Zones as Major Tools for Opening—up

In 1984, the Central Committee of the Communist Party of China and the State Council made the strategic decision to establish national economic and technological development zones. Over the past 40 years, these zones have evolved into one of the most concentrated industrial hubs, the most active platforms for an open economy, and the strongest drivers of regional development in China. They have played an essential role in deepening reform, expanding opening-up, and promoting new industrialization and urbanization. As important platforms for opening-up and industrial agglomeration, national economic and technological development zones account for 3‰ of China's land area but contribute 10% of GDP, 20% of utilized foreign investment, and 20% of foreign trade totals. They have made significant contributions to building China's modern industrial system and advancing reform and innovation. The latest comprehensive development assessment results[1], published by the Ministry of Commerce, show that these zones have maintained steady growth across key indicators, with growth rates exceeding national averages and their share of the national economy further increasing (see Table 3-1).

1. Enhancement of the quality of economic development

In 2022, national economic and technological development zones achieved a regional GDP of CNY 14 trillion, accounting for 12% of the national GDP. By the end of 2022, there

---

[1] The Ministry of Commerce conducts an annual assessment of the comprehensive development level of national economic and technological development zones between July and October, evaluating the performance of the previous year. The latest assessment results currently available are for 2022

were 1,765 manufacturing enterprises with annual revenues exceeding CNY 3 billion in the eastern zones and CNY 1.5 billion in the central and western zones, representing a significant year-on-year increase.

2. Promotion of the driving effect of opening-up

In 2022, the actual utilization of foreign capital in national economic and technological development zones reached USD 43.2 billion, accounting for 23% of the national total. The total import and export volume reached CNY 10.3 trillion, contributing 25% to the national trade total, including CNY 3 trillion in high-tech products, which made up 27% of the national high-tech trade.

3. Improvement of the capacity of technological innovation

By the end of 2022, national economic and technological development zones hosted 683 national-level incubators and makerspaces, 12,000 provincial or higher-level R&D institutions, and 65, 000 high-tech enterprises, all reflecting substantial growth from the previous year.

4. Improvement in green and low-carbon levels

In 2022, industrial enterprises in these zones above designated size saw significant reductions in energy and water consumption per unit of industrial added value, while the comprehensive utilization rate of industrial solid waste increased by 2 percentage points compared to the previous year.

5. Enhancement of the development of regional coordnation

By the end of 2022, the number of cooperative projects between eastern zones and central and western zones, as well as projects assisting Xinjiang, Xizang, and (cross-) border cooperation areas, had increased by 126 compared to the previous year.

Table 3-1: Some Indicators for the 230 National Economic and Technological Development Zones in 2022

Indicator	Value	Growth Rate (%)	Share of National Total (%)
Regional GDP	CNY 14 trillion	5.6	12
Actual utilization of foreign capital	USD 43.2 billion	11.5	23

Continued Table

Indicator	Value	Growth Rate (%)	Share of National Total (%)
Import and export volume	CNY 10.3 trillion	15	25
High-tech product trade	CNY 3 trillion	—	27

C. Enhanced Role of Large−Scale International Exhibitions

At the 5th China International Import Expo (CIIE), President Xi Jinping emphasized that "China's market should become the world's market, and global exhibitors should become investors in China[1]". Events such as the CIIE[2] and the China International Fair for Investment and Trade (CIFIT)[3] have become vital platforms for showcasing China's new development model, advancing high-level openness, and serving as a global public good for shared economic growth. These platforms also create new opportunities to expand bilateral investment cooperation, contributing to the global economic recovery.

The CIIE is the world's first national-level expo themed exclusively on imports, representing China's commitment to actively open its markets to the world. In November 2023, the 6th CIIE was held in Shanghai, achieving a record high in intended transaction volume, totaling USD 78.41 billion, a 6.7% increase compared to the previous edition. The event attracted representatives from 154 countries, regions, and international organizations, with 72 countries and organizations participating in the National Pavilion. China's pavilion, themed "China's New Achievements in Modernization Provide New Opportunities for Global Development", highlighted ten years of progress in the Free Trade Zone initiative, emphasizing high-level openness and high-quality development. The exhibition demonstrated

---

[1] Speech by Xi Jinping at the opening ceremony of the 5th China International Import Expo on November 4, 2022.

[2] China International Import Expo (CIIE).

[3] China International Fair for Investment and Trade (CIFIT).

how "a better China contributes to a better world". Nearly 200 events were hosted in the National Pavilion, offering a platform for countries at various development stages to promote cooperation and mutual benefit. The Enterprise Pavilion featured 3,486 companies from 128 countries and regions, showcasing 442 innovative products, technologies, and services being debuted. The Innovation Incubation Zone attracted over 300 innovation projects from 39 countries. Over five years, the CIIE has accumulated intended transaction volumes nearing USD 350 billion, with a significant spillover effect as exhibitors transform into investors, releasing continuous benefits from China's open market.

The CIFIT, held annually for 23 years, has become one of the most influential international investment events and a crucial platform for promoting two-way investment in China. It emphasizes three core functions: facilitating two-way investment, authoritative information release, and investment trend research. In September 2023, the 23rd CIFIT in Xiamen attracted over 100 countries and regions, 1,000 trade and economic delegations, and nearly 80, 000 domestic and international business participants[1]. Twelve international organizations, including UNCTAD, UNIDO, the Shanghai Cooperation Organization, and the OECD, participated in the event. During the conference, 638 projects were signed with a total planned investment of CNY 484.57 billion, setting a five-year high in both the number of participating institutions and the total investment amount.

In addition, a series of exhibitions, including the China Import and Export Fair, the China International Fair for Trade in Services, the China Hi-Tech Fair, the China-ASEAN Expo, and the Western China International Fair, have played a significant role in promoting trade and investment cooperation between China and countries around the world.

---

[1] https://www. gov. cn/yaowen/liebiao/202309/content_6903371. htm

Chapter 4   China's Promotion of Two-Way Investment and Global Mutual Benefit

Openness is a distinctive feature of China's modernization. China has steadily expanded institutional openness, continuously deepened reforms in the management systems for foreign investment and outbound investment, and achieved mutual benefit through two-way investment. Foreign-invested enterprises have embraced the vast opportunities of the Chinese market, leveraging their operations in China to support global business growth. Simultaneously, Chinese enterprises investing abroad have enhanced their long-term development capabilities and shared development achievements with host countries. Through two-way investment cooperation, China has contributed greater certainty and new growth momentum to the global economy.

I. Mutual Commitment and Win-Win Cooperation between Foreign-Invested Enterprises and the Chinese Market

In the historical process of China's reform and opening-up over the past 40 years, multinational corporations have played significant roles as participants, witnesses, and beneficiaries. They have seized the major opportunities and substantial dividends offered by China's market openness.

A. Strong Development of Foreign-Invested Enterprises in the Chinese Market

Foreign-invested enterprises in China have leveraged the policy and market dividends of reform and opening-up to achieve rapid development. Since 2013, the total profits of industrial enterprises with foreign investment above the designated size have remained stable, maintaining a profitability rate of approximately 7%. In 2021 and 2022, the total profits of these enterprises reached CNY 2.28 trillion and CNY 2 trillion, respectively, ranking as the highest and second-highest totals in history. In 2023, foreign-invested and Hong Kong, Macao, and Taiwan-invested enterprises achieved CNY 27.2 trillion in operating revenue and CNY 1.8 trillion in total profits, with a profit margin of 6.6%, nearly 1 percentage point higher than the national average profit margin for industrial enterprises above the designated size (5.76%)[1] (see Figure 4-1).

Figure 4–1: Profit Trends of Industrial Enterprises with Foreign Investment Above Designated Size, 2013—2023

Data Sources: *Statistical Bulletin of FDI in China* 2023, calculated and compiled by the research team.

In 2023, many foreign-funded enterprises in China achieved significant growth. For instance, both L'Oréal and Bosch saw sales increases of over 5%; Apple's revenue from the Greater China region accounted for about one-fifth of the company's total revenue; Merck's sales in China reached USD 6.71 billion, a year-on-year increase of 32%[2]; and Toyota's sales

---

① Data for 2023 is sourced from: https://www. gov. cn/lianbo/bumen/202401/content_6928596. htm, while data from 2013 to 2022 comes from the *Statistical Bulletin of FDI in China 2023*.

② https://www. gov. cn/yaowen/liebiao/202403/content_6939076. htm.

in the Chinese market exceeded 1.9 million units, making up 17% of its global total. The *White Paper on the Chinese Economy and Japanese Companies 2024*, released by the Japan Chamber of Commerce in China in July 2024, states that China provides enormous market opportunities for foreign enterprises, becoming a significant source of profit for many of them. A win-win relationship has been established between China and foreign enterprises.

B. Significant Contributions of Foreign-Invested Enterprises to China's Economic and Social Development

Foreign-invested enterprises play a critical role in advancing Chinese modernization and fostering the shared prosperity of the Chinese and global economies. Although they account for less than 2% of market entities in China, these enterprises drive over 8% of employment, contribute 1/6 of tax revenues, and generate 1/3 of total imports and exports. Therefore, substantial contributions have been made to the economic and social development of China.

Since the reform and opening-up, the share of foreign-invested enterprises in China's goods trade has steadily increased. In 2006, their share peaked at 58.9%, marking the highest level in history[1]. Subsequently, as domestic enterprises grew and foreign-invested enterprises expanded their focus to upstream sectors of the industrial chain, their share in goods trade decreased but remained significant. In 2023, foreign-invested enterprises accounted for over 30% of China's goods trade, providing strong support for the steady development of foreign trade. Foreign-invested enterprises have also been a significant source of tax revenue. Their contribution to China's total tax revenue peaked at 22.9% in 2006 and 2009[2]. Since 2013, this share has declined slightly but has consistently remained above 17%, underscoring their importance to China's fiscal revenue (see Figure 4-2).

---

[1] Data from 2012 to 2022 is sourced from the *Statistical Bulletin of FDI in China 2023*. The 2023 information comes from a press conference held by the State Council Information Office on January 12, 2024, where Wang Lingjun, Deputy Director of the General Administration of Customs, provided an introduction.

[2] *Statistical Bulletin of FDI in China 2023*.

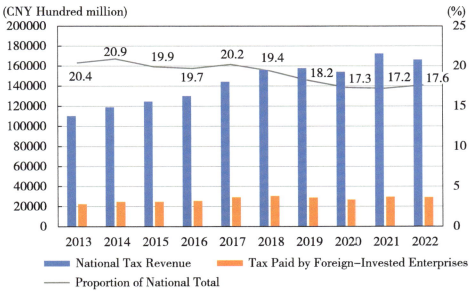

Figure 4-2: Contribution of Foreign-Invested Enterprises to China's Tax Revenue

Source: *Statistical Bulletin of FDI in China* 2023, calculated and compiled by the research team.

As foreign-invested enterprises have expanded alongside the Chinese market, they have created significant spillover effects in areas such as technology, management, and innovation. These effects have enhanced the ability of domestic enterprises to compete in international markets, promoted their deeper integration into global industrial, supply, and value chains, and accelerated industrial transformation, upgrading, and the improvement of international competitiveness.

C. Foreign-Invested Enterprises Committed to a Shared Future with China

Digitalization, green development, and innovation are emerging as new opportunities in the Chinese market. Since 2023, numerous multinational industry leaders have demonstrated their confidence in the Chinese market and their commitment to open cooperation with China by increasing investments. For example: Tesla established its first energy storage "Megafactory" outside the U.S. in Shanghai. Volkswagen Group (China) announced an investment of 2.5 billion euros to establish its largest overseas research and development center. ExxonMobil added CNY 10 billion in investment to the first phase of its ethylene project in Huizhou, located in the Daya Bay Petrochemical Zone. In February 2024, the American Chamber of Commerce in China released a survey report indicating the significant importance of the Chinese market to U.S. companies operating in China. Nearly half of the member enterprises projected profits in 2023[1], and nearly 50% of the members ranked China among their top three global investment destinations—a 5-percentage-point increase from 2022.

II. Enhancing Host Countries' Economic and Social Development Capacity through Chinese Outbound Investment

In recent years, Chinese enterprises have significantly improved their capacity for outbound investment and international operations. In the process, they have made substantial contributions to host countries, such as improving local infrastructure, creating jobs, increasing tax revenue, and cultivating technical talent. These contributions have actively supported the economic and social development of host countries and facilitated shared development outcomes.

A. Strong Overall Performance of Chinese Overseas Enterprises

In 2023, nearly 70% of Chinese overseas enterprises reported profits or broke even, with reinvested earnings reaching USD 78.46 billion, the third-highest in history, accounting for 44.2% of China's outward direct investment[2] flow during the same period. According to the *Survey on Current Conditions and Intention of Outbound Investment by Chinese Enterprises* released the March 2024, by the China Council for the Promotion of International Trade (CCPIT), over half of the surveyed enterprises reported stable or increased returns on

---

[1] The data collection period for this survey report is November 2023.

[2] Ministry of Commerce, National Bureau of Statistics, State Administration of Foreign Exchange: *2023 Statistical Bulletin of China's Outward Foreign Direct Investment*, China Commerce and Trade Press, 2024 edition.

overseas investments, and more than 30% reported increased profit margins. A survey by the China Chamber of Commerce to the EU indicated[1] that despite external challenges, 90% of Chinese enterprises in Europe achieved revenue growth in 2023, a significant increase from 70% the previous year. Furthermore, 58% of these enterprises expected their revenue to show "moderate" or "significant" growth, and 83% had plans to increase investment and deepen their presence in Europe. Similarly, a survey by the China General Chamber of Commerce-USA revealed that despite heightened tensions and uncertainty, most Chinese enterprises in the U.S. opted to maintain or expand their investments in the market. Nearly 90% of these enterprises planned to either maintain current levels or increase their investments, demonstrating continued optimism regarding future revenue trends[2].

B. Supporting Host Countries in Infrastructure Development and Long-Term Growth

Chinese enterprises have leveraged their strengths in fields such as transportation, water and energy infrastructure, and digital infrastructure to assist host countries in building and improving their infrastructure, boosting industrial development, and promoting long-term economic and social progress. For instance, in transportation, Chinese enterprises constructed the Algeria East-West Highway, spanning 1,216 kilometers and connecting 17 provinces in the country's north. This project reduced travel time from three days to just 10 hours[3] and was hailed by the media as a "road of transportation and tourism, a road of development and hope". In the field of water and energy infrastructure, Chinese enterprises collaborated with Laos to construct hydropower stations and cross-border power transmission networks. These

---

[1] China Chamber of Commerce to the EU: *Building Trust, Boosting Prosperity--CCCEU Report on the Development of Chinese Enterprises in the EU 2023/2024*, November 14, 2023.

[2] China General Chamber of Commerce-USA: *Annual Business Survey Report on Chinese Enterprises in the United States*, June 2024.

[3] *People's Daily*: Witnessing the Abundant Results of High-Quality Co-Building of the Belt and Road Initiative between China and Arab Countries, July 23, 2024.

initiatives enabled electricity exports to account for 30%[1] of Laos' total exports, helping Laos establish its position as the "battery of Southeast Asia" and significantly enhancing its long-term development capabilities.

Beyond large-scale infrastructure projects, Chinese enterprises have also implemented smaller-scale, community-focused projects that have been well-received by local populations. For example, during the construction of the China-Laos Railway, Chinese companies relocated 65 kilometers of power lines, built and renovated 743 kilometers of access roads, constructed 34 temporary bridges, leveled 140, 000 square meters of residential land, and built 272 kilometers of canals and 15 water wells. In Africa, projects such as the "Luban Workshop" and Tanzania's "Village Electrification" program have significantly improved local living conditions and contributed to host countries' long-term development capabilities.

C. Creating Jobs and Increasing Tax Revenue to Support Host Countries' Economic Growth

Chinese enterprises' investments and operations overseas have created numerous jobs, paid significant taxes, and directly contributed to the economic and social development of host countries. Since the 18th National Congress of the Communist Party of China, China has cumulatively made outward direct investments totaling USD 1.68 trillion, equivalent to 57% of its stock in 2023. For eight consecutive years, China's share of global outbound investment has exceeded 10%. Chinese enterprises have paid USD 518.5 billion in taxes to host countries and regions, and they have provided over 2 million jobs annually[2]. In 2023, Chinese overseas enterprises paid a total of USD 75.3 billion in taxes to host countries, an increase of 0.3% from the previous year. By the end of the year, they employed 4.289 million workers, of whom 2.57

---

[1] *The Nikkei*: Chinese Enterprises Increase Investment in Laos' Power Infrastructure, March 12, 2024.

[2] Ministry of Commerce, National Bureau of Statistics, State Administration of Foreign Exchange: *2023 Statistical Bulletin of China's Outward Foreign Direct Investment*, China Commerce and Trade Press, 2024 edition.

million were local hires, marking an increase of 77,000 (see Table 4-1). For example, Chinese enterprises[1] have been the largest Asian investors in France for three consecutive years. As of 2023, Chinese investors have invested in more than 900 French enterprises, creating over 50,000 jobs.

Table 4-1: Number of Foreign Employees Hired by Chinese Overseas Enterprises, 2017—2023

Year	2017	2018	2019	2020	2021	2022	2023
Foreign Employees Hired (10,000)	171	187.7	226.6	218.8	239	249.3	257

Source: Ministry of Commerce, National Bureau of Statistics, and State Administration of Foreign Exchange, *2023 Statistical Bulletin of China's Outward Foreign Direct Investment*, China Commerce and Trade Press, 2024

D. Increasing Investments in Digitalization and Green Development to Support Host Country Innovation and Transformation

Chinese enterprises have leveraged their strengths in the digital economy and green development to bring digital and green technologies to host countries, assisting their transitions to digitalization and sustainable growth. For example, the De Aar Wind Farm in South Africa is the first wind power project in Africa undertaken by Chinese companies that integrates investment, construction, and operation. Since it began operation in 2017, it has supplied approximately 760 million kWh of electricity annually, meeting the electricity needs of 300,000 households, and reducing carbon dioxide emissions by over 600,000 tons each year. The Garissa Solar Power Plant in Kenya, constructed by Chinese enterprises, provides electricity for 70,000 households and reduces tens of thousands of tons of carbon dioxide emissions annually. Kenya's former president, Uhuru Kenyatta, commended the plant for its role in promoting Kenya's green development and energy transformation[2]. In the European

---

[1] *People's Daily*: China, France see mutual benefit from bilateral economic, trade cooperation, January 29, 2024.

[2] Kenya Broadcasting Corporation (KBC) News: China: A Reliable Partner in Africa's Greener and Greater Future, May 23, 2024.

Union, China, as the leading investor among developing economies, has established R&D centers, data centers, cybersecurity hubs, and battery factories in Germany, Ireland, Belgium, and Hungary, significantly contributing to local economic development, job creation, and research innovation[1].

E. Providing Technical Assistance to Cultivate Talent in Host Countries

Chinese enterprises emphasize not only technical cooperation but also the training of management and technical personnel in host countries. For example: During the construction of the Algeria East-West Highway, Chinese companies established a large project management academy and a national quality control center, training over 16, 000 local infrastructure technicians. In Saudi Arabia, Chinese companies established an overseas training center focused on health, safety, environmental management systems, and drilling technology. Since its founding in 2008, the center has conducted over 1, 000 training sessions, training 40, 000 Saudi employees, and building a comprehensive pipeline of petroleum engineering talent to enhance the host country's capacity for independent oil extraction and refining[2].

III. China's Two-Way Investment Injects Certainty and Growth Momentum into the Global Economy

Amid slowing global economic growth, intensified geopolitical conflicts, and significant adjustments in national industrial policies, China's large, open market, efficient industrial system, and robust innovation capabilities offer enormous opportunities to multinational enterprises in China and contribute to global economic growth.

---

[1] China Chamber of Commerce to the EU: *Building Trust, Boosting Prosperity--CCCEU Report on the Development of Chinese Enterprises in the EU 2023/2024*, November 14, 2023.

[2] *China Discipline Inspection and Supervision Daily*: "Chinese Enterprises Actively Participate in High-Quality Belt and Road Construction, China Has Continued to Strengthen "Hard Connectivity" in Infrastructure to Building a Community with a Shared Future," October 18, 2023.

A. An Open Chinese Market Injects New Momentum into Global Economic Recovery

A market is the most valuable resource. China's super-sized market advantage, combined with its market-oriented, rule-of-law-based, and internationalized business environment, provides vast market space and cooperation opportunities for global enterprises. In recent years, China's resilient and dynamic economy has maintained stable growth, contributing around 30% to global economic growth. China has expanded imports of high-quality consumer goods, advanced technologies, essential equipment, key components, energy resources, and domestically scarce agricultural products. Through platforms like the China International Import Expo (CIIE), China has broadened its diversified import channels, improved import trade facilitation, and established national innovation demonstration zones for import trade promotion. These efforts have transformed China's massive market into a global marketplace, injecting new momentum into global economic recovery.

In July 2024, the International Monetary Fund (IMF) updated its *World Economic Outlook Report*, projecting China's economic growth to reach 5% in 2024, a 0.4 percentage-point increase from its April report. According to a survey by the German Chamber of Commerce in China, most surveyed German enterprises expect China's economy to rebound strongly within five years. In sectors such as electronics, machinery/industrial equipment, plastics/metal products, and automobiles, over 60% of enterprises anticipate robust growth within three years[1]. The *White Paper on the Chinese Economy and Japanese Companies 2024*, released by the Japan Chamber of Commerce in China, indicated that over 50% of Japanese enterprises view China as their most important or one of their top three markets. *The New York Times*, citing projections by global financial data provider FactSet, reported that while nearly 60% of the revenue of S&P 500 companies comes from the U.S., their largest overseas revenue source is China. According to Xinhua News Agency, J. P. Morgan's Asia-

---

[1] German Chamber of Commerce in China: *Business Confidence Survey 2023/24*, January 2024.

Pacific CEO emphasized that China's economic influence is undeniable, and for investors, it is an indispensable market.

B. Enhancing an Efficient Industrial System to Improve the Stability of Global Supply Chains

As one of the three major hubs in the global value chain, with the most comprehensive and largest-scale industrial system and the most robust supporting capabilities, China adheres to its fundamental national policy of openness and steadfastly pursues a win-win opening strategy. This has enabled China to make significant contributions to stabilizing global industrial and supply chains.

For example, Airbus officially began operating its first aircraft full lifecycle service center-Airbus Lifecycle Services Centre in China in January 2024. This marked the completion of Airbus' industrial chain in China, spanning research and development, component production, aircraft assembly, technical support and services, and recycling. An Airbus China representative noted that amid global supply chain tensions, Chinese partners have played a critical role in stabilizing the supply chain, demonstrating resilience and competitiveness. Similarly, in March 2024, multinational biopharmaceutical giant AstraZeneca signed an agreement to establish manufacturing facility in Wuxi, covering processes from formulation to packaging. This facility will join AstraZeneca's global production and supply network, providing high-quality innovative medicines "made in China" for both domestic and international markets, showcasing China's global value contributions.

C. Strengthening Technological Innovation and Industrialization to Energize Global Innovation and Progress

Amid the ongoing wave of technological revolution and industrial transformation, China has accelerated its efforts to build itself into a technological powerhouse, creating new domains and pathways for development. In 2023, China's R&D expenditure reached CNY 3.3278 trillion, an 8.1% increase from the previous year, accounting for 2.64% of its GDP—

a globally competitive level. The number of effective invention patents in China totaled 4.015 million, a 22.4% year-on-year increase, making China the first country to surpass 4 million patents. High-value invention patents accounted for more than 40% of this total. Additionally, China maintained its position as the global leader in invention patent filings and international patent applications under the *Patent Cooperation Treaty (PCT)* for consecutive years[1].

China's rapid advancements in technological innovation have enhanced the global competitiveness of domestic enterprises while providing multinational corporations with accelerated industrialization opportunities and new vitality. China encourages foreign investment in establishing R&D centers, collaborating with domestic enterprises on technology development and industrial applications. It also supports foreign-invested enterprises and their R&D centers in undertaking major scientific research projects, fostering an innovation-friendly ecosystem for global enterprises. By the end of June 2024, Shanghai had recognized 985 regional headquarters of multinational corporations and 575 foreign R&D centers, maintaining its position as the most concentrated city for such entities in mainland China. Numerous prominent multinational companies have established large-scale R&D and innovation centers in China[2]. Many foreign executives believe that China's open innovation ecosystem, forward-looking talent cultivation strategies, and policy support for industrial development position the country as a key driver shaping future technological and innovation trends. China's robust technological innovation capabilities, continuously optimized business environment, and well-developed industrial and supply chain foundations create significant growth potential. These strengths provide multinational corporations with ample opportunities

---

① *People's Daily*: "Courageously Taking on the Responsibilities of the Era and Accelerating the Construction of a Technological Powerhouse", July 31, 2024, by the CPC Leading Group of the Ministry of Science and Technology.

② https://www. jingan. gov. cn/rmtzx/003008/003008004/20240726/93db4e5d-d300-4b99-886e-d7c8ab58ac2a. html?type=2, Shanghai Jing'an District People's Government Website: *Shanghai Hosts 985 Regional Headquarters of Multinational Corporations, with Foreign Investment in China Set to Increase*.

to integrate global resources and deepen cooperation in supply chains and industrial chains, while also continuing to serve as an essential pillar for global economic stability and development.

Chapter 5   Investment Links the World, Opportunities Benefit the Globe

Openness is a defining feature of Chinese modernization. China adheres to its fundamental national policy of opening-up, leveraging its vast market advantages to deepen international cooperation and develop a higher-level open economic system. Looking ahead, China will continue to strengthen international investment cooperation, promoting mutual benefit and stable development of global two-way investment. By supporting collaboration in global supply chains and advancing digital and green transformations, China aims to contribute new dynamism to the global economy, implement the Global Development Initiative, and foster economic globalization toward greater openness, inclusiveness, and balance.

I. Promoting Global Cross-Border Investment and Economic Recovery

Currently, global landscape is marked by volatility, and foreign direct investment (FDI) faces numerous challenges in a sluggish global economy. More than ever, international cooperation and shared openness are needed. Mutual benefit, deeper participation in global industrial divisions, and cooperative development are essential for sustainability. Creating an open and inclusive international investment environment requires collective effort. Despite rising trade and investment protectionism and growing uncertainty in the international environment, China will steadfastly pursue high-level opening-up, institutional openness, and reforms. By aligning with international high-standard economic and trade rules, China will establish transparent, stable, and predictable institutional and market environments. These initiatives will bolster the "Invest China" brand, create vast opportunities for multinational corporations (MNCs), and enhance global investment confidence. China will continue to facilitate outward investment by improving regulatory frameworks and services, fostering high-quality Belt and Road cooperation, and encouraging Chinese enterprises to strengthen international capabilities in production, R&D, and green collaboration. This effort will generate jobs, drive economic growth in host countries, and promote mutual benefit.

II. Enhancing Efficiency and Resilience in Global Supply Chains

Economic globalization has faced headwinds in recent years, and global economic recovery remains challenging. President Xi Jinping has emphasized that maintaining resilient and stable global supply chains is critical to global economic development. Premier Li Qiang has highlighted the shared interests and urgent expectations of all parties in strengthening global supply chain cooperation. To safeguard supply chain stability and efficiency, countries must embrace openness and collaboration while avoiding exclusive, closed supply chain structures that risk geopolitical fragmentation in international investment. China plays a pivotal role as both a participant and builder in global supply chain cooperation. Leveraging its position as a supply chain hub in the Asia-Pacific region, along with its comprehensive industrial system and infrastructure, China promotes open cooperation in supply chains to create systems that are secure, stable, efficient, inclusive, and mutually beneficial. China will also support MNCs in utilizing China's manufacturing scale, cost advantages, and technological strengths to respond rapidly to global supply and demand shifts. By establishing regional headquarters, R&D centers, and other functional institutions in China, MNCs will find enhanced opportunities to expand their global businesses. Furthermore, China will foster trade and investment liberalization, expand its high-standard free trade agreement network, and support Belt and Road cooperation. In this way, China can provide greater convenience and better safeguards for foreign enterprises investing and operating in the country. It aims to support the industrial upgrading of host nations and contributes to the stable and efficient operation of global industrial supply chains.

III. Supporting Digitalization and Green Transitions

Emerging fields such as digitalization and green development are driving global economic growth and transformation. At the 4th China International Import Expo, President Xi Jinping stated, "China will actively participate in international cooperation on green, low-carbon, and digital economies. " In digitalization, as a global leader in the digital economy, China will further expand market access in the digital sector, improve regulatory frameworks through categorized management, enhance cross-border data flow, and foster AI and digital investment cooperation. Internationally, China will negotiate and implement multilateral and bilateral agreements on digital economy investment, promote digital trade, and encourage the globalization of e-commerce platforms, enabling industries like smart logistics and mobile payments to thrive globally. In green development, the global green investment gap remains significant. According to a 2021 report, *Carbon Neutrality Economy*, by China International Capital Corporation (CICC), the global green investment gap is estimated at USD 121.7 trillion. A 2024 report by the International Energy Agency (IEA) confirms that China will remain the largest global investor in clean energy, with an expected investment of USD 675 billion, surpassing the combined investments of the U.S. (USD 315 billion) and EU (USD 370 billion). China's commitment to green development accelerates its domestic green transition and encourages foreign clean energy investments in its market. By providing application scenarios for advanced green technologies, China supports global green transitions. Furthermore, China integrates green principles into its outbound investments, leveraging its expertise in sectors such as new energy vehicles (NEVs), batteries, and solar and wind energy. These efforts address power shortages and green investment gaps in developing countries, contributing significantly to sustainable global development.

IV. Supporting the Global Development Initiative and the Sustainable Development Agenda

Development embodies people's aspirations for a better life, serves as the ultimate key to resolving all challenges, and remains the eternal theme of human society. Sustainable growth is a common demand among developing countries worldwide. In September 2021, President Xi Jinping proposed the Global Development Initiative (GDI), offering a Chinese solution to address the global development deficit. In recent years, China has advanced 32 major initiatives to implement the GDI, hosting the first and second high-level meetings of the Forum on Global Action for Shared Development and releasing the *Shared Future Actions Plan*. This plan encompasses 50 items, including technical assistance, infrastructure development, and talent cultivation, aiming to achieve more robust, green, and healthy global development. These efforts enhance countries' autonomous development capabilities while providing new opportunities and spaces for advancing high-quality cross-border investment. In September 2015, the United Nations Development Summit formally adopted the 2030 Agenda for Sustainable Development, marking a critical global development roadmap. Looking ahead, China will continue to foster global development consensus, advance the implementation of the GDI, and assist developing countries in accelerating their efforts toward the 2030 Agenda for Sustainable Development. China will leverage the expertise of multilateral development banks to mobilize investments, advocate for increased contributions to global development cooperation, and take pragmatic measures to expand development resources. China's focus will remain on cross-border investment strategies that both "provide resources" and "build capacity", supporting developing countries in accelerating industrial transformation and enhancing their self-reliance. By working together to expand and equitably share the benefits of economic globalization, grounded in mutual benefit, China will continue to promote globalization toward greater openness, inclusiveness, and balance. Through its two-way investments, China aims to connect the world and bring shared prosperity to all!

Regional Section

Chapter 6　Shanghai Foreign Investment Utilization Report[1]

Foreign investment utilization is a key component of China's basic national policy of opening up. President Xi Jinping has repeatedly emphasized that "China will only open its door even wider to the outside world". As a pioneer in reform and opening up and a forerunner in innovative development, Shanghai has consistently regarded attracting foreign investment as a top priority in expanding openness. It was the first to implement a system of the access to pre-establishment national treatment with a negative list, continuously improving the levels of investment and trade liberalization and facilitation. Shanghai has become one of the world's most attractive destinations for foreign investment and a preferred location for multinational companies to establish global supply chains, industrial chains, and innovation chains.

I. Progress and Achievements in Foreign Investment

Shanghai serves as a window for the world to observe China and as a bridgehead for foreign investment entering the Chinese market. A significant number of foreign-funded enterprises have gathered and developed here, becoming a vital force in driving the development of both Shanghai and China.

First, steady growth in the scale of foreign investment.

---

① Provided by the Shanghai Municipal Commission of Commerce.

In 2023, Shanghai approved the establishment of 6,017 new foreign-invested enterprises, marking a 38.3% increase year-on-year. The actual utilized foreign capital reached USD 24.087 billion, setting a new record high and exceeding USD 20 billion for four consecutive years. By the end of 2023, Shanghai had cumulatively established over 120, 000 foreign-invested enterprises, with more than 75, 000 still active, and had attracted over USD 350 billion in actual utilized foreign capital.

Second, continuous optimization of the structure of foreign investment. Shanghai has gradually developed a foreign investment structure centered on the services and high-tech industries. In 2023, 90.0% of the actual utilized foreign capital was invested in the services sector, mainly in information services, business services, scientific and technological services, real estate, wholesale and retail, and financial services. Meanwhile, 10.0% was allocated to manufacturing, particularly in electronic components, new energy vehicles and auto parts, pharmaceuticals and medical devices, general equipment, non-metallic minerals, and food production. The ability of high-tech industries to attract foreign investment has continued to grow, with USD 10.56 billion of actual utilized foreign capital in 2023, an increase of 9.4%, accounting for 43.8%.

Third, continuous upgrading the energy level of foreign investment. Regional headquarters and R&D centers are highlights and unique features of Shanghai's foreign investment landscape. In 2023, Shanghai added 65 new regional headquarters of multinational companies and 30 foreign-funded R&D centers. By the end of 2023, it had established a total of 956 regional headquarters of multinational companies and 561 foreign-funded R&D centers, maintaining its position as the city with the most concentrated regional headquarters of multinational companies in Chinese Mainland. The energy level of headquarters projects has been gradually improved. Headquarters of Greater China and above accounted for 18%, and R&D centers established by Fortune 500 companies accounted for about 25%.

Fourth, stable main sources of foreign investment. In 2023, Shanghai's main sources of foreign investment were Hong Kong SAR China, Singapore, Europe, Japan, the United States, and South Korea, collectively contributing more than 95% of the actual utilized foreign capital. RCEP member countries invested a total of USD 3.19 billion in Shanghai, an increase of 27.5% year-on-year, accounting for 13.3% of total foreign investment. Countries participating in the Belt and Road Initiative invested a total of USD 2.43 billion in Shanghai, a year-on-year increase of 1.4%, accounting for 10.1%.

Fifth, significant contributions from foreign-invested enterprises. Central enterprises, Shanghai's state-owned enterprises, foreign enterprises, and private enterprises each account for about a quarter of Shanghai's economy. Among these, foreign-invested enterprises contribute more than a quarter of the city's GDP, about a third of tax revenue, nearly two-thirds of foreign trade imports and exports, about one-fifth of employment, over half of the industrial output value above a designated size, and two-fifths of R&D expenditure in industrial enterprises above a designated size. Foreign capital has become a crucial engine for Shanghai's economic growth, a key support for industrial structure adjustment, a driving force for technological innovation, and an important factor in enhancing urban functionality.

II. Key Points, Highlights, Initiatives, and Their Roles

The CPC Shanghai Municipal Committee and the Shanghai Municipal Government have consistently prioritized the attraction and utilization of foreign investment. They diligently implement President Xi Jinping's directives for Shanghai, resolutely advancing all-around opening-up and embracing, attracting, and servicing foreign capital with even greater vigor.

A. Driving High-Level Opening-up by Implementing National Strategies

Shanghai emphasizes expanding openness and attracting foreign investment by being the first to implement national-level opening measures.

Promoting broader and deeper opening-up. Shanghai has implemented the pre-establishment national treatment with a negative list system for foreign investment, adhering to the latest national negative list and the *Catalogue of Encouraged Industries Foreign Investment*. The city has introduced comprehensive service industry expansion pilot programs and released policies such as the "24 Measures to Stabilize Foreign Investment" and "20 Measures to Enhance Foreign Investment Attraction and Utilization". These initiatives encourage foreign investment in newly opened sectors. Several groundbreaking foreign-funded projects have been established in Shanghai, including the first wholly foreign-owned securities company, the first batch of wholly foreign-owned public fund companies, joint venture wealth management companies with foreign ownership, and wholly foreign-owned vocational skills training institutions. Additionally, China's first foreign liner company offering "foreign trade container coastal relay" services officially launched in Yangshan Port.

Deepening institutional-level high-standard opening-up in free trade zones. Shanghai has released 117 implementation measures for the *General Plan for Advancing Institutional Opening-up of China (Shanghai) Pilot Free Trade Zone in Alignment with High-Standard International Economic and Trade Rules*. These measures stress stress-testing in service trade, goods trade, digital trade, and post-border regulatory rules. Following the State Council's *Notice Regarding the Implementation of Several Measures to Promote Institutionalized Opening-up of Qualified Free Trade Pilot Zones and Free Trade Port in Accordance with International High Standards*, Volvo Construction Equipment (China) became the first enterprise nationwide to conduct import pilot projects for remanufactured products in key industries. Since the establishment of Shanghai's first free trade zone, numerous institutional innovation outcomes have been replicated across the country. Of the more than 300 free trade zone institutional innovations promoted nationwide, nearly half originated from or been initiated in Shanghai.

Leveraging the China International Import Expo (CIIE) platform. For five consecutive years, Shanghai has hosted city promotion conferences during the CIIE, with top city officials of the Shanghai Committee of the Communist Party of China and the Shanghai Municipal Government extending invitations to the global community. Nearly 100 thematic investment promotion events have been held, transforming exhibitors into investors. For instance, during the CIIE, Novo Nordisk (a Fortune Global 500 company) invested CNY 200 million in pharmaceutical R&D, product imports, and distribution. German pharmaceutical giant Boehringer Ingelheim invested USD 198 million in new drug development. Meanwhile, the LEGO Group invested USD 550 million to establish a LEGO theme park in Shanghai's Jinshan District, which will become one of the largest LEGO resorts globally. In the six years since the inception of the CIIE, Shanghai has seen an increase of USD 127 billion in actual utilized foreign capital, which represents one-third of the city's total foreign investment.

B. Enhancing Global Resource Allocation Capabilities and Fostering a Headquarters Economy

Shanghai has continuously refined policies for regional

headquarters and foreign R&D centers, supporting multinational corporations to consolidate their operations, expand functions, and upgrade capabilities in the city.

Strengthening headquarters expansion efforts. Shanghai has revised Provisions of *Shanghai Municipality on Encouraging Multinational Corporations to Establish Regional Headquarters*, introducing new provisions for business unit headquarters and increasing support measures. Eligible multinational regional headquarters can receive financial support and rewards per regulations. Complementary policies provide support for headquarters enterprises in areas like fund management, trade facilitation, technological innovation, business registration, talent recruitment, and immigration facilitation. Over recent years, the regional headquarters of multinational companies in Shanghai have steadily upgraded their operational scope. For example, Honeywell, Henkel, Ford, and Volvo Construction Equipment established Asia-Pacific headquarters, while companies like Corning and Panasonic were recognized as business unit headquarters. Headquarters' functions continue to expand. More than 95% of regional headquarters in Shanghai now fulfill multiple roles, including investment decision-making, fund management, procurement and sales, and trade settlement, reinforcing their resource concentration and radiating influence.

Introduction of foreign-invested R&D center upgrade plans. Shanghai has combined the utilization of foreign capital with enhancing its independent innovation capabilities, actively encouraging foreign enterprises to set up R&D centers in the city. The city has revised its support policies for foreign R&D centers, introducing two new upgraded categories: "Global R&D Centers" and "Foreign-Funded Open Innovation Platforms. " The upgrade plan includes nine measures, such as increasing R&D investment, encouraging open innovation, streamlining customs and supervision processes for research materials, supporting cross-border data flow under the law, strengthening intellectual property rights protection, and enhancing talent attraction and retention. Since the end of 2020, 15 enterprises, including Schindler, Carrier, and Carestream, have been recognized as global R&D centers. For example, Fuchs Lubricants' R&D center in Shanghai is one of the group's three global hubs, and Toshiba Elevator's R&D center is the largest outside of Japan. Open innovation platforms have also been developed, with companies like Johnson & Johnson and Siemens Healthineers establishing such platforms in Shanghai. The amplification of R&D spillover effects has led to a concentration of a vast array of international talents, capitals, and technologies, all crucial innovation elements, within foreign-invested R&D centers. Currently, foreign-invested R&D centers in key sectors such as biomedicine, information technology, and automotive parts account for over 60% of all foreign R&D centers in the city.

C. Strengthening Investment Promotion and Actively Expanding Foreign Investment Inflows

Establishing and improving a foreign investment promotion service system, intensifying efforts across all aspects, stages, and channels to attract foreign investment.

Strengthening mechanisms by issuing the *Shanghai Comprehensive Plan for Advancing Foreign Investment Promotion Work* and establishing the citywide coordination and dispatching mechanism for promoting foreign investment "1+9+18+X", led by municipal leaders. This mechanism ensures regular tracking of project progress, promotional activities, and issue resolution, advancing foreign investment promotion across the city. The *Global Partner Scheme to Promote Foreign Investment in Shanghai* was also launched to leverage partner projects and expand foreign investment channels.

Focusing on activities by organizing annual certification ceremonies for multinational regional headquarters and R&D centers and holding hundreds of investment promotion events domestically and abroad. Overseas promotion campaigns, such as the "Invest in Shanghai, Share the Future" initiative, feature keynote speeches by municipal leaders to highlight Shanghai's investment environment, significantly enhancing the visibility and influence of "Invest Shanghai".

Building platforms by establishing the Shanghai Foreign Investment Promotion Service Platform, which integrates online and offline services to provide policy information, project matching, and investment facilitation. The platform's bilingual visits have exceeded 1.35 million. Publications like the *White Paper on Environment for Foreign Investment in Shanghai* and the *Shanghai Foreign Investment Guide* are released annually to highlight the city's business environment.

Expanding networks by forming the Shanghai Investment Promotion Institutions Partnership (SIPP), with about 110 member organizations from over 30 countries and regions, which are Shanghai's main economic and trade partners including the US, UK, Germany, Japan, Korea, and Singapore. This network supports global investment promotion. Overseas offices also play a vital role by organizing trade and economic activities and facilitating information exchange and project matchmaking.

Strengthening teams by appointing professional consultants and specialists from business associations in Europe, the US, and Japan as "Promotion Ambassadors" for international investment. Districts and key zones hire "Service Ambassadors, " and the city conducts training programs to build a professional and international investment promotion team.

D. Strengthening Enterprise Services and Continuously Optimizing the Business Environment

Emphasizing collaboration between municipal and district authorities, government departments, and enterprises to foster a favorable environment for foreign investors.

Ensuring the landing of major foreign investment projects. A citywide list of key foreign investment projects has been established, with a dedicated task force and service mechanism to ensure collaboration between municipal and district authorities. Tasks include project access, planning, land use, energy provision, environmental protection, foreign exchange, and immigration, ensuring follow-ups, feedback, and progress for each project. A "Green Channel" has been established to expedite project launch, production, and realization. For example, Tesla's Shanghai Gigafactory delivered 947, 000 vehicles in 2023, a 33% year-on-year increase, accounting for over half of its global production. The localization rate of parts and components exceeded 95%. In 2024, construction began on Tesla's energy storage superfactory, which will produce 10, 000 large commercial energy storage batteries annually upon completion, with a storage capacity of nearly 40 GWh, demonstrating Tesla's confidence in the Chinese market.

Enhancing government-enterprise communication. Since 2019, Shanghai has established a regular "Government-Enterprise Communication Roundtable Meeting" mechanism for foreign investment. Municipal leaders have hosted 103 roundtable meetings with foreign enterprises and foreign business associations, providing face-to-face exchanges to explain the latest policies, listen to challenges and suggestions, and resolve issues. Over the past five years, nearly 1, 000 foreign enterprises and associations have participated, raising over

1, 000 issues and suggestions, with a resolution rate exceeding 90%. The roundtable meetings have become an important platform for foreign enterprises to voice their concerns and a shining brand of "Shanghai Service".

Improving services for expatriates. Shanghai has focused on the high-frequency needs of foreigners working and living in the city. The new Shanghai International Service Portal (english. shanghai. gov. cn) was launched on January 1, 2024, and is simultaneously available on three international social media platforms (Facebook, X, and WeChat English version). It integrates government, information, and market services from the perspective of expatriates, providing services in eight languages, including English, Japanese, and German. It offers authoritative policy services, precise consultation, and thoughtful living services for expatriates conducting business, working, traveling, studying, or shopping in Shanghai, covering the entire work and life cycle.

Implementing the "Service Package" system for key enterprises. Shanghai conducts regular visits, assigns dedicated service personnel, and customizes policies to help enterprises accurately understand policies, conveniently access services, and efficiently handle needs. Tools such as "Policy Express", "FAQ Hotline", and the direct communication mechanism for headquarters are used to interpret policies and widely promote their content, highlights, and application scenarios, helping enterprises make full use of various policies.

E. Establishing and Improving Mechanisms to Protect the Legal Rights of Foreign Investors

Focusing on improving the institutional arrangements for the business environment and advancing the establishment of a foreign investment enterprise complaint resolution mechanism, with an emphasis on solving key and difficult issues.

Strengthening legal protections. The rule of law is the cornerstone of an optimal business environment and a strong guarantee of high-level openness. Shanghai has fully implemented the *Foreign Investment Law of the People's Republic of China* and, in 2020, became the first city in the country to introduce local foreign investment regulations. These regulations emphasize "full-process" national treatment and ensure that foreign enterprises receive equal treatment after market entry when implementing policies.

Enhancing rights protection. Following the principle of "one mechanism, one name, one organization, one method, one process, and one platform", Shanghai has established a municipal joint meeting mechanism for foreign investment complaints and issued the *Rules on Handling Complaints of Foreign-Invested Enterprises in Shanghai*. The city has created a "1+16+2" network (one municipal center, 16 district centers, and centers in Lin-gang New Area and Hongqiao Business District) to handle complaints. This system ensures accessible online and offline application channels, standardizes acceptance, processing, and feedback procedures, and institutionalizes the protection of foreign enterprise rights.

Supporting participation in standardization work. In April 2024, Shanghai established the first nationwide Foreign-funded Enterprise Standardization Collaboration Platform. This platform addresses issues raised by foreign enterprises, such as unfamiliarity with standardization policies, unclear participation pathways, and limited access to comprehensive standards information. It provides precise one-stop services, listens to and responds to enterprise concerns, and ensures that their voices and contributions are recognized in standardization work. Shanghai currently has 44 local technical standard committees, with more than 10 of these committees including representatives from foreign enterprises, covering areas such as disease prevention and control, elevators, new energy, building materials, human resources, intelligent transportation, intelligent connected vehicles, and artificial intelligence.

Addressing key and challenging issues. To tackle difficulties in cross-district relocation, Shanghai has established a municipal-level "Three Committees and Three Bureaus" coordination mechanism, set up dedicated service windows, and optimized processes. Enterprises with annual tax revenue under CNY 100 million can directly process relocations. For enterprise deregistration challenges, Shanghai has introduced categorized handling, synchronized procedures, and one-time processing. A simplified deregistration procedure is also available, offering announcement services via the enterprise information disclosure system. To ensure equal participation in public resource transactions, foreign enterprises can participate in government procurement, tendering, bidding, land transfers, and property transactions through public resource platforms. Additionally, the *White Paper on the Protection of Intellectual Property Rights of Foreign-Invested Enterprises* compiles policies and cases to help foreign enterprises better safeguard their rights.

III. Case Study: Johnson & Johnson "JLABS@ Shanghai" Open Innovation Platform

As a key initiative of Johnson & Johnson's efforts to accelerate external innovation and build an open innovation ecosystem, the company launched its largest global and first Asia-Pacific innovation incubator, JLABS, in Zhangjiang, Shanghai, in June 2019. This was a collaboration between Johnson & Johnson, the Shanghai Municipal Government, the People's Government of Pudong New Area, and Shanghai Zhangjiang (Group) Co., Ltd. JLABS@Shanghai, with a total area of over 4,400 square meters, can host up to 50 innovative entities in life sciences and healthcare, covering fields such as pharmaceuticals and medical devices.

JLABS@Shanghai offers plug-and-play services for startups, providing an efficient and flexible one-stop innovation platform, world-class laboratory spaces and equipment, guidance from experts in technology, industry, and financing, as well as robust support from Johnson & Johnson's internal and external innovation networks. These collective resources are designed to accelerate innovation, offering high-quality healthcare solutions to enhance human health, combat diseases, save lives, and benefit patients in China and worldwide.

Since its launch, JLABS@Shanghai has supported 93 companies, including 57 graduates and 36 current residents. The companies hail from across the globe, with 49% being Chinese domestic firms and 51% international firms. Additionally, 40% are serial entrepreneurial companies. Collectively, the resident companies have securedUSD 5.7 billion in funding and strategic collaborations, including five IPOs, one acquisition, and 156 transactions. Over one-third of the companies have partnered with Johnson & Johnson or JLABS at least once.

On December 1, 2020, following the implementation of the *Regulations of Shanghai Municipality on Encouraging the Establishment and Development of Foreign-funded Research and Development Centers*, Johnson & Johnson became the first foreign-invested open innovation platform recognized by the Shanghai Municipal Government. It continues to play a leading role in strengthening global resource allocation and enhancing its innovation engine.

The development of this new model of open innovation platforms further integrates foreign-invested R&D centers into Shanghai's industrial and innovation chains, fostering innovation and entrepreneurship among SMEs and teams.

IV. Future Outlook

Moving forward, Shanghai will fully implement the guiding principles of the 20th CPC National Congress and the second and third plenary sessions of the 20th CPC Central Committee. The city will steadfastly expand its openness, strive to create a world-class business environment, and continue to position itself as the top choice for foreign investment and a hub for high-quality foreign capital in the new era.

First, advancing high-level opening-up. Shanghai will align with international high-standard trade and economic rules, such as the CPTPP and DEPA, steadily expanding rule-based, regulatory, managerial, and standard-oriented institutional opening-up. The city will actively seek pilot implementation, ensure the implementation of national strategies such as the Free Trade Pilot Zone, Lin-gang Special Area, Pudong Leading Zone, and Hongqiao International opening-up Hub, and accelerate the rollout of the "80 High-Level Institutional opening-up Measures". Comprehensive service sector opening trials will be deepened, and new rounds of service sector expansion measures will be implemented. The China International Import Expo platform will be fully leveraged to utilize market advantages and broaden the scope and depth of Shanghai's openness.

Second, strengthening investment promotion services. Efforts will be coordinated to advance foreign investment promotion, increase overseas promotional activities, and tell Shanghai's "introducing FDI" and "going global" story. Foreign investors will be encouraged to participate in green development and digital transformation, sharing development opportunities. Mechanisms such as the *Global Partnership Plan for Promoting Foreign Investment* and direct communication with headquarters decision-makers will be leveraged for targeted investment promotion. The potential of the equipment renewal market will be tapped to attract new investments, and foreign enterprises will be supported in collaborating with upstream and downstream supply chains. The dedicated service mechanism for key foreign investment projects will be enhanced, with strengthened support for land use, energy consumption, environmental assessment, and financing.

Third, enhancing and upgrading the headquarters economy. Shanghai will implement the new round of multinational company regional headquarters support policies, continually improving the lists for nurturing, empowering, and upgrading three lists. The city is directing its efforts toward augmenting the number of headquarters, broadening its operational scope, and enhancing its operational caliber. This will be achieved through innovative policies and pilot initiatives in the realms of fund management, research and development (R&D), talent attraction, and immigration policies. Additionally, the Foreign R&D Center Upgrade Plan will be put into action to bolster support for foreign entities engaged in R&D and innovation activities.

Fourth, continuously optimizing the foreign investment environment. Shanghai will maintain high-quality government-enterprise communication roundtable meetings across various levels and sectors, implement the "Service Package" system for key enterprises, and provide comprehensive point-to-point services for major foreign investment projects, effectively solving problems for enterprises. Business environment reforms will be deepened, with enhanced protection for the legal rights of foreign investors. Measures for managing data cross-border flows will be investigated and refined to ensure that data can be transferred in a tiered and categorized manner, under conditions that are secure and manageable. Efforts will be made to enhance the convenience for expatriates regarding work visas, immigration processes, payment systems, and talent services, all aimed at fostering a welcoming and business-conducive international environment.

Chapter 7   Zhejiang's Two-Way Investment Report[①]

2023 marked the 20th anniversary of Zhejiang Province's implementation of the "Double-Eight" strategy. Guided by Xi Jinping Thought on Socialism with Chinese Characteristics for a New Era, Zhejiang actively adapted to new circumstances and requirements. The province deepened the "Double-Eight" strategy, launched the "Sweet Potato Economy" enhancement and upgrading initiative as its "No.1 Open Project", and advanced the level of an open economy, its role as a dual-circulation strategic hub, and the institutionalized open system. This amplified the synergistic effects of high-level "going global" and high-quality "introducing FDI", providing robust support for national two-way investment development.

I. Progress and Achievements in Zhejiang Two–way Investment

A. "Introducing FDI" : Growth in Both Quantity and Quality, with Foreign Investment Increasing Against the Trend

1. Zhejiang maintains a leading position nationally in foreign investment volume, with significant scale growth and economic contribution

In 2023, Zhejiang had 4,281 foreign-funded enterprises

① Provided by the Department of Commerce of Zhejiang Province.

above designated size, accounting for 7.5% of such enterprises in the province. These enterprises contributed 18.9% of the province's revenue, 25.2% of total profits, 14.6% of total tax revenues, and 15.2% of total employment, playing a significant role in the provincial industrial economy. In terms of scale, the actual utilization of foreign investment in Zhejiang reaching a record high of USD 20.23 billion. Zhejiang accounted for 12.4% of the national total, ranking fourth in the country, one position higher than in 2022, marking the best performance in five years. The growth rate exceeded the national average by 18.5 percentage points.

2. Optimized and enhanced foreign investment structure with "Two Increases and Two Decreases"

The "two increases" are an increased proportion of foreign investment in manufacturing and a higher proportion of investment from developed economies. In 2023, guided by the emphasis on attracting advanced manufacturing foreign investment, Zhejiang's manufacturing sector utilizedUSD 9.1 billion of foreign investment, an 85.8% year-on-year increase, accounting for 45.0% of the province's total, up 19.6 percentage points from 2022, reaching a record high. Investment from developed economies also increased, with USD 3.77 billion from EU countries, accounting for 18.6% of the provincial total, up 16.7 percentage points from 2022. The "two decreases" are a lower proportion of investment in real estate and a declining share of investment from Hong Kong. In 2023, foreign investment in real estate was USD 1.2 billion, representing 5.9% of the provincial total, down 1.3 percentage points from 2022. Investment from Hong Kong reached USD 12.47 billion, accounting for 61.6%, down 16.7 percentage points from 2022.

3. Breakthroughs in landmark projects highlight the driving role of foreign investment

In terms of project agreements and landings, majorUSD 1 billion-plus foreign investment projects, such as Saudi Aramco's acquisition of Rongsheng Petrochemical and Stellantis Group's strategic cooperation with Leapmotor, successfully landed in collaboration with Hangzhou, Zhoushan, and Jinhua. High-quality manufacturing projects, including Novartis Radiopharmaceuticals and Swiss Sika, as well as functional foreign institutions like BD Medical's Greater China Innovation Center and Pfizer's Smart Healthcare Innovation Center, also settled in Zhejiang. Regarding actual foreign investment, there were 129 major projects with investments exceeding USD 30 million, totaling USD 14.37 billion, accounting for 71% of the provincial total, up 7.3 percentage points from 2022. Among these, 27 projects utilized over USD 100 million in foreign investment. In terms of key projects, Zhejiang had 67 projects included in the national list of key foreign investment projects in 2023, ranking second nationwide (after Jiangsu), an increase of 16 projects from 2022. At the provincial level, approximately 30 key foreign investment projects were dynamically managed on a "list of major foreign investment projects", which acted as a priority for ongoing endeavors to finalize agreements and attract investments.

B. "Going Global" : Global Expansion with Stable and Orderly Overseas Investment

1. Outbound investment remains stable with steady growth, and investment in emerging sectors is developing rapidly

In 2023, Zhejiang's actual overseas investment reached USD 17.273 billion, a year-on-year increase of 21.10%, accounting for 16.97% of the national total and ranking second nationwide. The province completed overseas engineering contract revenue ofUSD 6.94 billion, an 8.4% year-on-year increase, accounting for 4.3% of the national total and ranking fifth among provinces and cities, one place higher than the previous year. Newly signed contracts amounted to USD 4.92 billion, a 7.4% increase. Zhejiang established 454 overseas manufacturing enterprises with a total registered capital of USD 11.58 billion, accounting for 68.81%. This manufacturing investment effectively boosted the province's intermediate goods exports. Overseas investment in emerging sectors such as new energy and minerals, digital economy, biopharmaceuticals, and photovoltaics grew rapidly. In 2023, the new energy and minerals sector saw 14 overseas enterprises established with a registered capital of USD 3.592 billion, a 1.13% increase. The digital economy sector established 85 overseas enterprises with a registered capital of USD 811 million, a 331.38% increase. The biopharmaceutical sector established 49 overseas enterprises with a registered capital of USD 415 million, a 40.68% increase. The photovoltaics sector established 31 overseas enterprises with a registered capital of USD 751 million, a 212.92% increase.

2. Innovative overseas investment methods with growth in large-scale cross-border mergers and acquisitions

With continuous growth and expansion, Zhejiang enterprises are adopting more innovative approaches to outbound investment. They are transitioning from straightforward capital contributions to engaging in transnational mergers and acquisitions, as well as setting up overseas economic and trade cooperation zones. First, greenfield investments have grown significantly, with 1,203 new overseas enterprises established, representing a 77.17% increase. The total recorded investment amounted to USD 11.896 billion, up by 53.38%, accounting for 70.69% of the province's total. Second, large-scale mergers and acquisitions (M&A) have also increased, with the number of enterprises involved in M&A valued over USD 10 million rising to 35, an increase of 13 from the previous year, and a total recorded investment of USD 2.178 billion, constituting 90.90% of the total M&A recorded investment. These M&A activities were primarily concentrated in fields such as extraction and processing of minerals for new energy technologies, automotive component manufacturing, and pharmaceutical R&D. Third, overseas economic and trade cooperation zones have progressed steadily. In 2023, one new provincial-level overseas economic and trade cooperation zone was established, bringing the total to 19. These zones span 13 countries worldwide, with 15 located in Belt and Road Initiative countries, forming a Southeast Asia-centered, globally radiating pattern. These cooperation zones are playing an increasingly pivotal role as hubs in China's domestic and international dual circulation strategy. By the end of 2023, the total cumulative investment in these zones reached USD 20.77 billion, with Zhejiang enterprises contributing USD 11.766 billion, accounting for 56.65%. The total output value of the zones in 2023 was USD 29.984 billion, driving China's import and export activities to USD 21.333 billion, an increase of 27.79%.

3. Increasingly diverse outbound investment markets, and further expanded space for international cooperation

First, significant growth in investment in Belt and Road partner countries. Zhejiang enterprises recorded an outbound investment amount of USD 10.888 billion in Belt and Road partner countries (including Hong Kong, Macao, and Taiwan), up by 38.70%, accounting for 64.39% of the province's total. In RCEP member countries, 577 projects were initiated, representing a 96.93% increase, with Chinese investments totaling USD 9.858 billion, up by 56.80%. Thailand and Vietnam have attracted investments from domestic mid-to-low-end industries due to their labor cost advantages and geographical positioning. Second, investment in Europe reached a recorded amount of USD 1.889 billion, an increase of 13.15%. Enterprises invested in Europe primarily to expand market access, such as Inventronics Group's successful acquisition of Osram's Digital Lighting Systems Division in Germany. Investment in North America totaled USD 2.35 billion, up by 79.66%, with a particular focus on Mexico, where investments amounted to USD 856 million, up by 14.90%. Chinese electric vehicle enterprises showed a strong demand to enter the European market, prompting related supply chain enterprises to invest in Hungary. In 2023, Zhejiang enterprises initiated 29 projects in Hungary, with a recorded outbound investment of USD 477 million, up by 9.06%.

4. Leading enterprises playing a prominent role, and the strength of local private multinational corporations continuing to grow

In 2023, Zhejiang's private enterprises established 1,457 overseas enterprises, accounting for 97.59% of the provincial total. The recorded outbound investment reached USD 16.339 billion, up by 29.46%, representing 97.09% of the province's total. That year, 60 private multinational corporations were recognized as "Pilot Enterprises", with 34 of them establishing 68 overseas enterprises, recording an investment amount of USD 4.066 billion, accounting for 24.89% of the provincial total. To date, these 60 "Pilot Enterprises" have cumulatively established 504 overseas enterprises, with a total recorded investment of USD 35.36 billion, accounting for 27.76% of the province's total during the same period.

II. Policy Innovations, Key Points, Highlights, Initiatives, and Their Roles

A. Policy Innovation Situation

First, the policies focus on implementing the State Council's directives, issuing Zhejiang Province's *Outlining Its Guidelines Regarding Further Optimizing the Foreign Investment Environment and Intensifying Efforts to Attract Foreign Investments*. These include six areas with 22 specific Zhejiang-style measures aimed at improving the quality of foreign capital utilization, safeguarding national treatment for foreign-invested enterprises, strengthening foreign investment protection, enhancing the convenience of investment operations, increasing fiscal and tax support, and improving foreign investment promotion methods.

Second, Zhejiang Province introduced *Optimizing the Foreign Investment Environment and Increasing the Attraction of Foreign Investment*. These measures leverage provincial-level funding to support key projects in advanced manufacturing, major services, and Fortune 500 company headquarters, successfully attracting landmark foreign manufacturing projects such as Purolite under Ecolab.

Third, *Guidelines for Encouraging the Establishment and Development of Foreign-funded R&D Centers* were formulated to expand new investments through exceptional landing incentives and revitalize existing assets through scientific incentives, tax support, talent services, and intellectual property protection. Formulate identification standards based on the principles of "scientific flexibility and moderate relaxation", Zhejiang has recognized 20 provincial foreign R&D centers such as Ferrotec.

Fourth, the province also issued *Several Measures to Further Improve Foreign Investment in Manufacturing*, implementing "project specialist" tracking services and mechanisms to ensure the allocation of resources for major projects.

Fifth, Zhejiang launched the *Accelerate the Cultivation of Zhejiang Private Transnational Companies "Silk Road Pioneer" Action Plan.* This plan aims to fully leverage the exemplary and leading role of Zhejiang's private multinational companies, fostering a group of private multinationals with high transnational operation indices, strong comprehensive competitiveness, and significant international influence. It seeks to enhance the ability of Zhejiang enterprises to coordinate within the global industrial chain and allocate resources efficiently, promote the upgrading of the province's industries to the higher end of the global value chain, and advance the high-quality development of the "Belt and Road Initiative".

B. Key Points, Highlights, and Measures

1. Strategically expanded the opening-up of its service sector while integrating domestic and foreign investment promotion

First, the province accelerated the implementation of the Hangzhou national comprehensive pilot project of expanding and opening up service industry, emphasizing the use of foreign capital in modern services and fostering "Integration of two industries" partnerships between transnational corporations and Zhejiang's cities. Efforts focused on 12 key areas, including technology services and wholesale and retail services. Second, explore the establishment of a coordinated mechanism for attracting foreign investments throughout the province, integrate investment promotion efforts, ensure services for major foreign investment projects, and build an overall image for foreign investment attraction, forming an integrated network encompassing one Investment Office of Jiangsu Provincial

Department of Commerce, one Investment Promotion Bureau (Overseas Business Service Center, seven overseas representative offices), 90 counties, and 117 development zones. In 2023, Zhejiang attracted 165 major manufacturing projects involving over CNY 1 billion in domestic capital outside of privince and USD 100 million in foreign investment, achieving significant progress in integrated foreign investment and domestic investment attraction.

2. Deepen exhibition investment attraction, continuously enhance the core brand of "Investing in Zhejiang" for investment attraction

First, Zhejiang has launched the "Investing in Zhejiang" global investment promotion campaign. The province compiled the *"Investing in Zhejiang" Information Documentation For Investment Project*, the *"Investing in Zhejiang" Global Investment Promotion Guide*, and the *"Investing in Zhejiang" Provincial Innovation Cases in Investment Promotion*, empowering the provincial investment promotion system for precise targeting. Over the year, Zhejiang organized more than 200 delegations to over 30 countries and regions, hosting over 360 investment promotion and negotiation events both domestically and internationally. These efforts led to the signing of 175 cooperative projects with a total investment of approximately USD 13.17 billion, including high-quality foreign investment projects from Sika (Switzerland), Shin-Etsu Chemical (Japan), and LG Energy Solution (Korea). Second, Zhejiang utilized exhibition platforms for investment promotion. At the 24th China Zhejiang Investment and Trade Symposium, 62 foreign investment projects were signed, including 17 projects from Fortune 500 companies and leading industry enterprises. During the Hong Kong-Macao-Zhejiang event, 77 cooperative projects were signed, with a total investment of approximately USD 8 billion. At the 6th China International Import Expo, Zhejiang secured 24 foreign investment projects with a total investment value of USD 3.838 billion. The second Global Digital Trade Expo resulted in 11 foreign investment projects worth USD 1.7 billion being signed on-site.

3. Integrated and enhanced its investment promotion resources, continuously optimizing its approaches

First, the province has deepened fund-based investment promotion by launching the "Investing in Zhejiang" Fund Promotion Partner Program and establishing the "Investing in Zhejiang" Fund Promotion Alliance, which now includes over 100 members. For two consecutive years, Zhejiang has hosted fund investment promotion activities, conducting industry-themed project roadshows to connect cities with funding and project resources. Second, the province has optimized the layout of its overseas investment promotion network. By constructing a global overseas investment promotion network, Zhejiang has effectively integrated cross-border enterprise resources, overseas economic and trade zones, and Overseas Chinese Entrepreneurs (Zhejiang) business networks. It has also actively expanded channels for engaging overseas intermediaries and platforms.

4. Cultivate local multinational corporations, continues to implement the "Silk Road Pilot" initiative for private multinational companies

Zhejiang has implemented the "Silk Road Pilot" initiative for private multinational corporations, focusing on strengthening the construction of corporate headquarters and fostering private enterprises with robust international competitiveness, global resource allocation capabilities, and strong coordination within global industrial and supply chains. A total of 179 private enterprises are currently included in the initiative, with 60 recognized as "Pilot Enterprises" in 2023. These 60 enterprises achieved an averageTransnationality Index of 25.7%, surpassing the national average for China's top 100 multinational companies by 9.8 percentage points.

5. Strengthening hub construction to promote high-quality development of the Belt and Road Initiative

Zhejiang has enhanced the quality and efficiency of the China-Europe (Yiwu-Xinjiang-Europe) freight train services, supporting the establishment of a demonstration project for China-Europe Railway Express Assembly Center. In 2023, the China-Europe (Yiwu-Xinjiang-Europe) freight trains completed 2,300 runs. The province has optimized the layout of its overseas economic and trade cooperation zones, increased cultivation efforts, and continuously improved public service capabilities in these zones to encourage the clustering of foreign-invested enterprises. The "Alliance to Expand Markets" initiative has been advanced, facilitating the integration of overseas contracted projects with foreign investment and trade. Zhejiang has strengthened the linkage between domestic and overseas zones, explored the establishment of "Two Zones, Two Parks" at the provincial level, and innovatively creatively hosted events related to the China-Central and Eastern European Countries Expo.

6. Providing service guarantees and optimizing the business environment

First, Zhejiang has launched the "Zhejiang is Your Home" service brand for foreign enterprises. In 2023, over 200 foreign enterprises were visited to provide on-site services, ensuring precise implementation of policies. The province also implemented the foreign enterprise roundtable mechanism, resolving 68 issues to support business stability and retention. Second, Zhejiang has strengthened resource allocation guarantees for major foreign investment projects by establishing a coordination mechanism, actively recommending key foreign investment projects to the national level, and securing resource support from the central government. Currently, Zhejiang ranks second nationwide in the number of projects included in the Ministry of Commerce's national key foreign investment project list. Moreover, the province has leveraged the advantages of departments such as the Zhejiang Provincial Development and Reform Commission, the Economy and Information Technology Department of Zhejiang, and the Department of Science and Technology of Zhejiang Province to improve interdepartmental coordination mechanisms. These efforts align industrial categories with departmental involvement to attract projects effectively. Third, Zhejiang has enhanced full-process tracking services for projects by iterating the "Zhejiang Investment Promotion Online" system to provide routine tracking for provincial-level key foreign investment projects. The province has utilized its provincial coordination mechanism to address demands from leading enterprises such as BD Medical in the life sciences sector and Novartis Nuclear Medicine (Fortune Global 500), facilitating the successful implementation of these projects.

III. Cases of Enterprises Benefiting from Policy Innovations

Case 1: Huahai Pharmaceutical's Cross-Border M&A—Achieving Synergy in Technology and Market Expansion

Zhejiang Huahai Pharmaceutical Co., Ltd. (hereinafter referred to as "Huahai Pharmaceutical"), founded in 1989, is a comprehensive pharmaceutical enterprise specializing in chemical drugs, biopharmaceuticals, cell therapy, and trade circulation. After going public in 2003, it began to enter the international pharmaceutical market and established its first subsidiary overseas in 2004, becoming one of the domestic pharmaceutical companies with the most official certifications from international mainstream markets. Huahai Pharmaceutical is at the forefront of the domestic pharmaceutical industry in the fields of formulation exports and international development. At present, Huahai Pharmaceutical has entered the United States, Germany, Japan and other places through M&A, alliances, etc., and has nearly 20 overseas offices worldwide. In the U.S. market, Huahai Pharmaceutical has developed a multi-channel sales system, including direct sales, major wholesalers, retail chains, and commercial companies. In European market, 12 formulation products have been approved and launched across 28 European countries.

Through cross-border investment projects, Huahai Pharmaceutical has become the first pharmaceutical company in China to obtain FDA certification for its formulations, the first to independently hold an ANDA formulation license, the first to achieve large-scale formulation exports to the U.S. market, and the first to challenge original U.S. pharmaceutical patents. At the same time, the production area has been certified by multiple international mainstream official quality systems, including China, the U.S., the EU, WHO, Australia, Japan, and Mexico. The two major industrial chains of the company, raw materials and formulations, are becoming increasingly mature, showcasing a vertical integration advantage from raw materials to formulations. It boasts an annual production capacity of over 20 billion solid dose forms, certified by European and U.S. CGMP standards. It has workshops for anti-tumor solid dosage forms, water-based injections, and freeze-dried powder injections.

Project management experience. First, strengthen international strategic alliances. Fully utilize various advantageous resources at home and abroad, and carry out various forms of strategic alliances. Therefore, when exploring the international pharmaceutical market, Huahai Pharmaceutical first considers forming cooperative or alliance relationships with relevant pharmaceutical companies entering the market. By building international strategic alliances, it gradually establishes a foothold in the international market and has a certain degree of international market discourse power. Second, in alignment with its corporate development strategies, Huahai Pharmaceutical has integrated the approaches of "going global" and "introducing FDI". This strategy accelerates the absorption and transfer of technology while fostering information sharing. It facilitates deep integration in areas such as research and development, sales, strategy, and corporate culture, maximizing synergies and driving both efficiency and profitability. Third, when selecting investment projects, Huahai Pharmaceutical considers factors such as innovation and research capabilities, the size of the international market, and the potential impact on the company's long-term sustainable development. By carefully evaluating these criteria, the company ensures that its investments align with strategic goals. Fourth, to further mitigate risks, Huahai Pharmaceutical conducts comprehensive due diligence by engaging professional intermediaries. This thorough process focuses on critical aspects such as finance, law, and taxation, significantly reducing uncertainties and challenges associated with mergers and acquisitions.

Case 2: Risen Energy's Export of "Chinese Technology" and "Chinese Solutions"

Risen Energy Co., Ltd. (hereinafter referred to as "Risen Energy") was founded in 1986 and specializes in the research, development, production, and sales of solar modules, solar power plant EPC and transfers, photovoltaic powerstation, lighting, energy storage products, auxiliary photovoltaic products, and crystalline silicon materials. With offices and subsidiaries established worldwide, Risen Energy has built a global sales network. It currently operates 22 marketing and service centers in regions including China, Germany, Australia, Mexico, India, the United States, and Japan, with the aim of providing green energy solutions globally.

Major cross-border investment projects. In 2021, Risen Energy launched a "3GW High-Efficiency Solar Modules" manufacturing project in Malaysia, with an investment of approximately USD 300 million. On May 15, 2022, the Malaysian base's first production line became operational, successfully producing the initial batch of 210 high-efficiency modules. In collaboration with Vietnam's Tasco Corporation, Risen Energy's Hong Kong subsidiary signed EPC contracts with Vietnam Electricity Group for two solar power stations with capacities of 100MW and 50MW, respectively, totaling USD 66 million. Over time, Risen Energy has undertaken multiple EPC projects in Vietnam.

Project management experience. First, developing a scientific market strategy: Before investing in Vietnam, Risen Energy conducted thorough market research and established a comprehensive business development strategy. Once the project began operating, Risen Energy demonstrated flexibility in adjusting market strategies in response to changes. The company created a proactive, independent, flexible, and controllable sales network supported by a high-quality sales team. It hired experienced local consulting firms, accountants, and lawyers in Vietnam to conduct market risk assessments and ensure compliance with local laws when setting up operations. Second, enhancing risk prevention measures. The registration address (final destination) of Risen Energy's project is in Vietnam. Before investing, carefully study the local political climate, legal systems and cultural environment in Vietnam, with a particular focus on antitrust laws, capital market regulations and labor laws. At the same time, in order to avoid financial risks such as exchange rates, Risen Energy employed various financial instruments and opted for soft currency payments and hard currency settlements in cross-border transactions. Additionally, a dedicated project management department was established to strengthen investment budgeting, enhance monitoring of project execution, and ensure the rigorous oversight of implementation processes. Third, Cross-cultural management. Risen Energy recognized the differences in management philosophies and practices between Chinese and Vietnamese employees. The company emphasized cultural integration, striving to build a shared corporate culture accepted by employees from both sides, seeking a balance between maintaining cultural integration and respecting the autonomy of enterprise operations.

IV. Future Outlook

Next, Zhejiang will continue to implement the important directives of President Xi Jinping and the decisions and arrangements of the Party Central Committee and the State Council. The province will deepen reforms, advance the "No.1 opening-up Project" for upgrading the "Sweet Potato Economy", and adhere to the principle of "developing Zhejiang while leveraging resources beyond Zhejiang". Efforts will focus on integrating domestic and foreign investment attraction, optimizing the use of foreign capital, and seizing the "window of opportunity" to attract major projects. By guiding enterprises to orderly expand their global layouts and enhancing Zhejiang's value in the integrated development of international industrial and supply chains, the province aims to drive high-quality two-way investment and contribute "Zhejiang Power" to Chinese modernization.

Opening-up Platform Section

Chapter 8   Hainan Province's Progress in Utilizing Foreign Capital[1]

I. The Situation of Foreign Capital Utilization in Hainan Province

A. Recent Situations of Hainan's Actual Use of Foreign Capital

In recent years, Hainan Province has achieved significant progress in both the scale and quality of attracting and utilizing foreign capital. From 2018 to 2023, the province's total actual use of foreign capital reached USD 16.12 billion, exceeding the total actual use of foreign capital utilized during the 30 years prior to the establishment of the province (USD 9.607 billion). The average annual growth rate over the six years was 46%. Between 2018 and 2020, the utilization of foreign capital doubled for three consecutive years. In 2021 and 2022, it maintained rapid growth of over 15% year-on-year on a high basis, and the scale of attracting foreign investment in 2023 remains at a historical high. The structure of foreign capital has been continuously optimized, with the modern service industry emerging as the primary driver of growth and structural improvement. The actual proportion of foreign capital utilized in modern services increased from 61% in 2018 to 83% in 2023.

Over the past six years, investors from 149 countries and regions have invested in Hainan. A large number of

---

① Provided by the Department of Commerce of Hainan Province.

internationally renowned enterprises have settled in the province. In the medical field, globally recognized companies such as Viatris, IQVIA, and Merck from the United States have established operations in Hainan, driving a group of industry enterprises to invest and strengthen the industrial chain. In thehigh-end consumer goods sector, companies like LVMH, Richemont, Kering, and L'Oréal of France have accelerated their presence in Hainan, concentrating industry resources, extending the industrial chain, and effectively attracting overseas consumption back to China. In the financial sector, UBS bank established a private equity fund management company in Haikou. In the art auction sector, Sotheby's, a leading global auction house, has established operations in Hainan. In information technology services, leading organizations such as Dun & Bradstreet and Intel have also established a presence. In the high-end consumer food processing sector, Yihai Kerry, a subsidiary of Singapore's Wilmar International, has launched an integrated oil processing and central kitchen project in Hainan. In education, Germany's Bielefeld University of Applied Sciences has established an independent campus in Hainan, the first of its kind in China and the first German public university to independently set up a campus abroad. Additionally, the University of Edinburgh, Coventry University, Michigan State University, and Rutgers University have collaborated on education projects in Hainan. In the new energy vehicle sector, Tesla from the United States and Toyota from Japan have launched trade, sales, and mobility services in Hainan. In commercial real estate and property management, major players like Swire Group from the UK, Shimao Group from Hong Kong, and Savills from the UK have made successful entries. In logistics, Bolloré Logistics is building a regional distribution center in Hainan. In the energy and environmental sectors,

SUEZ from France is conducting wastewater treatment projects in Hainan, while Germany's ALBA Group is constructing food waste treatment facilities to manage organic waste safely and sustainably.

B. Actual Use of Foreign Capital in 2023

In 2023, although the growth rate of Hainan's actual use of foreign capital slowed, the scale remained at a historical high, and foreign investment activity in Hainan remained vibrant. The province's actual use of foreign capital totaled CNY 22.7 billion, a year-on-year decrease of 7.1% (compared to an 8% year-on-year decrease in actual use of foreign capital nationwide in the same period). The number of newly established foreign-invested enterprises reached 1,736, a year-on-year increase of 28.4%.

From a regional perspective, the top five sources of foreign capital were: Hong Kong SAR China (CNY 13.9 billion, 61%), the UK (CNY 5.83 billion, 25.7%), the British Virgin Islands (CNY 800 million, 3.5%), the Cayman Islands (CNY 570 million, 2.5%), and Singapore (CNY 530 million, 2.3%). Foreign capital from European countries grew the fastest, totaling CNY 6.22 billion, a year-on-year increase of 142%.

From an industry perspective, the actual use of foreign capital in the modern service industry utilized CNY 18.8 billion, accounting for 83% of the province's total actual foreign capital utilization. The top five sectors were: Leasing and business services (58.3%), Information transmission, software and IT services (17.8%), Scientific research and technical services (10.8%), Wholesale and retail trade (7.1%) and Financial services (2.8%).

From a corporate perspective, a number of internationally renowned enterprises have established operations in Hainan. In the high-end consumer sector, companies such as Tapestry from the US, Moët Hennessy from France, and BVLGARI from Italy, a group of participating companies in the China International Consumer Products Expo, have settled in Hainan. In the medical and healthcare sector, Merck from the US and Nestlé from Switzerland have established operations. In the financial sector, Stonewood established a private equity fund management company in Haikou. In logistics, Bolloré Logistics is building a regional distribution center in Hainan. In the information technology services sector, Intel has established operations in Sanya.

II. Key Measures to Attract Investment

A. Optimize the Policy Environment for Attracting Investment

1. Implementing national policies to stabilize foreign investment

Efforts have been made to thoroughly implement the central government's policies on stabilizing foreign investment, as well as the *Opinions of the State Council on Further Optimizing the Foreign Investment Environment to Strengthen Efforts in Attracting Foreign Investment* (hereinafter referred to as "Document No.11 of the State Council"). First, Strengthening leadership and high-level promotion: Secretary of the Provincial Party Committee, Feng Fei and the Governor, Liu Xiaoming attach great importance to the implementation of Document No.11 of the State Council, issuing instructions and specifying requirements. The Department of Commerce promptly organized a special task force to draft the *Several Measures to Further Optimize the Foreign Investment Environment and Promote Stable Utilization and Quality Improvement of Foreign Investment in Hainan Province* (hereinafter referred to as the *Several Measures*), which were approved by the

Executive Meeting of Provincial Government and issued by the General Office of the Provincial Government on November 5, 2023. Second, clarifying responsibilities and formulating implementation measures: The *Several Measures* outline 20 actions across four key areas: improving the quality of foreign investment utilization, enhancing investment facilitation, strengthening the protection of foreign investment, and optimizing investment promotion methods. Responsibilities for each measure have been clearly assigned to relevant departments, and progress is regularly reported to the Provincial Inspection Team. Third, conducting policy advocacy to strengthen investor confidence: The Department of Commerce has provided briefings on Document No.11 of the State Council to 18 municipal and county-level commerce departments and 13 key industrial parks. In collaboration with the Provincial Taxation Bureau and the Hainan Branch of the People's Bank of China, they organized sessions for over 150 foreign-invested enterprises and investment promotion personnel to explain the policy implications of Document No.11 of the State Council, along with free trade port tax incentives and financing facilitation measures. These efforts have stabilized investor expectations and bolstered confidence in investing in Hainan.

2. Editing and publishing the 2023 *Hainan Free Trade Port Investment Guide*

The guide comprehensively showcases the advantages, policies, industrial opportunities, and investment highlights of the Hainan Free Trade Port, as well as its law-based, internationalized, and business-friendly environment. It serves as a window for global investors to understand Hainan and a practical reference for companies conducting investment and trade activities in the region.

3. Promoting local legislation on foreign investment.

The Provincial Development and Reform Commission

and the Department of Commerce are jointly formulating the *Foreign Investment Regulations in Hainan Special Economic Zone* to strengthen the promotion, protection, and management of foreign investment from a legal perspective. For example, in expanding market access for foreign investment, we will promote the opening up of key areas; In terms of investment promotion, support the development of headquarters economy, etc; In terms of investment protection, the legitimate rights and interests of foreign investors in Hainan Free Trade Port are protected in accordance with the law.

B. Innovating Investment Promotion Methods and Implementing Precise Investment Promotion

1. Utilizing platforms such as international exhibitions and forums to expand investment flow

Hainan has utilized platforms like the Boao Forum for Asia Annual Conference 2023 to conduct "one-on-one" business meetings with major foreign enterprises such as AstraZeneca from the UK, SABIC from Saudi Arabia, and Goldman Sachs from the US. During the third China International Consumer Products Expo, various investment promotion activities were carefully planned, leading to the settlement of internationally renowned brands and leading enterprises such as Moët Hennessy from France, BVLGARI from Italy, and Estée Lauder from the US. Additionally, through the Ministry of Commerce's "Invest in China Year" platform, Hainan promoted its free trade port's policy advantages and new development opportunities to global investors, further advancing international cooperation.

2. Implementing a global investment promotion campaign

First, making good use of overseas visits to attract investment. In 2023, Hainan's provincial leaders led delegations to the UK,

Germany, Switzerland, Japan, the UAE, and Hong Kong SAR China, hosting dedicated promotional events and "one-on-one" business meetings. These efforts emphasized Hainan's free trade port policies and its commitment to high-level opening-up. A total of 11 overseas missions were conducted, comprising approximately 250 events, including 19 comprehensive and special promotion events for Hainan Free Trade Port, and about 80 one-on-one economic and trade negotiation activities. Key enterprises and institutions engaged included Oerlikon, Standard Chartered, the Kerry Group, and the École Hôtelière de Lausanne, yielding fruitful results. Second, holding special promotion activities targeting key countries: Special promotional events were held in Zurich, London, Tokyo, and Dubai, inviting local government officials and business leaders to learn about Hainan's free trade port policies and investment opportunities, encouraging enterprises to invest in Hainan. Third, deepening collaboration with foreign chambers of commerce in China: Meetings were held with investment promotion organizations such as the Japan External Trade Organization to enhance communication and jointly plan cooperative activities. Close ties were established with chambers such as the Association of German Chambers of Industry and Commerce and the American Chamber of Commerce in China, deepening connections with international enterprises and expanding investment cooperation.

C. Making Good Use of the Platform and Leveraging Its Role in Attracting Investment and Gathering

1. Advancing comprehensive pilot programs for opening-up the service sector

Focused on areas such as science and technology, business services, education, and finance, the comprehensive pilot programs have progressed steadily. Experiences, best practices, exemplary cases, and institutional innovations from these pilots have been promptly summarized. Six practical cases, including promoting the progress of pilot work, timely summarizing pilot experience and practices, typical cases, and institutional innovation achievements, relaxing restrictions on foreign high-level talents participating in science and technology projects, and opening a green channel for international talent title evaluation, were included in the second batch of national exemplary cases for the comprehensive pilot program on expanding the service sector.

2. Promoting innovation and upgrading in national economic development zones

Efforts have been made to support the Yangpu Economic Development Zone in participating in the 2023 national comprehensive development assessment for economic development zones. The zone has been guided to play a leading role in implementing the Regional Comprehensive Economic Partnership (RCEP), leveraging the synergistic effects of the "free trade port model area" and RCEP rules. It effectively utilizes the RCEP rules of origin and the free trade port's value-added tax incentives for processing.

D. Strengthening Service Support and Optimizing the Business Environment

1. Establishing a task force system for foreign investment

A provincial task force for stabilizing foreign trade and foreign investment has been set up, with the provincial leader in charge as the team leader, to make decisions, coordinate and solve the difficult demands of key foreign trade and foreign investment enterprises and prominent problems that restrict the development of foreign trade and foreign investment, and promote the stable development of foreign trade and foreign investment work. At the same time,

9 key foreign-investment municipalities and counties such as Haikou, Sanya, and Danzhou have established similar task forces led by local government heads. These local task forces provide comprehensive support for major foreign investment projects in their jurisdictions and maintain a standing book of key foreign-investment projects.

2. Establishing a two-tier complaint mechanism for foreign-invested enterprises covering both provincial and municipal levels

The *Hainan Provincial Rules on Handling Complaints of Foreign-Invested Enterprises* have been formulated and Hainan Province Foreign Investment Enterprise Complaints Guide released. Currently, 19 complaint-handling institutions have been established across the provincial and municipal levels, covering all 18 municipalities and counties. These institutions handle complaints in a tiered manner. Since 2024, the Provincial Department of Commerce has organized two training and exchange sessions for municipal commerce departments and foreign investment complaint staff, significantly enhancing service capacity for foreign investment. The Provincial Department of Commerce conducted a questionnaire survey on 186 foreign-invested enterprises revealed that 86% of respondents expressed satisfaction with Hainan's foreign investment complaint services.

3. Establishing a roundtable meeting mechanism for foreign-invested enterprises

The Provincial Department of Commerceof Hainan Province has formulated the *Implementation Plan for the Roundtable Meeting Mechanism for Foreign-Invested Enterprises in the Hainan Free Trade Port*. Together with the governments of Haikou, Sanya, Danzhou, Chengmai, and other municipalities and counties, it has organized five roundtable meetings with foreign-invested enterprises. These meetings invite representatives from "province-city (county)" government departments, industrial parks, and major foreign-invested enterprises. Through a cross-regional, cross-departmental communication and coordination mechanism, they address policies of common concern to enterprises on-site, efficiently resolving issues raised by businesses. After each meeting, the Provincial Department of Commerce collaborates with local governments to establish issue-specific task lists, assign responsibility to relevant departments, strengthen follow-up and supervision, and ensure a closed-loop service process.

III. Case Studies of Enterprises Landing

Hainan's vibrant foreign investment environment is the result of decades of preparation since its establishment as an economic special zone, the direct impact of Hainan Free Trade Port development, and the combined effects of policy advantages, improved business environment, solidified industrial foundation, increased investment opportunities, platform assistance for development support, and strengthened policy expectations.

A. Policy Dividends Released

Since the establishment of the Hainan Free Trade Port, a series of preferential policies have been implemented, continuously releasing policy dividends that enterprises have directly benefited from during their setup and operations.

Preferential policies inject strong vitality into the development of enterprises. Taking KPMG as an example, in the field of trade and investment, the introduction of the negative list for foreign investment access and cross-border service trade in Hainan Free Trade Port, as well as the implementation of three "zero tariff" lists, have attracted numerous enterprises to Hainan, providing KPMG with abundant market cooperation opportunities. In the financial and tax sectors, the "two 15%" income tax preferential policies of the Free Trade Port have allowed KPMG to enjoy relevant tax reductions. Moreover, the combined effects of RCEP's implementation and the Free Trade Port's preferential policies have further facilitated KPMG's growth.

Early opening of policies showing results: Compared with China's current negative lists for foreign investment in free trade zones, Hainan's negative list for foreign investment access is pioneering in four areas: education, value-added telecommunications, legal services, and mining. For example, the first independent campus of a foreign university in China, the Hainan Bielefeld University of Applied Sciences, has already opened.

The offshore tax exemption policy is constantly being optimized. Over the years, Hainan's offshore duty-free policies have undergone multiple rounds of optimization, effectively stimulating market vitality. Offshore duty-free shopping has flourished, benefiting many foreign-invested enterprises. For instance, since June 2020, the implementation of the offshore tax exemption policy has had a stimulating effect on the sales of Tapestry, while convenient measures like "buy-and-pick-up" have positively impacted the market.

B. Strengthening the Industrial Foundation

In recent years, Hainan has leveraged its abundant natural resources, unique geographical location, and proximity to a vast domestic market to accelerate the cultivation of new cooperation and competition advantages unique to Hainan. The industrial foundation has been continuously strengthened, with "chain-based investment" yielding notable success in various sectors, and key elements such as industry chains and talent pools rapidly converging. For instance, Huaxi Houyuan Biotechnology

(Hainan) Co., Ltd. settled in Meian Ecological Science and Technology New Town of Haikou High-tech Zone, largely due to the ongoing development of a billion-dollar biomedical industrial cluster there. Companies like Tapestry have taken advantage of Hainan's strong foundations in tourism and modern services, capitalizing on the Free Trade Port's offshore duty-free policies to explore the vast Chinese market. Some companies are opening new stores, launching new products, engaging in manufacturing and processing, or establishing regional headquarters, further amplifying the clustering effect.

C. Optimizing the Business Environment

Hainan continues to optimize its business environment, expedite policy implementation, and promote institutional integration and innovation, while also making efforts to transform government functions, provide refined services for enterprises, the province actively addresses challenges encountered by enterprises, boosting foreign investors' confidence.

Efficient services facilitate enterprise investment: For example, Jialvqiao Food Manufacturing Industry (Hainan) Co., Ltd. (referred to as "Jialvqiao Hainan"), invested by Canadian merchants, received attentive and efficient services from local authorities during license processing and production site selection, enabling the company to begin operations in a very short period. Similarly, with strong support from relevant departments and industrial parks, ALBA Hainan completed an expansion project for the harmless treatment of kitchen waste and sewage in Haikou within just six months, half the planned construction period.

Preferential policies attract foreign talents: To attract foreign talent, Hainan has intensified efforts in policy systems, career platforms, and the business environment, creating opportunities for foreign professionals to innovate, start businesses, and work in Hainan. Haikou has optimized its services for foreigners applying for work and residence permits. In addition to implementing "one window for all" services, the city has established a comprehensive service network for foreign talents, offering multifaceted support to enterprises and institutions in recruiting foreign professionals.

D. Platforms Empowering Cooperation

The Boao Forum for Asia Annual Conference, the China International Consumer Products Expo, and other platforms have showcased Hainan's openness to domestic and international guests, attracting numerous global investors to Hainan and facilitating the establishment of high-quality cooperation projects. The Consumer Products Expo served as a platform for Green Chocolate Works Ltd. to understand the Chinese market. After participating in the inaugural Expo in 2021, the company established Jialvqiao Hainan in September of the same year. Tapestry, encouraged by the Expo, solidified its confidence and determination to invest in the Hainan Free Trade Port, leading to the efficient establishment of its China tourism retail headquarters one year after the inaugural Expo. Charoen Pokphand Group has leveraged platforms like the Boao Forum and the Consumer Products Expo to deepen its engagement with Hainan and expand multi-sector cooperation.

IV. Future Outlook

Next, the province will fully implement the decisions and arrangements of the Central Committee of the Communist Party of China and the State Council to stabilize foreign investment, focusing on building a new highland for opening-up and advancing broader, deeper, and more comprehensive opening-up efforts. These measures aim to usher in a new phase of high-quality foreign investment utilization.

A. Continuing to Optimize the Environment for Foreign Investment

First, enhancing the policy environment for foreign investment: Fully implement the policies outlined by the State Council and Hainan Province on optimizing the foreign investment environment. Closely monitor the introduction of supplementary measures by relevant departments and ensure comprehensive release and explanation of these policies to foreign-invested enterprises. Second, strictly enforcing pre-establishment national treatment with negative list management: Leverage the *Catalogue of Encouraged Industries for Foreign Investment* to guide foreign investment toward advanced manufacturing and modern services. Third, regularly addressing unreasonable treatment disparities between domestic and foreign enterprises: Resolve issues such as "opening the big door while keeping small doors shut" or "access without operational approval" as raised by foreign enterprises, timely understanding of the situation, clearing up blockages, and continuously promoting the clearance of various hidden barriers, implementing the requirement of "entry without restriction". Fourth, conducting in-depth analysis of domestic reinvestment data by foreign enterprises: Analyze the structure of foreign enterprises' reinvestments by country and industry to comprehensively understand the operational status of existing foreign investments. This data will support accurate policy formulation and effective investment attraction strategies.

B. Continue to Carry Out the International Investment Promotion Campaign Well

First, utilizing overseas opportunities for overseas investment visits, targeting key regions such as the United States, France, the United Kingdom, Germany, Italy, Japan, South Korea, the United Arab Emirates, Singapore, and Hong Kong Special Administrative Region. Organize "face-to-face" business meetings and comprehensive promotional events abroad, establish communication mechanisms with Fortune Global five hundred companies and renowned multinational corporations, and lay a solid foundation for introducing high-impact foreign investment projects. Second, leveraging high-level platforms: Utilize platforms like the Boao Forum for Asia Annual Conference, the Ministry of Commerce's "Invest China" Summit, and other national-level platforms to conduct comprehensive investment promotion activities. Further strengthen the investment service functionality of the China International Consumer Products Expo, expand its promotional reach, and enhance the recognition and influence of the Hainan Free Trade Port. Third, focusing on industry-specific investment and business partnership promotion: Strengthen connections with leading enterprises in high-tech manufacturing, new energy vehicles, and healthcare. Encourage these companies to bring in partners and establish upstream and downstream enterprises in Hainan. Fourth, expanding indirect and mediated investment channels: Collaborate with major accounting firms, consulting firms, Chinese financial institutions with overseas networks, and similar entities to promote Hainan's policies and attract high-quality enterprises. Foster ties with foreign business associations such as the American Chamber of Commerce in China, the EU Chamber of Commerce in China, the China-Britain Business Council, and Hainan associations to broaden foreign investment channels. Fifth, promoting investment through funds: Strengthen coordination with financial regulators to advance overseas fund-type QFLP investment attraction work, attracting high-quality foreign capital. Leverage the cross-border financing advantages of the Hainan Free Trade Port to attract more high-value foreign investment projects. Focus on the quality of promotional activities to ensure effective project matching and high conversion rates from promotional efforts.

C. Strengthening Enterprise (Project) Service Guarantee

First, optimizing the "Roundtable Meeting" mechanism: Continue leveraging the roundtable meeting mechanism, organizing localized and sector-specific meetings at the municipal and industrial park levels. When appropriate, invite provincial leaders to host direct dialogues with enterprises to address their concerns, ensuring a stronger sense of satisfaction among businesses. Second, securing national-level support for key foreign investment projects: Advocate for the inclusion of priority projects in advanced manufacturing, high-tech industries, and modern services into the national coordination mechanism for foreign trade and investment services. Accelerate project implementation and construction while enhancing resource support for these projects. Third, improving the one-stop service platform for foreign investment: Enhance the "Free Trade Port Navigator" platform to provide end-to-end lifecycle support for foreign enterprises, including pre-establishment, establishment, and post-establishment services. Improve investment facilitation and continuously optimize the business environment for foreign investment.

Chapter 9   Report on the Construction of the National Comprehensive Demonstration Zone for Expanding Opening-up in the Service Sector[①]

In 2015, Beijing pioneered the launch of a comprehensive pilot program for expanding opening-up in the service sector, focusing on key areas of the service industry and implementing vertical reform and opening-up citywide. This initiative created a new model for industrial openness. In 2020, under the personal care, planning, and announcement of General Secretary Xi Jinping, the "pilots" was officially upgraded to a "demonstration zone", making Beijing the nation's only National Comprehensive Demonstration Zone for Expanding opening-up in the Service Sector (hereinafter referred to as the "Demonstration Zone"). The Beijing Municipal Party Committee and Beijing Municipal Government have prioritized the integration of the Demonstration Zone with the construction of the China (Beijing) Pilot Free Trade Zone (referred to as the "Two Zones"), opening a new chapter of reform and opening-up for the capital. Today, the construction of the Demonstration Zone has entered its 2.0 iteration and upgrade phase. Over the

---

[①] Contributed by the Beijing Municipal Commerce Bureau.

past eight years, Beijing has consistently promoted reform and development through opening-up, advancing both industrial and park-level openness, and driving progress through institutional innovation and project implementation. This initiative offers a local model for creating a broader, deeper, and more comprehensive opening-up framework, charting a Beijing path that promotes high-quality development through high-level openness.

I. Continuously Deepening the Demonstration Zone Construction to Build a New Highland for Opening-up

A. Leading High-level Institutional Opening-up with Policy Innovation

First, leading high-level institutional opening-up through policy innovation. Aligning with national strategies to pioneer high standards in international opening-up. By focusing on implementing the State Council's approved plan, Beijing has completed 98% of the first-phase Demonstration Zone construction tasks within three years. Building on this success, Beijing has proposed the *Work Plan for Supporting the Construction of Beijing's Comprehensive Demonstration Zone for Further Opening up the National Service Sector* (hereinafter referred to as the 2.0 Plan), driving the iterative upgrade of the Demonstration Zone. This plan aims to establish a high-level institutional system for opening up the service industry across seven areas: investment, trade, the digital economy, financial services, intellectual property, dispute resolution, and risk management. It also includes orderly alignment with the rules of the *Comprehensive and Progressive Agreement for Trans-Pacific Partnership (CPTPP) and the Digital Economy Partnership Agreement* (DEPA), with over 70 measures accounting for 40 % of the total pilot tasks. The Beijing Pilot Free Trade

Zone has become one of the first in the nation to conduct pilot programs for aligning with international high standards, pioneering institutional opening-up in areas such as innovation in goods trade, free and convenient service trade, optimizing the business environment, and strengthening risk management. The comprehensive implementation of pilot tasks is being advanced.

Second, expanding institutional opening-up steadily, rooted in the strategic positioning of the capital city. Based on the national tasks assigned to the Demonstration Zone, Beijing has focused on strategic sectors that align with the capital's unique positioning and strengths, such as technological innovation, the digital economy, green finance, and biopharmaceuticals. Efforts have been directed toward full-chain and full-process reform across key elements such as investment, trade, talent, intellectual property, and international payments. The first phase has seen the development and implementation of over ten specialized plans. Additionally, Beijing has conducted policy evaluations for niche sectors like offshore trade, wellness and health, cultural trade, and the low-altitude economy, supporting the development of regionally distinctive industries. For forward-looking and comprehensive sectors, a project-based management approach has been adopted to drive integrated policy and institutional innovations. This has resulted in the launch of forty-seven innovative tasks, including scenario-based integrated services for foreign-funded enterprises and foreign nationals, with nearly ninety percent of these tasks implemented successfully.

B. Leveraging Open Platforms to Create a Magnet for Foreign Investment

First, promoting distinctive and differentiated development in key parks to shape a diverse open framework. Beijing has introduced twenty-one key "Two Zones" parks (clusters) and launched a specialized development and enhancement action plan to guide each cluster in accelerating the growth of its advantageous industries. The Lize Financial Business District of Beijing has cautiously advanced the digital RMB pilot program, with Galaxy Securities implementing the first digital RMB application scenario in the securities industry nationwide. The global cross-border payment company Thunes has established its China headquarters in the district. The Beijing Sino-German Economic and Technological Cooperation Demonstration Zone has attracted over one hundred German-funded enterprises, including Mercedes-Benz and Ameco, achieving an industrial scale of CNY 40 billion in 2023. Meanwhile, the Beijing Sino-Japanese Innovation Cooperation Demonstration Zone has launched the first phase of a Sino-Japanese fund with an initial scale of CNY 20 billion, bringing in over one hundred foreign-invested enterprises. In 2023, these twenty-one parks, occupying less than two percent of the city's area, contributed over twenty percent of the city's revenue from above-designated-size enterprises and more than one-third of its tax revenue.

Second, enhancing the free trade pilot zone to strengthen open leadership. With a focus on major institutional innovations, key platforms, and critical projects, Beijing has shaped five "Free Trade Brands" emphasizing innovation, intelligence, green, convenience, and collaboration. Key achievements include the opening of Beijing GoBroad Hospital, accelerating the commercialization of pharmaceutical R&D results; the establishment of the first full-process cross-border trade digitalization pilot project between China and Singapore; and the launch of the nation's first integrated carbon chain platform combining "standards certification + production procurement + financial support", supporting the China Beijing Green Exchange in building a unified national voluntary greenhouse gas emission reduction trading center. Additionally, the Yizhuang Business Center 2.0 has started construction, creating the country's first "one-stop integrated service platform for zone entry". The Beijing-Hebei "Free Trade Office" model has enabled over three thousand six hundred government service items from Beijing and Tongzhou District to be processed without regional differences in the Hebei Free Trade Pilot Zone. As the main platform for open economic development, Beijing's Free Trade Pilot Zone contributed 19.3% of the city's actual utilized foreign investment in 2023 with just 0.7% of its area.

Third, advancing high-quality development of comprehensive bonded zones to optimize the open layout. The Beijing Tianzhu Comprehensive Bonded Zone, the nation's first airport-based comprehensive bonded zone, passed the cross-border trade facilitation standardization pilot evaluation and ranked as a Class A zone in the 2022 national comprehensive bonded zone performance assessment. Its import and export volume exceeded CNY 100 billion for the first time in history in 2023, a year-on-year increase of 41%. Efforts to accelerate the development of the Beijing Daxing International Airport Comprehensive Bonded Zone have included the launch of the cross-border e-commerce direct mail export model, the improvement of the cross-border e-commerce industry chain, and the operation of projects such as the bonded public service platform, bonded smart warehousing center, and logistics center. The Beijing Zhongguancun Comprehensive Bonded Zone, the nation's first comprehensive bonded zone focusing on R&D innovation and the first to eliminate physical fences, has been successfully approved. It is pioneering the exploration of intelligent regulatory models nationwide.

C. Creating a World-Class Business Environment for Domestic and Foreign Investment Cooperation

First, leveraging the project promotion mechanism. Projects are treated as the focal point for advancing the "Two Zones" initiative. The "Two Zones" project framework incorporates a "One Database and Four Mechanisms" approach: a centralized project management system and four mechanisms—target expectation management, regular coordination, government-enterprise matchmaking, and inspection and evaluation. To date, the database has included over 25,000 projects, with nearly 18,000 implemented, involving a total investment exceeding 3.6 trillion yuan.

Second, enhancing efforts to attract and utilize foreign investment. Tailored to Beijing's specific conditions, the city has implemented the State Council's "24 Measures" to attract foreign investment and issued the *Several Measures for Further Optimizing Foreign Investment Environment and Making Greater Efforts to Attract Foreign Investment to Beijing*. These measures focus on improving the quality of foreign investment, ensuring national treatment for foreign-invested enterprises, strengthening foreign investment protection, and increasing fiscal and tax support to achieve more effective and substantial foreign investment attraction and utilization. The *Beijing Plan for Expanding Opening-up in the Service Sector to Promote Foreign Investment* has been formulated to further expand foreign investment access.

Third, improving the foreign investment service system. Beijing has established smooth channels for regular communication between the government and enterprises. Meetings have been held between municipal leaders and international chambers of commerce and Fortune Global 500 companies based in Beijing. A "Roundtable Meeting"mechanism for foreign enterprises and a "closed-loop" enterprise demand response mechanism ensure that communication between the government and enterprises is "accessible at all times, conducted monthly, and aligned quarterly". This approach helps foreign enterprises resolve issues effectively. Additionally, a bilingual investment policy service package covering 10 key areas, including technological innovation and the digital economy, has been published. Using platforms such as the "Two Zones" global liaison stations, the "Close Partner Plan," the Global Cooperation Partner Mechanism for Invest Beijing, and the World Association of Investment Promotion Agencies, Beijing has promoted "Two Zone" policies to help foreign enterprises fully utilize available benefits.

Fourth, strengthening the legal protection framework. Beijing has implemented "One Regulation and One Decision" specific to the "Two Zones", ensuring that significant reforms and innovations have a solid legal basis. The city is expediting the enactment of the *Regulation of Beijing Municipality on Foreign Investment* to protect the legitimate rights and interests of foreign investors and regulate foreign investment services and management. Furthermore, the Beijing Court's "One-Stop" Diversified International Commercial Dispute Resolution Center have been established. Efforts are also underway to construct an international commercial arbitration center to provide diversified dispute resolution mechanisms. From 2020 to 2023, Beijing's actual utilized foreign investment amounted to nearly USD 59 billion, accounting for 8.8% of the national total, with over 90% of this investment concentrated in the service sector.

II. Deepening Reform and Opening-up to Stimulate Momentum for High-Quality Development

A. Aligning with the Construction of an International Center for Innovation in Science and Technology to Foster an Open and Shared Innovation Ecosystem

First, promoting the integration of resources to strengthen high-level international scientific cooperation. Leveraging its strengths in fundamental research and concentrated financial resources, Beijing has received approval to establish the Zhongguancun Pilot Financial Reform Zone for Scientific and Technological. Over five years, the goal is to build mechanisms for effectively supporting technological innovation and enhance financial services for tech enterprises. Key initiatives include piloting equity and venture capital share transfers, launching the first national pilot for comprehensive warrant services, and setting up the first national venture capital fund utilizing warrant strategies. These measures broaden financing channels for tech enterprises. The Beijing Equity Exchange Center launched the first national "Specialized and New" equity board to support high-quality, innovative "Specialized and New" enterprises in expediting their public listings. Major national science and technology infrastructure resources are now more open and shared. The Huairou Comprehensive National Science Center has formed a cluster of national science facilities, accelerating its development into a world-class innovation hub. Of the 37 planned platforms, 10, including the Synergetic Extreme Condition User Facility and the Earth System Numerical Simulation Facility, have opened for access. Additionally, Beijing has established the first national platform for international science organizations, attracting 12 entities, such as the International Society for Digital Earth and the International Coalition of Intelligent Manufacturing, further linking global innovation resources.

Second, accelerating the introduction of open innovation entities to strengthen key industrial chains. Beijing has promoted foreign enterprises' participation in international scientific cooperation and strengthened connections to global innovation resources. A comprehensive set of measures supporting foreign-funded R&D centers has been introduced. As of the end of 2023, 107 foreign R&D centers, including Airbus, Schneider Electric, and ABB, have been certified. Landmark foreign-invested projects include Toyota's fuel cell R&D and production base, GE Healthcare's high-end production line, SMC's China headquarters, and Bayer's new advanced production line.

Third, releasing development momentum through reform to translate scientific achievements into productivity. Beijing pioneered the "filing-based approval" policy for high-tech enterprises, streamlining processes for integrated circuits, AI, biopharmaceuticals, and critical materials. This reform implements a system of applying, recognizing, and filing on the spot, cuts approval times by over 80%, benefiting 377 enterprises. Beijing has also reformed the ownership and usage rights of scientific achievements, granting rights to 59 projects across nine pilot units. Additionally, tax incentives for technology transfers have benefited 108 enterprises, with tax reductions totaling CNY 742 million.

B. Focusing on the Opening-up of Key Service Sectors to Provide Beijing's Approach to Supporting Domestic and International Dual Circulation

First, deepening the opening-up of the financial sector. Beijing has attracted prominent financial entities such as Standard Chartered Securities (China), the nation's first wholly foreign-owned securities firm, and BlackRock's wholly owned subsidiary, Panyan Investment. Other major firms include CITIC Securities Asset Management. Supporting financial institutions to expand their services, Amundi Asset Management increased its capital and securing additional QDLP quotas in Beijing. HSBC Insurance Brokers Ltd. gained approval for fund distribution, and BMW (China) Insurance Brokers Co., Ltd. and ERGO-FESCO Broker Company Limited secured licenses for insurance brokerage operations. In green finance, Deutsche Bank (China) and Société Générale (China) were among the first foreign banks included in China's carbon reduction support tools. Beijing also saw the launch of the CAAC Beijing Photovoltaic REIT, one of China's first new energy REITs. Brokerages like China International Capital Corporation and China Securities Finance Co., Ltd. gained carbon emission trading qualifications. To support the Beijing Stock Exchange, a "Beijing + Hong Kong" mechanism was introduced in collaboration with the Hong Kong Stock Exchange, enabling eligible companies to list in both markets. By the end of 2023, the Beijing Stock Exchange had 239 listed companies, with a total market capitalization approaching CNY 450 billion.

Second, promoting reforms and opening-up in healthcare and professional services. In healthcare, 30 institutions are building or have established research-oriented wards, with 4,800 research beds under construction or completed. A series of measures to promote the high-quality development of the wellness and health industries were introduced, including China's first personalized cosmetics service experience center. Beijing also established two Medicine and Medical Device Innovation Service Station in Changping District and the Economic and Technological Development Zone, providing services to nearly 2,800 enterprises. In professional services, Beijing was the first to implement a trinity international certification mechanism for securities, fund, and futures professionals. It also launched a pilot program for accounting firms to establish branches in the Free Trade Zone. In aviation services, Beijing pioneered a bonded logistics supply chain regulatory model, allowing aircraft maintenance companies to apply VAT refund and exemption policies within comprehensive bonded zones. The city also advanced the construction of the "Air Silk Road" innovation demonstration zone, enhancing the international functions of its dual-hub.

C. Supporting the Creation of a Global Digital Economy Benchmark City and Strengthening Rule Exploration in the Digital Economy

First, cultivating and developing a data element market. Beijing has initiated the construction of the nation's first data infrastructure pilot zone, releasing a creation plan and policy list to build a comprehensive reform testbed for data infrastructure. The activation of data transactions has accelerated with the establishment of the Beijing International Big Data Exchange's Data Asset Service Center. This center provides data asset registration, evaluation, inclusion in financial statements, and financing services, with data transaction volumes exceeding CNY 2 billion. The Data Trading Alliance has grown to over 100 members. The nation's first industrial data section was launched to assist industrial enterprises in developing data products and trading data assets. In the spatial sector, the first national data asset registration and spatial data transaction were completed. Beijing has also pioneered intellectual property protection rules for new fields and business models, becoming the only city to fully complete the pilot tasks of rule creation, registration practices, case protection, transaction application, and data asset inclusion in financial statements. Additionally, it successfully concluded the nation's first data intellectual property registration certificate validation case.

Second, promoting the lawful and orderly cross-border flow of data. Beijing achieved the first national case of data outbound security assessment and filed the first standard contract for the outbound cross-border transfer of personal information, achieving the "two firsts" in compliance with data export regulations. In 2023, it successfully completed 38 security assessment projects and 27 standard contract filings, enabling compliant data outbound flows in six major industries: civil aviation, automotive, education, medicine, academic, and artificial intelligence. Beijing leads the country in data compliance approval rates and application scenarios. It has also developed the nation's first data hosting service platform for cross-border scenarios and a public service platform for data security and governance, and introduced social forces to participate in the governance of cross-border data flow.

Third, empowering innovation in key industries. Beijing has built the world's first cloud-controlled advanced autonomous driving demonstration zone and expanded the area to 580 square kilometers in its 3.0 phase. Over 700 vehicles, including intelligent connected vehicles, are deployed for testing in eight major scenarios, with more than 1,000 vehicles conducting demonstration applications in six districts citywide. These vehicles have provided over 7 million trips and retail services, with daily orders averaging nearly 3,000. Beijing released the nation's first real-scene-based vehicle-road collaboration autonomous driving dataset, an intelligent network roadside operating system, and the first autonomous driving demonstration zone data security management regulations and classification guidelines. In 2023, Beijing's digital economy added over 1.8 trillion yuan in value, an 8.5% year-on-year increase, accounting for more than 40% of the city's GDP.

D. Deepening Regionally Complementary Cooperation to Build a High-Level Beijing-Tianjin-Hebei Collaborative Open Platform

First, promoting collaborative innovation. The *Beijing-Tianjin-Hebei Free Trade Zone Collaborative Development Plan* was signed, focusing on trade and investment facilitation, port interconnectivity, financial innovation, industrial development, and resource mobility. These initiatives have elevated the region's collaborative development and led to the release of the "1+5+18" series of collaborative innovation achievements for the Beijing-Tianjin-Hebei Free Trade Zone. The nation's first comprehensive technology innovation center, the Jingjinji National Center of Technology Innovation (Jingjinji: Beijing, Tianjin, and Hebei), was completed, promoting the implementation and transformation of scientific achievements within the region. Beijing also established the first internet-based cross-regional corporate credit information chain platform, the "Beijing-Tianjin-Hebei Credit Chain. " This platform facilitates high-quality cross-regional sharing of credit information from multiple domains, including industry and commerce and judiciary sectors. The platform has processed nearly 25 million transactions and supported loans to nearly 20 million enterprises, with total disbursed loans exceeding 100 billion yuan.

Second, enhancing interconnectivity. Port cooperation has deepened, enabling the mutual recognition of user systems for the Beijing-Tianjin-Hebei International Trade "Single Window." A "Beijing-Tianjin-Hebei Collaborative Service Zone" has been launched, allowing enterprises to log into the "Single Window" in any of the three locations to access shared services. Administrative integration efforts have also progressed, with 203 unified administrative service items introduced in five batches across the Beijing-Tianjin-Hebei Free Trade Zone by the end of 2023. These initiatives ensure "same thing same standards." Additionally, 165 qualification recognition items have been introduced, enabling cross-regional mutual recognition of professional qualifications and certifications across the three areas.

III. Continuously Expanding Policy Coverage and Effectiveness to Shape the "Beijing Service" Brand

First, promoting free and convenient investment. Beijing continues to relax foreign investment access restrictions. Landmark projects such as the first foreign-invested futures company, the city's first foreign-invested vocational skills training institution, and the first foreign-invested commercial factoring company have been established in Beijing. HSBC Insurance Brokerage Company, the first wholly foreign-owned insurance brokerage firm under newly implemented measures for opening the insurance intermediary market, has successfully commenced operations in Beijing. Its registered capital increased from 10 million yuan to 1.108 billion yuan, making it the insurance intermediary institution with the highest paid-in registered capital in China. Efforts to streamline investment-related processes include promoting online applications for business licenses, tax-related matters, and bank account openings for foreign-invested enterprises, effectively reducing costs for setting up and operating businesses in Beijing.

Second, promoting free and convenient trade. Beijing has optimized its trade supervision model, establishing the nation's first public inspection platform for special items within a comprehensive bonded zone. This allows enterprises to complete "receiving, dispatching, tallying, and inspection" in a single operation. A unified platform for customs clearance and sampling of imported medicines has been established, enabling 24-hour completion of customs clearance and sampling for imported pharmaceuticals, significantly enhancing efficiency and reducing costs for enterprises. New business models such as duty-free bonded e-commerce, cross-border e-commerce for pharmaceutical imports, and "bonded + consumption upgrade" pilots have been introduced. Offshore trade has also seen development through the creation of "Jingmao Xing (Beijing Trade Prosperity)," the first public service platform providing cross-regional support for offshore trade. The National Base for International Cultural Trade (Beijing) has established a national-level cultural trade service platform, promoting emerging businesses such as bonded restoration of overseas artworks, with imports of artworks accounting for one-third of the national total.

Third, facilitating free and efficient capital flows. Beijing has strengthened capital management, becoming the first in China to pilot integrated cross-border currency operations. This "domestic and foreign currency integration + cross-border" capital pool policy benefits over 100 multinational corporations and nearly 5,000 domestic and foreign member entities in the city. The pilot for one-time registration of external debt in Zhongguancun Haidian Science Park has achieved a registered amount exceeding 100 billion yuan. The facilitation of trade-related foreign exchange payments has expanded to include 140 "specialized, refined, distinctive, and innovative" enterprises, hospitals, and research institutions, with over 230 pilot participants collectively handling amounts exceeding USD 360 billion. Cross-border financing facilitation pilots have expanded to include high-tech, specialized, and innovative enterprises. Beijing has also gained approval to conduct trials for high-level opening-up in cross-border trade and investment, streamlining compliance processes for more enterprises engaging in cross-border trade and investment.

Fourth, facilitating the entry, exit, and employment of talent. Beijing has enhanced talent services by reducing the processing time for work permits and work-related residence permits for foreign nationals to five working days. Over 4,000 foreign talents and their family members have benefited from these services. Pilot standards for recognizing "high-level and advanced talents in short supply" foreign talents have been implemented, expanding the categories of high-level foreign talents (Class A) and professional foreign talent (Class B) eligible for work permits. The Zhongguancun International Talent Service Area has been launched, providing 32 types of services across governance, living, and career development. Beijing has also facilitated professional qualification recognition for foreign nationals by releasing version 3.0 of its Catalogue of Recognized International Professional Qualifications in Beijing Municipality, covering 122 qualifications and highlighting 7 high-value qualifications such as ACM Fellows. The *Human Resources Development Catalog for the Integrated National Demonstration Zone for Opening up the Services Sector and the China (Beijing) Pilot Free Trade Zone (2023 Edition)* identified 130 key development directions and 58 urgently needed occupations.

Fifth, strengthening intellectual property protection and utilization. Beijing has promoted intellectual property financing by implementing high-quality development policies for IP pledge financing. Ten service mechanisms have been established, including IP evaluation, online registration inquiries, dual-channel white-list recommendations, and risk compensation. Since 2022, the total amount of patent and trademark pledges has exceeded 27.8 billion yuan, with satisfaction rates among enterprises surpassing 98% in 2023. Innovative models of IP protection include the nation's first

IP insurance pilot, supporting nearly 500 enterprises with over 4,800 patents insured under domestic patent enforcement and infringement loss insurance policies. The insured amount has reached approximately 5.4 billion yuan. Additionally, Beijing became the first city in China to pilot insurance for legal costs in international IP disputes, providing insurance coverage of 100 million yuan for 17 enterprises. The patent infringement administrative adjudication demonstration initiative has been launched, with over 300 cases concluded. The "preliminary decision and separate appeal" model for patent disputes has been promoted nationwide. A comprehensive IP protection service system has been established, achieving city-level coverage for public IP service institutions. Beijing has also built an overseas IP public service information database, containing over 100,000 entries and providing 37,000 instances of information services.

IV. Future Outlook

The Third Plenary Session of the 20th CPC Central Committee emphasized that opening up is a defining feature of Chinese modernization, we must remain committed to the basic state policy of opening to the outside world and continue to promote reform through opening up, and develop new institutions for a higher-standard open economy. Going forward, the construction of the Demonstration Zone will adhere to General Secretary Xi Jinping's important directives on high-level opening-up and his series of key instructions for Beijing. It will fully implement the guiding principles of the 20th CPC National Congress and the second and third plenary sessions of the 20th Central Committee. Accurately grasp the new situation and new requirements, based on the needs of in-depth reform, high-quality development, and open cooperation, create a high-level open model with distinctive capital features, demonstrate greater responsibility and action of the capital at a new starting point, and contribute to the construction of a higher-level open economic new system.

First, steadily expanding institutional opening-up. Guided by national needs, Beijing will leverage the Demonstration Zone's extensive scope, comprehensive industries, and diverse samples to align precisely with international high-standard trade and economic rules. This involves steadily expanding institutional opening-up in areas such as rules, regulations, management, and standards. While ensuring the implementation of the 2.0 plan for the Demonstration Zone, Beijing will simultaneously plan for a 3.0 version. These efforts will contribute local practices to China's efforts to join high international standards of economic and trade agreement and support the development of a high-standard service industry openness system.

Second, continuing to support the development of a modern industrial system. With a systemic perspective and goal-oriented approach, Beijing will focus on key sectors such as the digital economy, finance, and healthcare, as well as critical elements like talent and intellectual property. Comprehensive, full-chain, and full-process reform and opening-up will be deepened to optimize the industrial development ecosystem. Pressure tests for openness will be conducted in fields such as biopharmaceuticals, value-added telecommunications, and autonomous driving. New models for the open development of cutting-edge areas, such as stem cell and gene diagnosis and therapy, will be explored. Major projects, including breakthroughs in core technologies and the enhancement of clinical translation capabilities, will be implemented to accelerate the formation of world-class industrial clusters.

Third, building a diversified opening up framework.

Beijing will strengthen platforms such as key industrial parks and comprehensive bonded zones, adhering to differentiated and distinctive exploration. The city will accelerate the extraction and release of innovative results, forming practical, innovative methods that can be replicated and promoted nationwide.

Fourth, increasing efforts to attract foreign investment. Utilizing channels such as the Global Partners of "Invest Beijing" and the "Two Zones" global liaison stations, Beijing will create a "policy express" platform to promote its policies directly to businesses. International exhibitions like the China International Fair for Trade in Services and the China International Import Expo will be leveraged to introduce the "Two Zones" policies to enterprises. By engaging business entities and society, Beijing will help businesses fully utilize these policies, ensuring that implemented policies expand in coverage and effectiveness.

Fifth, balancing opening up and security. Beijing will ensure the positive interaction between high-quality development and high-level security by deeply integrating development and security. This includes implementing measures for foreign investment security reviews, export controls, content reviews for imported cultural products, and anti-monopoly reviews. The city will strengthen security capabilities in key areas, refine mechanisms for risk assessment, early warning, prevention, and management, and build a safety protection system that integrates institutional, managerial, and technical measures. These efforts will provide robust support for higher-level openness in the Demonstration Zone.

Chapter 10　CIFIT: Focusing on Building a Key Platform for a New Round of High-Level Opening-up to the Outside World[①]

The China International Fair for Investment and Trade (CIFIT) is an international investment promotion event approved by the State Council of the People's Republic of China. Hosted by the Ministry of Commerce, it is co-organized with entities such as the UN Trade and Development (UNCTAD), the United Nations Industrial Development Organization (UNIDO), the Organization for Economic Co-operation and Development (OECD), the International Finance Corporation (IFC) of the World Bank, the World Association of Investment Promotion Agencies (WAIPA), and the China Council for International Investment Promotion (CCIIP). The event is undertaken by the People's Government of Fujian Province, the Xiamen Municipal People's Government, and the Investment Promotion Agency of Ministry of Commerce. 31 provinces, autonomous regions, and municipalities of mainland China, as well as Hong Kong and Macao Special Administrative Regions, some of Chinese municipalities with independent planning status, relevant national departments, and major national business associations.

① Contributed by Chen Wenshui, General Manager of the Investment and Trade Promotion (Xiamen) Exhibition Co., Ltd.

These entities contribute to the organization and participate in exhibitions and delegations.

CIFIT is currently the only national-level international investment promotion event in China that focuses on facilitating two-way investment. It is also the largest global event of its kind. With the themes of "introducing FDI" and "going global", CIFIT provides a platform for showcasing, project matchmaking, and discussions to support investment cooperation between domestic and foreign entities. Guided by China's policies for attracting foreign investment and encouraging Chinese enterprises to "going global," CIFIT hosts the International Investment Forum and dozens of seminars on trending investment topics. The event actively invites foreign governments, business associations, and enterprises to showcase their policies for attracting foreign investment, highlight their investment environments, and present market opportunities. By doing so, CIFIT serves as a platform for bilateral and multilateral investment cooperation. Since its inception in 1997, CIFIT has been held annually from September 8 to 11 in Xiamen. It evolved from the Fujian Investment and Trade Fair, which was successfully held in Xiamen for ten sessions prior. CIFIT has pioneered a new international investment promotion model, growing into one of the world's most influential investment promotion platforms. It has significantly advanced China's efforts to utilize foreign investment and implement its strategy of opening up to the world, catalyzing the rapid development of investment-focused expos. CIFIT has also strongly promoted investment cooperation between China and developing countries, showcasing the Chinese government's commitment to mutual development and prosperity. It has effectively facilitated cross-strait economic and trade exchanges, while projecting a positive image of China's dedication to reform and opening-up, seeking shared growth through expanded investment cooperation. CIFIT has notably enhanced China's international standing.

In 2018, President Xi Jinping sent a congratulatory letter to the 20th CIFIT, expressing hope that the event would focus on promoting two-way investment, maintain a high standard of internationalization, professionalism, and branding, and establish itself as a premier platform for high-level opening-up. Xi emphasized that CIFIT should play an active role in fostering a new framework for comprehensive openness and in building an open global economy.

I. Development History and Strategic Value of Opening up of CIFIT

A. The Development History of CIFIT

The history of the China International Fair for Investment and Trade (CIFIT) reflects and embodies China's reform and opening-up process. On September 8, 2024, the 24th CIFIT was inaugurated. Including the ten-year history of the Fujian Investment and Trade Fair, CIFIT now boasts a remarkable 34-year journey. Over the past four decades, CIFIT has adapted to the changing domestic and global economic landscapes in alignment with China's overarching policies on opening up. By continually adjusting its themes and content, CIFIT has evolved from a regional economic and trade event into one of the most influential international investment promotion fairs worldwide.

Fujian Province, known as a crucial cradle and practiceplace for Xi Jinping Thought on Socialism with Chinese Characteristics for a New Era, holds a special connection to CIFIT. CIFIT was an initiative spearheaded and carefully nurtured during President Xi Jinping's tenure in Fujian. In 1987, the Xiamen Municipal People's Government established the "Southern Fujian Triangle Foreign Investment and Trade Fair", with Xi Jinping, then a member of the Standing Committee of the CPC Xiamen Municipal and Vice Mayor, actively participating in its creation. This laid a strong foundation for the future development of CIFIT. In 1988, the fair was renamed the "Fujian Investment and Trade Fair" and organized by the Fujian Provincial Government. In 1997, the fair was officially upgraded to the "China Investment and Trade Fair" with approval from the Ministry of Commerce (formerly the Ministry of Foreign Trade and Economic Cooperation), which became the sole organizer. In 2005, the event was further elevated and renamed the "China International Fair for Investment and Trade (CIFIT). " In 2014, the central government adjusted CIFIT's schedule to occur biennially in even-numbered years as part of its restructuring of state-led international expos.

Due to President Xi Jinping's high attention and concern for the development of CIFIT, he served as the Chairman of the CIFIT Organizing Committee for four consecutive sessions from 1999 to 2002. During this period, he also repeatedly proposed and personally promoted the development of CIFIT towards the goal of becoming an "International Investment Expo". In 2010, during his tenure as a member of the Standing Committee of the Political Bureau and Vice President of China, Xi Jinping attended the 14th CIFIT and the 2nd World Investment Forum in Xiamen. He delivered the keynote address and personally inaugurated the event with the symbolic "Golden Key. " In 2018, at the milestone of CIFIT's 20th session, President Xi Jinping sent a congratulatory letter, providing clear guidance for the fair's future development. He emphasized that over the past two decades, CIFIT had been committed to building three core platforms: for two-way investment promotion, authoritative information release, and investment trend discussions. It had grown into one of the most influential international investment fairs globally, making significant contributions to China's reform and opening-up, and socialist modernization.

Through more than three decades of exploration and growth, CIFIT has established a distinctive organizational model. Its core focus is investment promotion, with an integrated approach that combines investment and trade, exhibitions and project negotiations, project promotion and policy consulting, as well as policy discussions and information release. This model fosters two-way, diversified investment and cooperation, providing comprehensive services to participants. Today, CIFIT's global appeal as a premier investment expo brand continues to grow, solidifying its role as a pivotal platform for international investment promotion.

B. The Role of CIFIT in Advancing Opening up

As China's earliest investment and trade fair, CIFIT has transitioned from focusing primarily on attracting foreign investment to embracing both "introducing FDI" and "going global". It has actively integrated with and guided high-level openness, reflecting the extraordinary journey of China's comprehensive reform and opening-up. CIFIT embodies the pioneering spirit of reform and opening-up, showcases its remarkable achievements, and serves as a vital platform for implementing national development strategies in economic and trade investment.

First, building the world's most influential two-way investment promotion platform. Investment remains one of the most critical global priorities, contributing over 40% to economic growth in many countries. By centering its theme on investment promotion, CIFIT aligns with global economic trends and China's broader openness strategies. Every year, in line with the overall goal of introducing foreign investment in various regions, CIFIT organizes and selects a large number of investment projects. In addition, it also arranges various levels and forms of two-way communication and investment project docking and negotiation activities to create conditions for international capital to enter China and for Chinese enterprises to expand globally. Each session of the CIFIT sees provinces, autonomous regions, and municipalities in China organizing delegations to participate, resulting in numerous signed and implemented projects. International participants set up exhibitions, host investment briefings, and conduct promotional events to explore cooperation opportunities in the Chinese market. CIFIT enables global participants to gain a comprehensive understanding of China's investment environment and opportunities while connecting with suitable projects and partners. Over its 23 sessions, CIFIT's exhibition area has expanded from 28,000 square meters in its first session to 120,000 square meters. The number of member units has grown from 37 to 57. CIFIT has welcomed over 300,000 foreign participants from more than 200 countries and regions, along with over 1,000 business organizations and 450 Fortune Global 500 companies. More than 30,000 projects have been signed, channeling over USD 340 billion into China, while numerous Chinese enterprises have leveraged CIFIT to expand their presence worldwide.

Second, effectively supporting China's economic diplomacy. Six major international organizations, including the UN Trade and Development (UNCTAD), the United Nations Industrial Development Organization (UNIDO), the World Trade Organization (WTO), the Organisation for Economic Cooperation and Development (OECD), the World Bank's International Finance Corporation (IFC), and the World Association of Investment Promotion Agencies (WAIPA), co-host CIFIT. These organizations contribute by releasing investment reports, discussing trends, and coordinating investment mechanisms. CIFIT serves as a critical link to international economic organizations and an essential platform for advancing China's economic diplomacy. In recent years, against the backdrop of complex international political and economic dynamics, CIFIT has astutely tracked market trends, demonstrating its authority, foresight, and relevance. It showcases China's commitment and capacity for high-level openness, effectively supporting economic globalization and bolstering global confidence.

Third, promoting pragmatic multilateral and bilateral cooperation in international trade and investment. Each session of the CIFIT focuses on China's foreign investment policies, showcasing achievements in utilizing foreign capital and its contributions to national economic development. It highlights local investment environments and policies, as well as priority investment projects, providing an abundance of investment-related information for global investors in a "one-stop" format. In recent years, China has expanded its openness in breadth and depth, accelerating the establishment of an all-encompassing, multi-tiered, and broad-ranging framework. Initiatives like the Belt and Road Initiative (BRI), BRICS cooperation, and the implementation of the Regional Comprehensive Economic Partnership (RCEP) have positioned China as not just a participant but a driver and leader in economic globalization. Amid this new wave of high-level openness, CIFIT has delved deeply into the Belt and Road Initiative, working with participating countries to explore shared investment opportunities. It has expanded cooperation with BRICS nations, facilitating practical collaborations in trade, investment, and industry. Additionally, CIFIT supports the high-quality implementation of RCEP by offering platforms for domestic and international organizations to share the benefits of regional cooperation. CIFIT has effectively acted as both a "window" and "platform" for investment promotion, fostering pragmatic multilateral and bilateral cooperation, facilitating investment and trade liberalization, and contributing to the deeper integration of global economic ties.

C. CIFIT's Positive Role in Serving National Strategies

Beyond its contributions to opening up, CIFIT has confirmed four key characteristics: national and international prominence, focus on investment matchmaking and policy promotion, emphasis on coordinated regional economic development, and commitment to cross-strait economic exchanges. These four characteristics have effectively supported the implementation of China's economic development strategies and promoted balanced regional growth.

First, meeting the needs of high-quality economic development. Over the past three decades, CIFIT has aligned with the realities of national economic development and the overall strategy for opening up by launching a series of projects reflecting contemporary investment priorities in China. These include initiatives related to Western Development, Strategy for Revitalization of the Old Industrial Bases in Northeast China, the rise of Central China, the Belt and Road Initiative, Free Trade Pilot Zone construction, state-owned enterprise reform, trade in services, digital economy, technological innovation, and more. CIFIT has also highlighted cooperation needs in areas such as patent technology transfer, property rights transactions, and the disposal of financial non-performing assets. By introducing these investment hotspots, CIFIT has guided domestic and international capital toward collaboration, significantly expanding investment growth opportunities.

Second, facilitating cross-strait integration through the

construction of the Western Taiwan Strait (WTS) Economic Zone. Held annually in Xiamen, a city separated from Taiwan by only a narrow strait, CIFIT has effectively advanced cross-strait economic and trade exchanges and cooperation. In addition, by showcasing the economic achievements and enormous development potential of mainland China's reform and opening up, it effectively promotes cross-strait economic and trade exchanges and cooperation, and drives a large number of Taiwan funded enterprises to settle in mainland China. During CIFIT, events such as the Cross-Strait Economic and Trade Cooperation and Development Forum and the Cross-Strait Agricultural Products Procurement Fair are regularly held. These activities foster routine, multi-channel, and in-depth exchanges between business communities on both sides of the strait, broadening the scope for industrial cooperation.

Third, driving the development of investment promotion exhibitions domestically and internationally. With over three decades of experience, CIFIT has refined its organizational system and operational model, pioneering a unique approach in which government departments organize national-level investment exhibitions. Through project promotion, product showcases, policy announcements, and thematic discussions, CIFIT offers domestic and international participants comprehensive opportunities for investment matchmaking and consultation. This model, originally created by CIFIT, has become one of its defining features and is widely praised. Former British Prime Minister Gordon Brown once noted his pleasure that the UK has established a long-term cooperation with this grand fair. "Britain held a series of promotional activities via the platform, and we look forward to more bilateral investment between China and the UK," Brown added. Pascal Lamy, former director-general of the World Trade Organization once said: "I have known CIFIT for a long time. It shows China's image after reform and opening-up, and also delivers China's desire to cooperate with the world at a harmonious developing pace. CIFIT is conducive to the opening-up and development of different economic systems around the world. That's why so many international economic organizations come. " "China has made great achievements in the past 10 years. Especially in recent years, more and more overseas traders came to the fair, making the platform more beneficial to global traders. The platform is efficient and successful. As a sponsor of CIFIT, the UN Conference on Trade and Development will continue to support this grand international event, and support the overall development of the Chinese economy. " said Supachai Panitchpakdi, former secretary-general of the UN Conference on Trade and Development. Domestically, CIFIT has pioneered a new international investment promotion model, driving the rapid growth of investment-focused exhibitions. It has become a vital platform for showcasing China's openness and facilitating global economic cooperation.

II. Achievements of CIFIT in Promoting the New Wave of High–Level Opening–up

In recent years, CIFIT has actively implemented the spirit President Xi Jinping's congratulatory letter, aligning itself with national development strategies, anticipating global investment trends, and striving to become an international public platform for investment. Through continuous enhancement, efficiency improvement, and innovative development, CIFIT has delivered significant results.

A. Striving to Create a "Three-ization" Premium Event

1. Emphasizing internationalization

CIFIT has maintained a global perspective, overcoming

the challenges of the pandemic to support high-level opening up. From 2021 to 2023, over 40 foreign countries and regions participated annually with offline exhibitions, promotional events, or matchmaking sessions. The 23rd CIFIT emphasized the Global Development Initiative, integrating the Belt and Road Initiative (BRI), BRICS cooperation, and the Regional Comprehensive Economic Partnership (RCEP), highlighting CIFIT's increasing international influence.

2. Prioritizing professionalization

Adhering to a philosophy of specialization, refinement, and distinctive features, CIFIT has created high-quality projects for exhibitions, matchmaking sessions and conferences that emphasize its unique attributes. In terms of exhibitions, CIFIT has hosted events with distinct industrial focuses, such as the BRICS New Industrial Revolution Exhibition, the Industrial Internet Exhibition, the Green Innovation Technology Product Exhibition, the Investment Services and Financial Exhibition, and the China Foreign-Invested Enterprises Exhibition. These exhibitions showcase cutting-edge industries and technologies, aligning with global investment trends. For matchmaking, CIFIT launched the Project-Capital Docking Hall, an innovative platform that facilitates collaboration between emerging industries and critical resources like capital, talent, and industrial parks. This initiative enhances CIFIT's role as a bridge connecting industries with growth opportunities. On the digital front, CIFIT has embraced technological advancements by building a comprehensive digital ecosystem. Its "Cloud CIFIT" app, mini-program, and official website offer a robust online platform for investment promotion, enabling digitalized and continuous engagement between participants. This digital transformation ensures CIFIT remains accessible and effective in a globalized and rapidly evolving investment landscape.

3. Enhancing branding

CIFIT has cultivated over ten signature brands, including the Silk Road Maritime International Cooperation Forum, the Cross-Strait Economic and Trade Cooperation Forum, the World Business Leaders Roundtable, and the China International Green Innovation Development Conference. In recent years, new brands like the "Gulangyu Forum" have emerged, focusing on the Global Development Initiative with participation from foreign diplomats, international investment agencies, and multinational corporations. CIFIT also launched events such as the China Emerging Industries Investment and Financing Cooperation Summit, the Chinese and Foreign Investment Promotion Agencies Conference, the "going global" Development Series Activities, and Green and Low-Carbon Industry International Cooperation Activities, further enriching its brand ecosystem.

B. Continually Optimizing the "Three Platforms"

1. Optimizing the two—way investment promotion platform

CIFIT has deepened its focus on the dual themes of "Introducing FDI" and "going global", inviting over 90 countries and regions to participate annually. It has expanded partnerships with BRI countries, BRICS nations, and RCEP members, fostering broader mutual openness and investment. Events like the Silk Road Maritime International Cooperation Forum, the BRICS Initiative on Trade and Investment for Sustainable Development, and the RCEP International Cooperation Forum promote two-way, diversified investment cooperation.

2. Enhancing the authoritative information release platform

In recent years, CIFIT has actively invited international

organizations, national ministries, and well-known research institutions to release information, policies, and reports on the business environment, investment climate, and investment indices, focusing on attracting foreign investment, outward investment, international investment, and global development. These include *World Investment Report (Chinese Edition), BRICS Investment Report, Foreign Investment Guide of the People's Republic of China, Statistical Bulletin of FDI in China, Report on Foreign Investment in China, Report on the Development of Chinese Enterprises* and other public goods in the investment field, guiding cross-border investment and global cooperation.

3. Improving the investment trend research platform

With the International Investment Forum as its core, CIFIT drives the enhancement of a series of high-end conferences and forums for discussion, focusing on global investment and international cooperation. It aims to build an authoritative platform for international politicians, business leaders, and academics to discuss major frontier issues of the world economy, study global investment trends, and promote global economic growth. 2021 (21st CIFIT): Themed "New Opportunities for International Investment under New Development Patterns", it signaled China's commitment to further openness amid the global pandemic and economic recovery. 2022 (22nd CIFIT): Under the theme "Global Development: Sharing Digital Opportunities and Investing in a Green Future," CIFIT centered on high-level openness and international investment cooperation, amplifying China's investment voice. 2023 (23rd CIFIT): Themed "Openness, Integration, Leading Quality Development", CIFIT hosted a series of events, including the BRI High-Level Development Forum, the Silk Road Maritime International Cooperation Forum, the Maritime Silk Road Central Legal

District Forum, and the "Silk Road E-Commerce" Public-Private Dialogue, deepening pragmatic international investment cooperation.

C. Amplifying China's Investment "Good Voice"

Before the COVID-19 pandemic, each session of the CIFIT attracted a significant number of high-profile domestic and international attendees, including government officials, leaders of international organizations, renowned entrepreneurs, and corporate executives. This elevated CIFIT as a critical platform for high-level public relations. From the 6th CIFIT, the number of foreign attendees consistently exceeded 10,000, while domestic attendees remained above 40,000. Each session of the CIFIT saw the participation of central government officials, provincial leaders in charge of foreign economic cooperation, heads of major state-owned enterprises, and experts. Nearly 300 authoritative media outlets and over 1,200 journalists from around the world converged on the venue. High-level meetings and negotiations abounded, with extensive media coverage spreading CIFIT's influence globally. These events offered unparalleled opportunities for domestic and international enterprises to enhance their public relations and showcase their corporate images.

As one of the few major international events themed around investment promotion, CIFIT has steadily increased its global influence and reputation. Over nearly 40 years, China has become one of the world's top destinations for foreign direct investment. With the improvement of the level of hosting and the enhancement of international influence, CIFIT attracts a large number of international politicians, renowned scholars, and multinational company presidents to attend every year. Many domestic and foreign media report and promote China's development status, consumer market, and increasingly perfect investment environment to the world through various media such as newspapers, television, and the internet. As a result, the external world's understanding of China is further strengthened. China's peaceful development not only brings prosperity and progress domestically but also contributes significantly to the global economy. As a platform dedicated to investment promotion, CIFIT plays a crucial role in driving global economic development and facilitating the flow of international capital.

III. Future CIFIT: Building an International Public Platform for Investment

Entering a new development stage, CIFIT aims to align itself with Xi Jinping Thought on Socialism with Chinese Characteristics for a New Era. It will implement the guidance of President Xi Jinping's congratulatory message, focusing on attracting high-quality foreign investment, promoting outward investment, and facilitating international investment. Each session of the CIFIT will deepen its focus on the "Three-ization" strategy (internationalization, professionalization, and branding) and the "Three Platforms" (two-way investment promotion, authoritative information dissemination, and investment trend research) to amplify China's investment "good voice". It will seek new international investment opportunities, promote greater openness among nations, and position itself as the preferred platform for advancing the Global Development Initiative. By combining distinctive themes with pragmatic actions, CIFIT will support global cooperation, contribute to building an open global economy, and help establish a shared future for humanity.

A. Strengthening CIFIT's Mission as a National Strategic Platform

In the face of major changes and the pandemic unseen in a

century, openness and cooperation are the practical requirements for promoting the stable recovery of the world economy. Today, more than ever, in the face of global economic and cross-border investment recovery, there is a greater need for an open and cooperative international investment public platform. CIFIT must fully leverage its unique positioning and strengths in two-way investment promotion, defining its mission in the new development stage. It should create a stable and sustainable international economic and trade cooperation platform that not only benefits China but also serves as a stage for other countries to engage in two-way investment, ensuring mutual gains.

First, enhancing its role as an authoritative international investment platform. CIFIT will encourage more countries to use its platform to expand mutual openness and investment. It will promote globalization and investment liberalization and facilitation, showcasing China's commitment to sharing investment opportunities and driving global cooperation and shared development.

Second, building a hub for deepening pragmatic multilateral and bilateral cooperation. CIFIT will prioritize initiatives such as the Belt and Road Initiative, high-quality implementation of RCEP, and BRICS industrial cooperation. It will solidify mechanisms for exchanges and cooperation with relevant countries and regions. CIFIT will also strengthen its role as a "window" for cross-strait economic integration, facilitating routine, multi-channel, and in-depth exchanges between the business communities on both sides, fostering substantial economic integration.

Third, promoting global pragmatic cooperation. CIFIT will establish a broad platform to implement the Global Development Initiative through tangible actions. A dedicated exhibition area highlights China's achievements in advancing the initiative.

The Global Development Promotion Center under the China International Development Cooperation Agency hosts dialogues to enhance global exchanges. CIFIT launches alliances such as the Global Alliance of Special Economic Zones and collaborate with international institutions for joint exhibitions. The Ministry of Commerce organizes discussions on implementing the WTO's *Investment Facilitation for Development Agreement* to promote dialogue among representatives from various countries.

Fourth, focusing on high-quality foreign investment attraction. In line with central government policies, CIFIT will continue to organize the "Invest China" thematic events, including roundtables with foreign enterprises and cross-border investment dialogues. These events will release authoritative reports on foreign investment and invite multinational corporations and foreign investors to share in China's development dividends. CIFIT will also celebrate the achievements of national-level economic development zones over the past 40 years. It will organize exhibitions and exchange activities to highlight these zones' contributions to high-level openness and high-quality development, further solidifying their pivotal role in China's economic progress.

B. Seeking New Breakthroughs in Internationalization

CIFIT positions itself as an international public platform for investment, adhering to the principles of global leadership, cutting-edge innovation, and sectoral advancement. By focusing on high-quality "introducing FDI" and high-level "going global", CIFIT actively participates in global governance, serving as a driving force for international investment, promoting economic globalization, and supporting shared development.

Broadening global perspectives. CIFIT aligns with the

theme "Invest in a Shared Future" to strengthen its role as a public platform for international investment. It seeks to advance the mission of building an open global economy by establishing a cooperative and inclusive international dialogue mechanism. By addressing forward-looking and comprehensive global economic issues, CIFIT designs initiatives and discussions on sustainable development. Key topics include exploring new approaches to global economic governance, implementing measures for regional economic coordination, and addressing critical challenges in economic globalization, such as investment and trade liberalization and facilitation. These efforts solidify CIFIT's strategic position as a major platform for implementing China's "Global Development Initiative" and contribute Chinese wisdom to the improvement of global economic governance.

Harnessing high-end resources. Cooperation with international organizations, institutions, and key regions needs to be comprehensively strengthened. In addition, multilateral and bilateral investment discussions and matchmaking events need to be designed to share investment development opportunities around the multilateral and bilateral cooperation mechanisms and hot spots such as the Belt and Road Initiative (BRI), BRICS countries, Middle Eastern countries, Southeast Asian countries, RCEP, Shanghai Cooperation Organization and China-Africa Cooperation. Specific actions include: Encouraging CIFIT's six international co-organizers to host branded events annually, release authoritative investment reports, and expand their influence. Facilitating the Shanghai Cooperation Organization's (SCO) transition from security-focused cooperation to economic and trade collaboration by organizing SCO-themed exhibitions and forums at CIFIT. Relying on the construction of the BRICS Innovation Base, we will continue to successfully hold events such as the BRICS Forum on Sustainable Investment and the BRICS Digital Economy Dialogue, to promote practical cooperation in BRICS economic, trade, investment, and industrial fields. Focusing on regional coordinated development and practical multilateral cooperation, we will plan and organize events such as the Belt and Road Interconnectivity Investment and Financing Seminar and the RCEP Investment Cooperation Summit, to fully leverage the mechanisms of multilateral cooperation, overseas business (association) joint meetings, and mobilize members of the mechanism and partner organizations to participate in these events.

C. Focusing on the Investment Nature of the Exhibition, Achieving New Heights in Professionalization

Currently, there are numerous commodity trade exhibitions worldwide, but there are almost no well-known investment exhibitions. To enhance its professional level, CIFIT should actively explore new domains in financial investment, maintaining its position as China's most significant investment exhibition platform. In line with emerging international investment trends and characteristics, CIFIT can expand its showcased investment channels to include financial investment. Initiatives such as the International Investment Forum 2024 and financial capital matchmaking events could be developed, inviting China's financial regulatory bodies and major domestic and international financial institutions to discuss topics such as deepening financial reform, managing and mitigating financial risks, and promoting ways for financial capital to serve the real economy. These efforts will support high-level financial market openness.

In terms of exhibitions, CIFIT should focus on showcasing global industrial and technological innovation as its core theme. Using project roadshows and matchmaking as primary formats, CIFIT can organize complementary exhibitions on investment opportunities and services. It should further integrate exhibitions, forums, and discussions into a cohesive structure, emphasizing the development of a globally influential Global Industrial and Technological Innovation Exhibition. This exhibition can highlight cutting-edge industries such as new productivity models, new energy, new materials, advanced displays, integrated circuits, and artificial intelligence, inviting Fortune Global 500 companies, multinational corporations, leading enterprises, industry leaders, and research institutions to showcase their latest products and technologies. Additionally, CIFIT can leverage opportunities created by international exhibition organizers expanding their presence in China, partnering with them to co-host premium thematic exhibitions.

In terms of investment matchmaking, CIFIT should strengthen its"Project-Capital Docking Platform", hosting more activities like the "Leading China· Emerging Leading China Investment and Collaboration Conference" and the China Foreign-Invested Enterprises Exhibition. These integrated events can enhance the connection between key investment elements such as startups, industrial parks, talent, and investment service institutions. By building platforms for emerging industry project roadshows and investment services, CIFIT can increase the participation of professional exhibitors, investors, and visitors from both domestic and international markets, enhancing the effectiveness of investment and financing negotiations.

In investment services, CIFIT should continue to refine and elevate its Investment Services and Financial Exhibition, inviting investment banks, consulting firms, financial institutions, securities firms, insurance companies, law firms, and accounting firms to showcase and promote products and services related to investment. This initiative will ensure that CIFIT remains a functional hub for investment services. Furthermore, the investment hotspots exhibition is innovatively designed to grasp the future investment trend industries, and special exhibitions are held on hotspots such as new energy, smart networking, metaverse, etc.

D. Focusing on Quality and Efficiency to Create New Highlights in Branding

Uphold the dual strategy of inheriting traditions and embracing innovation. Benchmarking against national-level exhibitions such as the China International Import Expo (CIIE), the China International Fair for Trade in Services (CIFTIS), the Canton Fair, and the China International Consumer Products Expo (CICPE), we aim to create a national-level brand in the field of international investment promotion, highlighting the CIFIT's important role in serving the "Global Development Initiative" and promoting international two-way investment in the economic and trade field. In terms of brand building, with the core of optimizing and strengthening the International Investment Forum, we will not only consolidate the existing brand but also carefully cultivate innovative brands, forming a brand system and unique charm for the CIFIT.

To strengthen its branding, CIFIT should prioritize the International Investment Forum as a core feature. This forum can be developed into a high-level platform for implementing the"Global Development Initiative". A structured format, with "one main forum + several sub-forums", can amplify the central theme and inspire other professional meetings to attract high-end resources. Topics should focus on global shared development and new opportunities in international investment, emphasizing internationality, foresight, and professionalism. Greater efforts should be made to invite prominent figures such as foreign political leaders, heads of international economic organizations, renowned economists, and executives of large multinational corporations to deliver speeches and discuss major global economic and investment issues.

The "Gulangyu Forum" can also be cultivated as a unique feature. Building on its successful debut in 2022, the forum should integrate the rich multicultural heritage of the "historical international community" with contemporary global development ideals. The forum will annually invite 98 high-profile guests, including ambassadors to China, leaders of international investment promotion organizations and chambers of commerce, and multinational executives. By offering innovative and relaxed formats for discussions, the forum can become a premier platform for promoting international investment, supporting global development, and deepening cross-sector collaboration.

CIFIT can further highlight supply chain cooperation. Establishing a National Supply Chain Innovation Expo and hosting events such as the 2024 Supply Chain Cooperation and Innovation Conference, the Fifth China Supply Chain Management Annual Conference, and the fifth National Supply Chain Competition. These events will bring together leading supply chain enterprises and scholars to explore topics such as sustainable development, resilience and security, innovation and application, management strategies, and market trends. By doing so, CIFIT can demonstrate its active role in enhancing international supply chain cooperation and safeguarding supply chain stability.

To launch distinctive projects, CIFIT should integrate resources from national ministries, international organizations, and expert think tanks to gain greater support from the Ministry of Foreign Affairs, the National Development and Reform

Commission, the UN Trade and Development (UNCTAD), Wolrd bank and WTO. For example, we should make efforts to collaborate with the World Bank to organize a Global Business Environment Conference at the CIFIT seek to host the Summer Davos Forum in Xiamen in collaboration with the World Economic Forum Secretariat; proactively enhance communication with the National Development and Reform Commission to facilitate the release of a business environment report at the investment and trade fair; partnerships with leading China Top Think Tanks such as the Development Research Center of the State Council can facilitate flagship reports like the *China Two-Way Investment Report*, first published in 2023. Collaborations with the Center for International Knowledge on Development (CIKD) and other "Global Development Initiative" China Top Think Tanks, it can bring in thematic events aligned with international investment cooperation and global shared development. These events can feature the release of authoritative information, high-impact research reports, or actionable plans.

CIFIT should also enhance its existing brands, such as hosting the Ministry of Commerce's annual Foreign-Invested Enterprise Roundtable, which invites Fortune Global 500 companies and multinational corporations to engage deeply. Other established events like the Silk Road Maritime International Cooperation Forum, advance the construction of the "Core Area of Maritime Silk Road" to a high standard, serving the high-quality joint development of the Belt and Road; continue to cultivate and enhance featured brand projects such as the "Leading China · Emerging Industry Investment and Collaboration Conference," "Green China · Summit on International Cooperation of Low-Carbon Industry," and the "going global" green development series of activities.

Association
Section

Chapter 11　New Observation of the Investment of Multinational Corporations in China[1]

Over the past three decades, as economic globalization created favorable conditions for the development of multinational corporations in China, they were deeply involved in China's socio-economic development, vigorously supporting China's high-quality development and integrating China deeply into the global industrial chain and supply chain. However, global political and economic patterns have changed remarkably. It can also be observed that multinational corporations doing business in China are seeking new investment strategies and models.

I. Significantly Increasing Number of Joint Ventures

At the beginning of the reform and opening up, multinational corporations in partial industries had to adopt the form of Sino-foreign joint venture to enter China considering policy restrictions on foreign investment in China. Nonetheless, the market access restriction was loosened with a smaller proportion of joint ventures and wholly foreign-owned

---

[1] Contributed by Huang Feng and Ding Suiliang, from Shanghai Foreign Investment Association, and Zhou Yanqi and Wan Tiannan from Shanghai Foreign Investment Consulting Co., Ltd.

enterprises accounting for nearly 90% after China joined WTO in 2001. In recent years, a rising trend could be found in the number of joint ventures and multinational corporations pursued integrative development with local enterprises more proactively, thereby building an open ecosphere and achieving mutual benefit and win-win cooperation.

The above tendency is mainly caused by the following factors: First, a raft of internationally competitive local Chinese enterprises emerged, posing a threat to foreign capital and forcing it to embark on a quest for more cooperation with local enterprises. Second, foreign capital placed greater emphasis on localized operation and their collaboration with Chinese enterprises can foster complementary strengths. Third, joint venture means risk sharing with Chinese enterprises.

Case 1: A joint venture pure electric vehicle (PEV) R&D company established by Toyota and BYD

Amid the reform of the automotive industry featuring electrification, networking, intelligence and sharing, pursuing cooperation for cost reduction and efficiency improvement among global industrial chains has become a key solution for multinational corporations. In April 2020, BYD Toyota EV Technology Co., Ltd. was incorporated, a joint venture of Toyota and BYD, with either party contributing 50% of the fund. Its main business comprises the design and R&D of PEVs and their platforms and parts, etc. In the future, Toyota will manufacture EVs based on BYD's e-Platform production base, taking full advantage of BYD's existing EV platform technologies and parts system and introducing Toyota's quality and safety control standard requirements. This cooperation model is different from that of Toyota-FAW and Toyota-GAC cooperation, marking the complete vehicle development and cooperation characterized by "Technological Equality" between Toyota and a Chinese automobile brand for the first time, as well as the cooperative development of PEVs and power batteries. The collaboration between BYD and Toyota can fill the technical gap of Toyota in PEV field, tackling the problem of Toyota's lack of marketable and suitable EV products in the Chinese market and demonstrating high significance for the industry landscape and quicker EV technology progress and popularization worldwide.

Case 2: A joint venture established by China National Medical Device Co., Ltd. and GE Healthcare.

Multinational enterprises strengthened in-depth joint venture cooperation with local enterprises in biomedicines, becoming a growing trend for the localization strategy of enterprises. In February 2023, China National Medical Device Co., Ltd. under SINOPHARM concluded an agreement with GE Healthcare (China) in Beijing, to establish a joint venture medical device company in China. In the initial stage, the joint venture is mainly responsible for rendering inclusive medical devices including CT and ultrasound for primary-level medical institutions in China and the vast Chinese market. In the future, both parties will boost joint venture cooperation in high-end medical devices, with a focus on the high-end medical imaging device industry. The cooperation between China National Medical Device Co., Ltd. and GE Healthcare (China) facilitated innovation in the cooperation model between an internationally leading medical device manufacturer and a state-owned central enterprise and is conducive to consolidating international cooperation in the medical field, showing practical and symbolic significance for building a comprehensive high-end medical device industry platform made in China.

Case 3: A joint venture established by BorgWarner and Shaanxi Fast Auto Drive Group.

Multinational corporations realized complementation in

R&D capability and product lines as well as efficient resource integration by joining hands with domestic enterprises. In January 2023, BorgWarner and Shaanxi Fast Auto Drive Group, a company concentrated on transmissions and drive systems, reached a consensus on setting up a joint venture to jointly develop controller applications for commercial vehicles such as heavy trucks and engineering vehicles, in an attempt to continue to expand its commercial vehicle portfolio in the pure electric and hybrid vehicle sectors. BorgWarner has a strong technical strength and powerful R&D capability and supply chain integration capability in automotive controllers; while Fast Group is recorded as a leading supplier of comprehensive solutions to commercial vehicle transmissions, high-quality automotive drive systems and high-end intelligent manufacturing equipment in China. The joint venture will support the growth of both companies' power electronics product lines in the electric commercial vehicle market, introduce highly efficient controller products into the market, and furnish a wider range of high-quality, stable, and safe electronic control products and drivetrain solutions for the Chinese commercial vehicle market by jointly developing controller applications suitable for commercial vehicles such as heavy trucks and engineering vehicles.

Case 4: A joint venture established by Johnson Controls and EMAGING Technology.

Multinational corporations underlined the utilization of smart manufacturing and the green and low-carbon transition by working with domestic enterprises. In January 2024, Johnson Controls and EMAGING Technology—an integrated solution provider for magnetic levitation high-speed rotating machinery in China, established a joint venture. The joint venture will focus on advancing innovation, energy conservation and emission reduction in the HVAC industry. The collaboration between Johnson Controls and EMAGING Technology will drive the progress of oil-free magnetic levitation units, effectively alleviating the motion loss of components, escalating product energy efficiency and extending the service life of the units. Relying on its innovative experience in the construction field and nearly 30 years of innovative practice in China, Johnson Controls will deepen the collaboration with EMAGING Technology in technical innovation and complete machine integration, and enhance the upgrading of quality management and operation systems, with the aim to furnish more industries in the Chinese market with tailored, intelligent, efficient and environmentally friendly solutions. These solutions will form an impetus to boost industry transformation and upgrading and the accomplishment of the goal of sustainable development, making a milestone for the green development of the HVAC industry.

Case 5: Strategic cooperation between Jaguar Land Rover and Chery Automobile

The cooperation between multinational corporations and local enterprises is also beneficial to the "going global" of local enterprises. In June 2024, Jaguar Land Rover and Chery Automobile announced their strategic partnership, after which Chery Jaguar Land Rover will launch a brand—new line of electric vehicles. This product line is planned to be equipped with Chery's PEV platform and adopt the "Freelander" brand licensed by Jaguar Land Rover. This brand represents a once popular model of Land Rover with a strong market base and high consumer reputation, and it will embrace a rebirth and be revitalized on the Chery Jaguar Land Rover's platform now. By combining Chery's leading position in China's automotive market and Jaguar Land Rover's global branding and design strengths, the two companies are determined to create competitive electric products that will meet consumer demand for high-quality and high-performance electric vehicles. It is reported that the "Freelander" electric product line will initially be marketable in the Chinese market through a specific network, and then be exported overseas in the future. This strategic cooperation not only strengthens Chery Jaguar Land Rover's competitiveness in the Chinese market, but further enhances its position around the world. With the advent of the electrification age, in the automotive industry, the competitive landscape is undergoing profound changes. Hence, the cooperation between Jaguar Land Rover and Chery Automobile will undoubtedly bring about new development opportunities for the two companies and constitute a new driving force for the automotive industry in China and across the world.

II. Prevalence of Corporate Venture Capital (CVC)

Corporate Venture Capital (CVC), a type of venture capital by multinational corporations, is known for more prominent industry resource integration capabilities and strategic objectives compared with traditional venture capital institutions (IVC). The common strategic objectives for setting up CVCs are to respond to the long-term strategy of the parent company in most cases, drive innovation and model expansion through investment, and provide unique value-added services for the invested innovative enterprises based on the business strengths of the parent company.

Multinational corporations have become increasingly active in CVC investment activities in China in recent years. Against the background of the rapid economic growth in China and the perfection of the entrepreneurial ecosystem, an increasing number of multinational corporations started solidifying their dominant positions in the industry by getting involved in the upstream and downstream of the industrial chain through CVC investment.

The CVC investment patterns of multinational corporations in China are as follows. The first investment pattern is direct investment, in which large companies set up independent venture capital funds or institutions to invest in Chinese startups. This pattern enables multinational corporations to directly participate in the management and decision-making of the invested enterprises, so these corporations have greater control over the startups and can easily realize their strategic objectives in venture capital investment. The second pattern is indirect investment, in which large companies invest in investment companies (or funds), which in turn invest in Chinese startups. When compared with the direct investment pattern, indirect investment proves weaker controller over startups, but allows utilizing the resources and experience of specialized investment companies, to lower investment risks.

Typical cases of direct investment include:

Case 6:In 2018, Bosch (Shanghai) Venture Capital Investment Co., Ltd., a venture capital institution of Bosch Group was incorporated in China, which speeded up the construction of the group's venture capital team in China and its investment activities. In 2021, Bosch Group set up the first market-oriented investment platform with a local independent decision-making process in China: Boyuan Capital, in which Bosch Group holds 50% of the shares. Bosch Group also initiated the establishment of Bosch China Growth Fund I. As a venture capital institution of a multinational enterprise, Bosch's institution is quite active in the Chinese market. For instance, in 2021, the institution took the lead in investing in Momenta, an autonomous driving company, in the Series C round of financing. Additionally, Bosch's venture capital activities in China also assisted in the group's intelligent vehicle division in China. In August 2024, Black Sesame Technologies, a company also invested by Bosch, was successfully listed on the main board of the Hong Kong Stock Exchange, becoming the "No. 1 AI chip stock for intelligent vehicles in China".

Case 7:In 2022, L'ORÉAL set up its first investment company in Shanghai, i.e., Shanghai Meicifang Investment Co., Ltd., which was dedicated to investing in innovative beauty technologies. In September 2022, the company made an equity investment in DOCUMENTS, a local high-end Chinese perfume and fragrance brand. In January 2024, the company made a minority investment in another Chinese perfume and fragrance brand - to summer, marking its further step into the Chinese fragrance market.

Typical cases of indirect investment include:

Case 8: The Venture Capital Division of Evonik took part in a number of Chinese venture capital funds in the capacity of a limited partner (LP). Evonik invested in GRC SinoGreen Fund III in China in 2015 and another two Chinese funds in 2021, namely, GRC SinoGreen Fund V and Richland VC Fund III. The main investment sectors consist of circular economy, synthetic biology, carbon materials, digital manufacturing, and other emerging industries. Moreover, the investment sectors of these two funds are highly relevant to Chinese growth industries highly concerned by Evonik.

Case9: Nestle Group contributed USD 30 million for investment in a Chinese VC fund for the first time and became a cornerstone investor for Tiantu Capital VC USD Fund 1.

Case10: In 2020, Starbucks and Sequoia Capital China entered into a strategic partnership for strategic investments in China and business cooperation in new-generation food and beverage and retail technologies. They established a venture capital enterprise, with a capital contribution of CNY 50 million from Starbucks and Sequoia Capital China as the managing partner (GP).

The CVC investment activities of multinational corporations in China are of great significance for the healthy development of China's entrepreneurial ecosystem, technological innovation and industrial upgrading. Moreover, as the Chinese government launches more favorable policies to support venture capital and the entrepreneurial ecosystem keeps improving, multinational corporations will face more opportunities in terms of CVC investment in China.

III. Investment, Construction and Operation of Industrial Parks

Vigorous support has been input into industrial parks which are also important platforms for fostering cross-border economic cooperation, optimizing resource allocation and advancing industrial upgrading, from the central and local governments. In recent years, governments have released a series of policies and measures in fiscal support, financial support, talent introduction and other aspects, forming a strong policy guarantee for the development of industrial parks. However, despite rapid development, industrial parks are also challenged by multiple bottlenecks, such as narrow financing channels and long investment return periods, as well as the new requirements of customers for green, low-carbon and digitalization.

Over the past years, introducing multinational enterprises to participate directly in the investment and construction of industrial parks, attracting investments and strengthening the operation and management of industrial parks became key solutions to high-quality construction of industrial parks. Multinational enterprises are able to contribute to the development of industrial parks by expanding financing channels, advancing international cooperation, enhancing top-level design, reinforcing teamwork and upgrading brand influence. Several instances are as follows.

Case 11: In February 2022, NXpark under France's Aden Group, built a high-end automotive seat R&D and manufacturing base for Faurecia in Aden Xi'an High-end Auto Parts Industrial Base, which was honored with the American green building LEED (Leadership in Energy and Environmental Design) Gold Certification. Aden Xi'an High-end Auto Parts Industrial Base, located in Caotang Area of Xi'an High-tech Zone, covers a total area of 161 mu, with a total floor area of 82,142.55 square meters and a total project value of CNY 2 billion. In the industrial park are factory buildings, office buildings, staff apartments and supporting facilities necessary for the manufacturing of core components of the automotive industry, satisfying the diversified needs of enterprises and offering auto parts manufacturing services to leading enterprises in the neighboring areas. The high-end automotive seat R&D and manufacturing line of Faurecia has already settled in the park and started production at present. The project was also praised as one of the top ten excellent cases in CCTV Finance 2024 "Invest in China".

Case 12:In July 2023, France's Aden Group invested USD 150 million in Chinese-French (Wuxi) Industrial Cooperation Park with the aim to build the Green and Smart Industrial Park of Schneider Electric Group. Located in Wuxi Hi-Tech Zone, Chinese-French (Wuxi) Industrial Cooperation Park is the first "Chinese-French Cooperation Demonstration Park" in China under the guidance and support of the National Development and Reform Commission and the Consulate General of France, and was licensed by the French Chamber of Commerce and

Industry in China. The investment, construction, investment invitation and the operation and management of the park are the responsibility of France's Aden Group, with a total investment of USD 500 million in the core area, and its construction consists of two phases: The first phase is the construction of the intelligent manufacturing industrialization base, which is expected to be delivered by the end of 2024; the second phase involves the planning and construction of the Sino-French innovation center and commercial and office buildings, which are expected to be delivered by June 2025. After its completion, the park will become a new generation of "super factory" integrating production, sales and R&D, with a higher level of digitization and integration. As the first and most important "cornerstone project" in the core area of Chinese-French Industrial Cooperation Park, with a total investment of USD 150 million, the Schneider Electric Green Smart Industrial Park is designed to be green, low-carbon and intelligent, fully reflecting the characteristics of "green + smart". Cutting-edge technologies will be introduced, such as 5G communication, artificial intelligence, etc., in order to build a comprehensive park integrating the concepts of green and sustainable development, a digital factory and an innovation center.

Amid the investment, construction and operation of industrial parks, multinational corporations have not only facilitated local economic growth and industrial upgrading, but enhanced international economic exchanges and cooperation. They can also elevate the competitiveness of enterprises in the parks and drive the synergistic development of the whole industrial chain by bringing in advanced technologies and management experience.

IV. Exploration of Non–equity Arrangement Investment

Multinational corporations are involved in the international production system through direct investment and trade, and non-equity operation models. The non-equity operation models incorporate contract manufacturing, service outsourcing, contract farming, franchising, licensing, management contracts, and other types of contractual relationships, through which multinational corporations coordinate their activities in the global value chain and influence their management of companies in the host country without owning shares.

In the biological medicine sector, non-equity operational models are gaining popularity. Numerous multinational pharmaceutical corporations (MNC) have been transferring the sales of their products to local pharmaceutical corporations. Within the realm of innovative pharmaceuticals, collaborations through licensing agreements between MNC and Chinese local companies have been flourishing. In 2023, China's pharmaceutical BD transactions saw a surge, with 53 License out deals amounting to a staggering USD 42.59 billion, which constituted 84.2% of the total. Both the transaction volume and value have experienced a notable rise compared to previous years, with the majority of the projects being acquired by MNC operating in China.

Typical cases of License in include:

Case 13: In March 2022, Eli Lilly and Innovent jointly declared the establishment of two collaborative agreements: Lilly granted Innovent the exclusive commercial rights to market, distribute, promote, and sell Cyramza (Ramucirumab) and Retsevmo in Mainland China post-approval, as well as provided Innovent with the preferential right to negotiate the commercial rights of Pirtobrutinib in Mainland China in the future. This marks their fifth collaboration.

Typical cases of License out include:

Case 14: In December 2023, GlaxoSmithKline (GSK) and veteran domestic pharmaceutical corporation Hansoh Pharmaceutical declared a shared announcement regarding an exclusive licensing agreement for the drug ADC HS-20093, developed in-house by Hansoh. GSK is set to receive an exclusive, worldwide license (excluding Mainland China, Hong Kong, Macao, and Taiwan), with the transaction's total value, comprising an initial payment and milestone payments, surpassing USD 1.7 billion.

Case 15: December 2023 saw the announcement from Biokin Pharmaceutical stating that its wholly-owned subsidiary, SystImmune, has entered into an exclusive licensing and collaboration agreement with Bristol-Myers Squibb for the development of an EGFR×HER3 bispecific ADC, designated as BL-B01D1.

Case 16: MediLink Therapeutics announced in January 2024 the establishment of a global partnership and licensing agreement with Roche. The collaboration will focus on the development of YL211 (c-MET ADC), a next-generation antibody-drug conjugate targeting c-MET, for the treatment of solid tumors. As per the agreement, Roche is to secure exclusive rights to develop, manufacture, and commercialize MediLink Therapeutics's YL211 project on a global scale.

V. Conclusion

The evolving global political and economic landscape has compelled multinational corporations to reassess their investment approaches in China, resulting in a trend towards diversification, localization, cooperation, and agility in their Chinese investments. Multinational corporations are actively adapting to global shifts and pursuing sustainable growth by forging broad partnerships with local Chinese enterprises, investing in CVC, participating in the development and management of industrial parks, and employing non-equity arrangements. These strategies have not only sustained the growth of multinational corporations' operations in China and deepened their integration with the Chinese market but have also been instrumental in bolstering the high-quality development of China's economy.

Chapter 12　Investment and Development of Chinese Enterprises in Singapore[①]

In the wave of globalization of Chinese enterprises, the Southeast Asian market, with its vast scale, economic resilience, demographic dividend, and cultural similarities, has attracted significant attention from Chinese enterprises. Among these, Singapore, with its unique geographical location, favorable trade policies, and excellent business environment, has become an ideal gateway for Chinese enterprises entering Southeast Asia. The deepening economic and trade cooperation between China and ASEAN, including Singapore, the continuous benefits of the *Regional Comprehensive Economic Partnership* (RCEP), and China's engagement in negotiations to join the *Digital Economy Partnership Agreement* (DEPA) have all significantly boosted trade and investment activities of Chinese enterprises in Singapore and Southeast Asia.

This chapter aims to examine the trade and investment activities between China and Singapore from 2023 to the first half of 2024, analyzing the development of Chinese enterprises in Singapore, investment highlights, and their contributions to the local economy. Through specific case studies, this chapter

---

① Contributed by the China Enterprises Association (Singapore), Deloitte China, and Deloitte Southeast Asia.

is intended to provide insights and references for Chinese enterprises intending to expand into the Southeast Asian and Singaporean markets.

I. Current Status of China–Singapore Economic and Trade Cooperation

A. China Has Been Singapore's Largest Trading Partner for 11 Consecutive Years, While Singapore Has Been China's Largest Source of New Foreign Investment for 11 years

Since 2008, the Free Trade Agreement (FTA) between China and Singapore has undergone continuous upgrades and improvements. In April 2023, China and Singapore announced the substantive completion of follow-up negotiations on upgrading the FTA and signed a memorandum of understanding. Building on the original agreement, both parties further elevated their commitments to service trade and investment openness, introduced a telecommunications chapter, and incorporated high-level trade rules covering national treatment, market access, transparency, and the digital economy. Singapore made high-level commitments in areas of particular interest to China, such as environmental protection and maritime transport, creating greater opportunities for Chinese enterprises to expand into the Singaporean market. Meanwhile, China "eliminated" restrictions in the manufacturing sector and made more open commitments in fields such as cargo transportation, onshore oil extraction, distribution, and medical services[1]. The total bilateral trade volume of goods between China and Singapore reached USD 108.39 billion in 2023, a year-on-year decrease of 2.6%. Of this,

---

[1] Ministry of Commerce of China, "Interpretation of the Protocol on Further Upgrading the China-Singapore Free Trade Agreement by the Head of the Department of International Trade and Economic Affairs," December 2023.

377

China's exports amounted to USD 76.96 billion (a decline of 1.1% year-on-year), while imports totaled USD 31.43 billion (a decrease of 6% year-on-year)[1] (see Figure 12-1).

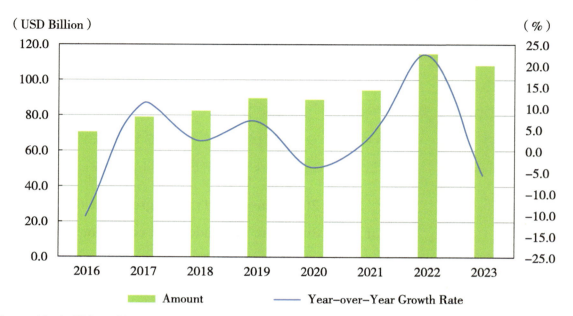

Figure 12-1: China-Singapore Bilateral Trade Volume of Goods and Year-on-Year Growth Rate (2015—2023)

Source: National Bureau of Statistics and Ministry of Foreign Affairs of China, Deloitte Research.

Since 2013, Singapore has been China's largest source of new foreign investment. In April 2022, Singapore surpassed Japan to become the largest cumulative source of foreign investment in China. Over the past few years, the bilateral direct investment between China and Singapore has steadily increased. By the end of 2023, Singapore's cumulative actual investment in China reached USD 141.23 billion, while China's cumulative investment in Singapore totaled USD 89.63 billion[2] (see Figure 12-2).

---

[1] Ministry of Foreign Affairs of China, "China-Singapore Relations," updated in April 2024.

[2] Ministry of Foreign Affairs of China, "China-Singapore Relations," updated in April 2024.

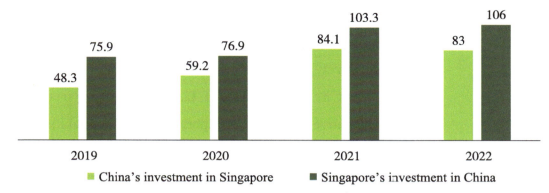

Figure 12–2: China–Singapore Bilateral Direct Investment Volume (2019—2022) (USD hundred million)

Source: National Bureau of Statisticsand Ministry of Foreign Affairs of China, Deloitte Research.

B. High Trade Interdependence and Strong Foundations for Industrial Cooperation between China and Singapore

Singapore's strengths in high-end manufacturing and commercial services are well-reflected in its trade cooperation with China. Singapore is not only the ASEAN country with the largest bilateral trade volume with China but also the only ASEAN country to consistently maintain a service trade surplus with China. On the goods trade front, Singapore has maintained significant exports to China in products such as semiconductors and precision equipment. In 2022, its exports to China of integrated circuits and semiconductor manufacturing machinery reached USD 7.08 billion and USD 4.39 billion, respectively. Conversely, Singapore's refined oil market is highly reliant on imports, making it China's largest refined oil export destination, with an export value of USD 9.62 billion in 2022[1]. Singapore is also one of China's major export destinations for integrated circuits, with a 2022 export value of USD 5.8 billion. In service trade, Singapore's main export categories to

---

[1] *Singapore Trade Guide (2023).*

China include transportation, other commercial services, and finance, accounting for 34.9%, 28.7%, and 13.7% of the total, respectively, in 2022[①].

● Characteristics of Goods Trade: First, China's comparative advantage in exports lies in industrial manufactured goods, particularly labor-intensive products, while Singapore's comparative advantage is concentrated in capital-intensive and resource-intensive industrial products. Second, Singapore's exports are relatively more dependent on the Chinese market (15.8% of total exports in 2022), reflecting strong complementarities in bilateral goods trade.

● Characteristics of Service Trade: Singapore demonstrates a higher overall competitiveness in service trade than China, with significant international competitiveness in transportation, finance, and commercial services. Future growth potential in service trade cooperation between the two countries is considerable.

From the perspective of industrial cooperation, Singaporean enterprises have established a deep-rooted presence in China over many years, providing a strong foundation for collaboration and significant potential for technological innovation. In the first three quarters of 2022, Singapore's investment in Jiangsu Province alone reached USD 2.1 billion (2.83 billion SGD), surpassing the USD 1.4 billion recorded for all of 2021 and marking a three-year high. Cooperation fields include green and sustainable development, advanced manufacturing, and biomedical exploration. For instance: In 2021, Sembcorp Industries acquired China's wind and solar energy assets for CNY 3.3 billion. Capital and Development, in partnership

---

① Ministry of Commerce of China, *Guide for Countries and Regions on Overseas Investment and Cooperation— Singapore (2023 Edition)*, April 2024.

with Mitsubishi Estate, established a joint venture to invest CNY 1.5 billion in developing a business park in Suzhou New District[①].

C. RCEP's Two-Year Impact: Enhanced Trade Facilitation and Investment Liberalization Between China and ASEAN

Since the *Regional Comprehensive Economic Partnership* (RCEP) came into effect in 2022, trade facilitation for goods among member states has significantly improved and investment environments have been continuously optimized. In addition, connectivity levels have increased. These changes have boosted the international competitiveness of small and medium-sized enterprises (SMEs) and driven the development of cross-border e-commerce in ASEAN. According to China Customs, the total trade volume between China and other RCEP members reached CNY 12.6 trillion in 2023, accounting for 30.2% of China's total foreign trade, a 5.3% increase compared to pre-agreement levels in 2021. By July 2023, cumulative two-way investment between China and ASEAN exceeded USD 380 billion, with over 6,500 direct investment enterprises established in ASEAN[②].

A survey conducted by the China Enterprises Association (Singapore) in June-July 2024 revealed the following insights (survey details available in the "About This Survey" section at the end of the chapter): 65% of Chinese enterprises believe that RCEP has expanded export markets and increased trade opportunities. 65% recognize the benefits of trade facilitation

---

① Economic and Commercial Office of the Embassy of the People's Republic of China in the Republic of Singapore, "Singapore's Investment in China".

② Mission of the People's Republic of China to ASEAN, 'Two Years Since RCEP's Implementation: Policy Benefits Continue to Inject Vitality into the Regional Economy', January 2024.

and tariff reductions brought by RCEP. 42% expressed concerns about intensified international competition due to RCEP. 38% believe the agreement creates a favorable environment for e-commerce (see Figure 12-3).

Figure 12–3: Impact of RCEP on Chinese Enterprises in Singapore

Source: China Enterprises Association (Singapore) Survey, Deloitte Research.

China formally applied to join the *Digital Economy Partnership Agreement* (DEPA) in 2021 and has continued to advance negotiations. Currently, China's highest commitments to digital trade governance in regional trade agreements are reflected in RCEP, serving as a foundation for its application to DEPA. Joining DEPA would strengthen China's digital economic and trade cooperation with DEPA members, create more opportunities for the outbound growth of China's digital economy, and enhance the international output of China's digital technologies. This would also expand the scale of China's digital trade and facilitate Chinese enterprises' global expansion. Survey results indicate that over two-thirds of Chinese enterprises believe that China's accession to DEPA would promote trade facilitation, improve cybersecurity, optimize the trust environment, and make cross-border data flows more convenient (see Figure 12-4).

Trade Facilitation
67%

65%

66%

Cross-border Data
Flow Facilitation

Cybersecurity and Trust
Environment Optimization

Figure 12-4: Anticipated Benefits or Positive Impacts of China Joining DEPA

Source: China Enterprises Association (Singapore) Survey, Deloitte Research.

II. Current Investment Status and Outlook of Chinese Enterprises in Singapore

A. Rising Investment of Chinese Enterprises in Singapore and Steady Recovery of M&A Activities

Amid the wave of Chinese enterprises expanding abroad, Singapore, with its advantageous geographical and strategic location, has become one of the top destinations for Chinese companies "going global". According to statistics from the Ministry of Commerce of China, the cumulative investment from China in Singapore is primarily concentrated in the financial and insurance industries, construction, and trade sectors. As of 2023, there were approximately 8,500 Chinese enterprises operating in Singapore.[1]

With the strengthening of economic integration in the Asia-Pacific region, the investment of Chinese enterprises in Singapore continues to grow. Over half of Chinese enterprises in Singapore plan to expand their investments there, while 60% of surveyed companies aim to expand their investments in other Southeast Asian countries beyond Singapore. Many Chinese

---

[1] Ministry of Commerce of China, *Guide for Countries and Regions on Overseas Investment and Cooperation — Singapore (2023 Edition)*, April 2024.

enterprises value the Southeast Asian market, with its population of over 600 million, using Singapore as a hub to efficiently manage and expand their operations in the region. Beyond technology and internet sectors, Chinese enterprises have also established a presence in energy and chemicals, infrastructure, fintech, and logistics. Survey data indicates an optimistic outlook among respondents regarding future investments in Singapore: 74% of enterprises anticipate an upward trend in Chinese investments in Singapore. 25% predict investments will remain stable, a higher percentage than the 19% recorded in the 2021/2022 survey.[1] Only 1% foresee a downward trend (see Figure 12-5).

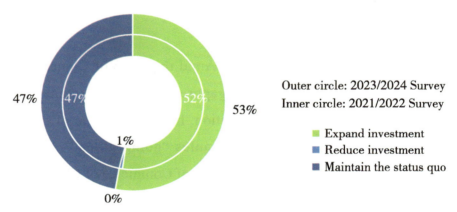

Outer circle: 2023/2024 Survey
Inner circle: 2021/2022 Survey

- Expand investment
- Reduce investment
- Maintain the status quo

Figure 12-5: Investment Intentions of Surveyed Enterprises in Singapore

Source: China Enterprises Association (Singapore) Survey, Deloitte Research.

Singapore is also a key destination for overseas mergers and acquisitions (M&A) by Chinese enterprises. From 2018 to the first half of 2024, M&A transactions by Chinese enterprises in Singapore accounted for half of all Chinese M&A transactions in Southeast Asia, totaling 118 deals. Vietnam and Indonesia were also active destinations, with 36 deals each. Although the activity level of Chinese enterprises' M&A in Southeast

---

[1] China Enterprises Association (Singapore), *2021-2022 Annual Development Report of Chinese Enterprises*, July 2023.

Asia in 2023 had not yet returned to pre-pandemic levels, the total number of transactions rebounded by 48% from the lows of 2022. From an industry perspective, sectors such as finance, manufacturing, wholesale and retail, and healthcare attracted significant attention from Chinese enterprises.

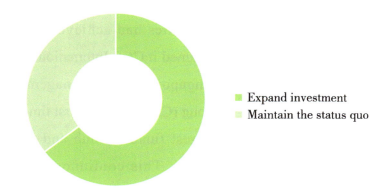

■ Expand investment
■ Maintain the status quo

Figure 12–6: Investment Intentions of Chinese Enterprises in Southeast Asia (Excluding Singapore) in 2024

Source: China Enterprises Association (Singapore) Survey, Deloitte Research.

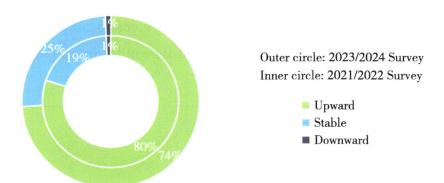

Outer circle: 2023/2024 Survey
Inner circle: 2021/2022 Survey

■ Upward
■ Stable
■ Downward

Figure 12–7: Surveyed Enterprises' Predictions for Future Investment Development of Chinese Enterprises in Singapore

Source: China Enterprises Association (Singapore) Survey, Deloitte Research.

The shift from "going-global products" to "going-global industry chain" has driven increasing demand for cross-border financial services among Chinese enterprises. Chinese brokerage firms have actively expanded their presence in asset management and investment banking, fostering the coordination of domestic and international operations to support the globalization of

Chinese enterprises. In April 2024, China Galaxy Securities officially launched its "CGS International" brand, marking its transition from a joint venture model to a 100% Chinese-owned securities firm. Back in 2018, China Galaxy Securities acquired the securities business of Malaysia's CIMB Group to establish the joint venture CGS-CIMB. By December 2023, China Galaxy Securities had achieved full ownership of CGS-CIMB and renamed it CGS International. In the wealth management sector, Singapore's asset management scale surpassed that of Hong Kong (China) for the first time in 2023, making Singapore Asia's largest financial hub and the world's third-largest financial center. This continuous inflow of wealth has encouraged financial institutions to enhance their wealth management operations in Singapore. In the same year, CITIC Securities established a wealth management platform in Singapore. Huatai International launched securities trading and corporate financing services in Singapore. Guotai Junan International increased its capital investment in its Singapore subsidiary.

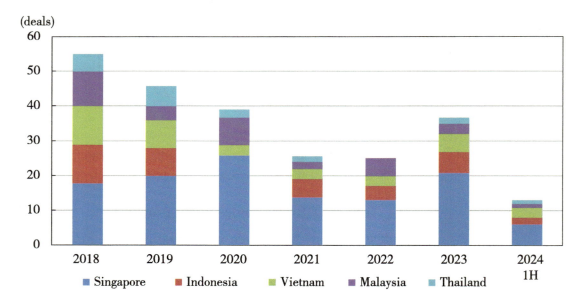

Figure 12–8: Regional Distribution of M&A Transactions by Chinese Enterprises in Singapore and Southeast Asia (2018–First Half of 2024)

Source: CVSource (www. chinaventure. com. cn), Deloitte Research.

Figure 12–9: Industry Distribution of M&A Transactions by Chinese Enterprises in Singapore and Southeast Asia (2018–First Half of 2024)
(Unit: Number of Deals)
Source: CVSource (www. chinaventure. com. cn), Deloitte Research.

B. Business Environment and Unique Geographical Advantages Are Key Factors Attracting Long-Term Investment from Chinese Enterprises

Survey data shows that an impressive 67% of Chinese enterprises rate Singapore's business environment as excellent. For many years, Singapore's business environment has consistently ranked among the first rank globally, earning high recognition from Chinese enterprises. In 2023, 67% of surveyed companies rated Singapore's business environment as excellent, 33% rated it as good, and only 1% considered it average, reflecting a slight 2% decrease compared to the previous survey conducted in 2021/2022 (see Figure 12-10).

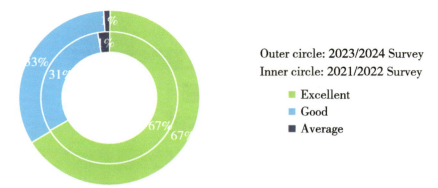

Outer circle: 2023/2024 Survey
Inner circle: 2021/2022 Survey

■ Excellent
■ Good
■ Average

Figure 12–10: Overall Evaluation of Singapore's Business
Environment by Chinese Enterprises

Source: China Enterprises Association (Singapore) Survey, Deloitte Research.

The top three factors that make Singapore's business environment most attractive to Chinese enterprises are government public services (78%), tax system (53%), and facilitation of international trade (49%). Compared to the 2021/2022 survey, enterprise approval rates for tax systems, financial services and capital markets, and labor and talent support have increased significantly (see Figure 12-11). According to the *World Competitiveness Booklet 2024* published by the IMD (International Institute for Management Development) in Switzerland, Singapore regained the top spot as the world's most competitive economy after a four-year gap, following its brief drop from first place between 2020 and 2023. Policies facilitating business activities and Singapore's open and innovative atmosphere provide an excellent platform for enterprises and individuals to thrive. These factors have attracted numerous international companies, including Chinese enterprises, to establish their regional headquarters in Singapore.

Surveyed enterprises identified Singapore's unique geographical advantage as a primary reason for increasing investment. 91% of enterprises believe that Singapore's location enables effective connectivity with the Southeast Asian market.

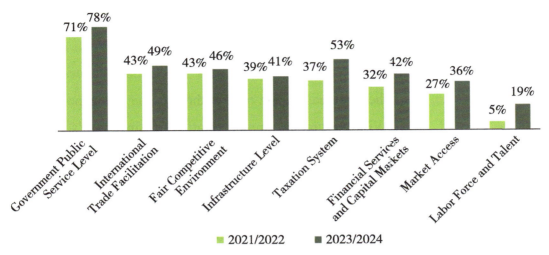

■ 2021/2022   ■ 2023/2024

Figure 12–11: Key Aspects of Singapore's Business Environment Attracting Enterprises

Source:China Enterprises Association (Singapore) Survey, Deloitte Research.

78% of enterprises view a Singaporean corporate identity as beneficial for overseas expansion. 46% of enterprises recognize that Singapore's capital market provides access to international capital beyond the United States and Hong Kong. Singapore has long been regarded as an ideal gateway for expanding into Southeast Asia and as a globalization laboratory. Other attractive factors include the availability of high-end international talent, a strong technology and innovation ecosystem, and significant demand for services catering to high-net-worth individuals.

In 2021, in response to the new trends of global supply chain restructuring and reshaping, Singapore launched the "Singapore+1" Strategy, attracting substantial international capital, including investments from Chinese enterprises. Spearheaded by the Economic Development Board of Singapore (EDB) under the Ministry of Trade and Industry, this strategy leverages Singapore's strengths as a global business hub and innovation ecosystem, combined with the manufacturing advantages of countries like Malaysia, Indonesia, and Vietnam. The approach aims to achieve a"1+1>2" synergy, enabling manufacturing enterprises to rapidly expand into regional markets while building diversified supply chains and fostering a new model of regionalization (see Figure 12-12).

Many Chinese enterprises, including WuXi AppTec, BYD, NIO, GDS Services, and LY iTech, have successfully entered the Southeast Asian market through the "Singapore+1" strategy. With the gradual implementation of Singapore's Manufacturing 2030 Vision and its Industry Transformation Maps (ITM), coupled with support for the digital economy, an increasing number of Chinese manufacturing companies can capitalize on the "Singapore+1" development model to achieve coordinated growth across the ASEAN region (see Figure 12-13).

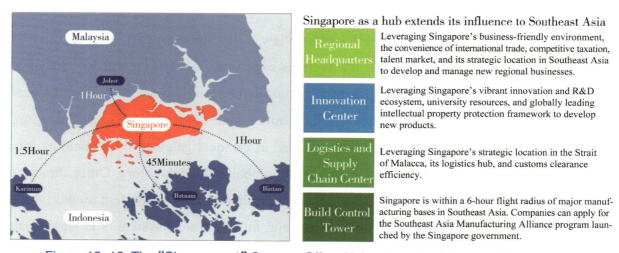

Figure 12–12: The "Singapore+1" Strategy Offers Unique Regional Synergy Opportunities

Source: Economic Development Board of Singapore, *Capturing New Manufacturing Opportunities in Southeast Asia.*

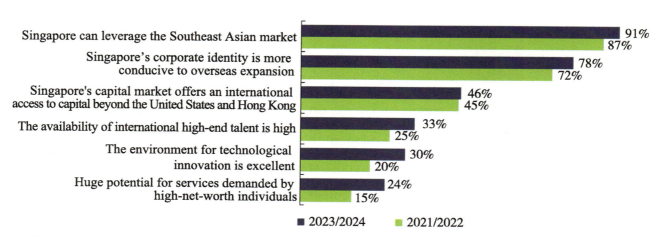

Figure 12–13: Reasons Why Chinese Enterprises Choose Singapore for Investment and Development

Source:China Enterprises Association (Singapore) Survey, Deloitte Research.

C. Chinese Enterprises' Investment Focus on Technology and Software, Emerging Financial Services, and Biotechnology

Technology and software, emerging financial services, and biotechnology are identified by Chinese enterprises as the top three fastest-growing industries, emphasizing technology enablement as a major growth driver. Additionally, transportation and logistics, intelligent manufacturing, and e-commerce are seen as high-growth sectors by some enterprises, while infrastructure construction is considered to have relatively limited growth potential.

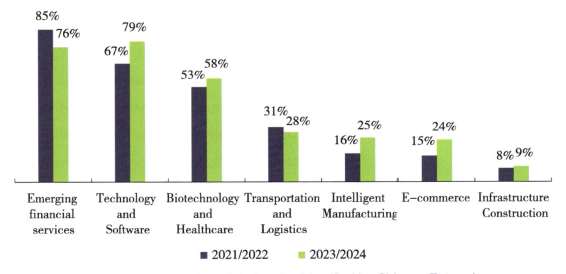

Figure 12–14: High–Growth Industries Identified by Chinese Enterprises

Source:China Enterprises Association (Singapore) Survey, Deloitte Research.

The fintech, software services, and biotechnology sectors in Singapore and Southeast Asia showcase long-term development potential in technology-enabled industries.

The fintech industry is thriving. As Asia's leading fintech market, the COVID-19 pandemic accelerated rapid development in Singapore's fintech sector, with surging demand for digital services such as online banking, digital payments, and e-commerce. As the scale of the payment and lending markets expands and the ecosystem matures, new players in the fintech sector are exploring opportunities in wealth management, capital markets, insurtech, regtech, and data analytics. Singapore's leadership in fintech and its robust infrastructure provide an advantageous space for innovation among these startups.

The B2B sector is emerging as a new frontier for technology. In the post-pandemic era, Southeast Asia's digital transformation has created significant business opportunities in the B2B sector. Singapore, home to many global technology companies, offers a rich industrial ecosystem that facilitates collaboration among tech companies and the co-development of solutions with end-user application firms. Promising areas in the B2B sector include Industry 4.0 technologies, enterprise service software, and B2B2C logistics solutions. Many B2B companies refine their technologies and validate their business models in Singapore, often establishing data centers and using Singapore as their regional headquarters to penetrate the Southeast Asian market.

The Southeast Asian pharmaceutical market, with its scale, growth rate, high population density, and relatively minor genetic differences from China, has attracted Chinese biopharmaceutical enterprises to accelerate their presence in Singapore. Supported by a strong manufacturing base and efficient transport and logistics networks, Singapore has become a global hub for international biopharmaceutical enterprises, attracting Chinese companies to engage in mergers and acquisitions or set up production facilities. Singapore's biotechnology innovation capabilities, leading-edge achievements, and robust intellectual property protection frameworks ensure the safety of R&D outcomes and encourage healthy growth in the industry. Since 2023, global mRNA vaccine leaders including BioNTech and Moderna, along with Chinese companies like Junshi Biosciences,

WuXi AppTec, GenScript, and Fosun Pharma, have established a presence in Singapore.

III. The Contribution of Chinese Enterprises to Local Economic Development

A. Chinese Enterprises Have Increased Local Employment in Singapore, Especially in Digital Technology and Finance

Not only have Chinese enterprises' investments in Singapore fostered economic development, but they have also boosted local employment. Currently, the proportion of local employees hired by Chinese enterprises in Singapore varies widely, with 54% of enterprises employing local staff at proportions exceeding 60% (see Figure 12-15). Chinese enterprises are continuously deepening mutual trust and cooperation with local business partners, exploring more efficient and practical paths toward sustainable development. These efforts not only create employment opportunities for local residents but also drive comprehensive innovation across multiple sectors, including trade, finance, shipping, logistics, and real estate.

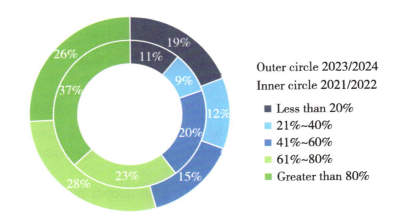

Outer circle 2023/2024
Inner circle 2021/2022

■ Less than 20%
■ 21%~40%
■ 41%~60%
■ 61%~80%
■ Greater than 80%

Figure 12–15: Proportion of Local Employees Employed by Chinese Enterprises in Singapore

Source: China Enterprises Association (Singapore) Survey, Deloitte Research.

B. Innovation by Chinese Enterprises in Five Key Fields: Products and Services, etc.

The contributions of Chinese enterprises to Singapore are particularly evident in the fields of product and service innovation, with an overall focus on enhancing customer value and providing strategic support. According to the survey, 58% of enterprises reported achievements in technology and service innovation by their Singapore subsidiaries, while 40% of enterprises noted progress in green development innovation, a 9% increase compared to the 2021—2022 survey. Additionally, Chinese enterprises have achieved breakthroughs in business model innovation, technological innovation, and management innovation, with contributions ranging between 20% and 30% (see Figure 12-16).

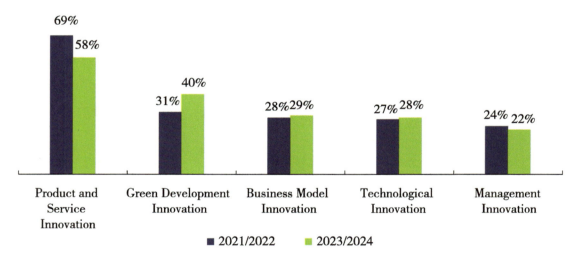

Figure 12–16: Fields of Innovation Contributions by Chinese Enterprises in Singapore

Source:China Enterprises Association (Singapore) Survey, Deloitte Research.

To gain deeper insights into the innovative achievements of Chinese enterprises in Singapore, the China Enterprises Association (Singapore) conducted a two-week video interview survey in mid-July 2024. Nearly 20 company executives shared their experiences, detailing the innovative contributions of

Chinese enterprises in five key fields to Singapore's economic and social development.

1. Product and service innovation

The development of Chinese enterprises in Singapore has introduced innovative products and services across various industries, significantly enhancing user experience and creating lasting market impact. By continuously innovating, these enterprises have been at the forefront of market advancement.

For example, China State Construction, a pioneer in international operations, established China Construction (South Pacific) Development Co. Pte Ltd., ("China Construction (South Pacific)") in Singapore in 1992. As one of the leading companies in Singapore's construction industry, China Construction (South Pacific) has been deeply rooted in the Singaporean market for 30 years. It has completed 214 high-quality projects across sectors such as education, commerce, hospitality, healthcare, and transportation, earning 223 awards to date. In recent years, China Construction (South Pacific) has actively supported the Singapore government's Construction Industry Transformation Map, exploring innovative business models to improve productivity. By focusing on cutting-edge technological applications, China Construction (South Pacific) has enhanced industrialized construction methods, reducing on-site labor-intensive processes. China Construction (South Pacific) continuously promotes digital construction by adopting Building Information Modeling (BIM) and virtual construction technologies to improve project accuracy and management efficiency. Additionally, in response to the "dual carbon" objectives, China Construction (South Pacific) has explored green, low-carbon industrial directions, employed new building materials, and strengthened collaboration among universities, research institutions, and industry to drive technological innovation. Since 2016, China Construction (South Pacific) has expanded its reach into neighboring markets, including Malaysia, successfully undertaking major projects such as the KL Eco City and IKEA Johor Bahru, demonstrating significant brand value.

2. Green development innovation

In the field of green development innovation, Chinese enterprises have made notable contributions by implementing environmentally friendly mechanisms and green technologies to achieve energy conservation and emissions reduction. Furthermore, these Chinese enterprises have achieved significant progress in social responsibility, advanced green technologies, and their practical and promotional aspects, showing improvement compared to 2023. However, gaps remain in foundational research on green innovative technologies.

For instance, MCC Singapore, a regional subsidiary of MCC Group under China Minmetals Corporation, has undergone four industrial upgrades since entering the Singapore market in 1996. It has evolved into a fully integrated urban construction enterprise, with many of its projects receiving Singapore Green Building Certification. MCC Singapore has completed influential projects such as the Singapore Convention & Exhibition Center, Universal Studios Singapore, and the Maritime Experiential Museum on Sentosa Island. One standout project is the Mandai Rainforest Park, a model for emissions reduction and green development. In May 2020, despite pandemic challenges, MCC Singapore secured the contract for the design and construction of the Mandai Rainforest Park. This large-scale ecological tourism project, championed by the Singapore government, aims to create a world-class ecological experience by integrating zoos, wildlife, and plant exhibits into a unified natural theme park. It will provide visitors with an unprecedented and unforgettable experience of nature and wildlife conservation. The Mandai Rainforest Park is the world's first rainforest-themed park, serving as a model project integrating wildlife conservation, education, research, and cultural tourism in Singapore. Phase 1, the Northern Zone, is set to be completed by the end of 2024, while Phase 2, the Southern Zone, is expected to be finished by the end of 2025. Once fully operational, the Mandai Ecological District is projected to welcome over 10 million visitors annually.

China Construction Bank (CCB) established a representative office in Singapore in 1993, upgraded to a branch in 1998, and was awarded a Qualifying Full Bank ("QFB") in 2020, becoming one of Singapore's 10 fully licensed banks. Leveraging its extensive client network, CCB Singapore provides comprehensive financial services to clients in China, Singapore, and along the Belt and Road Initiative and the New International Land-Sea Trade Corridor. CCB Singapore actively promotes green panda bonds, collaborates with the Singapore Monetary Authority's Project Greenprint, and explores the development of objective, quantifiable, and comparable ESG evaluation metrics. These efforts aim to help SMEs in China and the RCEP region access targeted green financing services, advancing regional sustainable development. Additionally, CCB Singapore leads or participates in green financing projects, supports the issuance of green bonds for Singapore's Housing & Development Board, and provides green loans for local public building rooftop solar projects.

3. Business model innovation

In the field of business model innovation, Chinese enterprises have contributed primarily by enhancing customer value, providing more cost-effective products and services, and delivering comprehensive customer service and follow-up surveys. While Chinese enterprises have a competitive edge in business models, they still have room for improvement in four aspects: resilience and stability, industry advancement, value reconstruction, and financial value, especially considering their relatively short history in the Southeast Asian market.

For example, China Life Insurance(Singapore) Pte. Ltd., the first overseas subsidiary established by China Life, entered the Singapore market in 2015. Singapore, now the world's third-largest financial center, boasts a highly developed and mature financial and insurance market. With intense competition in the life insurance sector, the market is saturated in terms of both scale and market development. As a latecomer, China Life (Singapore) adopted strategies such as product differentiation, digitalization of services, and refined sales processes, targeting high-net-worth Chinese customers familiar with China Life products. Based on business data over the past few years, the company has outperformed the market average in connecting with the Chinese market and expanding its customer base in Southeast Asia compared to local market averages and leading competitors.

4. Cutting–edge technology innovation

In the field of technology innovation, Chinese enterprises have made notable contributions by adopting leading-edge innovation strategies, aiming for industry leadership rather than merely catching up or imitating existing technologies. Leveraging their experiences and successes in China's vast and competitive market, Chinese enterprises have found it relatively easy to identify similar application scenarios in Southeast Asia.

For instance, China Unicom(Singapore) has experienced rapid business growth in the promotion of cutting-edge technologies such as 5G, data storage, security, server rooms, and AI applications. From 2020 to 2023, the company achieved substantial increases in revenue and profits, primarily driven by the growth of communication-related products, particularly IDC services, data centers, cloud computing, and cloud applications. China Unicom (Singapore) has engaged with local business associations, such as SME associations and manufacturing associations, to introduce China's successful 5G application cases to the Singapore market and industrial parks, fostering win-win collaboration. The company has enhanced its R&D capacity by establishing research institutions, investing more in R&D than the industry average, and participating in innovation alliances. In the field of computing and networking, China Unicom (Singapore) continues to explore new applications, leveraging its expertise as a leading 5G network application provider. For example, in Thailand, China Unicom achieved unmanned connectivity at industrial parks for Great Wall Motor and Midea factories, offering advanced digital solutions such as smart factories and unmanned operations. These proven cases have facilitated digital transformation across industries in the region.

5. Management model inncvation

In management innovation, Chinese enterprises have contributed by adopting superior concepts and practices in specific aspects of corporate management, such as organization and control, information management, and supply chain management. For example, Mergers and acquisitions (M&A) remain a key mode of international expansion for Chinese enterprises, and effective post-M&A integration requires the rapid establishment of management systems adapted to local markets. Chinese enterprises have also made significant contributions to management performance, earning market recognition for their innovative approaches.

For example, PetroChina International(Singapore), established in 2000, initially focused on exporting refined petroleum products and regional sales in Southeast Asia. In 2009, PetroChina (Singapore) acquired Singapore Petroleum Company (SPC), gaining upstream assets and production operations, including a refinery, jet fuel services at Changi Airport, and marine fuel services. Through post-acquisition business integration, PetroChina (Singapore) achieved significant advancements in the management of upstream operations, refining, and sales. After M&A, the company emphasized corporate culture development, respecting Singapore's multiculturalism, languages, and customs, while promoting cultural integration. The integration with SPC exceeded expectations, and by 2023, PetroChina (Singapore) had achieved record-high trading profits and trade volumes.

IV. Conclusion

The investments and innovation developments of Chinese enterprises in Singapore have achieved remarkable results, driving bilateral economic and trade cooperation as well as two-way investment between China and Singapore. In areas such as green development, technological innovation, and urban construction, Chinese enterprises have not only demonstrated strong competitiveness and adaptability but have also injected new vitality into Singapore's economic and social development.

With the further advancement of the *Regional Comprehensive Economic Partnership* (RCEP) and the *Digital Economy Partnership Agreement* (DEPA), opportunities for Chinese enterprises in Singapore and the broader Southeast Asian market will continue to grow. Singapore, with its unique geographical advantages and excellent business environment, remains an attractive destination for many Chinese enterprises to invest in and expand their operations.

Looking forward, both China and Singapore should deepen their collaboration and jointly explore more win-win investment opportunities. By continuously optimizing trade policies and the business environment, the two sides are poised to achieve closer economic ties, contributing more significantly to the prosperity and development of the regional economy. This report aims to provide valuable references and insights for Chinese enterprises interested in entering the Southeast Asian and Singaporean markets, helping them navigate the waves of globalization.

About This Survey

To gain a deeper understanding of the investment landscape of Chinese enterprises in Singapore, theChina Enterprises Association (Singapore) conducted the 2023/2024 annual development report survey from June to July 2024, receiving over 100 valid responses from association members. From an industry distribution perspective, the top three sectors represented were infrastructure and construction, finance, and international trade, each accounting for 14%. These were followed by transportation, communication technology, and energy (see Figure 12-17). From an ownership perspective, state-owned central enterprises accounted for 44%, private enterprises for 28%, and local state-owned enterprises for 14% (see Figure 12-18). The institutional types in Singapore were primarily regional headquarters and regional sales centers, with a smaller proportion categorized as regional logistics management centers and regional manufacturing and production centers.

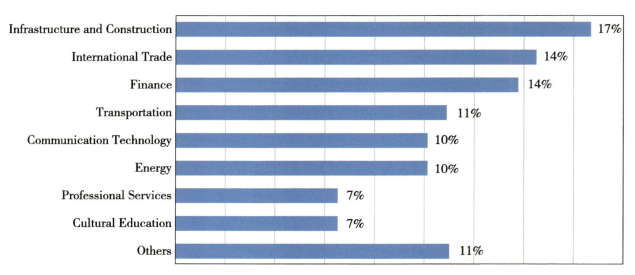

Figure 12-17: Industry Distribution of Surveyed Enterprises

Source:China Enterprises Association (Singapore) Survey, Deloitte Research.

Note: Other industries include advanced manufacturing, biotechnology and healthcare, and consumer goods production and retail.

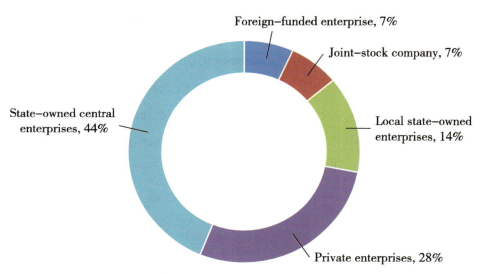

Figure 12-18: Ownership Types of Surveyed Enterprises

Source:China Enterprises Association (Singapore) Survey, Deloitte Research.

Industry
Section

Chapter 13 New Achievements in High-level Opening-up of the Financial Sector[1]

As an important part of China's high-level opening-up, since the 18th National Congress ofthe Communist Party of China, the pace of financial opening-up has accelerated significantly. Through a series of institutional measures, such as significantly relaxing market access in the financial sector, expanding the business scope of foreign financial institutions, promoting two-way connectivity in the capital market, The degree of financial openness in China has been significantly enhanced and deepened. In 2023, In the face of multiple challenges, including the recovery period of covid-19, the conflict between Russia and Ukraine, the divergence of monetary policies among major countries, and the inverted interest rate differential between China and the United States, China continued to unswervingly promote institutional opening-up in the financial sector, continued to improve the system of cross-border financial transactions and services, deepen financial market connectivity, steadily enhance the international monetary function of the RMB, and continued to promote the development of international financial centres in Shanghai and Hong Kong, their international competitiveness and regulatory influence have

---

[1] Contributed by Zhang Liping and Sun Fei, from the Institute of Finance,Development Research Center of the State Council.

continued to grow. Looking ahead, China's high-level financial opening-up will help build a new open economy system with better coordination between opening-up and security, as well as "introducing FDI" and "going global".

I. Continuously to Expand Institutional Opening-up in the Financial Sector

Since 2018, China has comprehensively promoted institutional opening-up of its financial sector, including granting national treatment to foreign-funded institutions,abolishing foreign investment restrictions on the proportion of capital holdings, expanding the scope of its business and improving its management rules. In October 2023, the central financial work conference further proposed"Steadily expanding the institutional opening-up of the financial sector," aiming to continue to optimize market rules, and strive to enhance the depth and breadth of financial opening-up.

A. Continuously Relax the Entry Threshold for Foreign-funded Institutions

At present, China has removed restrictions on foreign ownership in banking, securities, fund management and other fields, greatly lowering the threshold for foreign institutions to set up financial institutions.In the banking sector, by the end of 2019, China removed the shareholding restrictions on banks and total asset requirements for foreign banks to set up foreign-funded corporate banks and branches in China.By the end of 2023, foreign banks had set up 41 corporate banks, 116 branches and 132 representative offices of foreign and Hong Kong, Macao and Taiwan banks in China, bringing the total number of operating institutions to 888, total assets amounted to 3.86 trillion yuan.

In the securities and futures industry, Standard Chartered

Securities was approved for establishment in January 2023, becoming the first wholly-owned foreign-owned securities firm to be approved after the formal lifting of the foreign equity ratio restrictions on securities companies on April 1,2020. By the end of the 2023,17 foreign-owned securities companies with total assets of over 650 billion yuan and operating income of over 27.5 billion yuan had been approved for establishment. Insurance industry, before the end of 2020, China has removed the proportion of foreign ownership of life insurance companies, operating years and other requirements for access; In September 2022, China removed the cap on foreign-owned insurance companies. By the end of the 2023, foreign insurance companies had set up 67 operating agencies and 70 representative offices in China, with total assets of 2.4 trillion Yuan and a 10% share of the domestic insurance market. In addition, China also grants national treatment to foreign-funded institutions in areas such as payments, ratings and corporate credit ratings. In November 2023, Mastercard's joint venture bank card clearing agency in China, Mastercard Network was approved to open.

B. Continuously Expand the Scope of Quasi-business of Foreign-funded Institutions

While relaxing the entry threshold,China has further expanded the business qualifications of foreign-funded institutions and continuously improved the business environment. In 2023 January, Standard Chartered (China) became the first foreign bank in China to be allowed to trade government bond futures. According to the Dealer Association's announcement, based on the market evaluation results of 2023 non-financial corporate debt financing instruments related members applying to engage in underwriting related businesses, China has added

HSBC, Standard Chartered and Banque de l'Indochine as general lead underwriters of debt financing instruments for non-financial companies; Increase the number of JPMorgan Chase Banks, Mizuho Bank and MUFG Bank as special underwriters of debt financing instruments for non-financial enterprises abroad; Adding Bank of East Asia, Fubon Bank (China) , Sumitomo Mitsui Banking Corporation and DBS as underwriters of debt financing instruments for non-financial enterprises.In addition, China's financial authorities treat Chinese and foreign-funded institutions equally when conducting new business trials, financial institutions such as the People's Bank of China's carbon reduction support tool have now been incorporated into 13 foreign banks, including Deutsche Bank, Société Générale and HSBC.

C. Further Optimising Market Rules

In the process of institutional opening-up in the financial field, in accordance with the new changes in the market and the new needs of market entities, China is constantly optimizing market rules to better promote fair competition and innovative development of the financial market, and enhance the depth of financial opening-up.In the capital markets, in February 2023, the China Securities Regulatory Commission (CSRC)and the Hong Kong Securities Regulatory Commission have opened up the shanghai-shenzhen-hong Kong stock connect trading day closed due to non-compliance with settlement arrangements, and enhanced the Shanghai-shenzhen-hong Kong stock connect trading calendar;CSRC issued the"trial measures for the administration of overseas issuance of securities and listing of domestic enterprises"and five supporting guidelines to support enterprises to list overseas in accordance with the law and regulations.On foreign exchange management, in November of the 2023,the People's Bank of China and the State Administration of Foreign Exchange have revised the "Regulations on the Management of Domestic Securities and Futures Investment Funds of Foreign Institutional Investors" and issued the draft for consultation, it further simplifies the registration procedures, optimizes the management of Accounts, simplifies the exchange management, facilitates the management of foreign exchange risks, and eliminates the administrative licensing requirement for QFII/RQFII funds registration with the State Administration of Foreign Exchange.

D. Expediting the Implementation of Financial Opening-up Policies for Specific Regions

The financial opening-up policy for specific region is an important measure to promote institutional opening-up in the financial field. Optimizing the rules for financial market access, capital flows and financial services in these regions will attract more domestic and foreign financial institutions and investors, promoting efficient allocation of financial resources and deep integration of markets, leading to high-quality opening-up of regional economies, and reducing reform risks by playing a pilot role and accumulating replicable experiences, accelerate the opening-up process of China's financial sector.In recent years, China has paid particular attention to the relevant rules in the financial sector in international high-standard economic and trade agreements, and introduced a package of financial innovation policies in key regions.In February 2023, the People's Bank of China, the Banking and Insurance Regulatory Commission, the Securities Regulatory Commission, the State Administration of Foreign Exchange and the People's Government of Guangdong Province jointly issued the "Opinions on Financial Support for the Development of the Hengqin

Guangdong-Macao Deep Cooperation Zone" and the "Opinions on the Comprehensive Deepening of Reform and opening-up of the Financial Support Qianhai Shenzhen-Hong Kong Modern Service Industry Cooperation Zone", thirty innovative measures of financial reform were put forward respectively.Hengqin's new policy encourages the development of cross-border financial services for the economic co-operation between Guangdong and Macao.Qianhai's new policy encourages financial institutions in the co-operation zone to innovate in their products and services to meet the diversified financial needs of the modern services industry.

II. Continuously Improve the Cross—border Financial Services System

Improving the cross-border financial services system is an important part of the process of financial opening-up. In recent years, China has continuously improved its cross-border financial services system, not only to better meet the needs of enterprises and individuals for financial services such as cross-border investment and financing, but also to further promote the connectivity of financial markets, and pushing financial openness to a deeper and broader level.

A. Continuously Improve Supporting Policies for Cross—border Investment and Financing

On the one hand, on the basis of the continuous introduction of cross-border trade and investment facilitation measures in recent years, in December 2023, the State Administration of Foreign Exchange issued the "Circular on Further Deepening Reform to Promote the Facilitation of Cross-border Trade and Investment", nine trade, investment and financing facilitation policies were introduced in three major areas: facilitating foreign exchange receipts and payments in trade, expanding capital account facilitation, and optimizing foreign exchange management in capital account.The policy covers the whole country from the previous 17 provinces (cities) , increasing the facilitation quota of the previous 17 provinces (cities) to the equivalent of US $10 million, it reflects the support of financial opening-up to the scientific and technological enterprises with technological advantages and certain development potential.

On the other hand,China continued to increase its foreign exchange support for scientific and technological innovation and small and medium-sized enterprises.Pilot projects to facilitate cross-border financing will be carried out for small and medium-sized micro-high-tech Enterprises and "specialized and special new" enterprises with small net assets, enterprises ware allowed to borrow foreign debt on their own within the equivalent of US $10 million or US $5 million.According to the State Administration of Foreign Exchange, the pilot area covered about 80% of the country, 280,000 high-tech and "specialized and special new" enterprises.Through the establishment of a cross-border financial services platform, eight financing application scenarios and three facilitation application scenarios ware be launched, nearly 100,000 foreign-related enterprises, mainly small and medium-sized enterprises, have received more than US $290 billion in financing and US $1.2 trillion in foreign exchange payments.

B. Chinese-funded institutions Actively Expand Their Global Business

Chinese financial institutions expand their global business by "going global" and provide guarantee for service enterprises to "going global".In the 2023, Chinese financial institutions have stepped up their efforts to "going global". In the banking industry, Chinese financial institutions have set up overseas branches in order to give full play to the role of a window and bridge for international economic and trade exchanges and to provide security for service enterprises to"going global". By the end of June 2023, Chinese banks had set up 295 first-level institutions in 71 countries and regions outside China, playing an important role in supporting Chinese enterprises and enhancing their overseas competitiveness.Among them, the five major banks have set up operational institutions in 67 countries and regions outside China, basically covering major international and regional financial centres. In addition to the distribution of developed countries, the banking industry has also focused on setting up overseas institutions around China's key foreign economic and trade countries and regions, and continuously expanding the coverage of financial services to the Belt and Road partner countries. Since the second half of 2023, the Bank of China has opened new branches in July and September in Islamabad, Pakistan and Riyadh, Saudi Arabia; China Construction Bank opened a branch in Penang, Malaysia, in November 2023.

In the insurance sector, according to the Financial Supervisory Authority,by the end of June 2023, Chinese-funded insurance institutions had set up 74 branches in 17 countries and regions, providing high-quality financial services for Chinese enterprises "going global" and jointly building the Belt and Road. For example, by the end of 2023, China Re Property Insurance Company has provided more than 100 billion yuan of risk protection for hundreds of Belt and Road projects, more than 10,000 China-Europe freight trains and more than 800,000 TEU of cross-border trade goods.

III. Continuously Deepen Financial Market Connectivity

In recent years, by actively promoting the two-way opening-up of the financial market, China has initially formed an opening-up pattern covering the stock market, bond market, foreign exchange market and derivatives market. The Shanghai-Hong Kong Stock Connect, Shenzhen-Hong Kong Stock Connect, Bond Connect and Swap Connect have become the means of financial market connectivity that domestic and foreign investors actively participate in.By the end of 2023, the total transaction value of Shenzhen-Hong Kong Stock Connect has exceeded 75.43 trillion yuan; Cross-border financial Connect individual investors have reached 69,200, and the balance of cross-border financial Connect market value has reached 5.1 billion yuan. In 2023, the trading volume of Bond Connect "Northbound Connect" increased by 24%, and the annual turnover was 9.97 trillion yuan. From the perspective of the new highlights in 2023, the outstanding performance is as follows.

A. The Depth and Breadth of Bond Market Connectivity Were Further Expanded

In 2023, foreign capital increased its domestic bond holdings by a net US $23 billion. By the end of 2023, a total of 1,124 foreign investors, including sovereign and commercial investors from more than 70 countries and regions, had entered the Chinese bond market, holding a total of 3.7 trillion yuan of Chinese bonds. As at the end of December 2023, foreign investors have bought Chinese bonds on a net basis for 11 consecutive months, of which foreign investors bought about 360 billion yuan of Chinese bonds on a net basis in November 2023, increasing their holdings by about 250 billion yuan, a record high. According to the People's Bank of China, foreign institutions held about 3.67 trillion yuan of bonds in the interbank market at the end of 2023. In addition,the amount of

2023 panda bonds issued hit a record high, exceeding 150 billion yuan for the first time in the whole year.

B. The Interest Rate Swap Market Interconnection Was Officially Launched

To help foreign investors better manage interest rate risks, the interest rate swap market interconnection between the mainland and Hong Kong ("Swap lines") was officially launched in May 2023.

Through the arrangements for the financial market infrastructure institutions of the mainland and Hong Kong to be interconnected in the areas of transactions, clearing and settlement, without changing their trading habits and complying with the laws and regulations of the two markets, domestic and foreign investors can easily complete RMB interest rate swap transactions and central clearing.By the end of December 2023, there were 20 domestic bidders and 51 foreign investors, with a total of more than 2,000 transactions and a nominal principal of more than 900 billion yuan.

C. ETF Exchange Procucts Are Continuously Enriching

Since the introduction of etfs into the mainland and Hong Kong stock market trading connectivity mechanism in 2022, Shenzhen stock connect ETFs continue to expand capacity. In the 2023,25 new ETFs were added to the list of Shenzhen stock connect, continuously enriching foreign investors' A-share investment tools. In addition, Shenzhen-new ETF cooperation has also been deepening.As of the end of the 2023, there are 76 ETFs in Shanghai Stock Connect. 55 ETFs in Shenzhen Stock Connect, 8 ETFs in Hong Kong Stock Connect, and 139 ETF in total, compared with the first batch of Shanghai-Shenzhen-

Hong Kong stock connect ETF products increased by 60% . In addition, the Shenzhen-Singapore exchange product Galaxy Rich China Securities 1000 ETF is listed on the Singapore Exchange in November 2023 , providing Singapore investors with a new tool to allocate a-shares[①].

IV. Steadily Improve the International Monetary Function of the RMB

A. The use of RMB in Cross-border Trade Has Increased

In order to better meet the needs of foreign economic and trade enterprises, such as transaction settlement, investment and financing, risk management, and so on, in January 2023, the People's Bank of China and the Ministry of Commerce jointly issued the "Circular on further supporting foreign economic and trade enterprises to expand the cross-border use of RMB and promote trade and investment facilitation". In 2023, banks paid 52.3 trillion yuan in cross-border renminbi, up 24.2 percent year-on-year, RMB has become the largest cross-border payment and settlement currency in China. Of this total, cross-border RMB receipts and payments in goods trade amounted to 10.7 trillion yuan, accounting for 25% of cross-border receipts and payments in both local and foreign currencies in goods trade over the same period, an increase of 7 percentage points over 2022, maintaining a high level. According to the Society for Worldwide Interbank Financial Telecommunication (SWIFT) , in November 2023, the RMB accounted for 4.61 percent of all payments in global currencies, surpassing the yen as the world's fourth-largest payment currency. According to the People's Bank of China, the amount of cross-border RMB settlement under the

---

① https://baijiahao.baidu.com/s?id=1788506878680186396&wfr=spider&for=pc.

current account in 2023 is 14.03 trillion yuan, of which trade in goods, trade in services and other current accounts are 10.69 trillion yuan and 3.34 trillion yuan respectively; The amount of cross-border RMB settlement for direct investment was 7.6 trillion yuan, of which outbound direct investment and foreign direct investment were 2.6 trillion yuan and 5 trillion yuan respectively.

B. The Facilitation of Cross-border RMB Payments Has Been Deepened

Cross-border payments by foreign residents in China have become much more convenient.In 2023, the State Council General Office issued a document on "Releasing the Potential of Tourism Consumption to Promote the High-quality Development of the Tourism Industry". The document proposes to make it easier for inbound tourists to use overseas bank cards and various electronic payment methods, as well as facilitate foreign currency exchange.

Since 2023, Alipay and Caifutong have joined hands with commercial banks, clearing houses, and card organizations to take a series of measures to optimize their operations. On the one hand, they are promoting the "internal use of foreign cards," whereby foreign bank cards can be tied to Alipay or Wechat for consumption by domestic merchants. On the other hand, they are supporting the "external use of internal use," allowing more overseas e-wallets to be used in China. Both Alipay and Wechat have raised the limit for foreign nationals to use mobile payments from $1,000 to $5,000 per transaction and from $10,000 to $50,000 per year[1].

Cross-border payment convenience for Chinese residents

---

[1] https://baijiahao.baidu.com/s?id=1794221409212700185&wfr=spider&f or=pc.

continues to improve. The RMB cross-border payment system (CIPS) has expanded its service area and improved its service level, 2023 National Day, the mid-autumn Festival holiday for the first time to achieve a "non-closing", continued to provide cross-border RMB payment and settlement services to domestic and overseas customers, and fully play the role of the main channel for cross-border payments. By the end of 2023, CIPS had 139 direct participants and 1345 indirect participants, and its business scope covers 182 countries and regions with 4442 corporate banking institutions.

C. The International Network for the Use of the RMB Is Becoming More Sophisticated

In 2023, the People's Bank of China signed or renewed bilateral currency swap agreements with the central banks of Saudi Arabia and the United Arab Emirates. New RMB clearing banks have been set up in Brazil, Cambodia, Serbia and other countries, and 33 RMB clearing banks have been authorized in 31 countries and regions, covering major international financial centres.

V. Promote the Development of an International Financial Center in an Orderly Manner

In the important speech at the opening ceremony of the special seminar for major leaders at the provincial and ministerial levels on promoting high-quality financial development, General Secretary Xi Jinping, clearly pointed out that a strong international financial center is one of the key core financial elements of a strong financial nation. In recent years, Shanghai and Hong Kong, as international financial centers, are based on their respective international competitive advantages, continuously enhancing their global resource allocation capabilities and steadily increasing their international influence, playing an important role in promoting the construction of a strong financial nation.

A. The Shanghai International Financial Centre Has Made Steady Progress

Influenced by history and national conditions, international financial centres have their own characteristics, but they all have strong international competitive advantages in some fields. The outstanding advantage of Shanghai is that its construction of international financial center is an important national strategy put forward by the CPC Central Committee and the State Council from the perspective of the overall situation of China's reform and opening-up as well as socialist modernization.In 1992, the 14th National Congress of the Communist Party of China first proposed the establishment of Shanghai as an international financial center.In 2009, No. 19 document of the State Council further clarified the goals and main tasks of building Shanghai into an international financial center.Shanghai, taking this as a lead in deepening reform in cross-border RMB settlement and capital market connectivity, has become an important window for the reform and opening-up of China's financial sector.In 2020, an international financial center was established that is commensurate with China's economic strength and the international status of the RMB. Since 2021, Shanghai has entered a new stage of overall upgrading of its energy level. On the basis of continuing to improve the markets for financial elements such as stocks, bonds, currencies, gold, foreign exchange, commodity futures, financial futures, insurance exchanges and stock exchanges, Shanghai data exchange is used as a carrier to explore financial data flow, and Shanghai Environmental Energy Exchange is used to promote the development of carbon finance, which forms a more complete market function than other international financial centers.

In recent years, the resource agglomeration effect of Shanghai international financial center has become more and more obvious, at the same time, actively exerting both radiating and driving effects. Relying on the advantages of the pilot free trade zone and the first-to-try financial opening-up and innovation in the new port-adjacent area, Shanghai has launched in-depth high-level opening-up trials for cross-border trade and investment, to make it easier for foreign institutional investors to square deal in the Chinese capital markets. In terms of financial institutions, the total number of licensed financial institutions in Shanghai in 2023 is 1,771, with foreign financial institutions accounting for nearly one-third; foreign legal banks, joint venture fund management companies, and foreign insurance companies headquartered in Shanghai each account for approximately half of the total in mainland China; Shanghai ranks among the top 5 globally in various sub-sectors such as banking, investment, and insurance.In terms of capital and management, Shanghai accounts for nearly 30% of the country's capital management, with public offering, private placement and insurance capital management ranking first in the country. In terms of financial talent, there are approximately 500,000 financial professionals in Shanghai, with the proportion of financial talent in the Pudong New Area accounting for nearly 9% of the total employed population, ranking among the top in the world.

B. The Hong Kong International Financial Centre Plays an Important Role

Hong Kong has always been the Asian headquarters of many well-known international banks, insurance companies, securities companies and other financial institutions. It is also an important global wealth management market,continuing to play a leading role as an international financial center. At the end of 2023, the value of assets under management in Hong Kong's financial markets grew by an annualised 2.1% to HK $31.19 trillion[1], mainly for private banking and private financial management businesses, and 3,257 licensed securities institutions, there are 2,609 listed companies with a total market capitalisation of US $4.0 trillion, and Hong Kong is the largest international bond issuance center in Asia, with new international bonds issued in 2023 amounting to 175.4 billion USD. It is the largest offshore RMB market, possessing the largest offshore RMB fund pool. As of January 2024, the balance of RMB deposits is 954.7 billion[2].

Hong Kong's competitive advantage is mainly embodied in the common law-based legal framework covering the professional services system in the areas of accounting, auditing, law and consulting, low tax rates and the free flow of capital across borders.These advantages have laid the foundation for Hong Kong to consolidate its position as an international financial centre.

VI. Prospect of China's High—level Financial Opening—up

Against the backdrop of the decision of the third plenary session of the 20th Central Committee to further comprehensively deepen reform, China will continue to deepen institutional opening-up in the financial sector, with a better business environment, more efficient allocation of resources, a better market system and a more professional workforce to further enhance the quality and efficiency of opening-up

---

[1] Hong Kong Securities and Futures Commission, "2023 Asset and Wealth Management Activities Survey", https://baijiahao.baidu.com/s?Id=1805356594368225398&wfr=spider&for=pc, 2024-7-23.

[2] Sohu.com, Hong Kong vs. Singapore, who is the third city of an international financial center, https://www.sohu.com/a/789674319_121304879.

the financial sector. But at the same time, facing the complex international situation and the uncertainty of domestic and foreign financial markets, China's financial opening-up faces many challenges.With China's financial opening-up entering the deep-water area, how to better construct the financial security mechanism and actively participate in international financial governance in the process of more opening-up, to promote the international competitiveness of China's financial system has become an important issue of China's financial opening-up.

On the one hand, better coordination of financial opening-up and security. By actively participating in international financial governance and cooperation, in order to further deepen international financial collaboration and promote the coordination of global macroeconomic and financial policies. In recent years, China has taken the initiative to align itself with high-standard international rules in many aspects, such as rules, systems, management and standards, to initiate the establishment of the Belt and Road inter-bank regular cooperation mechanism (BRBR) , the Belt and Road Green Investment Principles (GIP) and so on.In the future, China will continue to integrate with high-standard international rules, actively participate in the formulation and revision of international financial standards, and constantly enhance the international level of the financial sector. At the same time, China will further promote dialogue and exchanges in the financial sector through mechanisms such as the china-us and china-eu financial working groups, and jointly explore new paths of financial opening, so as to promote the stability and development of the global financial market.

On the other hand, better coordination will be made between "introducing FDI" and "going global". In October 2023, the Central Financial Work Conference once again clearly stated the importance of "adhering to both 'introducing FDI' and 'going global' equally". In terms of "introducing FDI", China will continue to expand the business scope of foreign financial institutions and further improve the business environment. In the aspect of "going global", with the quickening pace of Chinese enterprises "going global", financial institutions will actively expand overseas markets, participate in international financial cooperation and competition, and enhance international competitiveness.

Chapter 14   Multinational Companies in China Actively Engaged in ESG Practice[①]

Transnational corporations actively fulfill their green responsibilities, which play an important role in China's green development. According to net-zero Tracker, among the world's largest 2,000 publicly listed companies, 1,142 have set net-zero targets, which is 2.7 times the 417 companies in 2020. Multinational companies' overseas investments place greater emphasis on environmental protection, social responsibility, and corporate governance (ESG) requirements, and pay more attention to leveraging the comparative advantages of host countries to promote the development of local green industries. In the context of China's accelerating green transition, multinational enterprises in China are also actively engaging in ESG practices to further enhance sustainability goals. At the same time, leverage the advantages of green technology to drive upstream and downstream enterprises in the supply chain to collectively enhance their ESG capabilities and levels. The Investment Company Working Committee of the China Foreign Investment Enterprises Association selected five multinational companies' ESG practice cases, showcasing successful experiences and innovative practices across different fields and industries.

---

① Contributions from the Investment Company Working Committee of the China Foreign Investment Enterprises Association.

Case 1: Ford's Sustainability Strategy

Ford's global sustainability strategy aims to increase the positive impact on society and the environment, the company has developed detailed strategies and targets for climate change, energy use, materials, water, waste, human rights and employees, and has released its commitment to carbon neutrality by 2050, it has also set medium-and long-term carbon reduction targets under the science-based carbon reduction targets initiative (SBTI), which aims to establish direct, open, transparent and frequent links and interactions with stakeholders.

Ford Motor Company is striving to translate its strategies and objectives into practical activities at its factories in China.

1. In terms of renewable energy usage, Ford China is taking proactive measures to promote the use of renewable energy and carbon neutrality; Ford has installed rooftop and parking lot solar photovoltaic panels with a total capacity of over 110 mwp in its factories in China,Significantly reduced carbon emissions, with an annual electricity generation exceeding 80 million kilowatt-hours.

2. In terms of water resources, Ford's latest global water management strategy not only continues to focus on improving water use efficiency but also ensures that everyone has access to clean water resources.Ford's manufacturing plants in China employ advanced water-saving technologies, such as the use of rotary immersion coating processes, dry spray booths, deep wastewater treatment, and reclaimed water systems in the painting workshop's pretreatment electrophoresis process. Reclaimed water is utilized for replenishing the painting process, irrigating green spaces with rainwater, maximizing the potential of cooling towers, and renovating pipeline leakage. These measures ensure a continuous reduction in water consumption during the manufacturing process.

3. Ford China continues to promote waste reduction,

recycling and reuse. Starting in 2021, all of Ford's factories in China are now"Zero landfill", with all of the waste generated by the plant no longer being disposed of in landfills, but instead being recycled or burned to generate electricity. In September 2021, the Chang'an Ford Hangzhou plant was awarded the title of "Zero Waste Factory" by the Hangzhou Municipal People's Government, in recognition of its efforts and achievements in waste management, achieving zero landfill of waste, promoting the classification of industrial and household waste, and reducing sludge, paint residue, and general solid waste. The Hangzhou plant has become an important component of the construction of a "Zero Waste City" in Hangzhou.

4. Changan Ford's Chongqing plant is committed to improving production processes and reducing volatile organic compounds (VOCs) emissions. The waste recovery solvents generated from the plant's painting process are reused in the production line after deep treatment, achieving a circular economy. Jiangling Motors' Fushan plant has installed a complete set of VOC waste gas treatment facilities for painting, making it one of the plants with the lowest VOC emissions in the world. Ford China has successfully been selected as a "2023 Outstanding Social Responsibility Practice Case" in the field of corporate ESG. In 2023, Changan Ford's Chongqing plant was recognized with the national-level green factory certification.

Case 2: Bayer's "Embrace Green" Project

The "Embrace Green" initiative has been ongoing for five years (2019—2023). Bayer Crop Science has a long-term vision, firm determination, and solid action for the transformation of agricultural production to green production and the development of high-quality agriculture.

The full name of the "Embrace Green" series of public welfare activities is "Embrace Green · Win-Win Future— Green Development Capability Enhancement Action Plan". It is a large-scale public welfare training project co-hosted by Bayer Crop Science and the National Agricultural Technology Extension Service Center, and it is a highlight of Sino-German agricultural cooperation. The initiative aims to provide professional and comprehensive training in green development skills, thereby offering strong talent support for the green and high-quality development of agriculture in China.

During the 5 years of implementing the "Embrace Green" project, a total of 15 offline training activities and 12 online live broadcasts were held in 18 provinces, autonomous regions, and municipalities including Jiangsu, Shandong, Guangdong, Yunnan,Xizang, Henan, Inner Mongolia, and Shanghai, creating 22 demonstration fields for 12 types of crops. More than 2,600 offline trainees from over 1,000 counties and cities participated in the training through various formats such as on-site observation, expert lectures, case sharing, and decision-making discussions, while the live training reached over 320,000 participants.

This public welfare training program disseminated new technologies and concepts such as high-quality development, green prevention and control, and the reduction and efficiency enhancement of pesticides, providing a great opportunity and platform for the knowledge updating, action optimization, and capacity enhancement of a wide range of students.

Case 3: IKEA Creates Sustainable Consumption

China is one of the fastest-growing and most important markets for IKEA globally, and it also possesses a complete value chain, with business activities encompassing product design, testing, production, procurement, warehousing and distribution, retail, and commercial real estate.IKEA integrates sustainability concepts throughout its entire value chain.

1. Product research and development

IKEA adheres to sustainable principles from the product development stage. There are more than 4,000 products that are particularly sustainable, such as energy-saving, water-saving, made from environmentally friendly or recyclable materials, certified in sustainability, and plant-based foods.

In the case of carpets, IKEA uses about 30,000 tonnes of polypropylene to make carpets worldwide each year. Polypropylene is made from propylene extracted from oil, which means IKEA consumes about 120,000 tonnes of crude oil a year. IKEA is currently attempting to use recycled polypropylene as a substitute for virgin polypropylene. The widely used recycled polyester yarn in the market is primarily made from plastic bottles. IKEA's partners have developed a technology that can recycle polyester waste generated during the textile manufacturing process, allowing the waste to be remade into polyester yarn and reused in production.Thanks to the breakthrough in this technology, IKEA has achieved a closed-loop recycling system for polyester textiles. Currently, this technology has been applied in the development of new products such as bedding, household textiles, and carpets.In 2030, IKEA's goal is to define the entire lifecycle of all products during the development phase, ensuring that all products produced use only renewable or recyclable materials.

2. Circular market

Currently, all 35 IKEA stores across the country have established "Sustainable Circular Markets". The products sold in the Circular Market mainly consist of display samples from the store, products with damaged transport packaging, and so on. Before being put on the shelves, the products undergo repairs and are sold only after ensuring their functionality and safety, at relatively affordable prices. As an important component of the sales area, the Circular Market not only inspires consumers to pay attention to a green and circular lifestyle but also gives products a second life, serving as an excellent space for consumer advocacy and education.

3. Green sustainable living products zone

IKEA has set up a dedicated space in its stores to display products that align with the concepts of green sustainability and home living, such as water-saving faucets, LED lights, and food sealing bags. The "Green sustainable living products zone" visually showcases sustainable products across multiple dimensions, including resource conservation, water savings, waste reduction, and reuse, helping to enhance public awareness of sustainable lifestyles.

4. Green movement line (Store 100% Implementation)

Sustainable development requires collaborative efforts from the entire society. Therefore, IKEA actively utilizes various platforms and channels to expand its green influence. Targeting consumers, IKEA optimizes the visual design of its stores, specifically creating sustainable green pathways within the stores to showcase the sustainable highlights of its products, encouraging more consumers to explore sustainable lifestyles. By enhancing in-store promotions, IKEA shares its insights on sustainable development in a more direct and locally relevant manner.

Case 4: Green Supply Chain— the Practices of Schneider Electric

According to calculations by the Global Environmental Information Research Center, the carbon emissions generated by a company's supply chain ecosystem are often 5.5 times greater than the carbon emissions from its operational scope. Many companies have already promoted green supply chains, such as Schneider Electric, which collaborates with partners to advance carbon neutrality, acting both as a practitioner of sustainability and as an enabler.

In terms of sustainable development in the supply chain, Schneider Electric has leveraged digital technology to create an end-to-end green supply chain that encompasses green design, green procurement, green production, green delivery, and green operation.

Schneider Electric integrates sustainability goals into its core business and leverages technology to collaborate with partners in advancing carbon neutrality. In China, Schneider Electric has 15 factories that have been certified as "green factories" by the Ministry of Industry and Information Technology, along with 19 "zero carbon factories" and 12 "carbon neutral factories", continuously providing green innovative products for both the Chinese and global markets. By 2025, Schneider Electric plans to help global customers save and avoid carbon dioxide emissions amounting to 800 million tons.

Based on its continuous outstanding performance in sustainable development, Schneider Electric has been named for 12 consecutive times in the annual "Global 100 Most Sustainable Corporations" list by Corporate Knights, and it is also the only company in the industry to have been included in the Carbon Disclosure Project (CDP) "A List" for 11 consecutive years.

Sustainable development requires the collective effort of the entire society. At this stage, many enterprises lack a comprehensive approach and capability for carbon reduction, and there is an urgent need for experience sharing and technical support. The empowerment of pioneers is of great significance for carbon reduction and sustainable development. As an enabler of sustainable development, Schneider Electric has established a wide-ranging carbon reduction ecosystem to continuously empower suppliers with experience and technology in response to systemic challenges.

To promote carbon reduction among suppliers, Schneider Electric launched the "Zero Carbon Program" in 2021, aimed at helping the top 1,000 suppliers worldwide reduce carbon emissions by 50% by 2025 through technical guidance, consulting services, and other means, including 230 core suppliers in China. By the end of 2023, the program achieved an average carbon emission reduction of 27%.

Specific measures include:

Deepeninggreen training for suppliers:Schneider Electric provides suppliers with technical training and decarbonization solutions such as carbon footprint analysis and carbon trajectory definition, as well as leading digital solutions to help them develop carbon reduction capabilities, enhance efficiency and reduce emissions, and achieve a green transformation.

1. Share leading experiences: By organizing on-site visits to Schneider Electric's smart factories and smart logistics centers, as well as exploration seminars related to carbon reduction, Schneider Electric provide advice and support to suppliers for emission reductions, harnessing the power of the ecosystem to collectively achieve carbon emission targets across the entire value chain.

2. Establishing a platform to follow up on the carbon reduction process: Within the framework of a 50% carbon reduction target, Schneider Electric has established a zero-carbon project platform for suppliers, which will assist each supplier in setting their own carbon reduction goals and monitoring project progress, enhancing the analysis of carbon reduction reports within the supplier system, while maintaining internal and external communication to share best practices.

Tianjin Jinrong Tianyu Precision Machinery Co., Ltd. (hereinafter referred to as "Jinrong Tianyu") is one of the carbon reduction benchmarks in Schneider Electric's supply chain.

Since participating in Schneider Electric's supplier "Zero Carbon Program" in 2021, Jinrong Tianyu has established its own top-level planning for sustainable development and long-term goals, aiming to achieve a 50% reduction in carbon emissions by 2025 compared to the baseline year (2019).Jinrong Tianyu integrates multiple energy-saving and carbon-reduction technologies based on Schneider Electric's EcoStruxure architecture. Among these, the installation of its own photovoltaic systems alone is expected to reduce carbon emissions by 1,100 tons annually. By the end of 2022, the carbon emission reduction per 100 million yuan in sales for Jinrong Tianyu has reached a decrease of 22.2%.

Case 5: ABB Xiamen Industrial Center Practices "Zero Emission Vision"

As a technological leader in the field of electrical and automation, ABB is one of the core forces driving the energy transition, supporting customers around the world in achieving energy efficiency, electrification, and decarbonization. It helps customers maintain competitiveness, reduce carbon footprints, and make transportation, production, work, and lifestyles more sustainable. ABB has long focused on and strategically positioned itself in ESG from multiple perspectives, and has currently received the highest AAA rating in the ESG field from the internationally recognized index organization MSCI.

To achieve the scientific net zero targets of ABB 2030 and 2050, ABB is actively promoting sustainable development in China, supporting the country in accelerating its green and low-carbon transition. By developing and promoting energy-efficient products and solutions, ABB helps customers in various sectors, including industry, transportation, construction, and data centers, to enhance energy efficiency, reduce carbon emissions, and minimize environmental impact.

Actively deploy sustainable development strategies, committed to moving towards a net—zero future.

The ABB Xiamen Industrial Center covers an area of 42,500 square meters and employs 3,000 people. By implementing ABB's global "Zero Emissions Vision Program," it is expected to reduce carbon emissions by 13,400 tons annually, clearly demonstrating how ABB's smart digital technology turns the vision of decarbonization and emission reduction (indirect emissions from electricity use) into reality. As a "carbon-neutral" park and a demonstration base for sustainable smart manufacturing, the ABB Xiamen Industrial Center employs an innovative energy regulation system, integrating applications of new energy generation and storage systems, significantly reducing carbon emissions and improving energy efficiency, thereby outlining a replicable and scalable low-carbon blueprint.

ABB Xiamen Industrial Center has advanced production lines for medium-voltage and low-voltage switchgear and circuit breakers. By installing 1,000,000 square meters of rooftop photovoltaics, it has achieved a 50% replacement with green electricity. Through multi-strategy precise flexible regulation technology, it maximizes the local consumption of clean energy and enhances energy utilization efficiency through coordinated source-load-storage. This smart energy solution is equipped with AI algorithms for power generation forecasting and load forecasting. By predicting the conditions of power generation and consumption, it deploys regulatory strategies to achieve a balance between low-carbon electricity usage and economic efficiency.

The project deploys ABB Ability™ ZEE600 Smart Energy Management Platform enables precise regulation of the "source-grid-load-storage" within the park. This platform integrates energy facilities such as photovoltaics, energy storage, distribution, heating, ventilation and air conditioning, lighting, and charging stations, achieving optimized energy management for the entire park. The estorage smart energy storage cabin solution includes distribution and control equipment, effectively balancing photovoltaic fluctuations and improving the local consumption rate of photovoltaics through regulation and management with the smart energy management system ZEE 600; The constructed direct current microgrid provides an effective demonstration for the widespread application of photovoltaic storage and flexible technology.

The power system of the ABB Xiamen Industrial Center is connected to the State Grid Xiamen Power Supply Company's virtual power plant platform. Through the demand-side response autonomously regulated by the energy management system, it creates "source-load interaction," effectively supporting the construction of a new type of power system.

Distributed rooftop photovoltaic distribution modules, smart energy storage modules, orderly charging management for building loads and charging piles are all modular solutions. This makes the solutions from ABB Xiamen Industrial Center easy to replicate at other sites, reducing installation time and project complexity. These packaged solutions and medium and low-voltage distribution equipment are all locally produced in China.

Chapter 15　China's Electronic Information Industry Foreign Investment Report[①]

The electronic information industry is an important pillar industry in China. In 2023, faced with a complex domestic and international environment and the pressures of a sluggish market cycle, the production of the electronic information industry showed signs of recovery, and the decline in exports narrowed. At the same time, the electronic information industry accelerated its pace of "going global". In 2023, China's foreign greenfield investment in the electronic information industry reached 40.85 billion USD, an increase of 132.8% compared to 2022; the amount of cross-border mergers and acquisitions in the electronic information industry was 18.07 billion USD, an increase of 38.8% compared to 2022.

I. The Progress of China's Electronic Information Industry in Promoting Foreign Openness in 2023

A. Production and Efficiency Are Steadily Recovering, Solidifying the Foundation for External Openness and Cooperation

In 2023, the added value of China's electronic information manufacturing industry above designated size grew by 3.4 percent year-on-year, compared with an average growth of

① Contributed by Guan Bing, Chen luping, Yang Jihan and Gao ya, from China Electronic Information Industry Development Research Institute.

5.5 percent in the same period from 2022 to 2023.The added value of information transmission, software, and information technology services grew by 11.9%, with an average growth of 12% over the same period in the past two years, indicating a steady recovery in production. In 2023, the revenue scale of the electronic information industry grew by 4.5% compared to the previous year. The software and information technology service industry achieved a cumulative business revenue of 12.3 trillion yuan, a year-on-year increase of 13.4%; The total profit of the software industry reached 1.5 trillion yuan, with a year-on-year growth of 13.6%, an increase of 7.9 percentage points compared to the same period last year. The main business profit margin increased by 0.1 percentage points to 9.2%, indicating a gradual growth in industry efficiency. The production and efficiency of China's electronic information industry are gradually recovering, laying a solid industrial foundation for enterprises to "going global".

B. Build a Modern Industrial System and Enhance International Competitiveness of the Industry

In 2023, the industrial structure of China's electronic information industry has been further optimized, promoting the development of key raw materials, core components, and high-end equipment, facilitating the integrated innovation and coordinated development of the upstream, midstream, and downstream of the industrial chain, and enhancing the resilience of the industrial and supply chains. In 2023, the mobile phone production reached 1.57 billion units, representing a year-on-year growth of 6.9%; The integrated circuit production totaled 351.4 billion pieces, also with a year-on-year growth of 6.9%; The revenue from software products amounted to 2.9 trillion yuan, reflecting a year-on-year increase of 11.1%; The revenue from information technology services reached 8.1 trillion yuan, with a year-on-year growth of 14.7%. Among these, cloud services and big data services generated a combined revenue of 1.2 trillion yuan, marking a year-on-year increase of 15.4%; The revenue from integrated circuit design was 306.9 billion yuan, showing a year-on-year growth of 6.4%; The revenue from e-commerce platform technology services reached 1.2 trillion yuan, with a year-on-year increase of 9.6%. The continuous optimization of the electronic information industry system is of great significance for enhancing the international competitiveness of the industry and promoting external cooperation in the industry.

C. The Pace of "going global" Is Accelerating, and the Ability to Layout Globally Is Improving

On one hand, the export of the electronic information industry remains sluggish. Affected by the complex international situation and the industrial cycle, in 2023, the export delivery value of large-scale electronic information manufacturing decreased by 6.3% year-on-year, which is 2.4 percentage points larger than the decline in the industrial sector during the same period; The export of software services saw a slight decline, with software exports amounting to 51.42 billion USD in 2023, down 3.6% year-on-year. Among these, the export of software outsourcing services increased by 5.4% year-on-year. On the other hand, the electronic information industry is accelerating its "going global" efforts. In 2023, China's electronic information enterprises made foreign greenfield investments totaling 40.85 billion USD, an increase of 132.8% compared to 2022; the amount of cross-border mergers and acquisitions in the electronic information industry reached 18.07 billion USD, an increase of 38.8% compared to 2022.

D. Policies Safeguard Stable Growth in Industries and Promote the Deepening of Foreign Openness

The electronic information manufacturing industry has a large scale, a long industrial chain, and a wide range of fields, making it an important sector for stabilizing industrial economic growth. In 2023, the Ministry of Industry and Information Technology and other departments issued the "Action Plan for the Electronic Information Manufacturing Industry 2023-2024", proposing to "stabilize the fundamentals of foreign trade and enhance the level of openness and cooperation in the industry". On one hand, stabilize the export market by proposing specific measures to optimize the export product structure, enhance brand international competitiveness, and develop cross-border e-commerce, thereby tapping into the potential of international markets. On the other hand, actively engage in international exchanges and cooperation, encourage foreign-invested enterprises to expand their investments in the electronic information sector in China, establish a normalized exchange and cooperation mechanism with relevant countries (regions), and promote the process of international production, capacity, and application cooperation.

II. Overview of China's Electronic Information Industry Foreign Investment in 2023

A. The Situation of Foreign Greenfield Investment in the Electronic Information Industry[1]

Firstly, from an overall perspective, in 2023, in the face of a complex economic situation both domestically and

---

[1] According to the classification of the FDI Markets database, the electronic information industry includes five categories: electronic components, semiconductors, communication products, consumer electronics, and software and IT services.

438

internationally, Chinese electronic information enterprises actively "going global" and promote industrial development through globalization strategies. According to data analysis from the fDI markets database, China's foreign greenfield investment in the electronic information industry in 2023 amounted to 40.85 billion USD.

Secondly, from a regional distribution perspective, greenfield investment is highly concentrated, primarily directed towards emerging economies. In 2023, the largest destination for China's outbound greenfield investment was Vietnam, followed by Morocco, Saudi Arabia, Turkey, Malaysia, and other countries. Statistical data shows that the top ten investment destinations account for 87.0% of China's outbound greenfield investment in the electronic information industry, indicating a high concentration of greenfield investment destinations in this sector, mainly focused on emerging markets and developing countries.

Thirdly, from the perspective of investment sectors and enterprises, in 2023, China's electronic information industry foreign greenfield investment covers ten areas, including terminal products and electronic components. In terms of investing enterprises, the foreign greenfield investment entities in China's electronic information industry are also concentrated among a few large companies. The top ten foreign greenfield investment enterprises account for 63.4% of the total investment amount, with large enterprises playing a leading role in promoting the internationalization of the industry.

B. The Situation of Cross-border Mergers and Acquisitions in the Electronic Information Industry in 2023

In 2023, cross-border mergers and acquisitions in the

electronic information industry maintained a rapid growth trend. According to calculations from the Orbis M&A database, in 2023, the amount of cross-border mergers and acquisitions in China's electronic information industry reached 18.07 billion USD. In terms of regional distribution, the cross-border M&A activities of Chinese electronic information companies are concentrated in a few economies, such as the Cayman Islands and Singapore. The total M&A amount in the top five target countries exceeded 17 billion USD, accounting for 92% of the total amount of cross-border M&A by Chinese enterprises. From the perspective of industry distribution, the information services sector is the preferred area for cross-border mergers and acquisitions. In 2023, the amount of multinational mergers and acquisitions reached 16.83 billion USD, accounting for 93.1% of the total merger and acquisition amount, while the share of other electronic information products was less than 7%, indicating a highly concentrated industry.

III. The Foreign Investment Models and Typical Experiences of China's Electronic Information Industry

A. Actively Expand the Global Market Through Product and Model Innovation

Firstly, based on mature products, enhance the brand and open up overseas markets through acquisitions. Having mature products is a prerequisite for enterprises to participate in international market competition.In 2018, ByteDance facilitated TikTok's rapid entry into the North American market and accelerated its international expansion by acquiring Musical.ly. After the acquisition, TikTok further enhanced its global brand recognition by integrating the Musical.ly brand with its own. The incorporation of Musical.ly's technology and content enriched the content library on the TikTok platform, increased user engagement, and attracted more users. As of April 2024, TikTok's global downloads have exceeded 4.92 billion, with monthly active users reaching 1.582 billion, making it one of the most popular short video platforms in the world.

Secondly, copy the mature development path, build C2M model to focus on overseas markets. Since its establishment in September 2022, Pinduoduo Group's overseas branch, Temu, has expanded its business footprint to over 50 countries and regions worldwide. On one hand, the success of Temu largely stems from the replication of Pinduoduo's successful experience in the domestic e-commerce market, with the core strategy being low pricing. Similar to Pinduoduo, Temu also emphasizes a cost-performance strategy, with its product pricing concentrated between 0.09 and 20 USD, and some products priced as low as 1 cent. It offers free return services and free shipping for orders of 29 USD and above. On the other hand, the C2M (Customer to Manufacturer) model created by Temu has innovated the business and marketing models of e-commerce retail, significantly reducing intermediary links. Abroad, products from e-commerce giants like Amazon and eBay mostly come from third-party sellers or distributors. Temu's C2M model bypasses these intermediaries, allowing Chinese suppliers to directly face overseas consumers. The platform takes on all aspects from promotion, warehousing, logistics to distribution and after-sales service, greatly alleviating the operational burden on merchants and ensuring that manufacturers can easily "go global".

B. Achieve Global Layout Through Supply Chain Expansion and Brand Enhancement

Firstly, it has transitioned from product export to supply chain export. Chinese home appliance companies have moved beyond the initial era of pursuing export orders and OEM production to a stage where some enterprises are achieving localized production and operations overseas, gradually becoming leaders in the global home appliance industry. For example, Midea Group has gradually evolved from the traditional model of "China supplying the world, with overseas operations as a supplement" to a global development model of "China supplying the world, with regional supply for regions" in its globalization strategy. This overseas expansion model is characterized by the external output of management models and talent cultivation, vigorously promoting the domestic lean manufacturing system and nurturing overseas lean talent at overseas manufacturing bases, thus no longer relying on domestic production. Currently, Midea has established 20 research and development centers and 18 major production bases overseas, with approximately 30,000 foreign employees and transactions conducted in 22 different currencies. Similarly, Skyworth Group's overseas operations have achieved standardized processes in local personnel allocation, supply chain, production manufacturing, testing quality control, sales supply, and after-sales service, forming a globally manageable and controllable professional service capability.

Secondly, the globalization layout involves multiple brands and multiple sectors. The development of multiple brands and sectors is of significant importance in the global strategy of enterprises, as it helps companies adapt to different market demands, diversify risks, enhance competitiveness, and promote innovation. In the development process of over 50 years, Midea Group has integrated global resources to establish three comprehensive brands: Toshiba, Midea, and Comfee, as well as 13 specialized brands in segmented categories, including Carrier and Eureka. Its business not only targets consumers with smart home products and various home appliances but also encompasses five major sectors: smart home, industrial technology, building technology, robotics and automation, and digital innovation. Since Haier Smart Home launched its global brand strategy in 2005, it has established a layout and global operations for seven world-class brands: Haier, Casarte, Leader, GE Appliances, Fisher & Paykel, AQUA, and Candy. Its business spans over 200 countries and regions across six continents, and it has established ten major research and development centers worldwide. On the path of global brand expansion, Chinese enterprises are gradually extending towards the high end of the industrial chain, attracting users with innovative technological strength. For example, Hisense's independently developed "Life Link" smart control platform, which was first launched in South Africa, integrates artificial intelligence and Internet of Things technologies to provide users with smarter, more convenient, and energy-efficient home appliance products and solutions.

C. Create Win–win Cooperation with Overseas Markets Through Localization Cooperation

Firstly, actively collaborate with local governments and non-governmental organizations to promote talent development and carry out the construction of digital infrastructure. On one hand, during the process of "going global", enterprises actively collaborate with local partners for talent development. For example, ZTE has partnered with the Ethiopian government to establish multiple communication technology training centers, cultivating a large number of local communication technology professionals. Additionally, ZTE has collaborated with several IT branches in India to create joint training and research programs focused on communication technology research and talent development, thereby nurturing a significant pool of technical talent for ZTE in the Indian market. On the other hand, enterprises actively collaborate with non-governmental sectors to build cybersecurity infrastructure and promote the widespread application of the internet. For example, ZTE Corporation has partnered with operators in Thailand to construct the largest 5G network in Southeast Asia; It has also collaborated with several telecommunications operators in Brazil to participate in the nationwide construction of the 4G network. Huawei supports South Africa in establishing Africa's first commercial 5G network.

Secondly, establish extensive cooperative relationships with local enterprises to achieve mutual benefits and win-win outcomes. On one hand, resource sharing and complementary advantages are achieved through the establishment of joint ventures. During their international expansion, photovoltaic companies can better adapt to local markets by forming joint ventures with local enterprises. For example, JinkoSolar's subsidiary Jinko Middle East, along with the Saudi Arabian Public Investment Fund's subsidiary RELC and VI, has made a total investment of approximately 985 million USD in Saudi Arabia to jointly establish a joint venture for the construction of a 10 GW high-efficiency battery and module project. This cooperation model helps photovoltaic companies establish a more solid foothold in the Middle Eastern market and promotes the development of the renewable energy industry in the region. On the other hand, collaborating with local enterprises to jointly promote local culture and brands. For example, TikTok partnered with the National Retail Federation (NRF) in the United States to launch a brand zone, working with retailers to showcase their products and brand stories. Through cross-border e-commerce and content platforms, ByteDance has assisted local small and medium-sized enterprises (SMEs) and individual merchants in expanding their markets, increasing business revenue and job opportunities. A report from the Oxford Economics Institute in Europe indicates that a significant number of SMEs in Europe, including those in France and Germany, have expanded their markets through TikTok, contributing 4.8 billion euros to the European economy in 2023 and supporting 51,000 jobs.

D. Strengthen Overseas Business Expansion by Deepening the Local Market

Firstly, fully respect and adapt to the local culture. Oppo does not emphasize national attributes when going to sea, but fully respects and adapts to the local market culture. When OPPO expands internationally, it does not emphasize national attributes but rather fully respects and adapts to the cultural context of the local market. On one hand, localization configurations are made in the team aspect by hiring executives and employees from overseas local markets. The brand operation management personnel, flagship store staff, and factory employees of OPPO in the Indonesian and Thailand markets are all locals, ensuring the effectiveness of operational methods. On the other hand, localized design innovation is being carried out on the product side. In the Southeast Asian market, OPPO has adjusted its product design and promotion to cater to the characteristics of young people who love taking selfies and are adept at socializing. In the Indian market, OPPO has localized improvements to Color OS 7, integrating it with India's DigiLocker platform to facilitate user identity verification while traveling. In the European market, adjustments have been made to accommodate users' preference for using the rear camera, focusing on enhancing the user experience of the rear camera. The first camera with physical-level image stabilization has been launched, allowing the phone to maintain stable performance even in special scenarios such as movement, enabling quicker adaptation to the local market.

Secondly, deepen the promotion of localized innovation and build a favorable ecosystem. Adhering to localized innovation is the key to Transsion Holdings' success. Transsion Holdings, upon entering the African market, conducted an in-depth understanding of local users' needs and preferences. For instance, it launched mobile phones specifically designed for the African market, equipped with larger capacity batteries and multiple SIM card slots to address the issues of unstable power supply and the use of multiple operators in Africa. It also implemented waterproof and corrosion-resistant designs, developed camera technology optimized for darker skin tones, and enhanced photo effects. Transsion Holdings is actively accelerating the popularization of smartphones in Africa while also building a robust ecosystem. It has developed applications such as an app store, an advertising distribution platform, a big data service platform, and a mobile management application around the mainstream operating system in Africa, Transsion OS. Additionally, it has engaged in strategic overseas cooperation with domestic internet companies like NetEase and Tencent to incubate mobile internet products.

IV. Trends and Outlook for China's Electronic Information Industry in Foreign Investment and Cooperation

Firstly, from "manufacturing" to "intelligent manufacturing", the strength of enterprises "going global" is becoming increasingly diversified. Chinese companies are experiencing a transition from exporting labor-intensive products such as consumer electronics to gradually upgrading to technology-intensive products like photovoltaics and lithium batteries. The capital and technological content are increasingly enhanced, achieving a shift from "Made in China" to "Intelligent

Manufacturing in China" on a global scale.

Secondly, the ecosystem of enterprises "going global" is becoming increasingly diverse, transitioning from manufacturing companies to internet enterprises. Chinese companies are shifting from processing products such as smartphones and laptop computer to enhancing service experiences, cross-border e-commerce, and localized experiences, continuously increasing the value of "Chinese experience" and "Chinese brands". The industry's "going global" is also gradually evolving from individual actions to a collective approach among upstream and downstream enterprises in the industrial chain.

Thirdly, the market for enterprises to "go global" is becoming increasingly diversified, extending from the European and American markets to the "Belt and Road" parter countries. Southeast Asia and other neighboring countries are the preferred regions for electronic information companies to expand overseas and are major investment partners for China. With the changes in domestic and international situations, the markets for companies "going global" are becoming increasingly diversified. On one hand, to avoid trade barriers, developed markets such as North America and Europe are becoming important destinations for large enterprises "going global"; on the other hand, to gain more markets and resources, South America, Africa, and the Middle East are also emerging as the "new blue oceans" for Chinese companies "going global".

Fourthly, the platform and market tend to be diversified from "productization for overseas markets" to "digitalization for overseas markets". With the advancement of a new round of technological revolution and industrial transformation, new technologies are gradually penetrating and being applied in the manufacturing industry. "New business formats" "new models" and "new products" are continuously emerging, driving Chinese enterprises to transition from purely manufacturing-oriented to digital and integrated approaches in their overseas ventures. The integration of emerging technologies such as industrial internet, internet of things, and artificial intelligence with fields like consumer electronics, mobile gaming, and cross-border e-commerce will inject more new momentum into enterprises' overseas expansion.

Chapter 16　Outward Investment in the Commercial Circulation Industry Achieving Quality Improvement and Upgrades[①]

In recent years, the global investment environment has undergone significant changes, with the rise of investment protectionism and disruptions to global industrial and supply chains. China's commercial circulation industry has actively responded to challenges, seized opportunities for global investment development, leveraged its service advantages, and advanced outbound direct investment (ODI) in a stable and prudent manner. By continuously optimizing its investment structure and enhancing the quality of outbound investment, the industry has provided strong support for smoothing domestic and international circulation, thereby contributing to the establishment of a new development pattern.

I. Overview of China's Outbound Investment in the Commercial Circulation Industry

The commercial circulation industry refers to the sectors involved in the circulation of goods and the services supporting such circulation. According to the classification of national economic industries, this industry primarily includes wholesale

---

① Contributed by Huang Qianyuan, from Institute of Market Economy, Development Research Center of the State Council.

and retail, accommodation and catering, transportation, warehousing, and postal services. The outbound direct investment (ODI) situation of China's commercial circulation industry is as follows:

A. Steady Growth in Outbound Investment Scale

From the perspective of investment stock (see Figure 16-1), the outbound direct investment stock of China's commercial circulation industry grew from USD 120.823 billion in 2013 to USD 530.01 billion in 2023, with an average annual growth rate of 17.9%. The proportion of the industry's ODI stock within the total national ODI stock remained relatively stable, accounting for around 16% from 2020 to 2023.

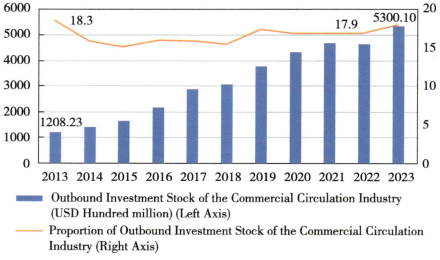

Outbound Investment Stock of the Commercial Circulation Industry (USD Hundred million) (Left Axis)

Proportion of Outbound Investment Stock of the Commercial Circulation Industry (Right Axis)

Figure 16–1: Outbound Investment Stock and Proportion of China's Commercial Circulation Industry (2013–2023)

Sources: Ministry of Commerce, National Bureau of Statistics, State Administration of Foreign Exchange, *2023 Statistical Bulletin of China's Outward Foreign Direct Investment*, China Commerce and Trade Press, 2024 edition.

From the perspective of investment flow (see Figure 16-2), the outbound direct investment flow in China's commercial circulation industry increased from USD 18.04 billion in 2013 to

USD 48.21 billion in 2023, with an average annual growth rate of 11.54%. Since 2018, ODI flow in the commercial circulation industry has shown a steady recovery trend, peaking in 2023. The ODI flow in this industry rose by approximately USD 12 billion in 2023 compared to 2022, representing a growth rate of 33.1%.

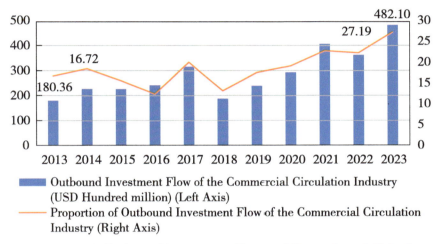

Outbound Investment Flow of the Commercial Circulation Industry (USD Hundred million) (Left Axis)

Proportion of Outbound Investment Flow of the Commercial Circulation Industry (Right Axis)

Figure 16–2: Outbound Investment Flow and Proportion of China's Commercial Circulation Industry (2013–2023)

Sources: Ministry of Commerce, National Bureau of Statistics, State Administration of Foreign Exchange, *2023 Statistical Bulletin of China's Outward Foreign Direct Investment*, China Commerce and Trade Press, 2024 edition.

B. Concentrated Outbound Investment Destinations

China's wholesale and retail industry's outbound direct investment in 2023 was mainly concentrated in Hong Kong, China; ASEAN; the EU; and the United States, accounting for 70.71%, 12.39%, 4.46%, and 3.17%, respectively (see Figure 16-3).

In 2023, outbound investment in the transportation, warehousing, and postal services sectors was concentrated in Hong Kong, China (65.02%), ASEAN (16.49%), and the United States (1.39%) (see Figure 16-4).

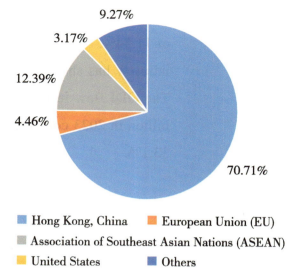

Hong Kong, China   European Union (EU)
Association of Southeast Asian Nations (ASEAN)
United States   Others

Figure 16–3: Distribution of Outbound Investment Destinations in the Wholesale and Retail Industry, 2023

Sources: Ministry of Commerce, National Bureau of Statistics, State Administration of Foreign Exchange, *2023 Statistical Bulletin of China's Outward Foreign Direct Investment*, China Commerce and Trade Press, 2024 edition.

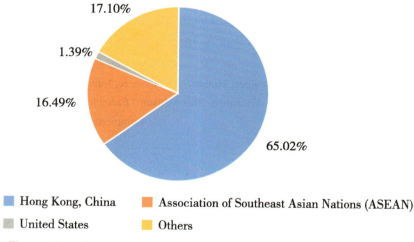

Figure16–4: Distribution of Outbound Investment Destinations in the Transportation, Warehousing, and Postal Services Sector, 2023

Sources: Ministry of Commerce, National Bureau of Statistics, State Administration of Foreign Exchange, *2023 Statistical Bulletin of China's Outward Foreign Direct Investment*, China Commerce and Trade Press, 2024 edition.

C. The Wholesale and Retail Sector Has a Large Scale of Outward Investment, a High Proportion, and a Slowing Growth Tate

The wholesale and retail industry demonstrated significant

outbound investment scale and proportion, with growth rates slowing in recent years. It ranks second in outbound investment stock across all sectors, following the leasing and business services industry. From 2013 to 2023, the wholesale and retail industry's outbound investment stock increased from USD 87.65 billion to USD 421.4 billion, with its share in the total stock of the commercial circulation industry rising from 72.54% to 79.51%. In terms of investment flow, outbound investment in the wholesale and retail industry grew from USD 14.65 billion in 2013 to USD 38.82 billion in 2023, with an average annual growth rate of 11.44%. The industry's share of total outbound investment flow in the commercial circulation sector recovered to 80.52% in 2023 (see Table 16-1).

Table 16–1: Outbound Investment Stock, Flow, and Proportion of the Wholesale and Retail Industry, 2013–2023

Year	Investment Stock		Investment Flow	
	Amount (USD Hundred Million)	Share	Amount (USD Hundred Million)	Share
2013	876.48	72.54%	146.47	81.21%
2014	1029.57	74.10%	182.91	81.21%
2015	1219.41	74.32%	192.18	80.54%
2016	1691.68	78.76%	208.94	84.78%
2017	2264.27	79.53%	263.11	86.35%
2018	2326.93	76.65%	122.38	83.28%
2019	2955.39	78.39%	194.71	65.26%
2020	3453.16	80.12%	229.98	81.28%
2021	3695.82	79.27%	281.52	78.36%
2022	3615.93	78.22%	211.69	69.26%
2023	4214.00	79.51%	388.2	80.52%

Continued Table

Year	Investment Stock		Investment Flow	
	Amount (USD Hundred Million)	Share	Amount (USD Hundred Million)	Share
Avg Annual Growth	19.06%	1.02%	11.44%	-0.09%

Sources: Ministry of Commerce, National Bureau of Statistics, State Administration of Foreign Exchange, *2022 Statistical Bulletin of China's Outward Foreign Direct Investment*, China Commerce and Trade Press, 2023 edition.

D. Transportation, Warehousing, and Postal Services See a Stable Yet Declining Trend in Foreign Investment

This sector's outbound investment mainly focuses on water transportation, multimodal transportation and logistics, air transportation, and pipeline transportation. In terms of investment stock, the sector ranked second after the wholesale and retail industry, with its outbound investment stock growing from USD 32.23 billion in 2013 to USD 104.26 billion in 2023. However, its share in the commercial circulation industry's total investment stock declined from 26.67% in 2013 to 19.67% in 2023, reflecting an average annual decline of 3.33%. In terms of investment flow, this sector experienced fluctuations in recent years. Investment flow reached its highest level in 2022, amounting to USD 15.04 billion and accounting for 30.08% of the sector's total investment flow. However, in 2023, outbound investment flow decreased significantly to USD 8.44 billion, representing a 43.88% decline compared to 2022, with its proportion falling to 17.51% (see Table 16-2).

Table 16–2: Outbound Investment Stock, Flow, and Proportion of the
Transportation, Warehousing, and Postal Services Sector, 2013–2023

Year	Investment Stock		Investment Flow	
	Amount (USD Hundred Million)	Share	Amount (USD Hundred Million)	Share
2013	322.28	26.67%	33.07	18.34%
2014	346.82	24.96%	41.75	18.34%
2015	399.06	24.32%	27.27	18.38%
2016	414.22	19.29%	16.79	12.03%
2017	547.68	19.24%	54.68	6.94%
2018	665.00	21.90%	51.61	17.31%
2019	765.34	20.30%	38.80	27.52%
2020	807.76	18.74%	62.33	16.20%
2021	917.23	19.67%	122.26	21.24%
2022	968.40	20.95%	150.38	30.08%
2023	1042.60	19.67%	84.40	17.51%
Avg Annual Growth	13.93%	-3.33%	10.97%	-0.51%

Sources: Ministry of Commerce, National Bureau of Statistics, State
Administration of Foreign Exchange, *2022 Statistical Bulletin of China's Outward
Foreign Direct Investment*, China Commerce and Trade Press, 2023 edition.

E. Relatively Small Scale and Proportion of Outbound Investment in Accommodation and Catering, Which Currently Show a Recovery in Outbound Investment

Since 2016, the outbound investment stock of the
accommodation and catering industry has remained within the
range of USD 4~5 billion, with its share of total investment stock
never exceeding 2%. In terms of investment flow, this sector
has exhibited high volatility. In 2023, outbound investment
in this sector reached USD 950 million, a significant increase
compared to 2022. Its share of investment in the commercial
circulation industry rose from 0.65% in 2022 to 1.97% in 2023.

Additionally, the investment stock of the accommodation and catering industry grew to USD 4.35 billion in 2023 (see Table 16-3).

Table 16–3: Outbound Investment Stock, Flow, and Proportion of the Accommodation and Catering Industry, 2013–2023

Year	Investment Stock		Investment Flow	
	Amount (USD Hundred Million)	Share	Amount (USD Hundred Million)	Share
2013	9.47	0.78%	0.82	0.08%
2014	13.07	0.94%	2.45	0.46%
2015	22.33	1.36%	7.23	1.08%
2016	41.94	1.95%	16.25	3.19%
2017	35.13	1.23%	-1.85	6.72%
2018	44.04	1.45%	13.54	-0.59%
2019	49.20	1.31%	6.04	7.22%
2020	49.26	1.14%	1.18	2.52%
2021	49.10	1.05%	2.69	0.40%
2022	38.32	0.83%	0.14	0.66%
2023	43.50	0.82%	9.5	1.97%
Avg Annual Growth	18.45%	0.51%	31.26%	43.54%

Sources: Ministry of Commerce, National Bureau of Statistics, State Administration of Foreign Exchange, *2023 Statistical Bulletin of China's Outward Foreign Direct Investment*, China Commerce and Trade Press, 2024 edition.

II. Main Characteristics of Outbound Investment in the Commercial Circulation Industry

A. Continuous Optimization of Investment Structure and Improvement of Investment Quality

The proportion of outbound investment in the wholesale and retail industry has slightly declined, stabilizing around 80%. In the past decade, the transportation, warehousing, and postal services sectors have shown fluctuating proportions, currently accounting for approximately 17%. Meanwhile, the accommodation and catering industry has seen a notable increase in its proportion, rising from 0.08% in 2013 to 1.97% in 2023 (see Figure 16-5). The investment structure among sub-sectors of the commercial circulation industry continues to adjust. Compared to 2022, the share of wholesale and retail investment in Hong Kong, China; the EU; and the United States increased in 2023, while the share in ASEAN decreased by 7.5 percentage points. For the transportation, warehousing, and postal services sector, Hong Kong remained the top destination in 2023; however, its proportion decreased by 15.61 percentage points compared to 2022 (81.01%). Investment in ASEAN increased from less than 1% in 2022 to 16.59% in 2023, while the proportion of investment in the EU showed negative growth (see Table 16-4).

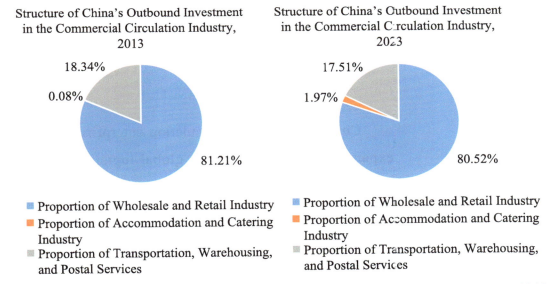

Figure 16–5: Changes in the Investment Structure of the Commercial Circulation Industry, 2013 and 2023

Sources: Compiled from annual editions of the *Statistical Bulletin of China's Outward Foreign Direct Investment*.

Table 16–4: Changes in the Proportion of Outbound Investment Destinations in the Commercial Circulation Industry, 2022–2023

	Proportion of Outbound Investment Destinations of Wholesale and Retail Investment Flow		Proportion of Outbound Investment Destinations of Transportation, Warehousing, and Postal Investment Flow	
	2023	2022	2023	2022
Hong Kong, China	70.71%	64.14%	65.40%	81.01%
EU	4.46%	3.05%	-0.62%	1.49%
ASEAN	12.39%	19.84%	16.59%	0.99%
United States	3.17%	2.78%	1.40%	1.80%
Others	9.27%	10.19%	17.20%	14.71%

Sources: Ministry of Commerce, National Bureau of Statistics, State Administration of Foreign Exchange, *2023 Statistical Bulletin of China's Outward Foreign Direct Investment*, China Commerce and Trade Press, 2024 edition.

B. Emphasis on Investment and Operations in Overseas Logistics Infrastructure

China's commercial circulation enterprises have actively expanded their investment in global logistics infrastructure construction, such as ports and aviation hubs, while enhancing the operation of related facilities. Leading central enterprises, such as China Merchants Group and COSCO Shipping, have extended their presence to over 100 countries and regions worldwide, covering nearly 2,000 ports globally and handling an annual freight volume exceeding 1.3 billion tons. Based on equity throughput, China Merchants Port and COSCO Shipping Ports rank second and third among global container terminal operators, with a combined market share of 12.6% (see Table 16-5).

Table16–5: Ranking of Global Container Terminal Operators, 2023

Operator	Equity Throughput (Million TEUs)	Growth Rate	Global Market Share
PSA International	62.6	4.60%	7.20%
China Merchants Port	55	8.70%	6.40%
COSCO Shipping Ports	53.8	1.40%	6.20%
APMT	48.9	-1.20%	5.60%
DP world	44.3	-4.70%	5.10%
Hutchison Ports	43	-4.60%	5.00%
MSC	42.3	10.30%	4.90%

Source: Drewry's *Global Container Terminal Operators Annual Review and Forecast 2024/25.*

C. Rapid Growth of the Cross-Border E-Commerce+Continuously Improvement of Global End-to-End Distribution Logistics System

Cross-border e-commerce has become a new engine of growth for China's foreign trade. Overseas warehouses, serving as key nodes in cross-border e-commerce logistics, have driven in the fast lane. According to the Ministry of Commerce, China has established over 2,500 overseas warehouses covering more than 30 million square meters. Among these, more than 1,800 warehouses are dedicated to cross-border e-commerce, with a combined area exceeding 22 million square meters. Investment in overseas warehouses bridges the "last mile" for cross-border e-commerce logistics, enhancing service efficiency. For example, Cainiao Network operates overseas warehouses spanning more than 800,000 square meters across 18 countries and regions, including Europe, the Asia-Pacific, and North America. These warehouses enable delivery within three days domestically, seven days across Europe, and three to seven days in the United States. In addition to providing storage and coordinated delivery services, these warehouses offer marketing, market data collection, and insights into overseas consumer markets, supporting Chinese enterprises in better serving global consumers.

D. Formation of International Circulation Hub Cities

Focusing on building a new development framework,and promoting the formation of a modern circulation network with smooth domestic and international linkages, a group of cities with strong circulation development foundations and extensive radiative driving capabilities have emerged as strategic international circulation hub cities that efficiently connect domestic and international markets. Among the 102 cities identified for their strategic role in modern circulation, 24 cities, including Beijing, Shanghai, Tianjin, Guangzhou, Shenzhen, and Xiamen, have been designated as comprehensive circulation hub cities. For example, Xiamen (China's Fujian Province), leveraging its status as a special economic zone and hub city of maritime cooperation strategy, has prioritized the development of supply chain services as a pillar industry. Xiamen's foreign trade accounted for nearly half of Fujian Province's total, ranking 11th nationally in comprehensive trade competitiveness. The city is home to over 23,000 supply chain enterprises, with three leading companies generating a combined revenue of over CNY 1.5 trillion. In 2023, key achievements include a 33.7% growth in the scale of imported bulk commodities, surpassing the national average by 18.5 percentage points. Xiamen leads the nation in the import scale of coal and granite and has maintained an average annual growth rate of 15% in grain imports and exports, it is striving to become a key center for the allocation of bulk commodities. In addition, Xiamen has strengthened logistics and trade ties with Taiwan, with 15.85 million cross-strait shipping parcels handled in 2023 (increase by 1.7 times). The number of newly approved Taiwan-invested projects and the actual use of Taiwan capital rose by 64% and 408%, respectively, positioning Xiamen as a logistics and trade center for Taiwan.

E. Enhancing International Competitiveness of the Circulation Industry

In the 2024 *Fortune Global 500 list,* 16 Chinese mainland circulation enterprises were included, with JD.com, Alibaba Group, China Post Group, and Xiamen C&D among the top 100. Collectively, these companies generated $1.2 trillion in revenue. Maritime transport, the backbone of international trade, highlights China's leading position in shipping capacity. By the end of 2022, the total capacity of China's maritime fleet reached 370 million deadweight tons, doubling over the past decade and establishing China as the world's second-largest fleet. In terms of global brand influence, Chinese circulation enterprises have achieved remarkable success. According to the Brand Finance *LOGISTICS 25 2024 RANKING* (25 Most Valuable Logistics Companies in the World in 2024), SF Express, China Post, and JD Logistics ranked 7th, 8th, and 16th, respectively, showcasing their growing prominence and competitiveness on the global stage.

Table 16–6: 2024 Fortune Global 500 Chinese Mainland Circulation Enterprises

Enterprise Name	Rank	Revenue (Million USD)	Industry
JD.com	47	153217.4	Retail

Continued Table

Enterprise Name	Rank	Revenue (Million USD)	Industry
Alibaba Group	70	131337.9	Retail
China Post Group	83	112778.5	Postal Services
Xiamen C&D	85	110665.6	Trade
COFCO	106	97765.1	Trade
Xiamen ITG Holding Group	142	85818.8	Trade
Wuchan Zhongda Group	150	81952.4	Trade
XMXYG	187	69286.9	Trade
COSCO Shipping	267	53929.6	Transport & Logistics
Zhejiang Communications Investment Group	330	45772	Transport & Logistics
Meituan	384	39092.5	Retail
Shandong Hi-Speed Group	412	36502.4	Transport & Logistics
S.F. Holding	415	36502.4	Transport & Logistics
Hailiang Group	429	69286.9	Trade
Pinduoduo	442	34981.1	Retail
China National Aviation Fuel Group	483	32984.2	Trade

Source: 2024 *Fortune Global 500* Rankings.

III. Future Trends and Outlook

A. Promoting Cross–Industry Collaboration in "Going Global"

A stable and efficient circulation system is a fundamental pillar for facilitating the dual domestic and international circulation and promoting high-quality outbound investment cooperation. As industries such as manufacturing, mining, and cross-border e-commerce accelerate their internationalization strategies, the commercial circulation sector, as a productive service industry, is deepening its integration with agriculture, manufacturing, and cross-border e-commerce. This integration aims to serve industrial internationalization, leverage comparative advantages within and across industries, and achieve collaborative success in outbound investment. For instance, with the growth of the new energy sector, some commercial logistics enterprises are actively establishing international resource supply chains, integrating"commercial logistics + mining" to deliver end-to-end supply chain services.

B. Enhancing the Global Commercial Logistics Network

Maximizing the role of the commercial circulation industry as a bridge between domestic and international markets, China aims to address gaps and improve weak points in the global circulation network. This involves optimizing the international layout of commercial logistics networks and enhancing the industry's capacity to provide globalized services. Efforts are being made to accelerate the construction of the "Two Belts and Ten Corridors" international logistics channels and align with agreements such as the Regional Comprehensive Economic Partnership (RCEP), strengthen the radiation capacity of diversified international logistics channels serving the joint construction of the "Belt and Road". This includes advancing multimodal transportation models such as rail-sea intermodal transport, river-sea intermodal transport, and international rail express lines, while improving the global land-sea transport corridor system. By constructing interconnected global commodity logistics transportation systems and enhancing cooperation in international logistics, China seeks to strengthen end-to-end full logistics services for key processes such as resource extraction, warehousing, transportation, and customs clearance. Additionally, significant attention is being directed toward key regions, such as Southeast Asia, Africa, and South America, by developing essential transportation hubs like ports and warehouses, thus improving localized service capabilities abroad.

C. Expanding Digital Outward Investments in the Commercial Circulation Sector

Digitalization is a critical area of growth for the commercial circulation industry's outbound investment. By adopting strategies such as mergers, equity investments, and capital injections, the industry seeks to boost its investment in new circulation technologies and enhance digital infrastructure connectivity in host countries. This will assist host countries in advancing their digital transformation in commerce and circulation. Strengthening insights into overseas consumer markets and fostering new technologies, business models, and platforms for international commercial logistics will better cater to global consumer needs and promote high-quality foreign trade development. The industry also focuses on upgrading the digital infrastructure of global trade and supply chains, enhancing the digitization of global commerce and logistics, and promoting innovations such as electronic bills of lading to increase trade efficiency. Additionally, there is an emphasis on creating synergies between overseas consumer platforms and domestic industrial platforms. This involves establishing overseas distribution centers, showrooms, and cross-border e-commerce service platforms through investments such as construction, mergers, equity participation, and capital increases. These initiatives aim to support related industries like smart logistics and mobile payments in expanding their global presence.

D. Strengthening Green and Low-Carbon Investments

As a foundational and leading industry, the commercial circulation sector's green and low-carbon transition not only directly impacts the broader green transformation of the economy but also plays a crucial role in greening the entire supply and industrial chains. By seizing global opportunities in green and low-carbon transitions, the industry is advancing its international competitiveness through strategic investments in this field. Efforts include increasing investments in green shipping and fostering international cooperation in clean energy and high-efficiency technologies. The sector is also investing in green upgrades for overseas-operated ships and ports while promoting the construction of zero-carbon smart ports globally. These initiatives aim to elevate the green infrastructure standards of the commercial circulation industry and establish international green logistics corridors. Moreover, the industry is enhancing international investments in green products and technologies, promoting their adoption globally, and strengthening investments in green procurement and packaging. This comprehensive approach supports the coordinated advancement of green supply chain management, ensuring that the commercial circulation sector plays a key role in the global push toward sustainability.

Postscript

The *China Two-way Investment Report* 2024 was jointly written by the Organizing Committee of the China International Fair for Investment and Trade (CIFIT) and the Information Centre and Department of Foreign Economic Relations of the Development Research Centre of the State Council, under the guidance of Vice Director Long Guoqiang of the Development Research Centre of the State Council. Chapter 1 was co-authored by James X. Zhan, Chairman of the Global Alliance of Special Economic Zones and Chairman of the Executive Committee of the World Investment Conference, alongside Professor Ge Shunqi of Nankai University. Chapters 2–5 were written by a team from the Development Research Centre of the State Council. Special thanks go to Research Fellow Li Feng from the Nanjing University Comprehensive Research Institute of Free Trade Zones and other experts for their research support. Chapters 6–10, for the Regional Section and Open Platform Section, we selected regions and open platforms with significant and distinctive achievements in two-way investments. These chapters feature contributions from the Shanghai Municipal Commission of Commerce, Department of Commerce of Zhejiang Province, Department of Commerce of Hainan Province, Beijing Municipal Commerce Bureau, and Investment and Trade (Xiamen) Exhibition Co., Ltd. Chapters 11–12,for the Association Section, we invited contributions from the Shanghai Foreign Investment Association, the Shanghai Foreign Investment Consulting Co., Ltd., the China Enterprises Association (Singapore), and Deloitte China/Deloitte Southeast Asia. These organizations shared insights on new investment trends of multinational corporations in China and provided case studies on two-way investment and cooperation between Chinese enterprises and other countries, with a focus on mutual benefit. Chapters13–16, for the Industry Section, we collaborated with experts from institutions such as the the Institute of Finance, Development Research Center of The State Council; Investment Company Working Committee of the China Foreign Investment Enterprises Association; China Electronic Information Industry Development Research Institute; Institute of Market Economy, Development Research Center of the State Council. Topics included financial openness, the "going global" of the commercial circulation industry, outbound investment in the electronic information industry, and ESG practices by multinational corporations in China. We extend our gratitude to the Department of Foreign Investment Administration, the Department of Outward Investment and Economic Cooperation, and the Investment Promotion Agency of the Ministry of Commerce for their research support! We also thank China Commerce and Trade Press for their support. Finally, we express our heartfelt appreciation to all experts and staff who dedicated their efforts to the drafting, proofreading, and publication of this report. Despite our best efforts, shortcomings in this report are inevitable. We sincerely welcome feedback and suggestions from readers.

September 2024